ARCHITECTURE, RITUAL PRACTICE AND CO-DETERMINATION IN THE SWEDISH OFFICE

ETHNOSCAPES
Current Challenges in the Environmental Social Sciences

Series Editors: *David Canter and David Stea*

For Rebecca, Amanda and Rachel

ARCHITECTURE RITUAL PRACTICE AND CO-DETERMINATION IN THE SWEDISH OFFICE

DENNIS DOXTATER
College of Architecture
University of Arizona

Avebury

Aldershot • Brookfield USA • Hong Kong • Singapore • Sydney

© D. Doxtater 1994

Published by
Avebury
Ashgate Publishing Limited
Gower House
Croft Road
Aldershot
Hants GU11 3HR
England

Ashgate Publishing Company
Old Post Road
Brookfield
Vermont 05036
USA

British Library Cataloguing in Publication Data

Doxtater, Dennis
   Architecture, Ritual Practice and
   Co-determination in the Swedish Office. –
   (Ethnoscapes: Current Challenges in the
   Environmental Social Sciences Series)
   I. Title II. Series
   720.9485

ISBN 1 85628 558 8

Printed and Bound in Great Britain by
Athenaeum Press Ltd, Newcastle upon Tyne.

Contents

vi

Figures

xi

Acknowledgements

This research was funded by a grant from the National Endowment for the Arts and Sabbatical Salary from the University of Arizona. These funds could not have been procured without the glowing reference letter written by Bill Bailey in the Communications Department, or without the full administrative support of Ronald Gourley, Dean of the College of Architecture. The author is greatly indebted to a long list of Swedish architects, scholars, office employees, public service workers, and friends, without whose gracious accommodation the work would have been impossible. I would particularly like to thank Hans Asplund, Jan Henriksson, Eva Sägerstrom, Mona Åhlund and Torsten Malmberg for their academic support and personal encouragement at my host institution, the University of Lund. A special thanks goes to our good friends and architects, Lars and Mia Landin, and many other wonderful people in Lund who made our family experience one of the most memorable of our lifetimes.

Introduction

0.1 Theoretical structure and summary of work

While this study of recent office settings in Sweden will hopefully have its most practical application in the fields of work organization and related architectural design, it is as well an introductory idea about the anthropology of human space. Why, then, is an anthropology of space significant to an understanding of contemporary culture in general and office organization in particular? First of all, our conventional Western approach to history, social science and philosophy has effected a somewhat misleading view of both preliterate primitive or traditional cultures, and contemporary organization.[1] Because of our particularly Western dependence upon written forms of expression, we have assumed that social experience is most effectively understood and mediated by language. The contemporary wisdom of cultural process works from the distinction between "oral" and "written" societies. Even McLuhan's ideas of a new electronic effect followed this basic paradigm, suggesting that television returns us to oral modes of communication and/or expression (McLuhan 1964). Given the ubiquity of linguistically dependent thinking in most areas of social and cultural research, corporate organization remains undistinguished as a special locus of inquiry. It is simply one of many forms of language based social and cultural phenomena.

What if, however, in the course of cultural "evolution" there had been a unique, indeed fundamental, contribution of spatially based experience, not so much as a medium of symbolic expression distinct from written texts, or even "talk" as Goffman (e.g. 1974) called it, but a different way of cognitively structuring and symbolically influencing social relationships. This is in fact what an

1

anthropology of space might establish. To radically oversimplify, one might consider both territorially based and symbolically constructed conceptions of space as experientially and theoretically separate from, or at least prior to, the effects of oral, written, or even electronic experience and texts. Such a shift in thinking sees medially based experience not as primary forms of cultural life or expression, but secondary modifiers to more fundamental, spatial strata. Even though the modern world has radically dissociated people from more permanent relationships with physical spaces, aspects of the spatial continuum from simple territoriality to complex ritual may still underlie important forms of contemporary social life. Because of its intensity of spatial experience, corporate organization may be seen as a socially and culturally unique focus of investigation, rather than being considered just one of many forms of modern life.

It is the author's belief that contemporary white collar organization, for some time the most ubiquitous form of work in many of our societies, has powerful influence over other aspects of modern life. Without defining for the moment the social reality of most office work, consider a culturally and medially diverse urban milieu, in which our places of work stand as unique islands of socio-spatial intensity. In most societies the white collar work environment is often perceived negatively. The family home and recreational loci are often characterized as escape from work. In Sweden, however, a very unusual phenomenon has occurred over the past twenty years or so. Corporate life has become so positive, so complete almost as a total social form itself, that it has come to compete with the family itself. Studies will be cited later that Swedish office workers actually "escape" back to work on Monday! Beyond the rhetorical tone of these statements, however, lies the possibility that not only are Swedish office workers happier in their work, but that these critical islands of social experience may have had, or are having, significant influence on wider spheres of Swedish life--namely the recent "democratic breakthrough" as the right to co-determination in virtually all organization.[2]

The logic of this argument, the loftiest hypothesis of the present work, rests on the assumption that major social change must rely upon changes in the way physical settings are used to structure experience, and that intensely experienced white collar settings will be critical in this regard. Because Swedish office settings appear to be kinds of spatial experience inherently different from their more typical contemporary counterparts, it is necessary to first ask more theoretical questions about the nature and origin of this experience.

2

Given the author's previous research in more traditional uses of space in Scandinavia, it became natural to construct a provisional evolutionary model of theoretically different ways space is used in social experience. As the reader will see, these ideas of a more spatially based continuum of socio-cultural experience and expression--an anthropology of space--ask very pertinent questions about the way immediate social experience links to more institutional structures and socio-cultural change itself.

The present provisional model rests first of all on a basic distinction between traditional and modern social uses of space. Simply put, uses of space more place dependent, i.e. those with the greatest amount of time lived in and overall expressive complexity developed, can be called "ritualistic". Contemporary uses of space, perhaps most characterized by common office settings, are in comparison, more territorial, presentational, rhetorical or "discursive". To a large extent, ritual uses of space both structure and operationalize powerful symbolism as a fundamental part of some pervasive, shared, traditional ethos or belief system. Most contemporary space operates, on the other hand, either in situations of ethnic diversity or ethnic absence. Its power lies less in the manipulation of deeply shared symbolic affect than in the discursive communication of partly territorial identities.[3]

Recent Swedish offices cannot be described as related to either the most traditional ritual forms, especially the "sacred", or to widespread contemporary organization in most countries, in spite of the fact that Swedish buildings are among the most modern and sophisticated built. There appears to be an interim form of space which relies upon shared ritual and ethnic meanings, but differs significantly from sacred space. At the same time these non-sacred but ritual places are not available to territorial, presentational or rhetorical manipulation. These are provisionally called "second order", standing theoretically between ritually sacred "first order" and rhetorical "third order" expression. A second order interpretation of space appears to have potential relevance to the general study of small scale, often autonomous "peasant" societies, and in the Swedish case suggests an actual historical linkage for the unusual form of recent office architecture. Because of the recency of the Scandinavian peasant or village tradition, and its hypothetically unique second order use of space, this spatially based ethos survived, though in a latent form, into the modern period. The political right to participate in decisions about physical settings, along with other effects of the 60's, allowed a reformation of traditional non-sacred ritual practice. Cooperative, co-

3

determination of work was then built upon these reintegrated definitions of social actors and experience. The expressive role of architecture was particularly significant in the overall process, a role which needs to be distinguished from architectural contributions to sacred and discursive "cultures".

The first two chapters of the book attempt, in the absence of a more fully developed anthropology of space, to outline the essential architectural distinction between the highly ritually organized indigenous Norse cultures, the "first order" or "sacred", and the more medially dependent societies which formed after industrialization, the "third order" or "discursive". It is however the transitional second order folk culture which occurred roughly, depending upon location, during the approximately eight hundred years after the introduction of Christianity and before modernization, which is defined in most detail in the first chapter. It provides the comparative and introductory theoretical basis for the chapters which follow. This book does not consider these highly sentimental, cooperative village-like clusters of Swedish farm families simply as the result of practical, ecological causes, as tends to be the case in Scandinavia. Rather it assumes a powerful effect as the old spatially based Norse symbolism and its primary ritual settings are severely compromised or outrightly destroyed by another sacred but new religion. Thus the formation of often quite formal villages during these periods represents not the sudden and dramatic changes in modes of production, but a new and different form of architectural and ritual expression.

First order Scandinavian expression set up powerful symbolic oppositions between ancestral or collective gods and individual family groups. Virtually all physical environments were informed by these spatial conceptions, with their emphasis on particular threshold locations and times for actual contact between "worlds". Although some occasions were obviously more ritualistic than others, even the most mundane daily activity performed in these settings could have immediate symbolic effect and implications for behavior. Expression was not for the most part textually removed from immediate experience, though related secondary expression in myth and folklore existed. The larger overall effect of first order ritual gave the egalitarian community of farmers power over the hierarchical individual farm. This social concept moderated competition for extremely scarce agricultural resources. The same ethos continues into the nominally Christian village period, though in more subtle ways. No longer able to ritually involve the ancient Norse gods in their traditional form, the spatial opposition

4

becomes architecturally focused on the two different social groups *per se*, the "community" and the "family", though still associated with many of the symbolic elements of this ancient Norse polarity. Not only is the ownership of even scarcer land effectively controlled, but also the new and related demand to farm cooperatively is given its underlying legitimacy. Ritually and ultimately politically, community must at times dominate family desires. It is this subtle form of architecturally framed ritual, presumably dependent upon the ancient oppositional symbolism of the ethos, which will be shown to reemerge in quite recent Swedish offices.

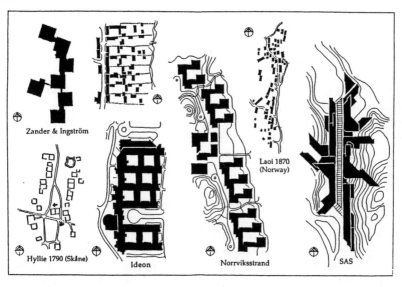

Figure 0.1 Plan comparison of cooperative settlements of Scandinavian farm families and recent democratic offices in Sweden--places with dates are traditional "villages"

In spite of the breakup of the highly traditional Swedish villages during the nineteenth century, Chapter Two argues that much of the ancient symbolic opposition, with its latent spatial associations, still existed (and exists) in modernizing Swedish society. During the early portion of the modern period, however, the two aspects of the experience of the Scandinavian self, the collective and the familial, ceased to be either contained in the same individual, or ritually integrated within commonly shared physical settings. Within a largely third order environment of the new cities, it was the working class which mostly maintained the meanings of

5

community, while the familial or "patriarchal" resided with the social elite of office workers. Relationships between the two entities were then highly territorial and often completely exclusive. While the workers' movement in Sweden roughly coincides with similar struggles in the Soviet Union and elsewhere, the values and organizational structure of the Scandinavian phenomenon are far more derivative from its indigenous cooperative history than from international ideology. The collective union activity of Sweden does gain political control, via the Social Democratic Party, of not only industrial work organization but the country as a whole.

In spite of union power for several decades, it was not until quite recently, during the past twenty years, that true participatory co-determination or the democratic breakthrough, has been achieved in work organization itself. This recency has frequently been attributed to the economic development of the post-war years, the logical abilities of modern Swedish corporations to plan, and generally to the informalization which has occurred in Sweden and elsewhere since the impact of the 1960's. Most of the accounts of Scandinavian work democracy read in other countries have focused on industrial groups, usually with little special attention to related architectural forms. The present work focuses on what appears to be a more widely spread form of participatory work, this in white collar settings. Such an exclusive interest in office democracy is unique in literature published outside Scandinavia, and is not even well represented within these countries. No major study anywhere has examined the relationship between architectural form and participatory office organization.

The present work goes much further, arguing that it was no accident that the major change in ways of working occurred only after the majority of workers occupy shared, relatively small scale physical settings as office buildings. White collar employees had always been the least interested in union activities, yet once they became the majority work force, the potential existed once again to play both individual/familial and collective roles--in a commonly shared setting. It is this traditional, second order and ritual potential, it is maintained, which operationalized traditional meanings, thereby legitimizing new forms of work. The expressive facilitation of this potential depended upon the "social availability" of office architecture, relatively unconstrained by critical functional demands such as in the layouts of manufacturing environments.

Chapter Three describes the initial circumstances which created the radical unwritten national norm of a separate room for each person, the individual/familial extension necessary for the

6

development of collective spaces and ritual which followed. The next chapter is devoted to the emergence of the work group as a participatory, horizontal form of organization, in contrast to strictly functional groups typical of highly vertical corporate structures. The new forms of architecture created by the demand for universal individual offices then become modified by subsequent needs, both functional and social, of the horizontal work group. Many architectural examples of these changes are provided in Chapter Five. Early in the 1980's a more integrated office form evolved in Sweden, one which finally and formally gave full expression of the relationship between individual office and collective spaces. Described in Chapter Six, this occurred almost simultaneously to the national legislative recognition of co-determination. The next two chapters turn the reader's attention to the more calendrical rituals of corporate life which during this same twenty year period have been increasing, particularly at the largest physical and organizational scales of offices. A rich yearly cycle of corporate *fests* are associated with major architectural changes at the larger scales of buildings. The climax of the breakthrough and its ritually meaningful architecture occurs quite recently as new architecture resolves expression of multiple scales of organization in a common physical form. Chapter Nine surveys several such recent buildings and focuses in greater depth on the spectacular SAS corporate headquarters in Stockholm.

0.2 Recent interests in the spatial basis of modern organization

An understanding of the unique phenomenon of Swedish office architecture offers an unusual and timely opportunity to link ideas about cultural processes in traditional societies with concepts of modern organization. It has been difficult to explain this interim or second order phenomenon in terms of either a more typical anthropological view of small, pre-literate societies, or orthodox models of modern corporate organization. The Swedish office is neither an obvious use of highly sacred ritual symbolism, nor of much more individually originated rhetorical "presentation" of social identities and status, which perhaps owe much of their power to written discourse. Eventually a true anthropology of space should clarify this major disjunction, leading to a more consistent understanding of the way change depends upon social space and differences in the effects of architectural expression. This anthropology must answer fundamental questions about the artifactual nature of the built environment, compared to more medial and potentially discursive texts.

Perhaps the most confusing thing at present is the nature of spatial social experience relative to its representation and expression in more medially specific forms of experience, e.g. talking or writing. In highly integrated sacred societies, for example, dwellings, settlements and the larger landscape are both symbolically structured and constantly experienced in terms of real or immediately potential social reality. Compared to other, more physically and experientially discrete expressive texts, such as myth or art, physical settings appear to be less available to political manipulation or other distortions in meaning. Their lived-in nature more firmly structures and binds symbolic association with the definitions and reality of social life.

The structuralist and post-structuralist preoccupation with (linguistic or linguistic-like) texts, and the assumed presence or absence of linkage to experiential reality, characterizes much discourse about even highly ritualistic, sacred life. Little recognition is given to the possibility that spatial or environmental experience may give rise to theoretically separate, perhaps more experientially prior forms of expression. At the other end of the potential continuum of society and culture, philosophers and others continue to devote most of their energies to the meaning and social reality of written texts. Thus until quite recently both ends of the spectrum were dominated by questions of structure and linkage of essentially linguistic meaning.

It has been stimulating in the effort to frame a theoretical context for the present work to review recent writings of the sociologist Giddens (1987) and others, particularly Meyrowitz (1985) in communication. They emphasize a special relationship between the physical spatial setting and society, particularly in relation to the presentational realities of social experience described by Goffman. Both use office settings as prime examples. There is however, still an implied discontinuity between more localized and intact traditional societies and the extended bureaucracies of most of today's world. Meyrowitz, in his creative fusion of McLuhan and Goffman, understandably sees the distinction between oral and written as paramount, the latter being supported to a large degree by physical settings. It is the physical setting, so important for Western "print" culture , which in turn is being significantly altered by the blurring of "front" and "back" regions by electronic media, especially television.

To Giddens, time and space are important in preliterate life, again in their role as organizers and maintainers of settings of interaction (1987:147). Again the emphasis remains on the oral

8

nature of these interactions, or "talk" as the fundamental aspect of social experience. Time and space are "integrated", or intrinsically linked to the places of oral experience, in contrast to "instrumentally" extended time and space of later organization. This view is somewhat contradicted by Giddens' earlier attempt to integrate the first order or sacred structures of space as man's being able to be "at home" in his environment (1984:144 - see Rosen, Orlikowski, Schmahmann 1990). The present author's own work, however, argues that sacred preliterate systems of space are as well capable of high degrees of organization across large geographical distances. The problem of structuration, or the link between small scale social reality and larger institutions, becomes extremely clear when one discovers the pervasiveness of ritual concepts and their systematic potential in integrating virtually all aspects of social space and time (Doxtater 1981, 1991).

As in Giddens, a seemingly parallel reference to media, expression, social reality and cultural evolution can also be understood in Foucault's widely read discourse on the origins of the modern prison (1977). One can interpret the earlier French preoccupation with ceremonial torture as integrally linked with the sacred symbolism of King who occupies the axial point of contact at the center (much sacred symbolic structure can be seen even in early prisons). In the evolution away from these forms of expression we see a shift to a much more politically motivated manipulation of spatial settings as a means of controlling social behavior. The change is from sacred spatial concept, and one could argue ritual performance, to a more immediate, perhaps inherently territorial manipulation of physical settings. Foucault makes little direct observation about the role of space or language in earlier punishment and therefore leaves open the question of a greater "spatial" continuity of socio-cultural experience from the traditional to the modern.

0.3 The implicit comparison of Swedish and other modern offices
Assume that the anthropology of space does one day thread together the "earlier" ritual basis of society with the "later" spatial dependence of Goffman-like situations or presentation as emphasized by Meyrowitz--questions of more recent electronic effect left aside for the moment. It will not have explained the uniqueness of Swedish offices as they have evolved over the past twenty years. They are neither sacred (ritual systems powered by contact with the other world) nor discursive (rhetorical or presentational systems probably dependent upon aspects of

territoriality). We may find other cultures, particularly in the Orient, where shrines and other obvious points of contact with spiritual powers do exist in modern office settings. They presumably, to some degree at least, ritually effect a sacred influence on social organization in these places. In spite of the relatively late existence of such systems in remote locations of Scandinavia, up until the eighteenth and even nineteenth centuries, most overt indigenous sacred practice was long ago prohibited by Christianity. Neither the dwelling nor the office in modern Scandinavia displays any shrine-like place, whether Norse or Christian. On the other hand, neither can we find much if any of the rampant presentational usage of space so common in contemporary office life, particularly in the U.S..

Much of Gidden's description of the phenomena of modern organization, and its reliance on physical or architectural form, turns out to be largely uncharacteristic of recent corporate life in Sweden. Giddens speaks, for example, of the special unsupervised role of private offices, their proximity to others of a similar authority level (for "presence-availability"), and their function as a sphere of autonomy within the larger hierarchic structure (1987:159). He continues by saying that such autonomy is most true toward the upper echelons of the organization, while at the lower levels "the physical setting of the office may very well resemble the shop floor" (ibid). The emphasis here is on the distinction between trust (the autonomous upper levels) and supervision (the open lower levels). Obviously this is not news to the vast majority of U.S. office workers, nor to organizational researchers, nor even pre-democratic offices in Sweden. Yet the recent office in Sweden absolutely confounds the conventional wisdom about current trends. "Office landscape" schemes, ubiquitous in other countries, are notoriously regarded, along with the supervision they often imply. Concomitantly, virtually all workers enjoy an autonomous individual office. While the universal glass wall of these countless offices may be seen by some as a means of hierarchical supervision, it will be shown to have been institutionalized as a later remodeling of initially opaque walls and doors. The glass wall permits communication and a form of group supervision of itself, considering the shift in responsibility from individual managers to the socially formed work group. Along with the *universal* trust and responsibility which all workers enjoy--not just those in higher positions--comes the commitment to the group to which one belongs. Obviously the physical form of highly participatory, co-determining organization will be radically different than that described by Giddens.

He discusses further the problematic nature of classic organization with smaller autonomous groups at the top and heavy supervision below. Unlike Foucault's treatment of prisons, to which Giddens refers more than once, the obvious inability of offices to involve physical force leaves room for frequent subversive activity at all levels. Again Goffman's situational distinction between "front" and "back regions" is used to describe the way various individuals and groups in such organizations either display or conceal themselves according to the best political advantage for doing so. Both an executive conference room and a customary *ad hoc* break locale for staff will be obvious physical settings for such back region behavior. A point which Giddens' essay spends little time on, is that a great deal of friendship formation and reformation will add to the situational play for power, both within and outside of the physical office setting. Recent Swedish offices, again to the contrary, appear to have effectively eliminated the phenomenon of back regions, whether as associated with hierarchical levels of work groups or smaller scale friendships. Such is not due to form itself but the overall symbolic definition of social identity which it structures, and its constant linkage to situational reality through ritual.

In his ideas of new kinds of behavior which take place outside the bounds of conventional physical frameworks, Meyrowitz describes a new, electronically influenced office organization. It eliminates much of the status or identity focused presentation of self or groups. He reflects primarily upon corporate settings in the U.S.:

> I have used the corporation as an analogy for general societal change, but since corporations are a part of our society as well, they too are being affected by the new patterns of information flow. There are significant moves away from traditional hierarchic secrecy and "lines" of authority. New techniques are being adopted such as "matrix management" (in which executives report to more than one supervisor) and "quality circles" (in which groups of employees who work in the same area meet to discuss and solve common problems--rather than depending upon "orders from above"). Linear and segregated situations are yielding to circular and integrated information systems. Furthermore, it is probably no coincidence that *electronics* companies such as Digital Equipment corporation

and Intel Corporation are leading the way in many of these innovations. In some high technology firms, there are few, if any, private offices or conference rooms, many executives report to multiple supervisors, and projects are often worked on by interdisciplinary teams composed of people from different offices. There is often significant "local decision power", with different branches of the same firm varying greatly in procedures, and there is extremely high mobility (in every direction--not just "up" in the hierarchy), with employees often selecting the position they wish to move to next. Significantly, many of these changes are affecting not only upper-level management, but also those on what were traditionally the "lower rungs" of corporate status. Many high tech companies encourage workers to participate at all decision levels (Meyrowitz 1985:163).

Aspects of the social organization described by Meyrowitz apply superficially to recent Swedish offices, not just to computer corporations but virtually all white collar organization in that country. Though the term "quality circles" (or more recently TQM, "total quality management") has only been associated with industrial organization in Scandinavia, participatory work in offices is much more broadly institutionalized not as adjacent to work organization, but as the fundamental basis of the work group itself. "Local decision power" and "participation" have become so indigenously pervasive that they are now defined in national law, again with no distinction between industrial or white collar organization. There are great differences between new Swedish and new U.S. electronic offices, even though both are considered as a change from customary, rhetorical, territorial processes of office organization.

To a large extent what Meyrowitz describes has been more specifically proposed by Stone & Luchetti (1982) as the solution to social problems in ordinary offices. Here, as also emphasized in Meyrowitz, the particular interest is in the way in which the physical setting is altered to achieve basic structural changes in the way people work. Similarly, the actual design scheme provided in Stone & Luchetti represents a kind of de-territorialized office landscape where virtually no space can be claimed by any individual or self-interested group. Individuals are only given closet-like spaces for storing personal things. All actual work occurs at a variety of shared workstations occupied only according to function, not status. This closely corresponds to Meyrowitz's

description of lack of private offices, shared spaces for such things as quality circle meetings, lack of enclosed conference rooms, and high mobility of the individual in and out of flexible, functional work situations.

These solutions imply a total elimination of social or cultural content in the form of the office--and the phenomenon of social space itself! Instead, physical form is to be used only for instrumental or functional purposes. This is not the case in Sweden. Everyone has a private office with an exterior view and small table for discussions with other workers; often one finds physically enclosed conference rooms; and in many cases the functional mobility of workers is difficult. The fact that the physical form of the current Swedish office is neither used for the classic political manipulation of situations, as in Giddens, nor a totally "informal", "middle stage" or purely functional use as described in Meyrowitz, points clearly toward some distinct, more cultural or ethnic purpose.

Figure 0.2 Radical architectural difference between "quality circle" office organization in the U.S. (above) and more indigenous and pervasive cultural phenomena of the democratic office in Sweden (below)

0.4 Historical contexts of different forms of architectural expression
Theoretically, a good deal of situationally manipulated behavior, in

particular that linked to physical form as emphasized in Giddens and Meyrowitz, can be associated with what is here being called "third order" (the presentational, rhetorical, territorial--discursive). Both authors (as well as Foucault) distinguish more "setting linked" situational behavior--with all its implications of role separation, front and back regions, and spatial extension of organization--from earlier oral cultures. Again, this juncture appears to correspond with and is integral to the historical shift from oral to print forms of linguistic media, in Western culture somewhere around the sixteenth century. The largely unexplained implication is that more formalized space and architecture at this point first become critical components in social organization, somehow also in relation to the advent of the printing press. It is natural for those living in discursive societies to see only discursive roles of architecture or to interpret the sacred discursively.

But the assumed relationship between oral cultures and what follows is problematic in both Giddens and Meyrowitz, and even perhaps in Foucault. An underlying assumption suggests that more formalized "space", as it were, not unlike some of the beliefs of U.S. computer firms, is largely absent as an organizational "device" in oral cultures. Once again, it is of course the dominance of the linguistic paradigm in modern thought which places situational talking as the foundation of traditional human social experience and then sees any significant medial alteration to that experience, i.e., printing, as crucial. This kind of thinking makes the sudden social use of space in the sixteenth century extremely difficult to theoretically integrate. What if Giddens' reference to Levi-Strauss, that primitive experience is primarily organized by oral myth, is actually wrong? To rephrase the question, what if the experiential basis of primitive societies was essentially spatial, with the structure of myth being a "secondary" reflection of or subordinate contribution to ritual performance?

What we would be dealing with, then, is not the major impact of print on essentially linguistic experience, but its effect in *shifting* the way in which space is used socio-culturally! The present distinction between sacred and discursive space/architecture attempts to capture this change, considering the most fundamental means of expressive experience to be physically spatial, rather than linguistic. The Swedish office not only represents an anomaly of use of space in a sacred, print or electronic culture, but perhaps something else, an opportunity to refine the overall continuum of social space.

The following chapters rely heavily upon this theoretical second order distinction in two respects. First is the recency of

14

modernization in Scandinavia and the persistence of unique cultural meanings traceable primarily to a folk or second order past. Such is the essential background to the recent reemergence of this unique expressive form of architecture, one neither sacred nor discursive. Second is the heuristic theoretical advantages which an "interim" second order kind of space provides, allowing a more accurate comparison between first and third order uses. Present interest does not lie in revealing any folk basis to the democratic breakthrough in a very modern Sweden; it is more theoretical, with a close eye to implications for corporate societies and cultures elsewhere. As an introduction, the idea may cast shadows on the notion that our recent electronic culture has returned to an "oral-like" way of experiencing and constructing social life. If all social life can be shown to have a fundamental basis in space, certainly including more immediate, animal-like, non-presentational uses of territoriality, then can we realistically design new corporate settings which presume to eliminate any socio-cultural use of space?

The powerful cognitive structures of first order space may not have been compatible with more individually initiated territorial or presentational uses. The medium of print, among other things perhaps, helped break down the effectiveness of all-pervasive sacred systems, leaving only vestiges of this form of space, such as Christian churches, surrounded by the presentational experience to which Giddens and Meyrowitz refer. Larger, integrated social spaces such as cities cannot under these circumstances be controlled by society as a whole. More ritualistic, symbolic forms of first order space are only effective among pockets of relatively autonomous religious communities. Certainly we cannot return to all encompassing sacred forms of society. Nor would we really want to, considering the symbolic power of these systems and difficulties in maintaining collectively controlled access to points of contact with the spiritual world. Second order uses of space, may solve many of the inherent political problems of both first and third order organization. They are in many respects historical or contact reactions to the same. Through a combination of limiting scale and increased reliance upon occupied architectural form, they manage to ward off the presentational uses of space so obvious to Foucault, while at the same time not relying upon the formalized spiritual relationships described by Eliade.

If, in corporate organization some sort of more culturally legitimized form of space is necessary to inhibit either a simple animal-like territoriality or more conventionalized, discursive evolutions of such, then both the idea of "second order" and

15

explanations of the actual Swedish phenomenon of this book may prove useful. It is likely that much of the organization of actual work always has been dependent upon spatially based socio-cultural expression, and it is unlikely that electronic society will eliminate either the need to socially found work, or to use space to do so. Sweden too has experienced the general informalization of situational life to which Meyrowitz continuously refers, perhaps even more dramatically than elsewhere. This informalization might actually have been one of the primary influences which destroyed existing discursive conventions, allowing a second order reformation. Most significantly, however, Swedish corporations have not chosen to attempt to eliminate either social definitions or the spatial/architectural basis of such. In fact, participatory groups at all scales are still in fact very formal, in spite of their apparent informality of clothing, modes of address and the like. It is true that they have cast off the conventional presentational ways of doing things in an increasingly discursive world. Yet the second order systems that have emerged are much less the result of simply breaking down "situational separation" by television, for example, than they are of a reintegration of ways of belief and organization from a richly expressive past.

Finally, while the present writing for the first time fully describes and theoretically integrates the unusual phenomenon of the Swedish office, it cannot answer questions of how smaller scale, folk like cultural systems of space might be used in societies where a coherent, national, second order ethos may not be available. Certainly corporations in countries such as the U.S., might be compared in their scale and intimacy to village life of the past. Much more obvious are recent efforts to understand, promote and actually create a positive relationship between a corporation's "culture" and its work (e.g. Deal & Kennedy 1982, et.al.). In spite of the fact that many of the proposed innovations to corporate culture remain fully entrenched in conventional third order processes--attempting to create change for example by giving the less powerful access to conventional symbols of identity and status--it may not be too unthinkable to consider the possibility of actually constructing both (non-presentational) symbolic contents and integrated second order frameworks for effective ritual.

Notes

[1] See particularly Catherine Bell's deconstruction of the conventionally imposed distinction between "thought" and "action" in symbolic anthropology (Bell

1992). The linguistic capacities of humans are often behind the causal preference given by anthropologists to "thought" in considering the origin of symbolic expression. Yet Bell's interest in a more authentic ritual "practice" (from Bourdieu) as a focus for symbolic studies still does not answer basic questions about special effects of environmental frameworks for practice. In other words, are there special structures created in the mind which come more from (environmental) "doing" than from (linguistic) "thinking"? The deconstructionist interest in what usually are linguistic or linguistically derived "texts" has tended to associate the idea of internal symbolic structure with the textual level of more individually minded expression rather than with some socially shared pattern of living in physical settings.

2   The relationship between "co-working", particularly in white collar settings, and "co-living" in cooperative housing (cohousing) has not been examined by architectural research. Although coworking in offices is much more pervasive than the small number of cohousing projects in Scandinavia, it is the latter which has received all the attention in the United States.

3   The most extensive treatment of the communicational aspects of space and architecture can be found in Rapoport (1990). Here theories primarily from non-verbal communication are extended to larger architectural and urban scales of physical settings.

1 The spatial basis of Swedish history

If the unique shapes of Swedish office buildings are in fact traceable to some sort of ritual meaning of space, then these patterns might logically be linked to the quite recent farm culture which persisted into this century. One intuitively seeks to connect the remarkable balance between authority and equality in offices with that same well recorded attribute in the cooperative farm societies. Yet a Scandinavian use of space, and its socio-cultural effects, probably can be traced back even to the late Iron Age societies that were called "Viking". Is it possible that in spite of major historical changes such as the introduction of Christianity (ca. 1000 AD), the Reformation (ca. 1600's), the radical restructuring of farm lands of the Enclosure Acts (ca. 1750-1850), and Industrialization and Urbanization (ca. 1850-1950), that some spatial aspect of an ethos persisted and can be most readily identified in the office societies of today? Again, many aspects of architecture, whether style or function, underwent seemingly major and influential changes. Yet some condition or set of spatial predispositions perhaps has not only reemerged but contributed significantly to the overall continuity of Scandinavian culture.

The image of the Viking fits the American notion of individualism, aggressive competition, and even nationalism. Within Scandinavia, however, educational and folklore material present this history in a more accurate framework. The Viking period was continuous with earlier Iron Age times which were just as much farm and fishing societies as were the Vikings and their nominally Christian successors. This has been essentially the ancient Germanic value of high autonomy of individual farm or fishing group and important relationship to their small scale spatially defined collectivity. These patterns of relatively separate valley, flatland, and coastal entities have remained in ways remarkably immune from the major external influences, whether Papal Catholicism, Feudalism, the Protestant Ethic, Mercantile economies, and even perhaps Industrialization, all of which may have more radically changed the basic patterns of life in the rest of Europe.

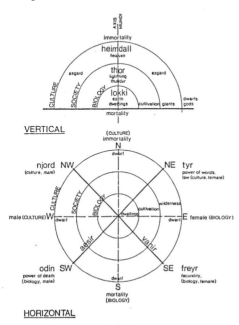

Figure 1.1 Sacred symbolism of Norse space evident in dwelling, settlement and landscape (Doxtater 1981:32)

From an architectural or socio-spatial point of view, one of the most interesting characteristics of Scandinavian space has been the absence of urban and village places in the overall context of human geography. Very few early market villages, such as on the small island of Birka near present day Stockholm, existed during Viking times. The vast majority of exchange occurred at unbuilt natural sites, a practice which persisted through most of the recent Christian period. The equally rare urban mercantile centers, such as 14th century Bergen, Norway, were inhabited and controlled primarily by other Europeans, a pattern which continued even into the establishment of present day cities during the latter part of the last century. The early twentieth century urbanization of native agrarian Scandinavia was by comparison to the rest of the western world, very late, as was its industrialization.

1.1 Indigenous Norse ritual: a first order of spatial usage

The most informationally powerful, and perhaps most socially effective human use of space is that experience found in first order or sacred ritual. The foundation of this very traditional ritual process lies in the function of shared abstract conceptions of symbolic spatial oppositions, evident as powerful directional meanings. The asymmetry of major directions, e.g. the power of the

19

spirit world and death over the world of the living, become available first of all to "frame" virtually all inhabited space: dwellings, settlements, and landscape. This framework is constantly available for the manipulation of symbolic power (symbolic content organized by space) through daily or ceremonial ritual acts. These are not "medial" texts but actual, multimedial settings immediate to one's experience of the world. Previous research by the author constructed such a sacred cosmology from the Viking Sagas, as seen in figure 1.1. This framework was then shown to still have been operational in the architecture and ritual of Norwegian valley communities even after the Reformation (Doxtater 1981).

Even though we may derive such ideal descriptions of sacred space from linguistic or text sources, as recorded by Icelandic saga authors in the 13th century, the primary source of such symbolism and effect is the actual environment itself. From the point of view of someone living in a remote farm community in Middle Ages Norway, for example, the visible symbolism of actual sacred directions and places of the built and natural environment, together with daily and more ceremonial practice in these frameworks, will be far more effective than any verbal or written "story" about mythical beings operating in some mythical space (even though the structure of myth will perhaps secondarily mimic actual ritual spaces--for a fuller discussion of this relationship see Doxtater 1981: 199). We will assume for the present that because the pattern was derived from Viking sources, and is evident in architectural and archaeological records of the Christian periods which followed, that the Viking farms and landscape were similarly symbolic. Just as in the folk societies of the Norwegian valleys, Viking ritual space and performance moderated the potential discord between highly individual farm and the collective place in which they were located.[1] The relationship between familial and community groups in these Scandinavian societies is related to Victor Turner's (1968) definition of socially opposite forces in primitive and perhaps traditional societies, i.e. "structure" as the hierarchical and "anti-structure" as the egalitarian. Individual farms have perhaps always been hierarchical entities with the male at the head (structure), ritually counterbalanced by the valley or coastal community (anti-structure).

First order space in the Viking and folk periods created powerful beliefs about the directions and dictated the orientation of dwellings and their location within the farm settlement, and perhaps even determined the location and relationships of natural ritual sites. To oversimplify, the all powerful ancestral spirits and gods resided in the North, while humans lived to the South. East was the location of things labeled "female", including birth, fertility, and probably the wealth of the individual farm. West maintained associations of "male", primarily that group of male heads of farms of the particular local collectivity. Virtually any daily activity, and all rite-of-passage or calendrical ritual events involved movement within or between some directionally labeled domain. Often a positioning at the center or *axis mundi* position of either the dwelling or natural ritual site created contact between the occupants of opposed directions and domains. This effect was much more ubiquitous and powerful than, yet similar to, today's only mini-mally sacred Christian churches. Here ritual movement down the aisle to the center position between altar and nave creates contact with the power of the spiritual world. The primary ritual site in the earlier Scandinavian culture, however, was not such a church or temple; it was a *pair* of opposed sites, the individual dwelling and collective ritual site in a natural setting.

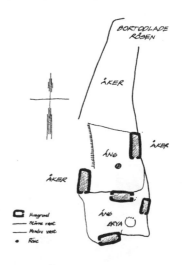

Figure 1.2 Spatially independent Iron Age or Viking farm from Gotland (Níhlen & Boethius 1962:14)

The major calendrical events of Winter and Summer Solstices illustrate how Viking and folk ritual used the positional frameworks and such contact to effectively maintain relationships between the structural (hierarchical) and anti-structural (egalitarian). During Winter Solstice the contact position within the dwelling created an occupation by major gods, Odin and others, as they seated themselves at the ritual table within the principal farm dwelling. Given the association of the collectivity with these ancestral spirits and gods, it was really the larger farm group which took over and otherwise showed at least symbolic domination over the hierarchical principle and individual farm.[2] The first order framework provided both the location of the gods, to the North, and the notion of contact at center. Spatial conceptions such as these provide not only the cognitive means of constructing

21

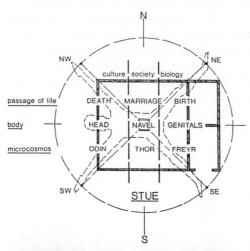

Figure 1.3 First order diagram of sacred power in the traditional Norwegian dwelling (above, from Doxtater 1981:107); interior of Åmli Stue, Setesdal (below, photo of a painting by Tidemand courtesy of the Riksantikvaren, Norway)

associations of powerful symbolic contact, but the means of ritually manipulating such content for social purposes. The meaning and effect of the Summer Solstice event was reversed. Instead of gods visiting or occupying the human dwelling, farmers and their families visited the major collective ritual site, the place where the gods lived. The notion of contact with spirits occurred at the high point of dancing around either a huge bonfire or decorated pole *(axis mundi),* thus cementing the important association of the collectivity with the power of the spiritual world.

In spite of the uneasy Middle Ages introduction of the architectural church, the site usually thought of as the place of "community" contact with the spiritual world, the basic opposition between individual dwelling and natural community site remained remarkably continuous in Scandinavia. The well known originally Viking *Ting* sites of Norway, Sweden, Denmark, and especially Iceland provide an excellent example of the persistence of these major meeting and ritual sites long after the nominal conversion to Christianity.

While the present volume does not permit a much more detailed and perhaps convincing description of first order space,[3] for purposes here it will suffice to form a relatively simple image of

22

first order Scandinavian space. The formal structure of space, its direction, geometry and symbolic meaning provide the ritual means of manipulating power relationships between the inherent counter forces of hierarchical individual family and egalitarian community. In the Norwegian valleys at least, the collective ritual group existed primarily for this purpose. Cooperative work exchange groups were much smaller given the largely self sufficient ability of each farm. The overall purpose was to control the ambitions of individual farms in an ecology of very limited land. This ancient first order "system" was the fundamental framework not only in the settings for daily, rite-of-passage and calendrical ritual, but as well ramified through virtually all expressive texts of the culture, e.g. decorative art and clothing, dance, and certainly folklore. Architectonic form and detail were highly conditioned by this underlying first order presence (see illustrations in figure 1.4 below).

Figure 1.4 First order graphic signifying sacred directional symbolism and position of contact: placed on or over hearth or fireplace in the Norwegian dwelling (Doxtater 1981:96,97)

One must try to briefly convince the reader of the fundamental cognitive, experiential differences between living in a ubiquitously sacred world and living in a typical modern milieu. To the Viking or folk farmer of Scandinavia, not unlike virtually all other primitive and traditional societies, all aspects of the social and physical environment were heavily imbued with spatially symbolic meaning. All formal concepts of time were intimately associated with direction and symbolic domains. In addition to the more obvious ritual usage of these conceptions, any daily activity also held the potential of being symbolically interpreted. The acts of moving from one part of the farm to another during the typical day had associational relevance.

Particularly feared was any act which might in some way upset the balance of the sacred axes, thus allowing an uncontrolled contact with the other world. These were "literally" concepts of spatial balance associated with most settings. If, while cooking on the central fire, which was also the powerful *axis mundi*, one were to accidentally spill some salt, immediately a bit of milk had to be poured on the fire as well. Salt was associated with the "male" and Western domain of the dwelling, while milk symbolized its opposite, the "female" and East. The spilling of salt is not so much a text metaphor of imbalance, but probably was perceived as integral to the immediate situational experience of acting and moving in real space. Though anthropologists and others have often described similar symbolic structures in many other cultures, seldom do they convey the fundamental experiential difference of living in first order worlds.

First order space must be seen as informationally very distant from what is being glossed as third order. While the opposed sites of individual farm dwelling and collective natural site might be thought of as more simple territorial forms occurring naturally between two different social groups with different interests, the presence of a relatively elaborate amount of formal, associational, religious meaning to those same spaces suggests the necessary and effective role of these expressive aspects.

History remains filled with examples, particularly of agricultural societies, where no natural (egalitarian) group territoriality exists or existed, in spite of acknowledged altruistic capacities in humans. Unlike the smaller and more evolutionarily common hunting and gathering "band", where altruism may be more natural, agricultural societies must deal not only with the independence of domestic groups working and occupying their land but with the constant potential for both individual scarcity and surplus. This danger seems to multiply when one considers the number of adjacent, culturally similar, inhabited areas, and the long term scarcity of land in each. In fact, the rich spatio-symbolic legacy which the Scandinavian folk period inherited may have been a result of the relatively higher degree and scale of social organization accomplished by the Viking religion. Throughout Pre-Christian Scandinavia the formal cultural balancing of the family/collective opposition existed on levels larger than the immediate valley or fishing community. The "All-Thing" on Iceland, for example, was the yearly collective event for the entire country, while other regional and local Things dealt with their own social and religious organization respectively.

Eventual consideration of the unique effects of sacred space in the much more complex and highly organized historical civilizations, rather than the superficial evaluation of their stylistic, artistic, or visual aspects, will probably reveal both the legitimate extent of and limits to first order social organization. Certainly in larger, more complex societies it has been possible for individuals or elite groups to control highly powerful places of sacred contact, creating and maintaining much less egalitarian human relationships. In the Scandinavian case, it appears as if, at least through the periods in which first order space was the dominant mode, the collectivity almost self-consciously maintained control over the most powerful sites, those associated with nature and the gods. Perhaps it is this collective will which prevails in spite of changes in economic and religious forms; it is a common recognition of the value of community over individual interests.

1.2 Transitions from first to second order space

The ideas of a fundamentally spatial aspect of the sacred sketched above are not as yet recognized as an essentially unique expressive phenomenon. Because most sacred ritual and other expression are felt, according to Eliade, to be essentially secondary to mythic or textual forms, there is no discontinuity perceived as society moves from sacred to other (still textual) means of expression. They simply stop speaking to god as it were. It follows, therefore, that the idea of a dissolution of sacred spatial forms, shifting to some next phenomenon or order in the course of cultural "evolution", is again quite new.[4] These hypothetical changes from first to second order space, and then to contemporary (discursive) territoriality, would seem to be critical to our understanding of the history of causes of built form.

What happens as a people no longer share the powerful meanings of the directions? Why and how does a society begin to discard the formal geometries of their ancient conceptual space, choosing instead to build, settle, and practice religion in places no longer symbolically contextual with each other? How do more conscious self-serving decisions of the individual or self-interested group modify or perhaps completely break down the collective perception and even control of first order space? How does the use of print help facilitate these changes? Does such a thing as second order space exist as an alternative to what can be extremely harsh transitions from the sacred to the rhetorical or presentational?

Within the relatively isolated folk farm valleys of Norway, the author has previously illustrated the minor impact which Catholicism and its intrusive architectural sites had on the indigenous first order system associated with individual farms and collective natural sites (Doxtater 1990a). At least until the Reformation reaches its 17th and 18th century extent, a solstice derived first order spatial concept or cosmos of Viking origins exists in the physical layout of dwelling, settlement and landscape, and in related ritual practice, as illustrated above. Given the essential disagreement of directional symbolism between the Catholic and

Norse cosmos (East is the place of the spirits to Christians rather than North) the first indication of external influence and first order change may have occurred not with the construction of the first East-West churches in the Early Middle Ages, but when Christianity finally manages to organizationally integrate the farm communities during the Reformation.[5] At this time many new churches are built and older ones are extensively remodeled. Essentially what is being emphasized is the East/West orientation of the churches, and the new power of the position of the clergy in this ritual context. A clear attempt is also being made to make the church rather than the dwelling the primary ritual site.

Prior to the Reformation, the first order orientation of the dwelling was obviously intimately coordinated with the larger conception of Norse space, and not with the intrusive associations of the anonymous churches. Further reading about the phenomenon of sacred space would show that coordination between sites is again one of the primary contributions of first order systems, and the lack of integration of Christian cosmos into the overall indigenous structure reveals its minor impact. But change in orientation finally did occur after the Reformation (see Doxtater 1990a). The new assertion of church architecture as primary ritual site demanded, at least initially, coordination of its sacred architectural space with that of the dwelling. For reasons almost exclusively symbolic, the domestic dwelling in the Norwegian valleys, still with its centuries old tripartite plan, reoriented itself, swinging its ridge direction from its ancient East-West orientation to North-South. The power of the Protestant Church had apparently successfully taken control of the formal system of space, making the church the most powerful collective site. Though in truth real power lay less in the collectivity and more in the hierarchies of religion and state, dependent as they were upon written text and discourse.

At first this would appear to be not so much the dissolution of first order space but its syncretization with intrusive culture. Yet the system does not maintain itself. The new orientations are not precise, and within less than a hundred years, perhaps, the Norwegian dwelling had lost its six-hundred year old tripartite plan and coordination with any first order directions. The church of course remained, increasingly defined as "sacred" in contrast to its "profane" surroundings. New things happened not only in the dwelling plan, but to the farm settlement patterns and perhaps even to landscape places, particularly the ancient natural collective sites.

During sacred periods in Scandinavia, individual farms had

26

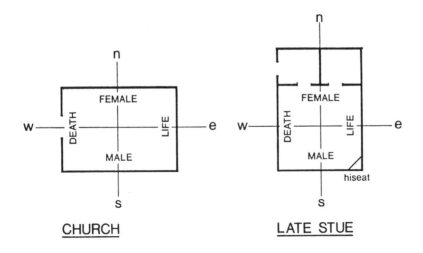

Figure 1.5 Historically brief sacred reorientation of Norse dwelling after the Reformation to conform to Christian cosmos (above, from Doxtater 1981:217); photo of Telemark congregation on "male" and "female" sides of the church, early twentieth century (below, photo courtesy Norwegian Folk Museum)

been physically separate from other farms. Whether in Viking times or in the valleys of folk Norway and Northern Sweden, the family farm had been a strong physical and conceptual entity unto itself.[6]   Again, no villages existed, one found only the non-contiguous farm units, some major natural ritual site, and after Christianity the intrusive church standing alone, as part of an individual farm or at some convenient or even ancient sacred site.[7] This pattern of separate farms remained in much of the less agriculturally intense areas of Norway and Northern Sweden. Individual farms can be found today with continuous inhabitation traceable to Viking times and before.   Yet during this period following the nominal Christianization of Norse sacred space, from the eleventh century to approximately the middle of the eighteenth or nineteenth century, at least two interesting changes in settlement pattern can be identified in these more remote valley and forest communities. These settlement effects are in addition to the major release of dwelling form from its ancient first order constraints.

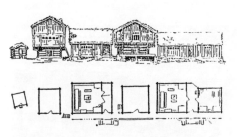

Figure 1.6 Contiguous grouping of multiple farms as occurred in Setesdal, Norway (drawing from the Norwegian Folk Museum)

When much of turn of the century Scandinavia was hurriedly attempting to document and even revive the remains of a then significantly altered folk society, one of the farm settlement patterns lifted intact from its valley locus to the new urban open air folk museums, was a "row" of contiguous individual farms as in the Setesdal illustration of figure 1.6. It is perhaps understandable that the more remote valley of Setesdal, one of the richest examples of Norwegian folk material, was one of the few places where the dwellings did not reorient in response to the Reformation church. Even today one can find log dwellings built through the long folk period which still accurately maintain the ancient Norse East-West orientation.

If there were a new second order tendency it may have been the phenomenon of placing two or three family farms together, with traditionally oriented dwellings (East-West) and storage lofts (North-South) contiguously fitted together in a row.   Animal buildings formed the southern row as was the old sacred Norse pattern within the individual farm. The now more pronounced *gata* (street) space between rows of buildings presumably became

28

more collective in association, while maintaining its functional and symbolic meaning as a part of the valley road of the larger community of farms. The row forms of these clusters of farms were usually occupied by related families.

It may not have been coincidental that this limited row tendency occurred in the place which possibly had the least apparent influence from the outside organization of the Reformation Church. This is in spite of the fact that in the seventeenth century the Telemark church too was extensively remodeled, including the addition of male (South) and female (North) pews which conformed to Christian space (see again figure 1.5). Churches did not have fixed seating prior to this time. The usual explanation of the clustering of farms emphasizes a scarcity of land for new separate farms as the primary motivation. The only culturally defined place of habitation was the farm, and the status of *husbond* (literally "house farmer")[8] was everything. Whether for a man or woman, only the individual farm provided the rights and obligations so ancient to the Scandinavian society. The row farms were but an evolutionary step away from the previously common pattern of creating more homesteads (considering the frequent scarcity of land) by partitioning the original farm into smaller, but functionally and culturally separate "North", "Middle", and "South" farms for example. The actual movement of architectural farm dwellings together, appears to have represented new expressive function. Emigration, either as Viking colonists or American settlers, was another solution to land scarcity.

Yet the individual farm had been the dominant and exclusive rule for over a thousand years! This pattern did not change in the majority of valley and forest regions of Norway and Northern Sweden. Other farms appear to have functioned just as well as smaller separate units rather than operate as a limited group. The change in the very traditional Setesdal could not have been made superficially. It may represent the local emergence of some limited second order condition of cultural space precipitated by both the dissolution of first order meaning and contact with external institutions. Given the importance of first order space in the contextual coordination of isolated and separate family farms into a ritual collective area, one would expect interesting effects as first order space dissolves.

Another example of this possibly new kind of expressive use of space occurred also in Norway during the same time period. Unlike the interior valley of Setesdal, the farms of the Western fjords and their adjacent valleys have always been subject to much greater

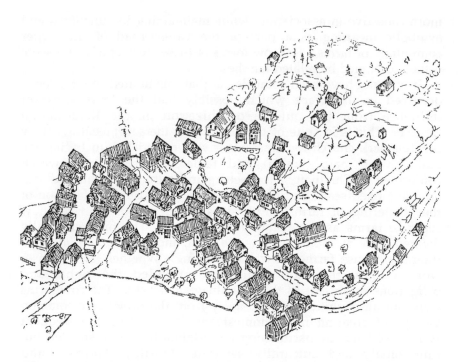

Figure 1.7 Cluster of individual farms in Western Norway, without church or other "village" characteristics (drawing from Berg 1968:192)

rainfall and have therefore continuously been rebuilt. First order patterns have been difficult to detect because of the lack of any wood building more than two or three hundred years old, compared with the still standing early Middle Ages structures of the dryer interior valleys. It is primarily archaeological evidence which suggests a continuity of the pattern of separate farms, until we find an unusual clustering of a small number of farms into what in Norwegian is called *Kling-tun* (cluster of farm buildings). Drawings like that of figure 1.7 were made in the mid-l900's from the memory of older people from or knowledgeable about a particular farm (Berg 1968). While clearly prominent in the 1800's, and obviously not part of the ancient sacred pattern of first order farms, a more exact date of the phenomenon is difficult to establish, though Middle Ages origins are not impossible.

Perhaps the most striking aspect of these agglomerations which look like villages but really are only clusters of individual farms and buildings, i.e. no churches, craft, or other non-farm entities or buildings, is the apparent lack of formal organization of space. No first order orientations and the like are in effect, and neither does one find distinct geometric notions of "row" as might have been one indication of second order space in Setesdal. The concept of collective space as "street" or even more bounded "common" may have existed. Was this something of an over-reaction to the dissolution of first order space with its spatially isolated farm schema? Given the greater frequency of rebuilding and less economic isolation, particularly due to commercial fishing, one could imagine an earlier breakdown of first order space, perhaps at the very beginning of the Reformation in the sixteenth or seventeenth century. Thus without the ancient East-West orientations of the dwellings, as was still the case in nineteenth century Setesdal, a presumed second order row tendency might be less formal in the Western part of the country. A greater period of separation from first order space may also account for the fact that the cluster pattern became the norm in the Western region of Norway, while the Setesdal valley example remained largely confined to that smaller area.

1.3 Older second order patterns of Denmark and Sweden

While evidence of first order Scandinavian space has been most extensive in Norway and to a lesser extent the forest and valley areas of Northern Sweden, more widespread and longer term examples of second order space appear in the more intensely agricultural flatlands of Denmark, areas of Middle Sweden and its larger islands of Öland and Gotland, and in Skåne (the southern portion of Sweden which was Danish until the middle of the seventeenth century). The rich and accessible flatlands of Scandinavia did not have the luxury of political and economic isolation more typical of the northern valley and forest areas. During the Viking period and before, the ancient pattern of dispersed individual farms prevailed in the flatland areas as well. Exceptions to these were the rare trading locus, or the novel and short lived warrior camps such as Trelleborg.

Apparently soon after these areas became Christian in the eleventh century, one sees a new form of contiguous farm "villages", this time built adjacent to a church. Such becomes the dominant pattern, with initially few separate standing individual farms.[9] Several reasons are given for this change. The external influence of regional and national political formulation was strong in association with the Catholic Church and its social organization. Farming practices may have changed necessitating more cooperation, or once the ritual and socially integrating power of the

31

individual Viking patterns diminished, with the prohibition of much indigenous religion, farms may have clustered out of purely territorial need to group together against external forces.

Given the greater strength and political interest of the Catholic Church in these areas, it is not unreasonable to speculate that the building of the church structure itself, with its defined geographic congregation, may have precipitated an initial territorial proximity of farm to church. Such was of course impossible in the northern forest and valley areas because of the dispersed nature of agricultural lands. Compared to the northern areas, greater spatial variability and more frequent examples of clustered farms existed in the fishing dependent western areas of Norway. These did not cluster around a church site as almost always occurred in the south. Given the scarcity of information about local social and religious life of the Middle Ages southern communities, one cannot pretend to speak definitively of the effects of becoming Christian eight or nine hundred years ago.

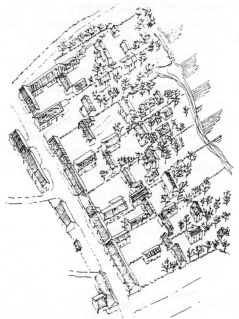

Figure 1.8 "Systematic" organization of farms in Testa 1916, a community in central Sweden (from Werne 1980:16)

In looking at the so-called "systematic" row farms of middle and island Sweden (see figures 1.8 and 1.9), and even those of Skåne and Denmark, the formality of these hypothetically second order groupings can be quite striking. Yet no such geometric rule appears to apply to the position of the church relative to the farm row, if one is even present. Typically the church is adjacent but perhaps not formally related with the same system as the individual farm units. Perhaps it is on the Swedish islands of Öland and Gotland that the formality of second order space reaches it greatest extent. It cannot be topography itself which causes clustering or formal organization, given the flat topography of the island communities.

Certainly agricultural land is most scarce on the naturally bounded islands, and something like a simple compression to the smallest possible space for non-productive farmyard sites might be an explanation. More persuasive, is the fact that these islands tend to maintain stronger subcultural continuity and independence within the larger Scandinavian culture. No dialect, with the possible exception of that of formerly Danish Skåne, is said to be as strong as that of Gotland. Certainly the ecological explanation does not preclude a more expressive one. The pattern could save space *and* expressively frame some essentially non-sacred form of ritual practice.

These extreme examples of formalization must be seen against the ancient background of dispersed, physically separate individual farms where overall productive efficiency was not markedly less than with the cooperative systems which followed. Until the Enclosure Acts of the 1800s, which will be discussed in Chapter Two, collective farming has been described as relatively inefficient because of the way in which large numbers of individual parcels were distributed in the larger collective area. The land reallocation of the Enclosure Acts, was in fact a return to unified parcels farmed by individual families once again.

Given the possibility that the major reason for the physical aggregation of farms was the huge cultural impact of dissolving first order Norse space, further study might show that the extreme of formalization on the islands relates to the extreme of indigenous, highly spatialized Scandinavian ethos which existed or exists there. It is also here that one can begin to more specifically identify the elements of second order space in clustered farm communities, as well as in the offices which we will shortly visit. First of all, some ancient East-West orientation of principal dwelling (a conceptual division between North and South) could persist within the flexibility of the now contiguous farm unit, even on Öland and Gotland. Even today people in Scandinavia are generally aware, and even suspicious of North as a powerful direction. Yet the major ritual places which were actually and conceptually to the North have long disappeared from active ritual and folklore practice. The frequent orientation of dwelling East-West could have lingering association, but no essential ritual function.[10]

Orientation still seems to exist in second order space, but now may be more a locally constructed direction of major collective space and road. Where possible these might, according to ancient first order associations, have run East-West. Their significance lies primarily in their ability to perceptually structure the new collective form; functional, topographic conditions dictated the actual directional orientation of many "village" roads or market spaces.[11] Without extensive further research, one cannot really be sure that the term "orientation" is appropriate, particularly in comparison

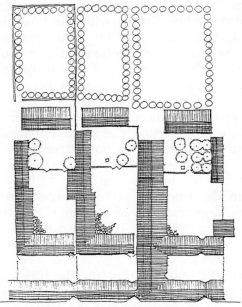

with its meaning in first order space. One assumes that the old East-West associations of the "passage of life" or complementary "alliance" between farm and "warrior" or guild aspects (Doxtater 1981:73) were not attached to second order village street *bygata* as they were called. In this case the direction of the open space, and hence its orientation may become non-associational and culturally meaningless in itself. The geometric axis seems to create a non-hierarchical linear contiguity, where conceptually each unit fronts independently and equally to its collective complement, the

Figure 1.9 A portion of Torp, a highly formalized group of farms on the Swedish island of Öland (from Werne 1980:48)

bygata. Differentiated positions along the row are not acceptable as sources of status. Herein lies the definition of the row as both uniquely second order, and Scandinavian.[12]

Given the loss of powerful orientational association, what remains at the cultural level of space may be the conceptual notion of opposition between individual farm unit and a new collective place, remembering that the old natural (collective) ritual sites eventually disappeared. The ritual dominance of Northern collective sites in nature, with the older dispersed farms, could have been replaced by the inherent dominance of the new aggregated form now as major collective site. The egalitarian row within is the *de facto* product of the conceptual association between individual farm and most powerful collective image, the street and its market/ritual area. To this space may have aggregated many of the old ritual practices of the ancient natural sites.

The initial meanings of the farm village, particularly the opposition between family farm and central "natural" collective ritual place, the *bygata*, must have initially maintained much of the old sacred symbolic associations. These meanings could have provided the primary expressive power to newly aggregated groups during initial changes from first to second order space. Without the daily and ceremonial contribution of symbolically oriented dwelling, settlement, and landscape space, one can hypothesize the gradual replacement of meaning attached to the spatial framework. What may be partly substituted for the symbolic orientational power of first order space, acting as it did to organize farms separated some distance from one another, is a social intensity of space which comes from radically increased physical proximity. There appears to have been a shift from relationships conceptualized primarily as between gods and humans to perceived relationships between two particular kinds of human groups. There is also a shift away from "obeying the gods" as it were,[13] and more consciously developing two aspects of the social self, one for each kind of group. While these same meanings were inherent in the earlier associations of the collectivity with the gods (the egalitarian), and the family with humans (the hierarchical), this more spiritually mediated form of expression could presumably only be effective through first order frameworks of axial contact.

To an extent, the symbolic meanings associated with places in first order space may be replaced in part by an associational frequency of behavioral acts within a less symbolically powerful framework of space. These more frequent acts may still be associated with a very rich complement of folk expression. During first order space, most if not all expressive media, e.g. decorative art, sculpture, architectural detail, and folklore, are informed or structured by sacred conceptions of space. In second order space symbolic content is somewhat "cut loose" from its positional meaning which provided much of its mnemonic and performative importance. It remains to be seen the degree to which this powerful, affective symbolic content from first order systems becomes reattached to the more architectural second order forms. This question arises because the actual usage of symbols is much less evident or overt in the latter folk life. Certainly these "Christians" cannot carve dragon images on the four corners of their dwellings, or paint images with "male" and "female" associations in formally designated domains. Overt symbolism, and particularly its attachment to cosmic directions, is intentionally focused on the Christian Church.[14] The job of keeping much of the old Norse symbolism alive, and perhaps reattaching it to modest folk villages and architecture, may rely largely on the discursive use of media such as folklore. These remain huge questions for future research.

1.4 The social intensity of the second order Skånsk *by*

The final segment of this overview of Scandinavian space focuses on the daily and ceremonial life of those "systematically" aggregated villages of Southern Sweden or Skåne, that formerly Danish area in many ways identical to the flatland farm history of present day Denmark. In reality the term *by* (pronounced "bee") should not directly translate to the English "village", because of the more common connotations of village as religious or economic focus, e.g. with a dominant and spatially central church with craft, commercial, and state administrative components. The meaning of the word *by* in Norwegian is reserved for more "European" villages and cities, and is distinguished from the term *bygd* which defines the topographical area of communally related dispersed farms (in inland areas where clustering did not occur). In Sweden, where the aggregated row form has much longer and more thoroughly been the pattern, *by* refers to the immediate village like cluster of farm dwellings, while the German related term *stad* applies to more European villages, towns and cities. Like the Norwegian, the Swedish *bygd* refers to the topographical area surrounding the *by*, but without of course the dispersed farms. In daily life, the proper name of such a farm community in Skåne refers to both the physical *by* and the surrounding *bygd*.

The reasons this chapter is concluded with an account of Skånsk *by* life is that first, the larger flatland societies were probably the most socially and spatially intense of all the second order examples, and second, it is here in Skåne that initial investigation of contemporary office buildings occurred. The link between the Skånsk/Scandinavian *by* and the *kontor* (office), was not direct in time or space. It is likely that these more intense and longer term Skånsk examples may have been principal carriers of Scandinavian second order culture, at least up until early twentieth century industrialization. Chapter Two more fully addresses the issue of how aspects of this symbolism and practice maintained themselves in spite of nineteenth and twentieth century changes in virtually all physical places where Scandinavians lived and worked.

The following image of the Skånsk *by* is one of intense collective life in aggregated second order settings. A central presupposition of this highly participatory and egalitarian balance between individual and group is its strong independence from the larger political, economic and religious sphere of both Catholic and Reformation periods. The limited role of parish council and church will be mentioned. More important for the present is a clear reader's view of the *by* in relationship to land owned by the nobility, Church, and Crown. While all three groups maintained for the most part large farm like estates, they all held other lands, sometimes adjacent, on which typical *byar* stood. Thus the vast majority of the population participated in the basic form of collective *by*. The greatest possibility of external control over these typically autonomous entities occurred in the case of the count or countess who lived on an adjacent estate. Rather than reapportion the *by* farms into more efficient productive units, as was the case during the nineteenth century enclosures, the nobility simply demanded some form of labor or product payment for the right to live in their *by*. Occupants of Church and Crown lands were taxed at a somewhat higher rate than farmers with clear title to their land within the *by*.

From the Middle Ages through the nineteenth century, the landed farmers (owning their own land), controlled about half the agricultural land in a country where less than ten percent of the population did not live in *by* communities. Deviation from this percentage occurred most markedly during the Post-Reformation period when Sweden became a major European power. The lands of both the Crown and the Nobility increased to about one-third each, leaving the remaining third still belonging to the landed farmer. The Church had lost virtually all of its land to the state which now controlled the new Lutheran religion (Löfgren 1972 :20). By the middle of the nineteenth century, the landed farmers had not only regained but increased their portion to about sixty percent, primarily because of new political power at the national level. Add to this historically stable percentage the numbers of other farmers who lived in similar *byar* as well (but with a somewhat greater, though seldom oppressive form of tax to the nobility or the Crown). One cannot fail to be impressed by the relative economic and political independence of the collective *by*, as well as its dominance and continuity as a form.

The most frequent pattern of aggregation in the Skånsk *by*, again, is the linear open space and road with facing rows of individual farms on both sides. As the illustrations of figure 1.10 show, these rows were not as geometrically precise as on the islands. Examples can be found where the *bygata* space takes a more circular form. Seemingly seldom is the church a formal organizing element for

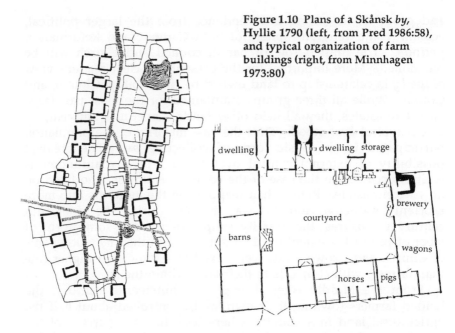

Figure 1.10 Plans of a Skånsk *by*, Hyllie 1790 (left, from Pred 1986:58), and typical organization of farm buildings (right, from Minnhagen 1973:80)

dwelling | dwelling storage

brewery

courtyard

barns

wagons

horses | pigs

either the row or oval shaped interior space. The formal effect of some island *byar* is contrasted further by the narrow spaces which separate one Skånsk farm group of dwellings from another. These create greater individual variation in setback and orientation.

At this scale, one sees again the product of the dissolution of first order space, specifically the conceptual relationships between dispersed individual farm and some major natural site to the symbolic North or perhaps Above. Formerly these natural communal places had probably been topographically and perceptually separate from any immediate farm areas. Their location in some high and mountain place "to the north" was probably not in any way geometrically related to individual farms. At the largest of community scale, an identical relationship between natural ritual site and all the farms would be difficult. Within the Norwegian folk farm, at least, a fairly precise directional geometry was possible between the group of farm buildings and the natural mound and tree of the farm spirit, located to the north (see figure 1.14). This orientational association and its ritual appears to have been similar to the larger opposition between entire farm area and the natural collective site. With the disappearance of the first order context, and the loss of control over the major natural ritual site, the society may have re integrated the natural site into a form controllable by second order practices.

This aggregated, architectural definition of what was to become the new collective open space, might with further research, be shown to have been something of a transitional phase during the Catholic Middle Ages. It could have been that the new churches, some of them built on ancient natural ritual sites, conceptually became the new place of the gods at first associated with collective ritual. How many of these churches were actually located to the north of the *by*, as in the example of Horup, Skåne? Many if not most of the Skånsk churches have principal entrances which emphasize not the Christian East-West axis but the ancient, powerful Norse contact axis of North-South. Some have no Western entrance, so essential to Christian sacred space.

The ritual calendar had been radically changed. Much of the former meaning of winter solstice with its feared and dominating visits of the gods to individual farms, a ritual death of the individual or familial perhaps, had been shifted to the symbolic death of Christ at Easter.[15] The intended subordination now was to Christ and Christian organization as source of individual salvation, rather than to the collective local community as before. Winter solstice was transformed into the time of God's gift to the world, his son, with the visitation of now friendly and benevolent spirits (see Doxtater 1981:171).

Yet major collective ritual continued outside of the church and Christianity in the form of political and judicial Thing meetings and the celebration of the ancient ritual of *Midsommer*. Presumably the sites used were no longer those of heathen Viking times in the Middle Ages, but were increasingly incorporated into the new collective spaces created in the *by* form. While it is most likely that the intrusive sacred concept of Christian space was never ritually persuasive, still it must have had the effect of diminishing the overall importance of first order space and symbolism. By the time of the Reformation, when the Church reasserted its architectural orientation and symbolism, it is possible that the meaning of the new collective *by* space had already reached very effective dimensions of practice. It may be that the Skånsk (and Danish) society was more successful in resisting the final attempt to implant Christian first order space, than the still dispersed Norwegian farm communities. In the flatland parts of Scandinavia a ready, second order, highly successful, physically integrated collective alternative existed to the more national and individually interested Lutheran church.

Figure 1.11 *Midsommer* rites in a Swedish *by* (1934 Dalarna, photo courtesy of the Nordiska Museet, Stockholm)

While the description of Middle Ages usage of these more intense, more architecturally defined second order spaces is difficult to reconstruct, one can perhaps paint a probable image of *by* social and particularly ceremonial life from more recent nineteenth century accounts. At the largest scale existed events in which the entire *by* participated. These were either calendrical ceremonies, or the yearly meeting of the *by* council. This was perhaps a replacement or evolution of Thing events which had disappeared during the changes of the Reformation.

As second order forms of ritual, one might expect less regional consistency and even formalization of performance, given the loss of orientational symbolism by which to organize particularly larger scale society. Gone to a large extent was the powerful symbolic effect of moving from the human to spiritual world during ritual. The legitimate ability to make contact with the other world had of course been exclusively focused on the physical place of the church. Not that much superstition about gnome like little beings, trolls, and even ancestors did not persist well into this century, but contact or access to them was no longer an important aspect of community scale rites. The Church prohibited such competition. Places where the spirits lived were no longer ritually organized or available in the second order *by* landscape. In ancient times major collective rituals outside the church structure involved either visits *from* gods or visits *to* gods, both of which required strong symbolic associations to real sacred places. The places where the gods lived were collectively known and directionally organized for ritual practice.

In contrast, the major collective space of the second order *by*, the *bygata* and *torg* or market space, had an intensive ritual focus but was probably not strongly associated with a spirit abode or place of origination. These largest scale *by* spaces were above all now permanently defined by the enclosing architectural form of the individual farms. No symbolic sacred space was necessary to construct and consecrate the collective ritual setting, the *bygata* (though perhaps still associated with Nature). To this architectural permanence is added the associational weight of egalitarian events in which all the farms and their families participated, especially *Midsommer* and the yearly council meeting of the farmers. Both occurred out-of-doors in the *bygata*. The social meaning of this space continued the basic first order social opposition between egalitarian collective and more hierarchical family. The opposed hierarchical element at this largest scale of the second order *by* may have been the architectural and institutional aspect of the Church. Certainly the Lutheran organization was hierarchical, with the priest occupying the highest local level of authority. Given more time to study this new symbolism in depth, one might find strong associational parallels between priest as hierarchical opposite to the community and the traditional symbolically similar role of the hierarchical master of the farm. Priests were generally farmers as well.

After the Reformation it is as if *by* society came to define the increasingly important national and economic role of the Church as similar to or associated with the very ancient individually interested and inherently hierarchical structure of the farm itself. Such a view is more continuous with old Norse culture in that many of these churches, at least in Norway, were actually built by important, individual farmers. The author has suggested that conceptually even the East-West orientations of the churches may have linked them with the power of the individual farm, whose principal dwelling also had a first order orientation of East-West (Doxtater 1990a). It is observed that the rites of passage which took place primarily in the dwelling, and were essentially legitimizing rituals of status, eventually shifted to the church in the form of the birth and death of Christ, the new image of farmer at the level of the *by* community. This farmer, operates, as individual farmers increasingly do, in terms of monetary economics and national politics. The architectural entity of church perhaps developed these associations in traditional opposition to the community open place, only the boundary of which is defined architecturally .

The form and meaning of marriage in the Skånsk *by* is particularly interesting because of its ancient importance as the most important ritual in an individual's life, the source of the most vital status of all, membership in the community of farms. Marriage meant the occupation of one's own farm, even though legally it might be rented or leased. The focus of the marriage rite had been on the farm dwelling. While the effective shift of one's "birth" and "death" to the church (as also occurred with Easter and Christmas) was perhaps symbolically effective, particularly in relation to more conscious selves, the movement of the critical marriage rites may have been more problematic for Lutheran organization.

Nominally people were to be married in the church by the priest, yet a large number simply formed households together as they still do in Sweden today. Christ did not himself marry, which may have been an illogical aspect to the image of Christ as farmer, though the local Lutheran priests could marry. This lack of major marriage ritual in the liturgy of the Church, either symbolically or factually, may be related to the observation that the most important collective ritual in the *by* open space, *Midsommer*, had strong overtones of marriage (Svensson 1977:14). Earlier the major collective association with the gods at their natural site had been the principal expression of equality or communitas and the most important rite of the community. This now becomes, with the disappearance of the gods and the natural collective site, a new expression of community through marriage. Previously, first order structure provided a symbolically permanent and known group of spirits primarily through sacred places. The second order community, placed more emphasis on the living to carry on and maintain

42

collective associations. The *Midsommer* rites understandably emphasized not only marriage, but marriage within the *by*.

During the 1920's, an elderly villager described the middle nineteenth century *Midsommer* celebration in the Skånsk *by* of Rorum:

> Everybody gathered in the open place near the church where the *Maistång* (maypole, *axis mundi*) had been raised. When everybody was there, we rode out a certain distance from the *by*....the young men were riding with their high hats on. The first rode with a trumpet. He had a young man at each side who held the horse while he blew...Then came all the other young men riding in pairs. And then came the young girls riding in a cart driven by one of the farmers. When they came to the place where they should turn back, each of the girls lay her garland on the hat of her fellow. The front riders received a wreath of flowers on their arm as well. Then they danced a little at that place, each with their own. When they came back to the *by*, the whole group rode around the *Maistång* one time and then went to the farm where they were to have the *fest*. There they danced. Later in the evening they would go again to the open place and dance around the *Maistång*. (Svensson 1973:93)

Other accounts from Skåne exhibit similar elements and meanings. The most apparent content involves the ritual pairing of the young unmarried men and women of the *by*. In some places the girls were given the opportunity to secretly choose the boy of their choice before the ceremony, then showing to all their preference during *Midsommer*. While much of the theme is common to European May rites of fertility and spring--usually not held specifically at summer solstice or midsummer--the association with weddings is much more particularly Skånsk and Scandinavian. Together with this marriage component, perhaps displaced in second order space from rites in the old Norse dwelling, one sees strong expression of the relationship between the individual farms and the collective *by*. The riding and dancing events at the communal open place, and out into the landscape, are contrasted with the ensuing *fest* of food and more dancing held at a particular farm. In many *byar* the location of the *fest* shifted yearly from farm to farm. Certainly the procession out to some natural place, a point on the road or field, is a remnant not only of the ancient trip out to the sacred place of the gods at midsummer, but the famous wedding journey to a conceptually similar place, often a church.

Figure 1.12 Painting of a *by* council in Skåne by Frans Lindberg (courtesy of Lund's folkmuseum, Kulturen)

This major collective rite in the open place may have been opposed spatially, temporally and symbolically to the major "hierarchical" rite of the church, *Jul*, at midwinter, or Christmas. Similarly opposed were the *by* council and the parish council. The *by* council of all individual farmers met yearly to plan cooperative activities. These were particularly strong in Skåne (Löfgren 1973:13) and the similar second order farms of Denmark. Spatially, in opposition to the parish council which met in some church building, the *by* council traditionally met at the village "stone" or marker, outside, located probably at a central point in the *bygata*. The council spokesperson, a position which shifted yearly, would call the yearly meeting, usually in the Fall, by blowing the distinctive Skånsk horn. This was an important business meeting, during which decisions had to be made about the maintenance of common grazing land, water supply, roads, fencing, and about the pattern of shared sowing and harvesting made necessary by the intricate collage of tiny individually owned parcels of land. The far greater cooperative work required on these flatland farms translated into strong *by* councils which appeared to very much hold their own against the spatially, politically and ideologically opposed parish councils, composed of some *by* members but dominated by the clergy.

During the *by* council meetings fines could be levied on those negligent in cooperation. The fines were usually in measurements of beer and schnapps which were communally disposed of in the *fest* or *gille* which followed the outdoor meeting (Löfgren 1973:19). The location of the *fest*, a particular farm, would shift from year to year. The ancient Viking individualism of the farmer is particularly evident from prohibitions against having knives on one's person during these traditional drinking *fests*. Much cooperative effort was required of each farmer and family. Produce was divided up and along with animals individually owned. Each farm was a physical and largely economic entity unto itself. Many activities, including vegetable gardening were the province of the individual family. As the tendency for fighting during *fests* suggests, these farmers were strongly independent and competitive, as always defined in the opposition between community and isolated Nordic farm. The Skånsk farmers were known for their independent status as masters of the farm. We can at this point use the term "patriarchal" to refer to this individual or familial component of the ancient Norse opposition.[16] Naturally, not only the traditional drinking among the collectivity of "patriarchs", but the political power of the *by* council was always a bone of contention with the Church, which frequently attempted to exert greater influence--particularly over the communally focused *fest*.

The pattern of cooperative work followed by the *gille* existed on many scales of space and time, and was the hallmark of Skånsk *by* society. The number of participants could range from those of a farm or two up to over a hundred at the largest scale of the entire *by* (Löfgren 1973:27). In the literature, the *gille* is described primarily as a principle of *by* culture, i.e. that every cooperative work event must be followed by a *fest*. The taking out of the summer's manure to the fields, for example, was one occasion for a relatively large and even formal *fest* (ibid:19). This was too much of a job for the individual farmer, since his particular pieces of land were dispersed in the *by* field fabric and could be some distance away from each other. Through an established order of rotation, each farm in turn would be the object of one day's cooperative labor, usually sufficient to clean out all the accumulated manure from the stalls. The most characteristic aspect of the ensuing *fest* was clearly plentiful food and drink, provided by many farms for the larger *fests*. Other activities occurred as well (ibid:26). With some of the larger *fests*, dancing might be included. People would play cards and tell stories.

The number of occasions for cooperative work in the flatland farms was large, e.g. sowing, harvesting, preparing new fields, slaughtering, house building, cheese making, moving, carding wool, preparing flax, transporting, and others.

Figure 1.13 *Slåttergillen* **(harvest festival), Gotland (photo by M. Klintberg 1914, courtesy Nordiska Museet)**

After working out in the fields, the communal group *fest* focused on a particular individual farm and dwelling. Some cooperative work, such as carding wool, took place in the dwelling at a particular farm. House building as well was an exception to the spatial oppositions expressed in most cooperative work events. Even in these cases where both the work and *fest* activity took place within the walls of the particular farm, at this smallest scale of space too, the spatial opposition between dwellings and enclosed courtyard may have structured these commonly opposed sentiments in *by* society. Just as the first order community site in nature had been incorporated into second order *by* form, this same phenomenon seems to have occurred as well at the scale of the individual farm. In first order Norwegian space, at least, the sacred natural place at the scale of the farm represented the ancestors as a collectivity. This was clearly the mound and tree standing North of and physically non-contiguous with the cluster of farm buildings.

46

The presence of unusually large and even formally placed trees in the courtyards of second order Scandinavian farms, as well as undoubtedly much folklore, suggests a similar incorporation of the natural site into a more architecturally expressive and associationally available form--this time at the scale of the farm itself.

Before looking more specifically at the apparent changes in Skånsk and Swedish farm society which took place over roughly the last two hundred years one needs to reiterate the essence of the second order *by* which served several hundred years from the Catholic Middle Ages through the Reformation. In the most general of terms, this long period maintained the first order social balance between the individual farm and the community. Along with the change in expressive processes, especially with regard to space and architecture, a certain atomization of culture existed as the larger ritually supported scales of Norse society condensed into the local form of the *by*. At least two scales of spatial and associational oppositions emerge. Each scale of opposition--village street/row of farms, courtyard/dwellings--carries the ancient association between the collective and familial. These are every bit symbolic concepts which exist as separate and opposed themes in the minds of *by* folk. Unlike the power of first order associations, which comes through the spatial organization of highly affective symbolic contents *per se*, here in second order space, many symbolic "objects" have lost their positional association to the frameworks of ritual space, in both architecture and landscape. In their place comes an intensity of ritual practice perhaps only marginally influenced by symbolic "residue" in verbal folklore content (which attempt to compensate for the breakup of sacred ritual). The organization of village experience into belief structures is still highly dependent upon spatial cognition, yet more upon architectural formalities than the coordination of symbolic directions in dwelling, settlement and landscape.

In first order societies, expressive effects depend upon the highly coordinated function of powerful symbols and spatial position. These produce structures in the minds of the participants, which together with the potential for convergence provided by actual symbolic frameworks in real settings, creates a ritual capacity and ability to influence social organization. These are here taken to be the *primary* bases of expressive culture in sacred societies. In hypothetical second order expression, social space continues to structure oppositional meaning in the minds of its inhabitants, still without primary contributions from texts. But the power of sym-

47

Figure 1.14 Sacred tree of the ancestors: ritually explicit first order (above), ritually implicit second order (below)

bolism and positional separation/contact have been replaced by associations much closer to the socio-political realities of actual life, i.e. by oppositions between actual social groups. To a large extent, the fear of death and the spirits, and its asymmetrical opposition to the living, gives way to an asymmetrical opposition within the emerging sense of self. A dominance of community over the individual can only be accomplished if that person participates in both situations, and has a developed sense of self in both domains.

The presumed effect of second order space is to provide a needed cognitive structuring of these fundamental relationships of selves. Not only is definition just as important in defining first order gods and their symbolism, but second order space provides as well the congruence between internal concept and social action or ritual. Definition is not in itself sufficient. There is probably always a tendency for the individual aspect of self to avoid collective control. The primary purpose of purely expressive acts of ritual is to maintain the power of community over the individual. Living in second order places not only gives the individual a strong sense of personal self, but demands frequent and obligatory participation in collective events. Hypothetically, the expressive function of architecture and ritual *precede* the ability to reach consensus during cooperative work--hence the separation of *fest* and function.

Unlike first order extension of ritual effect to larger scales, as in Iceland for example, expressive effect in second order societies such as the *by* is first of all limited to those spaces where an intensity of socially real and opposed events can be maintained, i.e. the *by* itself. Cognitive structure, its permanence, and shared usefulness over social time, become more dependent upon architectural form. In the absence of much first order expression, the form of settlement and dwelling become the expressive mold of social action and thought. The community pole of thought is not as we in the U.S. would quickly judge, an opposed discursive "other" which is essentially foreign to the individual, but is really a well-developed, essential, and dominant aspect of the self.

Certainly the second order *by* is a topic which demands more detailed research and consideration than presently possible. Regional variations in sustenance and settlement patterns must be given close attention while developing second order ideas. Attention must be paid, for example, to differences between those *byar* in which the land was owned by the *by* occupants and those where the land was owned by others, particularly an aristocrat or priest who lived nearby. One Swedish author briefly mentions the possibility that political and economic dependence upon a local patriarch created social disruption within the *by* and actually reduced the formality and presumably the expressive effectiveness of the *by* architecture and overall form (Gaunt 1977). Yet in spite of much work still to be done, the present outline of second order Skånsk and Swedish space serves to raise significant ideas about the continuity and theory of the way Swedes use space today, specifically in socially and economically vital office settings.

49

Notes

1   About the same time as the author's dissertation work in Norway, Kirsten Hastrup was similarly using textual sources of Nordic myth to first extract a spatial/symbolic conception(s) and then apply these concepts to actual socio-spatial experience and organization (Hastrup 1985). Because of the relative lack of data about real architectural, settlement and landscape usage in Viking Iceland, Hastrup's association between mythic space and actual society remains more sociologically abstract than experiential. Given the stated limitations of such a study, the work is an important parallel source to the similar but more spatially and experientially grounded efforts by the author. Most important, perhaps, is Hastrup's interests in changes in Icelandic socio-political and cultural processes. Interesting issues are raised about shifts from more ritualistic (sacred) systems of meaning to those more influenced by writing or textual expression. No theoretical distinction is made between the two in terms of expressive process (space vs. text), since the sacred is assumed to flow from verbal and written myth.

2   Artistic reflections of this ancient practice may be seen in Bergman's film "Fanny and Alexander". They do not eat their Christmas Eve dinner (winter solstice) in the customary dining room, leaving it implicitly vacant for visiting spirits. They, like their ancestors, find some other place of considerably lower status in which to convene the family meal.

3   The ritual use of (first order) sacred space forms the basis of the author's dissertation on folk periods in Norway. See again Doxtater 1981.

4   Though the idea of three orders of expressive or cultural space emerged during the present work--as a simple means of temporarily labeling things which were neither sacred (first order) nor territorial (as we will see third order)--a brief introduction to this theoretical idea was published earlier (Doxtater 1990b). A different ethnographic area, the Pueblo Indians of the American Southwest, was used for examples of similar changes in architectural form through the three different kinds of expressive space.

5   Interestingly enough, this is also the time of greatest impact of print on society. If in fact the largest social change in the Scandinavian farm culture took place during or after the Reformation, rather than at the time of the introduction of Christianity, then this might point to a greater importance of the change in expressive process, i.e. in its fundamental spatial aspects, rather than to more outwardly obvious cultural forms such as Religion, *per se*.

6   Recently, more intensive archeological research on Iron Age (Viking) farms in the agriculturally rich flatlands of Denmark and Sweden is probing the question of whether village like groupings of farms existed prior to the Middle Ages in these areas. Some evidence exists of prototypical clusterings prior to the long established historical forms (e.g. Hvass 1979, Callmer 1985). Whether these forms actually pre-date the introduction of Christianity remains to be seen. Throughout the majority of Viking Scandinavia, including Iceland, the spatially separate family farm is well documented.

7   An entire genre of folktale exists about the attempts of and reactions by the indigenous spirits to early Christian construction of churches on communally

sacred natural sites. Christiansen states that there are at least 125 variants for Norway alone; examples are provided (1964).

8 English "husband" and its traditional meaning of male head of the family or house appears to be derived from or related to old Scandinavian: "hus" (house), "bond" (farm or farmer).

9 The Swedish folk ethnographer, Sigurd Erixon, working primarily during the first half of this century, described the differences of settlement pattern we are speaking of as that between "systematically ordered and non-systematically ordered" farms (1960). These differences are explained primarily in terms of ecological causes.

10 Remember that second order space in these areas developed in response to the earlier Catholic period of the Middle Ages, rather than the more organizationally demanding Reformation in the valley and forest areas of Norway, for example, where the new dwelling orientation was still for a short time integrated with the larger Christian framework.

11 These village spaces were not "commons" in the sense of the English term. They were not commonly held grazing areas, but much smaller, circulation, meeting, market, ritual spaces defined by the buildings of individual farms.

12 The phenomenon of row housing or building certainly has not gone unnoticed in the architectural history of Scandinavia, e.g. a recent volume on Danish housing by Jørn Ørum-Nielsen (in Danish only).

13 This shift recalls the general hypothesis of Julian Jaynes (1990) that at some point in human history, people stopped listening to internal voices of the gods, as he defines it, and began to exercise greater consciousness. Certainly an increased awareness of the self can be seen as integral to presentational or discursive processes. The retreat of indigenous societies into collapsed, highly localized, largely autonomous entities within some larger "foreign" or non-integrated organization would produce immediate self-awareness.

14 This is not to say that much syncretism does not occur between Christian and Norse expression. The author recalls photographing the inscription "Adam and Eve" over the traditional interior doorways in a nineteenth century log dwelling in Norway. Earlier in this centuries old dwelling layout, other more indigenous symbols of male and femaleness would have been attached to this same location. This is probably made more likely by the syncretized sacred orientations between church and dwelling which briefly existed in some of these Norwegian valleys, ending less than a century ago (see again Doxtater 1990a).

15 The incorporation of essentially space based calendrical rituals into a really textually dependent now sacred form of rites of passage, of Christ, adds more evidence to the present introductory argument about possible expressive orders and their dependence upon changes in the vehicles of expressive process.

16 It seems quite possible that the patriarchal emphasis on a male master of the farm is part of the overall reaction to and integration with the Reformation. We know that the actual chair of honor or "highseat" for the master was introduced sometime in the sixteen or seventeenth centuries. Its obvious dominance of the formerly collective ritual table says much about larger scale influences on local equality.

2 Transitions to modernity

2.1 The Enclosure Acts

Swedish researchers, scholars, and laymen have been extremely interested in their own historical processes of agricultural intensification, industrialization and urbanization. Implicit in much of this interest is the motivation to illustrate the presence or absence of influence of the ancient farm culture on the uniquely democratic society that is Sweden today. Many of the research approaches closely parallel specialization elsewhere, e.g. economic, political, religious, or architectural history. From within anthropology has emerged a unique and now separate field called "ethnography". These are individuals who, very much like their anthropologist cousins, deal with general processes of culture. Unlike anthropologists in Sweden, ethnographers focus only on Swedish society. This research, much of which involves the transitions to modernity, has proven particularly useful to present efforts to understand the cultural meanings of Swedish space and architecture.

Within the issues significant to the emergence of modern Sweden, the Enclosure Acts from the middle of the 18th through the early part of the 19th centuries have been considered to be extremely critical (e.g. Åberg 1953, Christiansen 1978, Löfström 1984, Pred 1986). Because of the stability and cultural importance of the very old *by* pattern (perhaps up to eight hundred years in places), the physical breakup of these villages during enclosure has obviously been felt to be the potential source of much change to ancient Scandinavian values and ways of living. Much discussion still remains as to why it was necessary for the state to pass laws which allowed and actually promoted the reassembling of the dispersed individual fragments of land, which had been collectively

52

farmed, into spatially consolidated family farms (see figure 2.1 below).

Economists have pointed out the need for intensification of agriculture in Sweden during this period, both to provide for a rapidly increasing population, and to create greater international market capital. The argument here is that the collective method of farming was less efficient than individual farms on which things could not only be run better, but a greater amount of land could be kept in cultivation. This line of reasoning lends weight to the present idea that the original shift away from the individual, consolidated farm, into *byar*, was primarily a spatio-cultural, rather than economic or technological, response to the demise of first order culture. The author has found no source, which mentions or theoretically integrates the fact that for most Scandinavians enclosure was essentially a return to the ancient autonomous (Viking) farm pattern.

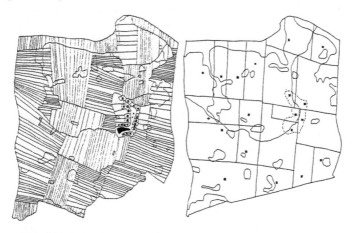

Figure 2.1 Changes in field ownership and location of individual farms in Lockarp Skåne, before (left) and after (right) enclosure (from Werne 1980:207)

Somewhat independent of economics and new technology *per se*, is the hypothesis that the enclosure acts were the means by which an alliance between large land owners (usually the aristocracy) and the state attempted to undermine or even destroy the cultural and political solidarity of the *by* communities of landed folk. The enclosure laws allowed any individual owner of parcels within the *by*, whether resident of that *by* or larger non-resident noble, to call for the enclosure of his, and by necessity, all lands within the *by*. Once the law had been invoked, a state surveyor began the process of mapping and meetings which sometimes only after several years produced a viable plan. While a small percentage of Skånsk *byar* never reorganized, either for political or topographical reasons, the large majority eventually came to agreement as to the new locations of now spatially independent farms. For functional and cultural reasons dating back to ancient times, farm buildings needed to be part of the individual farm site. For many, in spite of possible economic advantages of the reassembled individual farm, the new building of virtually all structures meant considerable expense; a fortunate few were able to remain in their old *by* location, gathering as it were their parcels around them.

As we have seen, it was hypothetically the second order architectural and settlement form which provided socio-cultural continuity to the Scandinavian ethos of community/individual balance. Perhaps different than other European experiences, Swedish landed folk managed to maintain a great deal of identity and solidarity at scales external to the *by*. This identity was always politically powerful against all outside influences: church, state, aristocracy. The increasing commerce and communication of the 18th century appears to have fostered a somewhat reactionary solidarity of landed peasant at the national level. Early in this same century the landed peasant farmers had nationally won the legal right to buy back into individual ownership much of the *by* farm land owned by the Crown. If the state, increasingly independent from the Crown, together with the aristocracy sought a means to counter the growing political power of the landed peasant, nothing could seemingly be more debilitating to farm solidarity than the physical breakup of the second order *by* form, perhaps *the* expressive basis of its collective success.

From the literature it is difficult to come to a clear conclusion about the effect of enclosure on *by* society. Many changes were dramatic. Daily interaction among the farm families was radically diminished by sheer distances between the now isolated farm sites. The incidence of cooperative work and ensuing *fest* diminished greatly. Competition among farmers became more pronounced. Some writers believe that all this was accompanied by the breakdown of collective sentiment. The ancient history and folklore of the Scandinavian farm community was being replaced by the increasingly self-interested, commercial identity of the individual farm and family. In terms of the aboriginal Scandinavian settlement pattern, the isolated individual farm pattern had been socially controllable, but only with the more powerful first order system of symbol, space, and ritual. It was not for reasons of any reemerged first order framework, that some have maintained that the enclosure acts did not in fact influence the farm culture as radically as often supposed.

Cooperative work and *fest* activity did after all continue, along with the "yearly" *by* council meeting, although with less frequency. The calendrical ritual of *Midsommer* continued to use the traditional spaces within and around the *by* as did rite-of-passage celebrations. After all, most of the previous accounts of these cultural events actually came from periods during or after the enclosures. The most important argument for a greater continuity of farm ethic, however, comes from a closer examination of actual changes in the physical form of the *by*.

To a large extent, the *by* continued to exist in spite of the departure of many of the landed patriarchs. New non-landed people moved in (Grandlund 1943). The powerful population growth of this period had produced large numbers of individuals who economically and culturally required their own familial identity, but were unable to acquire the actual land on which to farm. Particularly in the flatland farms of Skåne, the tendency was strong not to subdivide the farm through inheritance, leaving the intact farm instead to the fortunate son or daughter. The result was that many hired on to the farms of their own and neighboring *byar*. This was not a significant deviation from the long established pattern of sending one's own sons and daughters, before time of possible inheritance, to work on the other farms of the *by*. It was even felt that one could not get as much work out of one's own in comparison with a hired hand. This traditional situation has been described as producing less emphasis on kinship *per se* than on the actual farm as economic and social group. Clear are the accounts which describe the equal social consideration of one's own and one's hired young people by the farm "patriarch".

What this means is that the second order form of the *by* actually continued to exist in spite of the absence of many of the land owning farmers and their farm buildings, see example in figure 2.2 below.[1] The increasingly large number of landless farmers, together with the remaining landed farmers, provided in many cases essentially continuous *by* forms which may still exist today.[2] Given the lack of need for collective work in these evolving *byar*, either because of the more self sufficient farm pattern or the fact that the new majority of the *by* did not own land, one appreciates the parallel reduction in collective socio-cultural activities, particularly the work related *fests*. The probable continuity of the second order *by* patterns of socially defined space, suggests that for a large number, even a majority of the still dominantly agrarian population, the ancient Scandinavian balance between individual and collective still existed at the level of expressive culture. The reader should be aware that many exceptions to enclosure can be found. Either communities managed to politically inhibit individual requests for aggregation of land, as generally was the case on the islands of Öland and Gotland, or in the forested Northern areas such as Dalarna the economic value of enclosing agricultural land was considerably less and produced virtually no disruption of the settlement pattern, though the clustering of farms had always created forms less dense and formal (Brück 1971).

2.2 New class distinctions between farmers
The combination of the removal of many landed farmers from the *by*, along with the proportionally larger population growth of those with very little or no land created class distinctions for the first time within the *by* (Christiansen 1978, Ek 1980, Löfgren 1972, Pred 1986). For a very long period of time this group had been egalitarian in its frequent collective relationships (even though small differences existed in the amount of land owned). The enclosures provided an opportunity for self-interested, wealth accumulating orientations of the landed farmers. Much of the literature expresses obvious Marxist orientations. The agricultural (second order) "proletariat" becomes (third order) "bourgeois".

Landed farmers in many ways attempted to emulate the small but growing group of affluent city dwellers. Fashions of clothing and other objects of status increasingly became the focus of accumulated wealth. Wider was the sphere of "cultural", political, and educational activities for those landed, increasingly less folk like families. These farmers also created new self-preserving institutions nationally (Christiansen 1978). One would think that the new physical separation of many farms from the *by* would, along with the new individual emphasis on wealth, encourage the use of architectural form for discursive expression of family identity and status. This was not initially the case. Apparently the altered but culturally continuous *by* form continued to constrain the expression of the individual family in relation to the spatially and symbolically opposed community.

Logically, the separated farmers maintained the traditional second order associations not only through continued, though less frequent usage of *by* space, but through the fact that some number of similar landed farms remained in the *by*. Perhaps these farms in their physical second order context can be thought of as associational representatives for the now dispersed other farms of the traditional *by* council. More individual stylistic changes of the larger Skånsk farm houses only begin to occur several decades after relocation and rebuilding. Even then the basic plan forms show little deviation from the traditional (Minnhagen 1973). For the cottars and farm workers of the *by*, the increased numbers of which also demand new buildings, the traditional architectural forms are kept longer. This growing economic segment of the population has become the primary heir to second order Scandinavian culture, hypothetically founded on the traditional architectural and settlement forms of the *by*.

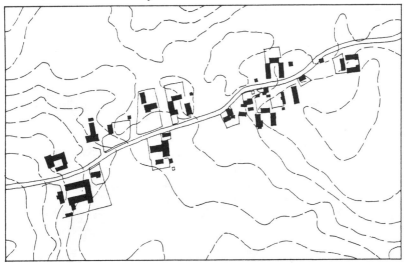

Figure 2.2 Plan of Östra Torn *by* near Lund, after enclosure during the early 1900's (from Ek 1968:96)

Architectural expression continued to be limited to the overall and largely external *by* form during the period after the enclosures and before true industrialization of the 1870's and on. Yet bourgeois inspired changes did occur at this time within the dwelling portion of the farm compound. Influenced by the expressive parlor so fashionable to urban Europeans, including a small but growing number in Sweden, the landed farmers in particular began to incorporate a similar "fine room" within the traditional dwelling (see figure 2.3). Prior to this time no special room had been set aside for formal, presentational (third order) events and expressions of family status. Both daily and ceremonial activities previously took place in the one major room of the dwelling wing. The highly decorated bourgeois character of these seldom used, but expensive new spaces has been one of the greatest sources of evidence for a major socio-cultural shift within the Scandinavian folk culture, particularly among the landed farmers. Yet it has also been pointed out, to the contrary, that these parlors also occurred within the dwellings of the forest *byar* to the north, where no class distinction was developing within the traditional farm society (Ek 1980). One even finds the argument that these new individualized uses of interior architecture were neither the expression of class within folk society, as in the Skånsk flatland *byar*, nor the adoption of bourgeois values by the entire *by* culture. In both flatland and forest, perhaps, they were primarily a syncretic expression of an emerging national folk identity as Christiansen argues (1978).

Figure 2.3 Urban model for the rural "fine room" or parlor within the "bourgeois" farm (Stockholm dwelling 1898, photo courtesy Nordiska Museet)

More important, from our present perspective, is the consideration of possible changes in the usage and association of second order *by* space which may have occurred because of the adoption of the parlor. Much of the discussion of bourgeois impact upon the traditional egalitarian farm society operates from more political science definitions. Here an entire society is labeled

58

"egalitarian", primarily because of a preoccupation with the more unusual, visible, collective aspects of their experience. Even ethnographers interested in architecture have tended to lose sight of the ancient reality of expressive *opposition* between the collective and the individual or patriarchical. The architectural dwelling had always been strongly associated with that family oriented, individual, and competitive pole of the opposition. Ever since the dissolution of first order symbolic and ritual meaning within the family dwelling, its almost logical use to express individual and competitive status had only been inhibited--not eliminated--by the intensity of ritual practice within the second order *by* form. In particular, the constant invitation of community into the dwelling itself during the *fest* component of collective work and ritual, must have been the most powerful inhibitor of status expression within the dwelling. This was culturally continuous, though only on the scale of the *by*, with the more symbolically effected ritual occupation of dwelling by communal spirits during first order periods.

The dispersal of farms during enclosure meant a reduction of opportunity for community *fest* occasions within the dwellings of the isolated farms. Eventually these large farms become more exclusively and expressively family oriented; the "fine room" becomes a sign of family status with formal events focusing more on individual family related rites of passage rather than collective *by* perspectives. The appearance of the parlor in the more economically homogeneous forest *byar* may be explained in part by the smaller size, less density and more informality of what is presumably a second order pattern. It is only logical, given the reduced formal and associational constraints by the community on the individual pole of the opposition, that expressions of the ancient meaning of the individual family would appear in terms of status and identity.[3] While second order culture must also be supported by folklore and even folk ideology, without the requisite amount of practice by which to build the cultural opposition, the system must begin to decay, particularly for those farmers living more physically isolated.

The question arises as to whether the larger farms remaining in the *by* built parlors as did their isolated counterparts. Again, the cottars of the *by* appeared not to, either for reasons of cost or second order constraints. Clarification of these issues will only come with specific research. Whatever the result, the building of parlors within the dwelling remains consistent with the ancient Scandinavian meaning of the individual farm and family, though one may be witnessing the first social ability to use architecture as discursive medium (diverging from first and second order ritual uses). It appears to have been some time before exterior architectural form was released from its highly constraining second order context, even in the new farms outside of the traditional *by*. This in spite of the fact that larger farmers were increasingly living in a much wider social and economic sphere.

It is the present thesis that in spite of the development of a class of large, isolated farms, much of traditional second order *by* practice survived the Enclosure Acts. The increasing number of cottars during the middle of the nineteenth century served to maintain the physical form and ritual of the *by* well into the industrialization and urbanization period from about 1870 through the early twentieth century. Yet cooperative purpose decreased significantly. Unlike more industrialized countries, Sweden still had half of its population on the farm as late as the turn of the century. At this time in England, for example, only eight percent of the population remained on the farm (Löfgren 1972:35).

Not only were there large numbers of Swedes still living on the land, the crofter majority of these in the traditional *byar*, but this period is strongly characterized by popular revivals of folk culture. Running parallel to or in outright conflict with European fashion, the arts and architecture of turn of the century Scandinavia were heavily influenced by folk themes. This is the period in which one finds rich written and graphic description of folk costume, art, architecture, and ceremony. Within professional architecture, it is not until the development of the modern movement, and the Stockholm exposition of the thirties, that the indigenous, largely folk influence diminishes significantly in Scandinavia. Just because a largely urban and European architecture of style and fashion no longer exhibits indigenous Scandinavian expression, does not necessarily mean that aspects of traditional second order culture have not made the transition from *by* to city.

2.3 Early urban phenomena

The most obvious evidence of importation of second order *by* practice into turn of the century Scandinavian cities lies in the phenomenon of the folk museum. Nowhere else in Europe or perhaps the world are open-air folk museums so ubiquitous or prominently located in the urban context. Foremost examples in Oslo (Bygdøy), Stockholm (Skansen) and the smaller museum in Lund (Kulturen) maintain a strong associational even visual relationship with the city center, as illustrated in figure 2.4. In the latter part of the nineteenth century, concerned citizen groups and

60

Figure 2.4 Views of folk museums of Skansen (Stockholm, above) and Kulturen (Lund, below) illustrating central location of these second order experiences in Scandinavian cities (photos courtesy of Kulturen and Skansen)

61

governments began buying and relocating the best examples of traditional architecture still standing on original farm sites. Urban open-air museum sites were limited in size by practical considerations of land cost and future urban growth. Yet a large number of examples from all the different regions of the country were assembled into these uniquely Scandinavian "urban" experiences. The effect may have been remarkably second order. Many of the farms moved in were from the more isolated valley and forest areas, where second order clustering never occurred (a latter day clustering as it were); and only individual flatland farms not pre-enclosure entire *byar* were included. The resulting density and physical contiguity of the museum effectively recreated at least a strong reminiscence of second order Scandinavian *by* within the city center.

The pilgrimage of either new urban dwellers or rural visitors to the "*by* in the city" must have evoked strong memories of the second order meaning and rhythm of the old *by* life. While traditional farmers had worked cooperatively out in the fields, urban workers in their factory and service jobs were struggling to follow this tradition (Frykman and Löfgren 1985:134). Much of the early activity in the folk museums involved the celebration of *fests*, many of which would have occurred in the traditional *by* spaces. People worked together and then held *fest* activities in the folk-museum. The new urban situation had significant differences. First it is difficult to see how the group who *fested* together would always be the same group who worked together. This is the essential ingredient for the structure/anti-structure rituals and "aspects of same selves" in second order societies. A greater expressive effectiveness must occur where people working together also perform social, communal celebrations in their same group.[4] The Scandinavian folk-museums continue to function today, though to a lessor extent as urban scale pilgrimage sites where communitas (anti-structure) celebration continues with strong associations to the ancient farm culture.[5]

Much of the educational interpretation of the museums lays heavy emphasis on work activities and implements. Spatially this tends to occur within the dwellings or other farm buildings. The museum sites are far too small to reproduce the major collective work which took place out in the fields. External spaces are experienced by the visitor as very much associated with collective *fest* or communitas activities. Coffee places are often expressly out-of-doors as are the majority of activities where visitors actually interact for more purely social or cultural motivations. Folk dancing and other more calendrical rites, with the exception of Christmas events in the dwellings, also appear to be expressively out-of-doors. While this opposition clearly recalls the old Norse polarity between the patriarchical work oriented family farm and the collective space in nature, it also may serve to actually oppose more industrial kinds of work with a collective experience in the largely open-air museum settings. Gone is the occupation of the individual farm by the community group which occurred during virtually all traditional *by fests* and celebrations. The expression of community dominance over structured (work) setting by actually moving into the formerly subordinate (and increasingly complementary) setting becomes less effective. It is conditioned by the economic and political autonomy of industrial work within the urbanizing Swedish culture.

Spatially the museums did and perhaps continue to function as second order culture, very much like the traditional *by*. Architecturally, the external forms of traditional fencing and gates make a strong statement of *by* identity vis-a-vis the surrounding cityscape. Internally, the architectural units become perceptually subservient to the roads and larger open spaces which their arrangement defines. Unlike traditional *by* constraints on the dwelling image, is the expression of regional identity in segments within the overall museum as *by*. The interiors as well show a range of variation representative of the late classes which emerged within the farm society. The presence or absence of the parlor may or may not have significance to second order culture of the *by*. Most important are the conventional behaviors brought into more formal cultural association by the spatial oppositions between dwellings and external spaces. If "work" to the industrial worker meant the possibilities of wealth and individual competition, then the associations of museum dwellings as settings for work behaviors seems clearly opposed to the communal events of the exterior spaces.

2.4 The workers' movements and their places

Although the folk movement and its most evident manifestation as folk museum possibly carried much of second order meaning (if not practice) into the urbanizing scene, for the new industrial worker the message was a mixed one. During the early industrialization period from the 1870's to the 1930's, most workers came from those same second order farm *byar* composed as they were of a majority of small farms and crofters. Large numbers also emigrated to the United States at this time. Coming from the *byar*, one would expect the meaning of the popularized folk culture and the folk museums to be particularly potent to these new urban, industrial workers. Yet much of the content and actual farm structures moved in to the museums, for example, clearly were associated with the larger farms and their separate and higher status which had emerged after the Enclosure Acts. So while much of the particularly second order culture and space must have been positively felt by workers and their families, the more conscious and obvious signs of large farm status could have created negative responses.

Swedish ethnologists speak of the existence of a socially clear urban class distinction between the new industrial "workers" or "underclass" and the more traditional "bourgeois" or "upperclass" during this time (Frykman and Löfgren 1985, Lindquist 1985). The so called middle class does not emerge until the period of the modern Swedish society. The academic, mercantile, and administrative powers of the city were instrumental in both the folk movement and the building of the many folk museums. Was this an attempt to somehow incorporate the newer status of large farmer with urban bourgeois values? Should one take a somewhat larger view of the very ancient meaning of Scandinavian farm culture and ask whether even in the small but growing cities, some second order presence existed? Before the Enclosure Acts, examples of *by* relationships between landed farmers certainly existed in close proximity to all urban places. Most city dwellers kept animals and maintained rural aspects in courtyard dwellings, in plan not unlike those of the *byar*. Most likely, the culture of these pre-industrial Scandinavian cities--small and limited as they were--was strongly influenced by the surrounding ethos, in spite of bourgeois differences. After enclosure, the decreasing status of the farm workers and crofters of the *byar* perhaps made association with the more status conscious city dwellers difficult.

Industrializing urban places, including the folk museums, probably were full of cultural contradictions, perhaps for both emigrating workers and established city dwellers. Much of the urban experience, outside of islands of second order meaning like the open-air museums, appears to have been determined by a kind of third order space and culture where classes vie for physical territories and symbols of identity (Frykman and Löfgren 1985:25). Unlike the more purely socio-cultural formation of second order *byar* from first order systems, urban forms even in Sweden were much less created in the first instance by purely socio-cultural consideration than by functional priorities of market and administration communication. Ancient religious centers such as Lund and Uppsala are obvious exceptions.

Figure 2.5 Discursive character of urban space during the early 1900's (Stockholm, photo courtesy of Nordiska Museet)

One finds ethnographic description of the central urban streets as "strange territories for the worker class, patrolled by bourgeois culture police with an eye for appropriate behavior" (ibid:119). There were music cafes where worker youth did not dare enter; just as the city hotel and central park pavilion were clearly territories of the *rena noblessen* (the clean nobility) or *de verkligt fina* (the really fine). In the central streets white student caps of the upperclass youth sharply contrasted with the dress of the older children of workers, as did the clothing of their parents (ibid:118-119). Yet if the central places of the city territorially or rhetorically belonged to the more European, traditional city dwellers, the workers appear to have created their own places. In contrast with the bourgeois who maintained a social life more focused on an overly patriarchical family and private residence, the workers, perhaps true to their origins in second order *by* society, maintained a much more evident collective life in public:

65

In a description of worker memories of the industrial city of Landskrona, 'One remembers how the neighbor on the second floor bought the block's first phonograph and played it in front of an open window while youngsters crowded together below. One remembers how women with their handwork sat on the stairs and talked across the street, while the men were in the back playing cards. In the summertime their world expanded. Then children could go out on expeditions, and on Sunday the entire family could cycle or take the train out to the country, and with their picnic basket visit relatives who still remained in farm worker houses or the street houses in the *byar*. Social life bloomed in the *kolonialer* (small garden plots clustered in marginal urban space, e.g. adjacent to the railroad tracks), in the open spaces of the apartment buildings, and on the local street corners...In Landskrona as elsewhere the normal family dwelling was only one room and a kitchen, which offered little opportunity for socialization within' (Frykman and Löfgren 1985:113). (author's translation, text in parenthesis added)

At the larger scale of the city as a whole, one finds unique expression of the worker community or collective in the construction of "folkhouses" and "folkparks". Nominally the result of growing worker identity and bargaining power, where surface imagery was superfically similar to communist prototypes, these centrally located assembly buildings and recreation parks provided a more formal territorial (discursive) statement of collective values vis-a-vis the urban territories of the bourgeois. One would like to interpret these expressions of collectivity as more dependent upon the linkage of workers to the second order *by* practice, than to the discursive rhetoric of socialist ideology. Particularly reminiscent of traditional community behavior in the street and open place of the *byar* are the folk parks such as illustrated in figure 2.6. Their intense social activity and general noise levels created negative impressions to the bourgeois more accustomed to quiet, aesthetic parks (ibid:122-23). Before either the folk houses or folk parks were built, the early organizational meetings of the worker movement took place in natural settings, more as picnic like collective events than strident inflammation to revolution (see figure 2.6). Large and occasionally violent strikes did however take place at industrial sites and elsewhere in the city during this early period of the worker movement.

Figure 2.6 Folkets Park in Lund, early twentieth century (above, photo courtesy Kulturen); mass workers' meeting near Stockholm, 1901 (below, photo courtesy the Nordiska Museet)

One can see the early meetings and the eventual folk parks in the city proper as closely akin to the activities of the open spaces of the *byar*. This phenomena may be unique to the Scandinavian urban experience, as are the folk museums. The relation between folk parks and folk museums in time and usage needs further study. Perhaps the centrally located folk park provided one of the greatest contributions to the maintenance of actual second order practice, or at least the collective aspect of such. For the later worker movement in the 1930's, the folk museum at Skansen in Stockholm seems to function at a more national level. This is the place where various unions held their yearly meetings (ibid:134). The Swedish interpretation emphasizes the discursive attachment of images of Swedish nationalism--park as symbol--to the emerging

67

social democratic middle class, a kind of fusion of worker and bourgeois values. One may alternatively stress the second order continuity of worker association and even practices with folk museums or folk parks, in this case at the national level.

Yet the building of often architecturally ornate "folks" buildings to express worker identity, clearly represents the adaptation of the third order, discursive uses of territory and architectural style. These were uses traditionally associated with the urban European bourgeois and mercantile economies in general. Inside seating during meetings was even used to formally express the hierarchies among different kinds of workers. This is said to be a period where the old Scandinavian farm values, largely that of localized community, blend with those of the city dwellers, that of the competitive and individual. In these terms, the architectural folk house and the natural folk park may as a pair express the newer third order purposes of competitive identity and power in place of the more culturally based integration of meanings accomplished by the old second order *by* society (the pair may also have replicated actual ritual practice *within* the worker class). By now this opposition should sound familiar. It is not the Marxist clash between capitalist and powerless worker, nor even the strife between a traditional Swedish agricultural society and the European city dweller. Instead, one sees attempts of the "folk-workers" to maintain traditional practices within themselves, while at the same time developing discursive strategies not so much to destroy the (non-ritually integrated) upperclass, as to eventually *reintegrate* them.

2.5 The patriarchal office
While urban industrial workers of the early nineteenth century apparently maintained viable connections with their second order *by* past, the small number of predominantly male office workers of this time associated very strongly with the bourgeois values of their employers. The Swedish term *tjänsteman* (service person) was sharply, and to some degree still is, distinguished from the industrial *arbetare* (worker). While many of the symbols of the urban bourgeoisie were borrowed from abroad, particularly from the rest of Europe, the basic familial or patriarchical social structure had strong ancestry within the traditional cultural system of Scandinavia. The patriarchical had always focused on the individual farm and family dwelling. The first offices in Sweden were very much associated with this past. At the early Bolinders

factory, for example, the office was actually (and typically) in the ground floor of an old house (Bedoire 1985:443).

In more urban settings, late nineteenth and early twentieth century offices took the form of apartments, often on the floors immediately above a retail ground level (Bedoire 1979:17). The central location and European architecture of these buildings carried strong discursive associations, not only of retail style and fashion, but more importantly of the upper class families who owned the buildings and often lived in the apartments above. This was the image in turn associated with the prestigious profession of *tjänsteman*. Growth in banking and insurance was the initial white collar response to the rapid industrialization occurring during this period. The palatial third order architecture of the first decades of this century belonged for the most part to these early forms of Swedish capitalism. While increasingly using larger portions of the entire building for offices, still, the often Chicago School exterior image and interior scale of rooms remained urban residential.

Figure 2.7 Italianesque bank building in central Lund directly in front of Scandinavia's largest and oldest cathedral (photo courtesy of Kulturen)

In Conradson's unique ethno-historical study of one of the original insurance companies in Stockholm, we are given specific description of what the primary amenities of working in these early offices were. Several have clear territorial implications. First was the importance of the location of the building in the most prestigious part of the city center. Second was the cleanliness of office work. Then came the desire to work with educated people. Fourth was being spatially near to the patriarch. Fifth consisted of an appreciation of the formally proscribed hours of work; and finally the employees liked the free midday meal and not having to carry a lunch box like common workers (Conradson 1988:75).

The patriarchical metaphor of office group as "family" appears frequently in interviews of now retired *tjänstemän* who began their career, usually as errand boys (Stigsdotter 1985). Most often the sons of *arbetare* families, these highly ambitious individuals sought identity as members of bourgeois white collar "families" whose fashionable clothing and clean hands created clear status separation from the class in which they had grown up (Conradson 1988:15). The small number of women in the very early offices were from well established families. Working often for little pay, and having attained their position through family ties, office work served as a temporary, socially acceptable activity until marriage (Conradson 1984:79). To the upwardly ambitious men, being a *tjänsteman* was serious business, not just a job but one's career. Long hours, extensive nightschool, and pay often lower than that of *arbetare*, were constant conditions of working one's way up in the office family.

A clear hierarchical authority is evident in status titles and formality of daily office life. Even an errand boy who at the age of seventeen or eighteen had become an "office assistant" could not be referred to in the informal *du* (you), but the formal *Ni*, by his replacement only a year or two his junior. Seating for *fests*, arrangements for photographs, customary places in the dining room, and the privilege of instigating *du* usages with subordinates, was dependent upon commonly understood rank order, with the patriarch of course at the head. Though advancement up the ladder depended upon sometimes extreme individual motivation, effort, and ability, strong feelings of office loyalty undoubtedly modified perceptions of competition among employees. It was felt that individual ambition adapted itself to a somewhat naturally occurring evolution of available higher positions or even an impersonal form of luck (Stigsdotter 1985:274). Employees always used the term "one" rather than "I" when discussing advancement among themselves. Camaraderie with fellow employees appears to have been part and parcel of loyalty to one's office, even to one's patriarch.[6]

Such a strong patriarchical sentiment had surely also been the case among the landed farmers after and perhaps even before enclosure, and even among rural and industrial *arbetare* families as well. This, represented in Scandinavia the ancient, family, hierarchical pole in the opposition with some community group. Yet, was there a major cultural or psychological difference between being a hired hand for a farm family other than one's own, as occurred for virtually all young farm people, and being a *tjänsteman* for an office patriarch? One recalls that the status of *tjänsteman* derived its superiority primarily from its distinctions from *arbetare*. We can only speculate whether, as sons of worker families with still active connections to the old second order *by*

70

society, being a *tjänsteman* during this period was socially parallel to becoming a farmer (at least when ideally possible for each to eventually own and be master of the farm). We are left with a unmistakable impression of early office as an hierarchical, patriarchical, family like organization, an extreme version of, yet not totally dissimilar from, the traditional individual farm. What is missing, perhaps, in the case of the office, is some sort of collective or community experience *between* office "families", one which at times dominates and controls for some greater good.

The ornate architectural exteriors of these early office buildings in Sweden, as seen in figure 2.7, were strongly influenced by American and European discourse of the time and clearly represented third order usage of form for purposes of identity and status. Particularly from the exterior, one can think of these buildings as elite territories within the spatially and culturally undefined flux of evolving Swedish cities. No shared, oppositional conceptions of space organized the whole, or even aspects of it. The architectural images were signs of status; their richness of mass, material, and ornamentation not only communicated the prestige of the occupants, but also rhetorically persuaded at a more emotional level. Compared with the limited expression of status through architectural exteriors of the landed farmer, even well after the breakup of the *byar*, the opulence of these images must have been heady stuff indeed. Not unlike the "fine rooms" or parlors which eventually made their way into the farm dwelling, the publicly visited interiors of the banks and insurance offices strongly communicated social and communicational importance, just as the exteriors did. The specific work rooms which received similar design treatment were reception areas, board rooms, private offices of a very limited number of executives, and often the dining rooms used by all *tjänstemän*, including those higher up in the organization (Conradson 1988:119).

Clerical work occurred in comparatively puritanical interior rooms seldom seen by the public. Most common were shared rooms, each of which would accommodate a small number of occupants, perhaps from three to twelve, as in the photograph of figure 2.8. These very unelaborated interior work areas, unlike the grand patriarchical public interface, had little or no decorative association with home or the family (Conradson 1988:119). When Conradson describes the lack of "home like" atmosphere of these sterile work rooms in early offices, she is comparing these images with those of internal office spaces after the second world war, when carpets, curtains and other decoration are said to have created

71

more residential images. It may be that only certain portions of the office provided positive patriarchical symbols available to the employee, for example going to work at a prestigious location or eating in the "family" dining room.

Figure 2.8 Early patriarchal office interior, a Stockholm insurance company (photo courtesy of the Nordiska Museet)

Yet the interior rooms were not simply functional to the extreme, but also authoritarian, very much an extension of patriarchical power. Work was a duty; only clocks and calendars were permitted on the wall. The message was discipline (ibid:122). Furthermore, these were highly territorial places. Such was the means of increasing one's position; the higher the rank the more the space. One began with a shared desk, then achieved one's own desk, then access to a telephone, then a position nearest or farthest from the window, and finally ownership of a private office (ibid: 123). In Conradson's chapter on the symbolism of the office, territoriality is the first (and presumably most important) category described. Somewhat later in her book, she speaks about the limited mobility of workers (ibid:145). Unless one were a *chef* (boss) one had very little opportunity to move about the building. Employees were watched where they sat and had little opportunity to leave their station. Doors to the corridor were always closed as part of the internal control over each work space (ibid:147). Work was to proceed with the least possible noise, with only work conversation allowed (ibid: 148).

It may be that much of the prominent third order signage of the public spaces of these buildings, including dining room, can be easily associated with the patriarchical domain of the Scandinavian ethos, while much of the actual behavior within the offices was essentially non-cultural, or territorial. As we will discuss in the book's conclusion, (Goffman's) "front spaces" communicating the public image of *tjänstemän* may be positive compensation for the negative territorial reality of working in "back spaces". In this view, the patriarchical meanings from the ethnic Scandinavian past are less a provision of overall legitimacy to the work organization than symbolic compensation for the territorial reality of work.[7]

Aside from the extreme territoriality which occurred within the interior work rooms, aspects other than their decoration may have had additional connotations of the familial Scandinavian dwelling. The size of these rooms, in addition to being in scale with those of apartments, was undoubtedly conditioned by the linear plan form of the buildings. One could argue that the relatively narrow building width was a vestige of the need for natural light before electric lighting was used. On the other hand, a large percentage of these office/apartment plans show a linear form wrapped around an exterior courtyard called *gård*, the Scandinavian term for farmyard, backyard, and even farm itself (see figure 2.9). Schematically, we are reminded of the traditional image of courtyard created by the arrangement of dwellings in individual *by* farms.

It is tempting to suggest that the "natural" courtyard represented a collective, cultural opposition to the more individually and hierarchically focused building interiors which surrounded. Yet just as the urban street has been defined as a setting for class territoriality rather than collective unity and control, the courtyard as well probably carried only vague associations with the meanings of its *by* counterpart. Although the actual usage of the courtyards of these early office buildings is not here, or apparently elsewhere well documented, retail occupation of the first floors would logically have inhibited the collective use of the *gård* by the patriarchal *tjänstemän*. Furthermore, the most seemingly "collective" room in the office organization was the restaurant dining room. Historically these are located on the top floors, where the association with courtyard is far less than with wider views of the cityscape, and the rhetoric of being highest up and in the city center. We will return to the location of true collective dining rooms, and their relationship to exterior spaces, in contemporary office examples.

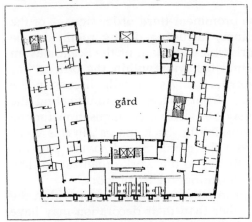

gård

Figure 2.9 Typical courtyard or *gård* of early office: Amerikahuset in Göteborg 1925 (from Byggnadsvärlden 1925)

The size and decoration of dining rooms in early white collar offices may be uniquely Swedish, while, for example, the light seeking courtyard plan probably was a more universal response to an urban site. In spite of the fact that rank order was clearly communicated by seating positions within the office dining rooms of this period, still, all employees, with the possible exception of errand boys, were included (see figure 2.10 below). Rather than expressing the later and more universal distinctions between executives and non-salaried clerical workers, for example, the meaning of the dining rooms and their hierarchical seating order lay in the particularly Swedish definition of patriarchal family as a cultural unit, the "individual" pole of the ancient opposition with the collective. In this sense, being a *tjänsteman* was the conceptual equivalent to being a member of that culturally defined unit, the patriarchal family. One asks whether the motivation to be a Swedish office person during the first decades of this century was less the bourgeois definition of self and class superiority, than the seeking of "family" identity in response to very old cultural definitions in Scandinavian culture.

What one sees in these early offices is an obviously novel, transitional, and evolving set of influences on architectural form. The physical urban setting and the legacy of need of natural light are largely responsible for the overall plan form and building massing. Just as clear are new third order exterior and interior expressions of the identity and status of the particular bank or insurance organization vis-a-vis others in the early twentieth century urban flux. Yet a substantial amount of patriarchal family meaning, as apparent in the apartment scale of rooms and inclusive dining rooms, can only be understood as maintained aspects of traditional

74

Scandinavian culture. What apparently is not carried into this new milieu is the community or collective opposite spaces and ritual practice of *by* courtyards, streets and major open space.

In the traditional farm societies, the community spaces and associations were dominant and thus useful in the control of patriarchical entities. No such meanings or places occur within or adjacent to early office buildings. With the possible exception of rare *frukost* (breakfast) rooms for men and women, no egalitarian break spaces existed to oppose the power of the patriarch. Nor was the dining room such a place at the largest scale. True to the *tjänsteman* and family concept, all was hierarchy. No dominant, or even equal place of collective power existed in relation to the expression of patriarch's private office with its privileged size and location.

Figure 2.10 Early dining room, *"matsal"*, in an insurance office, Livförsäkrings Svecia (photo courtesy of Nordiska Museet)

Perhaps the interiors of early Swedish offices were, however, less available to the extremes of territoriality which occur in U.S. offices today. First, the linear form produced by the legacy of natural light and the metaphor of apartment limited the positional importance of the location of individual offices and the sizes of the typically shared office rooms. It is more difficult for a *chef* or *V.D.* (CEO or chief executive officer) to signal dominance of position along a linear plan since power corners on the plan exterior do not generally occur. In Sweden the important direct association of *chef* to public entrance, expressing reception of guests, remains historically continuous through the evolution of the office. To a large extent, the *chef 's* office is spatially separated from the office spaces of the employees, thereby strongly limiting positional dominance in relation to the large office organization.

In sum then, the highly patriarchical way of doing business in early twentieth century Sweden created limitations to processes of change which eventually would create a very modern industrialized economy with a highly social-democratic labor organization. To a large extent, the prestigious office settings of the time were divorced from the places and people most active in generating the forces which eventually would lead to the emergence of the modern Swedish state.

2.6 Labor influences on early office organization

It was the industrial *arbetare* who were most responsible for the creation of the strong labor organization that was to become the basis for the dominant political party in modern Sweden, the Social Democrats (Olofsson 1984). The party, founded in 1889, fueled by agitation and strikes of the first two decades of this century, became Sweden's largest political organization by the 1920's. Though not yet in control of parliament, its influence at this time led to the institution of the general vote and other more democratic processes in government. The Social Democratic movement in Sweden, already by 1920 much more successful than in other Western European countries, was founded less upon the organization of new urban and industrial kinds of power, than upon national rural and folk associations (Olofsson 1984:439). Unusually immune to factionalism of work type or ideology, including Communism, the Swedish labor movement was and is characteristically unified. In addition to more purely philosophical or ideological links with the second order *by* tradition, the associations *arbetare* maintained with novel places such as workplace clubs, urban folk houses, folk museums and parks in the evolving urban milieu are felt to have been uniquely important to the Swedish movement. While the political and economic successes of the Social Democratic movement may have been built upon a shared, collective sense of their second order past, the industrial settings in which they actually worked remained, in Fredric Bedoire's view, places where normal social rules about the human environment did not apply (1985:437).

Within offices, highly patriarchical social and cultural values clearly created much of the spatial usage and architectural form of these settings. The amenities of washrooms, coatrooms, and especially restaurants were part of the necessary provisions for the patriarchical "family". In the industrial Swedish workplace of the early twentieth century, however, even such basic facilities as toilets might still be absent. Other countries were farther ahead in the provision of worker amenities in industry. While the growing labor and Social Democratic movement appeared to have created a spatial basis for its collective ethos--in parks, locales and museums-- still, these community places and practices remained largely independent from the actual workplace. Industrial work settings were primarily patterned after the functional requirements of production rather than any social or cultural processes. Subsequent emphases on rationalization and modernization in Swedish industry, up even to the 1960's, would as well provide the primary influence to the human use of space and form, continuing to inhibit the emergence of an expressive, lived-in, second order milieu.

While *arbetare* of the early decades of the twentieth century maintained, perhaps, the second order collective pole from traditional *by* society, *tjänstemän* appear to have emphasized the opposite, i.e. the individual, hierarchical or familial. The urban, industrial process had for a time separated the two meanings of what were spatially and socially related in virtually every scale of traditional places. Ritual practice had integrated the two aspects of self which now resided in different minds. The *arbetare* were struggling to maintain the collective, surely sensing the difficulty of achieving a family status even remotely equivalent to that of the traditional farmer. At the same time, the *tjänstemän* were working just as hard to keep the patriarchical aspect functioning, sensing on the other hand the improbability of collective equality in a capitalist economy. To the *tjänsteman* of this period, union organization was anathema to their belief and behavior, even though here too could a certain but limited collective sentiment be discerned. It was not until the 1940's, after major changes in the office, that *tjänstemän* reluctantly allowed themselves to be organized into unions.

2.7 Rationalization of the office

The becoming of a modern capitalist economy during the two or three decades before the 1950's generated seemingly significant changes in the patriarchical office. Greater numbers of office workers found themselves increasingly subjected to "rational", industrial or Tayloristic scrutiny. Important aspects of the patriarchical way of doing things could no longer function with the larger numbers of *tjänstemän*, many of whom were doing increasingly specialized work. Like industrial settings, presumably, the spatial patterns of offices could be influenced by "rational" ideas. Even in the first two decades of the century, one could find rare and ominous examples of *tralhav* (sea of slaves) where large numbers of low level, routine workers were assembled in one expansive but crowded and noisy space (Bedoire 1979). As evident in figure 2.11, these were not status territories of the patriarchy but rationalized production places, particularly as the distinction between skilled and unskilled employees.

Figure 2.11 View of so-called *trälhav*, Svenska Livförsäkrings, Stockholm (photo courtesy of Nordiska Museet)

78

Specific references of Tayloristic influences in Swedish offices occur in the years 1929 and 1935, for example (Bedoire 1979:10). From a biographic account of the life and philosophy of a Swedish industrial engineer one witnesses the essence of rationalization, i.e. the managerial control and supervision over employees (Lindqvist 1985:151). The same is clearly true within the expanding more Tayloristic office settings as well. The *trälhav* was surrounded and visually controlled by smaller offices. In most buildings of this time, glass walls were common as it was felt necessary for supervisors to visually oversee their subordinates. This was the case in the vast open spaces of routine work and in the more specialized smaller shared offices (Bedoire 1979:23). Earlier apartment like offices maintained the privacy or family definition of the room through traditional solid walls, entryways, individual doors, and the like. With the new windows on interior room surfaces and even entrances, the corridors became far more useful for the visual control of workers. Though the linear, double loaded office of the patriarchical period essentially remains, corridors become specifically functional and geometrically clean, intended as they were for efficient control and movement of "goods".

In spite of the fact that the rationalization of interior plan was taking place at the same time that architects were purifying themselves with the application of "modern" or "functional" styles, as a type of design project, offices were far from the mainstream of architectural interest. One immediately recognizes the endemic predisposition of architects everywhere to give less consideration to the social/functional program than to the discursive expression of style. While the visual style of offices throughout the Western industrial world was following the lead of popular examples such as Lescaze's Philadelphia Saving Fund Society Building (Bedoire 1979:23), the form of their interiors was far more dependent upon a philosophically related but politically separate set of decisions coming from executives rather than architects.

The relatively sudden shift of facade image from the bourgeois and urban residential to the rational and modern clearly signaled the loss of status which many *tjänstemän* were experiencing. The old familial, achievable hierarchy was being threatened by production as an end in itself, something quite different from the traditional definition which had been dominant. The larger overall scale of the buildings, together with specialized work within, reinforced the separation which was taking place between the employees and administration. While separated before from the "discursive" zones of the building they nonetheless had access to these places as compensatory, presentational symbolic capital. Now they were increasingly denied this capital and were even severed from a symbolic place in some overall hierarchical or familial scheme. At the same time, office workers from this period report a loss of camaraderie (Stigsdotter 1985:278). Increasingly, specialized high school and even university education was replacing what had been largely an apprentice system of learning how to work in an

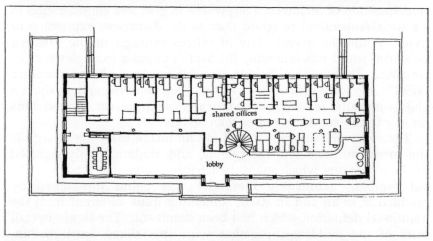

Figure 2.12 Shared room in modernizing office, Singer & Co., 1934 (above, photo courtesy of Nordic Museum); plan of "modern" office published in Byggmästaren, 1940 (below)

80

office. Individuals could enter the system immediately, particularly in areas of specialization, rather than rely upon a socially intense process of "family socialization".

Again from Conradson's ethnographic history of a Stockholm insurance office during the 1930's, one further understands the detail of daily life which accompanied the rationalized office space and decor. The formality of the patriarchical shifted quite easily, it would seem, to the formality of the rational. The strict rules and authoritarianism of the good bourgeois family became the obedience to production goals and flows of information. Forms of address maintained their rigidity. The traditional formal "family" clothing of the earlier and more prestigious *tjänsteman* was for a time in this insurance office replaced by actual uniforms during rationalization (Conradson 1980:55). The chief executive of the industrialized office continued to have the only private room which would be well decorated, while the shared employee work spaces remained functionally and visually austere, lacking either expression of style or personalization.

Lunches continued to be subsidized by the employer and the seating in the office restaurant or lunch room still signaled differences in rank, though presumably family statuses are being replaced by a ranking of work specialization, skilled or unskilled, salaried or unsalaried. Referring back to the interviews of retired *tjänstemän*, they actually recalled the differences between the greater individual choices of food in earlier offices and the standardization of menu which followed (Stigsdotter 1985:293). This might be interpreted as a contrast between the bourgeois importance of food as third order expression and the rational view of food as energy for workers. In the Stockholm insurance office, no coffee break times or places were allowed as part of the efficient work process, only lunch (Conradson 1980:55). Physically, what had been the separation between the "domestic" work rooms and "family" dining room becomes the necessary separation of work from the non-productive necessity to eat.

The periodic use of often elaborate dining rooms had been a reaffirmation of the statuses and identities which permeated the daily work relationships between *tjänstemän*. In the more rationalized office, the intention was to completely divorce things which were social from things which were efficient and productive. The fact that rank seating orders in often distant dining rooms appear to have persisted through much of the 1930's and 40's, suggests that a certain amount of patriarchical tradition remained. It seems that the described similarities between patriarchical and rational behaviors and the lack of change in overall layout of offices casts some doubt as how much the strictly discursive idea of rationalism changed the way things worked.

There appears to be little evolution of the essential territorial basis of social organization in the major work spaces of the office. It is probably the case that the overt third order symbolism of *tjänstemän*, the elaborate public spaces and facades, had been replaced by a new rhetoric of functionalism. These new signs probably provided little symbolic capital to the average worker by which to compensate for the hierarchical, territorial reality of work. Undoubtedly, as we will examine to greater length in the conclusion, the facade of functional instrumentality was but a rhetorical device to more consciously assuage the political inequalities of work. It did not have the symbolic value of the traditional, patriarchical meanings of *tjänstemän*, with its underlying roots in a Scandinavian past.

When the old integration of opposite aspects of selves was broken up in the move from rural to urban lives, both *arbetare* and *tjänstemän* compensated for their loss of (other) self in part through a sort of discursive exaggeration of the self which remained. The expressive deemphasis of these extremes of symbolic capital by rationalization and the modern movement, especially in the case of office workers, removed the "capital" without substituting new or reintegrating old selves. Both older and even younger office workers, and particularly the increasing number of women, probably still thought of their relationships to each other as familial, even though the bosses (and architects) were discursively deep into practices of rationalization. One recalls Conradson's discussion of offices becoming more decoratively "homelike" during this period.

2.8 Rationalism as source of the democratic breakthrough

During the period of modernization, one could idealize the maintenance of the power of collective meanings through actual practices of the *arbetare* (ritual), while individual or patriarchal meanings were emphasized by *tjänstemän* through more presentational capital (discourse). Though it is also true that collectivity itself had to become externally discursive in its power relationships with a newly separate class of Swedes. The critical dimension of resolution of this dilema--at the level of expressive culture and tradition of egalitarianism--was perhaps the ability of Swedish society to find appropriate spatial expression within a urban shape created primarily by functional, communicational and territorial (third order) forces. To a certain degree this contrasts with indigenous ethnographic views of the modernization process. The Sweden which emerges as the "democratic breakthrough" of the 1940's, and the Sweden which the outsider more immediately sees, is a very rational, socially sensitive, health conscious people bound together by an educated history of Swedish history and culture. It is felt that the discourse of industrial processes, including Taylorism (Lindquist 1985:161), and the conscious, discursive struggle against the bourgeoisie (Fyrkman and Löfgren 1985:137, Conradson 1988:13) produced this overriding rationalism. In spite of early movements of religious fundamentalism and abstinence, which related in time and substance to the organizational efforts of the rural and urban worker class, and in spite of the state Lutheran church to which most Swedes nominally belong, organized religion is given a relatively a minor role in the evolution of modern Swedish society.[8]

At the level of culture, the relatively swift but substantial move from *by* society to modern social democracy is seen as a contrast between clearly collective beliefs of temporally cyclical farm society, economy, or mythic landscape, and newer meanings of strongly individually and competitively focused values about linear time, education for a better life, the atomization of the nuclear family, and consumption of things including recreation (Frykman and Löfgren 1979:21-73).[9] Yet this latter definition can to a large extent be applied to most modern industrial societies; it feels particularly descriptive of processes in the United States, an influential conscious model in fact for much industrial modernization in early twentieth century Sweden (Lindquist 1985). Discursive industrial ideals certainly can and have been the source of individual and group values which function more broadly in the society. There is something very unique about the way Sweden organizes itself at several scales, something beyond the more universal psychology and philosophy of industrial societies. It goes beyond the possibility of a historically and demographically unique "national rationalism" as the seemingly discursive accommodation of worker groups and bourgeois mentality--less the non-discursive or ritual reintegration of ancient Scandinavian selves, than a presumed conscious enlightenment of social individuals.

In a recent work assembling evidence for a Swedish national character, the popular ethnographer, Åke Daun, exhaustively details many of the typical traits: shyness, independence, conflict avoidance, honor, exactness, rational approach, order, puritanical morality, work ethic, etc. (1989, 1991). Origins of this are open to debate, but Daun proposes some tentative ideas in his conclusion.

First and foremost was a necessary rational interface with the uncompromising climate and overall ecology of the North. To this basic "survival" characteristic he adds the independence created by the diminished social and cooperative contact which occurred with the enclosure acts or breakup of the villages. These characteristics in turn lead to a belief in objectivity and rationality, not only in terms of one's own life, but as an accepted and trusted *modus operandi* of governmental and other institutions as well (Daun 1989:215). Thus the long tenure of the Social Democratic government in Sweden is seen as a kind of magnification of basic character. Presumably, given the ultimate political control of society and the expansive post-war economy, the emergence of the rational modern Swedish society was "characteristically" inevitable.

Daun's accurate description of the typical Swede establishes such character, while perhaps, like so many other Scandinavian scholars, leaving out possible links to the rich symbolic and ritual past. Stromberg, while echoing the fascination with what he calls "cooperative individualism" and speaking also of the existence of both strong self-independence and cooperation and consensus, places more emphasis on a cultural or expressive origin of both aspects (1991). He maintains that a highly discursive Christian fundamentalism provided the cultural means to these developing ends. While Stromberg's interest in explaining this emergent phenomenon strongly parallels the present essay, fundamentalists appear to use different expressive processes than ritual societies. Baptists, for example, seem to be clearly third order in their absolute dependence upon the "word", while pre-ecumental Catholics maintain the symbolic and spatial power of first order expression (though in a very spatially limited setting).

In most explanations of the Swedish phenomenon, the social practices of collectivity tend to be left out of discursive processes. Collective experience is recognized, but its purposes tend to be defined as functional, a logical means of protecting the overriding individual belief in independence and objectivity. If one were to take a more ritual practice view of Swedish history, as the present work does, many of these same personality characteristics may be seen as very much the *result* of such expressive process.

The real question is whether these personality characteristics are belief systems in themselves--even only in terms of the discursive-- or are products of other, more obviously symbolic phenomena. Given the present hypothesis of an evident second order ethos in Scandinavia, one based on traditional symbols, conceptions of space, and ritual practice, one tends to treat the idea of personality based

84

beliefs as somewhat epiphenomenal (given the linkage between behavior and institution accomplished by second order ritual). The presumed ethno-historical basis of these beliefs in the interpretation of Swedish evolution amounts to a reification of the mythic instrumentalism which accompanies any modernizing society. One can see why Tayloristic thinking from abroad has easily fused with indigenous ideas of Swedish culture.

In terms of the rationalized offices of this relatively brief period before the modern breakthrough, one again sees territorial continuity with the earlier patriarchical forms. Certainly many of the compensatory symbols have been removed, but it seems unlikely that the new rationalism represented either a socially based alternative belief system, or a compensatory philosophy. Perhaps the most important thing which rationalization provided, in a milieu previously shaped by social and cultural meanings, was the executive control of the overall shape of the office workplace. The issue of whether rational offices were in fact more productive can probably be dismissed rather quickly. The interviews with retired *tjänstemän* again and again illustrated their perception that people worked harder in the patriarchical office. Compared with early and contemporary offices, the greater amount of routine work during the period that followed might be argument for more efficiency, but probably the crowded workspace and often extreme supervisory control created the opposite effect, as it often does today.

It has become axiomatic, at least for this researcher, that the key to office productivity is, and always has been, not primarily the functional arrangement of workers, but the degree to which positive social and cultural relationships are an institutionalized part of the activity. This is true both in the case of the elaborated Swedish office family of the early period, and the more recent reintegration of traditional selves.

2.9 The larger urban-industrial context

Compared to the physical setting of industrial workers, office places in Sweden were always more susceptible to social and cultural expression, though the employees' control over office layout was considerably mitigated by the combination of traditional Scandinavian patriarchy and executive ideologies of rationalization. Quite early in the industrial development, the *arbetare* had been quite successful in achieving both worker rights in the shop and national power. Because of the dominance of manufacturing function in the design of the workspace, however, the industrial workers could not control the shape of their major life space. Thus

85

the collective pole of the old Scandinavian opposition was excluded from these essential social and economic places. It did appear elsewhere, either physically separated in the factory or in the larger urban setting. In the more culturally and ideologically dominated offices, it was only very late in the period of rationalization that unionization became politically necessary, though probably not even then ethically acceptable. The right for *tjänstemän* to organize was won with comparatively little fanfare in 1939. The first labor agreement between the new union of office workers, the TCO (*Tjänstemännens Centralorganisation*) and corporate management did not occur until 1946 (Conradson 1980:54, 55).

Although unionization occurs late in the "rational" period, and makes significant improvements to salary, pension, titles, and work hours, change in the control and shape of the socially sensitive physical setting could only take place at some later time. One finishes this chapter with a hoped for sense of expectation for future resolution of the Swedish office. Will a collective union aspect of office life develop, one which is assumed to associate with the traditional second order *by* as did the larger social-democratic movement? How will this new presence relate to a continuation of the individual, familial, or patriarchical?

While our foregoing discussion of the continuity of separated aspects of second order culture and space into the urban industrial process has been short and very speculative, and as an issue deserves extensive work itself, the exercise will hopefully be seen as useful. It appears axiomatic that the functional and social forces of industrialization have in most countries produced predominantly third order uses of space and architecture. Under these conditions, the architecturally defined spaces of the city cannot owe their form primarily to anything like ritual practice in the culture. Within the larger constraints of transportation patterns and the like, space becomes available for the more immediate play of territoriality of individuals and self-interested groups. Status, identity, and commercial or political rhetoric become the largest motivation for the design of architectural form itself. Though associated with particular territories, whether as building or urban area, this linkage of sign and space is more a communication of powerful discursive bodies, than an evolution of more systematic, subconscious, and evocative cultural space developed and shared by the society as a whole.

The fact that socio-cultural space cannot, at least originally, be the primary determinant of industrial urban form has led to the implicit assumption, even in Sweden, that the cultural dependence upon and traditional uses of space had come to an end. Third order expression has become the dominant mode, functioning more superficially as culture in terms of style, fashion, or rhetorical message. Thus discussion of the modern social democratic Sweden logically emphasizes linguistically and medially based processes of communicational or educational discourse available to individuals. Absent are considerations of evocative symbolic themes or shared concepts of spatial oppositions.

This is not to say that an understanding of the spatial contribution to cultural processes occurs elsewhere, either internationally or in terms of other disciplines. Most cultural research which either wholly or partially includes aspects of the physical environment is still highly predjudiced by the fact that scholars either live in extremely third order situations, e.g. the U.S., or are influenced by theory and literature from such places. It is especially true that researchers from the field of architecture live in and work with extremely rhetorical settings, rather than ritually determined places such as occur in both first order and second order societies.

In spite of probable segmented second order content in portions of the early industrial cities of Sweden, these overall forms are primarily determined by non-expressive factors. The period from 1870 to the emergence of the modern Swedish society in the 1940's must be seen as a time when very old expressive *by* practices and spaces sought urban expression. Third order experience in the cities might be seen less conventionally as the competition of bourgeois values than as the potential breakdown of a significant aspect of prior cultural process, i.e. the spatial basis of symbolic expression and practice. The second and third order tension of this critical time in Swedish history does not begin to find resolution until relatively large numbers of the population once again find the opportunity to establish and practice second order expression.

Notes

1   The present emphasis on the continuity of expressive village form, in spite the enclosure acts, varies from Pred's recent focus where the "spotlight has been turned on landed-peasant households rather than on street-house and crofter households" (1986:198). While his interests in "structuration", i.e. the linkage between local practice and the structures of larger socio-economic scales, is very much in keeping with our present interests in space and the evolution of society, his work seems to leave much of the symbolic and ritual traditions of Scandinavian space out of the discussion. His more economically and politically motivated view of practice, and the use of local place, naturally

leads to the preoccupation with the more situationally influential, third order activities of the landed farmers which become evident after moving out of the *byar*. This does not invalidate his approach to this aspect of rural life, even from present perspectives. It simply leaves undefined, as Pred himself states (ibid), those other (village) aspects of post-enclosure life. This "place" separation of collective (village) and patriarchal (landed farm) becomes, as the reader will see, a major theme to the present work.

2   Ethnographic studies of *byar* such as Ek's of Östra Torn, just outside of Lund, document the post enclosure addition of new dwellings along the *bygata* (1970). A broader overview of the architectural of the landless peasant (*de obesuttna*) in Sweden may be found in Granlund (1943).

3   Future research may also determine with greater accuracy whether these new upper class farmers are for the first time, in the long tradition of Scandinavian farm culture, using symbols and images for the expression of territorial identities and status. When the idea of third order uses of signs and images related to territoriality is discussed at greater length in Chapter Three and elsewhere, the reader might consider the newly decorated "fine-room" and eventually facade of the now upper class farmers as part of this phenomenon. The territorial character of the spatially independent farms must produce a significant psychological effect, independent of first and second order expressive meanings.

4   See again the origin of these ideas in smaller African societies (Turner 1968). Pilgrimages in larger, more complex societies, whether to Mecca or Las Vegas, do on the other hand appear to function as the communitas opposite to the structure of daily work oriented life, in spite of the fact that the journey is made with friends or travel companions not fellow workers. Fyrkman (1988) also uses these structure / anti-structure ideas of Turner to talk about the much more recent image of informality seen in today's Sweden. This view is even less ritualistic, as described in his article, since it involves primarily (third order) expressions of dress and language, rather actual ritual places such as folk museums or as we will see offices.

5   A biographical example of the ritual use of folk museums occurs in one of the accounts of a female office worker from the 1940's to the 80's (Bohman 1987:235). An employee of a textile factory in Ulricehamn, the woman in the 1960's was the only union member among the office workers. She met her husband at a dance in the Folkets (People's) Park in Borås. In 1970 they became engaged and exchanged rings in front of Seglora church in Skansen, the folk museum in Stockholm.

6   Conradson describes the use of sport competition as a means of promoting company solidarity (1988:111). The third order metaphor of participating in team athletics was essentially the competition of insurance "families" for scarce resources. They played in leagues of commercially competing insurance companies. Camaraderie among one's fellow players remained just as formal as within office work itself; they continued to use formal modes of address even while playing. Most likely, as we will see, today's companies use organized athletics far less as an expression of family solidarity and external competitiveness. Getting together on a team today undoubtedly is much more expressively related to social processes *within* the organization, i.e. to the

resolution of competitive conflicts between any of the many collective sub-groups of the office.

7　Though not specifically applied to the present discussion of architectural expression, Conradson does mention in her introduction the notion of "symbolic capital" by Bourdieu (Conradson 1988:15). Further work might illustrate symbolic capital as essentially part of the discursive usage of symbolism, where territorial realities are either reinforced or compensated for by such associational strategies. Presumably much of these processes cannot be part of first and second order systems.

8　In his work on Swedish Popular (religious) Movements, Peter Stromberg (1983) places much greater emphasis on these forces as change agents in the democratization of modern Sweden.

9　Much of what these widely read ethnographers discuss in their work about becoming "cultured", as Sweden modernized, deals with the discursive, third order signs which more affluent and urban Swedes begin to use (Fyrkman and Löfgren 1979). Even nature itself becomes "picturesque" and "recreational" in contrast to more traditional uses in ritual practice.

3 The linear extreme

During the interim between the viable second order *by* and the democratic breakthrough of the 60's the spatial basis of traditional oppositional values was tentative. In effect, it became the cultural image and practices of *tjänstemän* and *arbetare* which carried on the two ancient aspects of Scandinavian life, though in spatially, ritually and socially severed forms more dependent upon third order expression (at least in their relationships between each other). We have seen the normal second order process in which a group of known individuals participate in both aspects of the opposition as they are alternatively masters of the farm, and members of the farm *by*. It has been described how a pair or pairs of physically integrated and expressive places, i.e. in the second order *by*, is essential to the effective ritual practice which alternates between settings, creating symbolic and social balance between the forces.

The absence of such a structure in a techno-economic, presentational urban setting, and the independence of the oppositional themes undoubtedly created what appeared to be typical class conflict within the urban Swedish society. Rather than move toward a more typical presentational system of modern organization, as in other western countries, Sweden appears to have managed to keep its cultural meanings intact, and perhaps restructure them as the democratic breakthrough of the 60's. Spatially and culturally, this happens nowhere else as expressively as in office buildings when the meaning of *tjänsteman* (the individual) finally is reintegrated with that of *arbetare* (the communal).[1]

3.1 The fascination with modern Sweden

In the modern period a great deal more information becomes

90

available about everyday life in Swedish offices. Unlike historical description, including ethnographic accounts by older, individual informants, a much wider range of disciplines and methodologies can be used to create a more detailed profile of contemporary offices. Plans can be collected and interviews conducted in existing offices.[2] This information can be analyzed in comparison to research literature from architecture, psychology, sociology, business, and contemporary culture, especially ethnography. The foreign researcher is immediately impressed with the level of education of all Swedes and the amount of total research which a relatively small nation like Sweden funds and publishes. It becomes evident that a considerable portion of research is focused on *work* with its historical, social, political, and individual implications. The relatively recent large numbers of white collar office workers in Sweden has produced an introspective research response as part of long term interests in work.

It may be that such broad, accepted research particularly on social conditions has helped maintain the communal aspect of traditional second order Swedish culture, at least on the discursive level. Unlike the U.S. for example, the Swedes have not been that interested in the "psychological".[3] A particularly good example of research interests not only in social life generally, but also in relations between individuals and their groups is an account of anthropological fieldwork with a community of Swedish fishermen in 1967. Its title was "leadership and consensus: decision making in an egalitarian community" (Yngvesson 1978). Here were groups of men participating in a modern international economy, yet their complete "team" model of organization totally defied the typical hierarchies of contemporary work both in ships and on land. Unlike the composition of the urban patriarchal office, but like the cooperative relationships among farmers of the *by*, the fishermen maintained no differences in rank or occupational roles, nor was there a difference in power or authority between adults. All decisions, on board or off, were reached by consensus and were anonymous. When leadership did necessarily occur from time to time, it was masked (ibid:81). This is the same characteristic of decision making reported as one of the primary distinctions between working in a Swedish and a U.S. firm. Any decision in a Swedish corporation is painstaking and time consuming. In the U.S. individuals are encouraged to take the initiative with decisions, providing greater opportunity for personal success and failure (Mortensen 1983:31).

The cooperative Swedish ethic which applies, even today, in both fishing and white collar group was captured by the author Sandemose in his 1933 description of a small town, Jante, which imposed its collective will on the main character of the novel. The *Janteloven* (the vow to Jante), well known to Scandinavians today, requires that:

1) you shall not believe that you *are* someone; 2) you shall not believe that you are as powerful as *we*; 3) you shall not believe you are smarter than *us*; 4) you shall not tell yourself that you are better than *we*; 5) you shall not believe that you know more than *we*; 6) you shall not believe that you are more important than *we*; 7) you shall not believe that *you* are good at doing something; 8) you shall not smile at *us*; 9) you shall not believe that anyone will bother about *you*; 10) you shall not believe that you can teach *us* something. (translation by author, italics from the original encyclopedia description)

Ever since the Viking periods, and probably before, ostracism from the group has been a principal means of collective enforcement. Banishment, not capital punishment, was the ultimate penalty on Viking Iceland. In spite of several synonyms in modern usage, e.g. *uteslutning* (to shut out) and *social utfrysning* (being socially frozen out), the term seen most frequently in news accounts and other literature is *mobbning*. The typical translation to the English "mobbing" is a poor one in that these group actions toward individuals are almost always social or psychological rather than physical as the English term connotes. *Mobbning* is the term used by Swedish psychologists and others to describe group ostracism and its powerful effects on the individuals in question. Earlier, most news coverage and social science literature focused on the problem as it occurred among children in various group settings, particularly school. Within the elementary schools efforts are made to keep students in the same class group from kindergarten at least up through the sixth grade. Class solidarities are understandably strong (a companion study of the effects of school architecture would be interesting).

More recently, beginning with the 1980's, literature can be found for *mobbning* among adults in those settings most sensitive to social relationships, white collar offices (Helmersson 1987; Ortmark 1989; Nivesjö 1988). This period coincides with the recent democratic breakthrough. Some researchers feel because it is very difficult to get people to talk about the subject, whether one is a victim or not, much extreme ostracism has simply been previously unreported. One particular book, entitled *Vuxenmobbning* ("adult ostracism", Leymann 1986) describes examples in everyday detail from office societies. Individuals at all levels of the organization for one reason or another find themselves painfully outside of usually small and intimate work groups. *Mobbning* occurs primarily among employees as coworkers, but can also happen as a case of manager against an employee, or an employee against a manager (Nivesjö 1988:3). One can ostracize by: not talking or listening to the victim, gossiping about psychological problems of the victim, writing notes, excluding the victim from office breaks or other group events, withholding information, being placed in a lesser work position, being criticized publicly, and by being the object of letter or telephone terror (ibid:4). The causes of *mobbning* remain elusive to Swedish social scientists. Some say that high work demands together with little freedom to create solutions is a major cause.[4] Most work demands come not from supervisors but from one's coworkers.

This particularly Swedish orientation toward group identity and participation is reflected frequently in an account, based upon some 170 interviews, of how foreign business people perceive their Swedish counterparts (Phillips-Martinsson 1981). One response maintained that:

> ...in other countries people aren't afraid to be individuals, but in Sweden all follow the common opinion, stay on the ground and look quietly around to observe other reactions. Be a part of the flock, group, and a common idea, but never take risks on your own" (ibid:63).

We see from these interviews that this ethos of group membership is restricted to more formal or structured relationships at the community level, particularly business organization. Being part of a group does not translate into spontaneous public relationships between friends or friendship groups, as in more Southern European cultures, the pubs of England,[5] or the U.S.. This kind of street life in Sweden is conspicuously absent to several interviewees (ibid:21). In other cultures personal relationships mean so much more, where people are valued more for their loyalty toward family and friends rather than for purely professional identities (ibid:22). Loyalty to the group in Sweden seems a part of some cultural set of values or norms about collectivity. This contrasts with culturally defined fictive family metaphor (as in many Latin societies), or with the more temporary, politically based formation of friendship or like-interest groups.[6]

It becomes easier to understand the frequency with which foreign executives in the above study describe the strong separation between business and private life in Sweden (Phillips-Martinsson 1981:17, 57, 58, 71). Visiting business people can easily misconstrue the Swede's reluctance to invite foreigners home as a negative statement about personal and business relationships. The sphere of life associated with the Swedish office is, in effect, complete in itself. Using the power of personal or family relationships to influence the corporate society would threaten the autonomy of the office as a cultural system. In one article from a business journal, Swedish executives are statistically less likely than their European counterparts to even use family connections, particularly marriage, as a means to career advancement; most are the sons of *arbetare* families (*Veckans affärer* 1971). Within the normal sphere of office life, neither visitors nor family fall within the collective definition of work group. At home, neither business visitors nor coworkers can comfortably be part of a totally separate set of relationships in which the Swedish family perhaps still plays a patriarchal role (in relation to some usually rural collective place?). Boholm (1983) finds a patriarchal emphasis in her anthropological account of modern Swedish kinship.

It is almost as if the two spheres of life are separately struggling to either maintain (the family home and rural connections) or perhaps reestablish (the office setting) traditional second order Scandinavian practice. Two conditions must hypothetically be satisfied. Given its traditional dependence upon space, such practice must be realized in one social place where oppositions are structured contiguously. The same individuals (selves) must participate in both hierarchical and egalitarian relationships. The private family may be connected to a residual second order experience. Its locus exists, perhaps, not in the apartments and single family areas of the city, but in rural places associated with friends or relatives, places not unlike traditional *byar*. A very interesting question arises as to whether separate cultural spheres can co-exist, or whether competition is inevitable.

Culturally, the Swedish family is somewhat fragile, as evidenced by a very high rate of divorce, whether from legal marriage or from living together unwed as a "permanent" form of union. Perhaps this in part is due to the extensive support which the larger society provides all members of the family. This support will continue regardless of the condition of the nuclear family. In the traditional *byar*, families were in many respects less important than the domestic group who lived and worked together, often including the sons and daughters of neighbors and even excluding one's older children. Is the recent office a related form of socio-economic unit? Evidence of outright competition between office and family appears in one ethnographer's assertion that private life in Sweden is impoverished by the greater time and sense of community in office life (Holm-Löfgren 1980:81).

The author was surprised when office workers described some major office *fest* or party, often a formal dance, to which spouses *wouldn't* be invited. In the U.S., the advice columnist Ann Landers provides evidence of the contrast with Swedish custom. She responds to an American wife who complains of being not invited with her husband to his office parties:

> Dear Hurting: I can't believe they are still doing this sort of thing. I thought businesses cut out that nonsense in the '60's. You have every right to tell your husband you don't approve of it and that he should take a pass (Arizona Citizen, Oct. 26, 1990).

The relation between office and home was studied in the European Values System Study. Compared with other countries, very few Swedes complained about having to go back to work after the weekend (Daun 1989:100). Yet free time and summer vacations remain powerful attractors away from the office. Seldom do coworkers participate in an office *Midsommer*, where the emphasis seems to be on connections with some traditional rural place, perhaps even more so than on one's immediate family.

The phenomenon of the democratic breakthrough, whether as office or industrial setting, is to a large extent one of having achieved or still striving toward work groups as complete, democratic, socio-economic entities--just as in the traditional *by* societies. Wages, working conditions, economic health security, and the ideological projection of this image to Sweden are today partially the byproducts of the power of essentially localized groups of workers. Clearly, from our external perspective, this unique phenomenon may have hypothetically been linked to second order traditions of Scandinavian culture. Internally, however, Swedish researchers, particularly within the national umbrella union organization called *SIFO*, describe the success of the 60's and 70's as dependent upon the recognition of individual needs for personal development and influence in one's work. The "social competence" phase of Swedish development, as it is called, follows

95

the emphasis on work for sustenance in the 1930's, and the rational preoccupation with production for its own sake in the 1950's (Lyttkens 1985:149). The most recent view of modern work stresses individual participation in and dependence upon the social group, creating personal benefit in terms of added meaning and content of life (*Veckans affärer* 1982:54). Is this not another way of describing the very positive balance of collective and individual selves in second order society?

The cultural tendency to participate in groups certainly existed during the delocalized, third order interim between the traditional farm society and the democratic breakthrough. One of the most frequent sources of collective participation during this period was in the multitude of groups associated with the unions. Whether work oriented, purely social, or educational, these activities still remained outside of the actual socio-political framework of work and its physical setting. Even the political and legal power of the local group did not become effectively integrated into actual work processes and decisions until relatively recently. This may have been easier to do in a white collar organization where technical and mechanical process do not dominate as in manufacturing. Not until 1977 was legislation created which mandated worker participation in actual decisions, *Medbestämmanderätt* (the right of co-determination), as distinct from previous negotiation for worker benefits and the like. Researchers debate whether the law was primarily a confirmation of existing practice or a major social reform (Sjöstrand 1978:107). Ample evidence exists that all through the 1960's and 70's, new formal collective entities appeared within work organizations, entities whose concern was the actual decision process of work itself (ibid:107). This was in addition to the widespread horizontal organization of employees into work groups, especially in offices.

So pervasive is the ethos of participatory democracy that even national statistics clearly communicate this bias in Sweden. In a recent publication by the government bureau of statistics, entitled *Hur jämställda ar vi?* (How equal are we?) (Rapport nr. 20:1980), one of the major categories of information about Swedes, in addition to education, occupation, sex, and health, was "social communication and isolation". Measures were developed to describe the possibilities of belonging to a group, according to one's profession, sex, age, etc.. Incidences of individuals spending much time alone, "isolation", were also integrated into the category. Male office workers, for example, were found to have a somewhat greater opportunity to have contact with a group of coworkers (71%) than did women office workers (56%), or men in industrial work settings. Not even considering the actual work group as a source of coworker contact, the opportunities for participation are great in themselves simply considering the nine or more separate, national *tjänsteman* (white collar) unions in Sweden (*Ordets Makt* 1974:33). Through all the literature, both current and historical, one is constantly impressed with the amount of participation in union organized groups of all kinds (Link 1974:45), though much more so in the case of industrial workers.

One is fascinated by these unique characteristics of modern Swedish culture. The present attempt is not the first to recognize the unusual blend of the traditional opposites into the democratic breakthrough. One can mention again the recent anthropological discussion of the fundamentalist Christian movement of the early 20th century as a key integrative device of culture, useful in the reconciliation of contradictions of modernizing industrial society. Stromberg maintains that "this dual language of *simultaneous* individualism and social welfare is so often invoked to discuss Sweden as a nation...the blending of socialist and bourgeois, communitarian and individualism" (Stromberg 1983:79, italics added, see also Stromberg 1991, Daun 1991).

In terms of the specific proposal of the article, i.e. the importance of religious fundamentalism to the present success of modern Sweden, it remains difficult to see the ultimate causality of a minority religious movement which peaked some forty years before the breakthrough. Even though there were associations between fundamentalism and the worker movement, and even though a small number of people still belong to these religious groups, the effect in the new organizational forms of today , such as offices, appears limited. The author recalls interviewing a middle management individual in a large office organization. His expressed physical and social isolation within the department may have been largely due to his very active membership in one such fundamentalist religion. As a rule, the vast majority of office workers, like the vast majority of Swedes, profess extremely limited religious belief or practice, though most have been confirmed in the state church and may attend services from time to time.[7]

3.2 Individual choices

What does the democratic breakthrough or even the reintegration of the "patriarchal" *(tjänstemän)* with the "communal" *(arbetare)* actually mean in terms of expressive practice and architectural form? Certainly this is the period in time when form becomes more socially sensitive, in distinction to the prior expression of the rational with its clear continuity with the patriarchal. If we witness something reminiscent of the patterns of traditional *byar*, does one attempt to define this as a contemporary example of second order architectural phenomena? Without question a significant change in office form takes place quite early in the democratization process of the sixties. Yet this change, both socially and architecturally striking, is nowhere commented upon in the diverse literature surveyed, architectural sources included. These new impulses in office buildings are precisely what distinguishes them from their contemporary counterparts in other countries, and were the first step to far reaching evolutions in very recent Swedish offices.

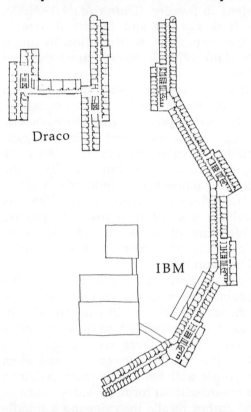

A first glance at these examples from varied types and scales of buildings, all built during or after the breakthrough, reveals a simple intensification of the linearity found during the rationalization period (see figure 3.1). Yet those readers with architectural background, particularly with office types in the U.S., Great Britain or even Japan,[8] will respond to the cross-cultural uniqueness of such extreme linearity, contrasting it with the "thick" shapes of our techno-economically determined buildings. Some may even laugh as they sense the difficulty of rendering and marketing an external (third order) image of these buildings. The immediate cause of such form is easy to identify. It is the result of giving virtually every employee an individual office with an exterior window. The

Figure 3.1 The radical effect on building form of universal individual offices; *smårumskontor* examples from Draco (Lund) and IBM (Stockholm)

Draco

IBM

resulting interior space is either a simple double loaded corridor or a linear core which contains opaque common spaces such as restrooms, storage, copy rooms, etc.. By the mid-sixties, the *smårumskontor* (small roomed office building) was becoming the conventional form in Sweden, and was referred to as such in professional journals and government documents. It was not, however, recognized as a unique phenomenon.

We can associate having one's own office with the fundamental principles of the democratic breakthrough, a basic sign, perhaps, of the equality essential to democracy. The timing of the change in architectural form seems to precede the actual democratization of day to day work activities characteristic of the mid-seventies to early eighties. Was the normative right to one's own office therefore essentially a political right which was won early, as part of the larger national Social Democratic phenomenon and the realization of power by white collar unions? Such an image does not exist in the memories of many interviewees whose careers had been played out in recent individual offices, and in earlier *stor* (large) rooms typically occupied by several workers. There is no recollection of a political struggle for the individual *rum* (room). In spite of the nine white collar unions in Sweden, and their accepted presence during transitions to the modern breakthrough period, having an individual office is not immediately associated with or attributed to union activity *per se*.

Not until the late 1960's did the unions begin their demands for legal definitions of work environments and rights to participate in planning processes. Even today there is no government recommendation or law about individual offices and windows.[9] Change is perceived as a more continuous and natural evolution of both earlier architectural form and ways of working. Many of the older employees said that it was customary in the shared rooms of the forties and fifties for most to have a desk by the window. The natural functional reason given for a private office is to minimize noise and visual distractions to work.

The obvious question remains: why then did the "one person, one office" standard occur during the seminal moments of major social and political change in Sweden? We must remember that office life was still quite formal up until the late 1960's. Formal titles of address were the rule. Offices still had strong overtones of hierarchical rationalization, fused with more traditional values of patriarchy and back-room territoriality. How was it possible that such a radical change in form emerged from the still very hierarchical atmosphere of those office organizations? This

99

investigation takes the point of view that functional reasons such as greater work privacy, could not have been the essential motivation for the shift to individual rooms. Such appears to be the conscious rationale. If visual and noise distraction had been such a problem, then one would have expected the individual room solution earlier during the rationalist period, patriarchal traditions not withstanding. Furthermore, acoustic screens of open landscape schemes solve such purely task performance problems. But these have not been acceptable in Swedish offices.

Should one attempt to define the individual office as the simple, almost animal like territorial privacy which provides the primary place of individual escape from the social demands of others? It is commonly known among environmental psychologists that in non-work institutional, particularly long term settings such as hospitals, having one's own defined space increases prospects for positive social interaction in public spaces. In the early Swedish *smårumskontor* one will see that individual rooms produced the opposite reaction, a reduction of contact and social relationships. As a result, the architectural form continues to change in response. Both the individual room in the long term hospital and the individual room in more territorial offices do in fact function as refuge from a larger territorial flux in which social relationships are constantly changing in relationship to the use of space. Certainly the individual need for territoriality might be the individual motivation to have his or her own room. How is it that everyone decided this at once, and if this was in fact due to a larger collective decision, then does this alter the interpretation of individual territoriality? Under what conditions will some number of individuals, all of whom seek individual territories, decide as a group to have equal spaces?

If the patriarchal had in reality diminished radically into more purely territorial forms of the rationalized modern office, then individual offices may have been seen on that level. Certainly one would not have thought that having one's own office would provide the kind of identity previously associated with executives. All of the offices would be the same, with little or no expression of differences. What universal offices might have provided was a fundamental equality in the distribution of resources. Because of the leveling effects of Swedish taxation, space may have been one of the most available commodities in office societies.[10] This raises the question of whether some precondition of material equality exists for "deritualized" second order systems.

3.3 Collective participation in planning

Other clues to understanding what took place might be found in the government publication of *Arbetsmiljö* (Work environments) (1982). Little is specifically said about individual rooms or even individual windows, agreeing with memories that the individual room itself was never a major political issue. One of the four major chapters in the document captures our attention...*De anställdas möjlighter att påverka arbetsmiljön* (the employees' possibilities to influence work environments). The first section of this chapter deals with definitions of physical planning. Most of *Arbetsmilijö* is oriented toward the problems of industrial work environments, in particular concerns for health, safety and comfort of the worker. There is a general lack of definitions specific to white collar settings, but the weight given to worker participation is significant. Participation is more important than specification![11]

Yet one cannot be certain of the degree to which participation represented a conscious goal of office unions, in comparison with other more tangible goals of salary, employment security, retirement benefits and the like. Literature about industrial work life in Sweden is rich in description of union participation of virtually all workers in political, social, educational, "cultural" activities . This was and is the basis of the political success of the Social Democratic Party. In other words, participation in decision making at all levels had always been perhaps the fundamental tenet of the worker's movement. As Daun says, the largely subconscious nature of this aspect of Swedish collectivity could be understandable as traditional personality traits. The big difference, however, between earlier Social Democratic success (presumably due in part to these traits of Swedish character) and the traditional *byar*, was that collective participation remained confined to the union organizations *per se*, and had relatively little effect on the actual process of decision making in the industrial workplace. Character traits themselves, in other words, were not enough.

The reason that collective participation had made few inroads into the actual decision making processes of industrial or office work, was that actual work participation required the involvement of both management and employees. Although unions in Sweden politically achieved, as in other countries, better work and economic conditions, most decision making in the workplace remained in the hands of patriarchally defined office groups. Given the cultural basis of decision making, and its traditional connection to second order space, it is here argued that the basis of the democratic breakthrough lay not in the immediate political leverage of union

101

might, but in a more subconscious manipulation of social order perhaps facilitated by spatial form.

To change day-to-day decision making, the basic social order had to be changed. To change the basic culturally and spatially defined social order--supported by third order expression--established space had to be changed. Furthermore, because of the dominance of the technical and functional in industrial settings, those spaces would remain largely non-cultural and immune to collective influence over social space. Office settings are much more susceptible to social processes, whether territorial or ritual. Is it possible that the democratic breakthrough began in office environments, with the changes in architectural form occurring early in the process? Remember it is not until the majority of Swedish workers are in offices, and remarkably different offices at that, that the breakthrough occurs.

The most plausible scenario suggests that the first collective decision making eventually to influence actual social structure may have occurred in the late fifties and early sixties as office workers began to participate in decisions about changes in their physical environments. While industrial workers had been making decisions about safety and health, and had perhaps stimulated environmental concern on the part of their office cousins, the same rights subconsciously involved far greater potential for social impact when applied to decisions about office settings.

Furthermore, one cannot discount possible early effects of "informalization" as discussed previously in the introduction, especially the electronic effects emphasized by Meyrowitz (1985). Yet one might argue that television in Sweden was at that time much more formal in its presentational tone, and was (and still is) less available to the Swedish viewer. Whether these or other effects made any major contribution to architectural processes at this time is a difficult question to answer. As discussed in the introduction and Chapter Ten, a "medial informalization" does not in itself appear to predict or create the eventual forms of office work in Sweden, unlike Meyrowitz's description of electronic offices in the U. S..

A better understanding may lie in the actual process of design itself. From the interviews and literature one finds typical examples of the almost extreme processes of participation as organizations program new buildings, both today and during the last two decades. In one published account of programming a new office for about 200 employees, two committees were set up: a building committee composed of board members and executives, and a building work group committee composed of department managers and union representatives (Örum 1980:54). The latter work group committee, where the essential social and functional problems were resolved, met seventy-seven times over three and a half years, amounting to about 1617 work hours of meetings. In one of the buildings studied by the author, a large quasi-governmental engineering, architectural, and planning firm, written records of the similarly extensive, highly participatory programming process were made available. Most impressive was the way in which the group, not some "top-down"[12] executive entity, made decisions about the future physical environment.

Several of the buildings of the present study had been built within the last two or three years. In each case employees remembered a great deal of programmatic discussion, much of it inherently social involving spatial location of individual offices and departments. In strong distinction to the territorial processes which *begin* when employees move into "thick" essentially non-socially or culturally programmed, techno-economic office spaces, political manipulation of office space in Sweden *stops* when the building is occupied! Unlike the use of space in the United States, where it seems that everybody, whether office worker or single family suburbanite, always has an eye out for some better, more socially advantageous place, once a Swede moves in to an individual room, little thought is given to other locations. None of the author's interviewees were ever able to describe some other place in the building where that individual would rather be. Even when functional reorganization is required, both individuals and working groups are reported to be quite difficult to move, though one personnel director felt that women were easier to move than men. More will be said about these differences later.

As we will see in the following chapter, there exists a very practical political reason that Swedes cannot live in office landscapes, predicated as they are upon their abilities to physically change as the organization evolves. Any modification of the setting requires so much employee participation in the planning process that small and more frequent changes in environment simply take too much worker time. As explained by a manager of the physical layout for several office buildings of an internationally competitive Swedish firm (one of the organizations which had tried the open landscape idea in the early 1970's) it is much easier simply to move employees in and out of equal, individual offices as the work organization requires. They had recently in 1986 retrofitted much of the originally open landscape into individual offices.

This more political consideration cannot be taken as the initial cause of individual offices because the participatory process certainly was not fully developed that early; remember that the actual laws of co-determination in the work place did not occur until 1977. It seems unlikely that the early participation in planning processes were highly formalized or politically and legally defined. Participation would not yet be a great enough drain on employee time, nor would it be recognized to the extent that it would create a conscious design solution of individual offices. It is also true that even in today's offices, in spite of the well developed participation in everyday work decisions, much of the design of work groups and work organization is initiated by mid-level managers and higher executives. In terms of the strictly functional, work oriented aspects of the physical setting, interviewees frequently reported that much was "top-down". This is seen as a natural component of the necessary hierarchical component of office work. What is not top-down are the social aspects of the settings. Individual offices provide a means of giving group leaders and executives the ability to make functional changes in employee organization *without changing the basic socio-cultural situation*, and without spending the huge amounts of time such social changes demand. Later in the evolution of the Swedish office, even this functional ability will cause problems in the socio-cultural system.

The fact that early collective participation in environmental decisions never appeared as formal, conscious elements in any remembered change in either functional or political process, leads us back to our central theme, i.e. that changes in offices were more related to initial, mostly subconscious evolution of meaning on the expressive level. Certainly the larger outside, discursive political pressures can be said to facilitate this phenomenon within the now major workforce of *tjänstemän*. Yet the legitimizing basis of actual work participation could not occur without prior change in cultural definitions of offices.

To the individual employee, participation in decisions about new or modified office settings perhaps gave vent to the Scandinavian ethos of the patriarchal or individual, whether in terms of traditional farm family or office *tjänsteman*. The cultural result of collective design responsibility may have been the declaration of each individual's right to this ancient identification of basic autonomous unit. In the *by*, this expression was the individual farm, in the office, its equivalent is the individual room. The fact that the individual office may be seen primarily as an expression of the authority of the individual Swede--at whatever

104

level of the organization--suggests that the first changes were not consciously collective or social, just as they were not immediately functional. Even though the decisions to build with all individual offices could only have been made through collective, participatory processes, the first cultural decision appears to have been the re-establishment of an individualized domain of the traditional patriarchal.

3.4 *Mitt rum*
In English the term "office" is used to designate either one's own individual work room or the larger socio-functional organization and place. The original meaning of course came from the largely presentational association with things "official", governmental or perhaps bureaucratic. In English usage, this essential meaning of authority is associated with either the private place of the actual official, or the larger building which often expresses the legitimizing authority of these officials. Historically in Sweden, the term *tjänsteman* (one in service of an institution or government) probably preceded the modern term for office, *kontor*, and certainly had third order class associations with the urban patriarchal, aristocratic, and bourgeois--though no physical places were so labeled. *Kontor* (*konto*, "account") comes from twentieth century accounting practice and seems to reflect more functional than class meanings. By the time of the major democratic inroads into Swedish office life of the sixties, the term used indigenously to refer to individual places was simply *mitt rum* (my room). One usually doesn't say *mitt kontor*, the equivalent to the English "my office" when speaking about one's individual room.[13]

Though etymologically and perhaps cross-culturally, the Swedish designation of individual room appears to invoke less association of official authority than its English counterpart, within the traditional second order ethos, *mitt rum* appears to have connotations of the patriarchal. Perhaps the distinction is between associations of political authority and territorial control with the American English use of "my office", while in Swedish, "my space" may have much deeper, cultural meanings associated with long Germanic traditions of individual and family autonomy. In Conradson's discussion of the historical meaning of the private office, she says that here "one could feel almost at home", obviously equating the individual office space with family dwelling (1988:147) Even the term *rum* in German and Swedish may have far greater cultural meaning than the English "space" or "room".

The individual meaning that comes from this kind of space in Sweden was very nicely expressed by the personnel director of the central Malmö municipal office of about 600 employees. While mentioning the more instrumental function of privacy, the greater portion of his response was dedicated to issues of "authority", "identity" and the "individual's recognition of his or her worth". His continued interpretation, in direct contradiction to what we would hear from an American executive, is that the lower on the status scale the individual is, the greater the need for the individual room. It is the typical employee (with not really lower but more universal status) who also must work most collectively in groups.

Figure 3.2 Typical individual offices in *smårumskontor*

A long term employee from the same organization, a kind of special projects person within the administrative area, clearly identified the importance of the individual rooms. He recalled the story of an older man who finally after some years, and probably as part of the changes of the sixties, was given his own room. Unfortunately, a relatively short time after, his space was needed for other purposes (not recalled by the informant). The loss of his newly won definition and individual room proved to be extremely traumatic. Several comparable accounts were recalled by the interviewed employees. The right to one's own room in Sweden may be much less the conscious (third order) choice for a sign of individual achievement and manipulation of one's position in real and social space--one person's gain is usually another's loss[14]--than it is of one's rights to be an equal member in full standing of the group.

Since many organizations have moved from pre-breakthrough

106

buildings to newer space within the last few years, participatory discussions about whether to build open larger rooms or individual rooms occur again and again. No written standard exists within governmental or professional publications. Invariably the choice is for individual rooms. In an office for an electronics applications firm built in the late sixties with virtually all individual rooms, a merger with another small company brought about discussions of the possibility of placing two people to a space (the individual rooms were ample enough to suggest this as a possibility). The employees quickly discarded this idea in favor of an addition to the existing building. The next question of participatory focus was how to solve the problem of the limited number of individual rooms possible with a window to the outside view, an amenity of all existing offices. The implication of early proposals was that in the resulting larger office, even though all might have an individual room, some would have outside windows and some would not. This concern brought about the final solution in which an enclosed but exterior courtyard provided some form of exterior view to all new individual offices (see plan of figure 3.3).

The electrical engineer who provided some of the information about this process was also consciously aware of recent governmental guidelines (in *Arbetsmiljö* 1982) which describe the need for all employees to have visual access to outdoor views, without designating the occupancy of the room. There was some question in his mind whether the new views into the courtyard were equivalent to their existing "standard" view out into a minimally landscaped industrial park setting. The personnel director for one of the three agricultural cooperatives which share a 1974 high rise office building of seven stories (figure 5.6) described the importance of having a window to the outside. One must have access out to the *fri* (free, open, at large). People want to view the landscape to see whether the trees are green, whether there is snow on the ground, or whether it is cloudy or rainy. He could not remember any office setting he had ever seen, including the older, larger shared rooms, where most individuals did not have a place with a window to the outside. Furthermore, one must be able to open these windows. Operable windows in individual rooms are another unwritten standard in Sweden. An architect who followed the American norm of sealed windows for a large office building in Stockholm, for reasons of (third order) external aesthetics, was sharply criticized for this lack of "functional" consideration (Örum 1980:58).

107

It is true that Swedes are aware that the operable window has functional purpose, either for climate control or for providing daylight for work activities. Such a provision does appear in the *Arbetsmiljö* guidelines, although the worker's distance from natural light is not specified. Yet neither the functional nor cultural purposes of the window *per se* can be argued to have been a motivating factor behind the individual rooms of the sixties, since many of the older shared rooms measured up favorably to these standards and partially explain the very early linear tendencies in

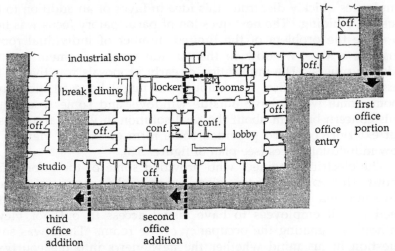

Figure 3.3 Plan of Electro-Sandberg, Lund, illustrating the strategy for additions to maximize the number of individual rooms with exterior views

Swedish offices. Still it may be true that in the earlier shared rooms of Swedish offices, owning a window individually may have been a third order symbol of personal identity and authority within the larger image of patriarchal family. Such could have contributed some motivation for universal individual rooms during the breakthrough. Though if one compares the earlier linear offices with more typically "thick" offices in other countries, the Swedes already possessed far greater exterior view than the rest, even by today's standards. In U.S. offices, past and present, the window view is again most often a commodity, not unlike salary, to be distributed according to merit and political favor.

In the individual Swedish room, at least, the window view might be considered an essential visual expression of the basic second order meaning of the patriarchal. The visual and spatial relationship between room and the natural landscape and the

108

"free", "open" or "at large", could have deep traditional associations. The window might play a threshold role as the primary symbolic link between individual and greater powers of collective spirituality. In the ancient Scandinavian ethos, one recalls, the dwelling threshold had always been the ritual link between these opposed meanings. For thousands of years Scandinavian dwellings had no windows, a result less of technical capabilities than of the symbolic dangers associated with any penetration, or threshold, which held the potential of making contact between the worlds of humans and spirits, especially at night. The fashionable European inspired windows which began to appear in dwellings of the Middle Ages or Reformation (depending upon location and degree of cultural isolation) created a wealth of folklore which described the new possibilities, both good and bad, of multiplied potential contact with the other world (see Doxtater 1981:113).

Just what kinds of associations remain of this traditional, extremely important ritual symbolism, is a question whose answer depends upon extensive research. What were the meanings of threshold in the second order *by*, and did such meaning carry into contemporary times and places of Sweden? Certainly one can appreciate the increased amount of control which the individual Swedish office provides its occupant. It is not just functional control, nor the control of social contact through privacy, but perhaps a sense of access to an important threshold, and of the patriarchal rights to the ritual practice and participation it implies. A certain ambivalence occurs between the window as threshold and the door to the room. This issue will be developed shortly.

The possible meaning which appears to be associated with the individual Swedish office window, as well as other culturally determined aspects, may have a negative effect on the way in which one personalizes his or her room. In the highly territorial, presentational milieu of third order offices, the individual's attachment of objects having either personal or status meanings, called "personalization", is often the means by which territorial identity, occupancy, and authority are communicated. In some offices, executives go so far as to limit the amount of personalization by assigning smaller bulletin boards to employees with less status. Type and content of employee personalization are often controlled as well. In Swedish offices, by contrast, few if any regulations about personalization are reported. Yet by comparison with individual American workstations in general, whether private office or open plan, the number of objects with personal or status meaning in Swedish individual offices is extremely small.

Because the individual office tends to be a culturally defined entity, expressions of individual personality and individually created images of status appear to be unnecessary in terms of one's workspace and identity. This follows both the lack of rules about personalization in Swedish offices, and the lack of evidence or sense of informal pressures to keep highly personalized images to a minimum. Pictures of nude women were the only things mentioned, by men half in jest, that would be offensive. For other reasons, virtually none of the forty individuals interviewed had pictures of their family displayed in their office. This reinforces the separation of office and family life. A woman in her early sixties recalled that as the daughter of a *tjänsteman* in the 1930s, she never once visited the office in which he worked! The standard individual office in Sweden is not representative of the domestic family of the worker, nor can images of family be used to create personal identity. It does appear to be the case, however, that a *chef* would be more inclined to have family photos, perhaps as part of his/her more public role with clients.[15]

Most of the potentially symbolic or associational objects in individual offices are part of a more collective definition of the individual or patriarchal role in the organization. This includes work related objects, expressions of participation in collective office activities such as sport clubs, furniture, and art. Although office workers often had some choice in their furniture, and often could change the modular portions of storage and work surface units, still, the overall furniture scheme was part of the participatory process of collectively controlling the physical setting. Like many other Swedish settings, two-dimensional art can be very prominent in individual offices, though the more collective office spaces are primary places for display. An interesting painting will be less an expression of individual taste, status or identity, than of a wider, socially shared appreciation of art culture. In several cases the art objects for individual rooms would be provided by the company either through selection by some committee or representative, or by a lottery usually as a part of an office *fest*.

Related perhaps to these collectively controlled definitions of rooms is the somewhat traditional way in which the public is received in these culturally defined, individual domains. Virtually all standard individual offices have enough space and at times even separate tables to accommodate visits from outsiders and fellow workers. Most of the visits are work oriented conferences of two or

110

three people. Limited information from the interviews suggests that conversations of a personal nature, though relatively infrequent, tend to occur in someone's room rather than in a "public" space such as the corridor. This appears to be consistent with the more cultural definition of space and social relationships in the Swedish office where to a certain extent, no place exists for strictly personal relationships such as friendships. While we will see that workers do in fact "socialize" a great deal together, these relationships are fairly ordered and institutional compared with the typical spontaneity and fragility of friendship. It is almost as one anthropologist put it, "the difference between a relative and a friend" (Schneider 1968). Swedish office workers are more like relatives than friends.[16] One can find quite a different scenario in presentational office spaces where more transient, less institutional friendship relationships are an accepted part of establishing political and social order.

Korda (1975) describes what he calls "neutral zones" in U.S. offices, e.g. reception areas, hallways, copy machines, etc., as those places removed from the territorial authority of private offices or supervisor workstations. It is here primarily that much of the personal politics occurs in informal, spontaneous conversation. Public spaces in U.S. office buildings have much the character of the street, a neutral space quite appropriate to friendship formation and personal politics. The reader may recall the accounts mentioned earlier of Sweden's reputation for a lack of street life. The hallways and other public spaces of the standard linear office building in Sweden have little of this street behavior. The invitation into one's individual office for occasional, probably non-political personal conversation probably is more comfortable than using a public space, but still may carry connotations of the contemporary, highly competitive, status manipulating visits between Swedish kin members and their homes (Boholm 1983:203). In comparison with the Swedish dwelling, the individual office exists under much greater communal control. A conversation in a Swedish individual office seems to carry far less implication of either personal politics or asymmetrical exercise of status and authority. The private U.S. office, by comparison, often has strong associations with personal position and authority and will influence both work and personal conversation. Neutral spaces are therefore important.

3.5 Locations of executives
There appears to be a traditional, cultural meaning associated with a visit to a Swedish executive's office, particularly in its location and

decor. Unlike executive offices in techno-economically generated buildings which gravitate territorially to the "power corners" (Korda 1975), the Swedish *chef* clearly prefers his or her office to be directly adjacent a building or floor's entry.[17] One of the principal roles of the *chef* and his or her larger than standard *rum* is the reception of public clients.

Figure 3.4 Location of *chef* near the main floor entrance of K-konsult, Lund

Perhaps because there is today less status and authority associated with a Swedish executive's office, it is therefore a comfortable place to discuss business. Perhaps relationships with clients, individuals not part of the collective corporate group, tend toward other, more transient definitions like friendship. While U.S. executive offices also have conference capabilities, these tend to be used more for internal purposes where authority is to be exercised. In the U.S. office an impressive (third order) conference room, often located adjacent to the entry, tends to be the focus of more neutral meetings between executives and clients.

Confirmation of this normative basis of the *chef's* location comes additionally from a description of ideal physical office planning found in a business school textbook. The director is said to require "central and representative placing" (Skare 1967:215). The ideal of a central location seems to be more an expression of his/her role in representing the work group to the public and functional accessibility to employees, than it is of territorial control. Because of the visual and acoustic separation required in the centrally located *chef's* office, there is virtually no direct supervision of employee work or socialization. The power corner is a much more powerful territorial sign of control. In one interview I was told that "if the *chef* sat in the corner he would be disconnected from the workers". The plan of figure 3.5 illustrates an interesting example of *chef* location in the office portion of a wholesale bakery. Here one sees a clear preference for a central position between the manufacturing and office portions of the building (the original location of the *chef's* office was by the main office entry). A potentially territorially

112

strong corner office is not appropriated by the *chef*, either initially or during a major remodel. Without two sets of windows, the one preferred is essentially an ordinary, though somewhat larger office.

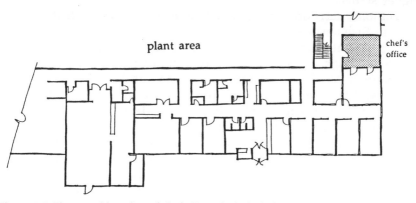

Figure 3.5 Photo and location of *chef*, Skogaholm's bakery, Lund.

Other perhaps culturally determined spatial distinctions exist between the expression of Swedish and other executives. Site analysis illustrated an unusual position of the *chef* at the conference table in the Malmö city building. In contrast to the usual U.S. territorial position at the "head" of the rectangular or oblong table, this Swedish *chef* sits squarely in the middle of one of the long sides, clearly another central and representative placement. The individual describing these positions used the rural analogy of the cows all knowing and using their own stall (the image of cows along a linear placement of stalls was chosen over the more hierarchical pecking order of hens!) The apparent lack of hierarchical order in the linear cow barn--even though individual cows will have strong attachment to their particular places--is also an appropriate analogy to the lack of positional status of individual rooms of the long corridors of these offices.

Even though a sign may tell the visitor that the *chef's* office is more directly adjacent to an entry, little distinguishes this room from all the others down the hallway. All the doors look alike. Similar to the linear second order farms of Sweden and Denmark, the social logic of the linear row of offices inhibits uses of positional location in plan layout as a source of territorial status.[18] In Swedish offices, one finds few indications that individuals use locations of their rooms along the core as sources of identity or status. There was no reported ranking of individuals according to their proximity to entry or *chef*, nor do the rooms at the ends of the corridor, most often designed identically to the rest, provide special status. In U.S. buildings, both the proximity to the boss's office and a long length of executive office distance from the entry are often used as signs of higher status.

The only territorial example apparently possible with the linear form in Sweden is the case in which an entire wing is occupied by an administrative department composed of several executives. One of the buildings studied, the large central office for a pharmaceutical company (refer again to figure 3.1), had the board room, CEO's office, and personnel director's office, plus other staff, all in one wing. From the corridor, this wing looked identical to all the others and its overall position in the building created no unusual territorial effect. In a similar situation described in one of the few major ethnographic studies of Swedish office society (referring only incidentally to the physical settings) the executive wing of one very large corporate headquarters had the nickname of "kings street" (Holm-Löfgren 1980:39). Yet in all probability this corridor too received no locational or detail designation of special status. While the public linear corridor in *smårumskontor* appears to be culturally designated as "egalitarian", it is interior differences in size and kinds of furnishings which provide relatively shallow hierarchical conventions within the *smårumskontor* concept of the "patriarchal".

114

Unquestionably the most conventional designation of status of office interiors is the size of the room measured in terms of the building module, at least in the *smårumskontor*. Not only do we find the Swedish term *modul* used in early business textbooks on planning the office (Skare 1967:214), but the term and its concept of status is again and again used by interviewees to designate the size of individual rooms in their building. In the extremely linear plan of the Malmö city building (figure 5.13), the modules created by windows and their separating mullion are actually numbered, presumably to aid in the designation of interior sizes and statuses.

At the large savings bank in central Malmö (figure 4.1), a "two module" was the basic size used by ordinary office workers; "three modules" meant a middle manager or ordinary *tjänsteman* with special need for client visitation; finally "four modules" was allocated for the department, section, or corporate *chef*. In the federal tax authority building of the same illustration, the designation became somewhat more complex. After the "two module" room which again related to the ordinary *kontorist* (a term for the ordinary office worker), the "two-and-a-half" belonged to *handleggare*(perhaps an employee doing special paperwork requiring more space), the "three module" was occupied by middle level managers, the "three-and-a-half" represented the rare situation where two receptionists or word processing specialists would share a space, and the "four module" designated an upper level department or section *chef*. Virtually all of the larger and many of the smaller offices made use of such a system in the *smårumskontor*, until the eventual evolution of fully second order forms to be described in subsequent chapters.

The module convention is not just a natural byproduct of linear buildings where virtually all employees have their own offices. Not unlike other hierarchical ordering conventions in offices in England and Japan, the patriarchal aspect of Swedish offices demands a firm definition of its limits and extent. Yet in many more purely territorial U.S. offices, in contrast, office size is also used as a sign of status, but without conventionalized designations of such. It appears to be a more *ad hoc*, immediately territorial than discursively developed situation, dependent upon the socially undesigned disposition of the techno-economic office plan and whatever spatial advantages the political situation creates. There are exceptions to be found, especially in larger and governmental organizations, both in the U.S. and other countries. In Sweden today, one participates in the patriarchal hierarchy in very controlled ways. At whichever of the few hierarchical levels, the use of one's private office as a status sign is not only conventionally defined, but perhaps culturally controlled. There appear to be major differences in who decides what the conventional meanings will be, whether executive or committee.

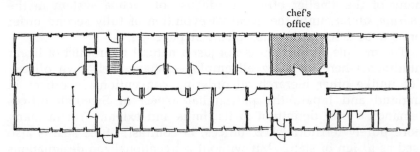

chef's
office

Figure 3.6 *Chef's* office at Lundafrakt, Lund; photo on wall depicts traditional scene of Skånsk farm

The conventionalized module system appears to be primarily the result of providing individual offices for all employees. It is unclear if module terminology was used earlier with "rational" linear offices. Yet given the variation of functional types of office spaces, it is highly doubtful that any standardized association of module size and functional need developed. Standard individual offices and the relatively standard number of hierarchical levels in today's Swedish offices, about three (*kontorist, grupp ledar*, and *chef*) provide ready ingredients for a conventionalized system of differentiation. In fact one must see the system as the natural complement to our hypothesized first collective, participatory demand for universal private offices. Politically, one cannot imagine a situation in which all employees had individual offices, but there were no conventionalized rules about office size. In the evolving participatory climate, no executive could make this decision on his/her own. While eventually "one size fits all" will become the solution, conventionalization during the initial stages of the breakthrough is in effect part of the larger influence of the collectivity over processes of hierarchy and the patriarchal.

This greater collective control of status designation is reflected in the differences in the kinds of individuals who became *chef* before and after office democracy. The literature provides interview statements about the fact that "many bosses are no longer brutal like one reads about 20 to 50 years ago" (Leymann 1986:33). Or there is mention of a strong military like presence which existed in Swedish offices, along with the typical patriarch (Lindgren 1985:137, 138). Today when one asks employees about the character of the "boss" and his or her larger "three or four module" office, it is maintained that these offices are somewhat larger with a conference table and are a little finer or are more decorated with furniture or carpeting. This is because of the executive's centrally located role in playing host to important clients. Often these differences are not even reported as sources of status, just functional in terms of company hospitality. During this line of questioning, an interviewed *chef* said that he did not feel his room, a module larger than others and furnished somewhat more extensively, was really as much his own (than typical rooms) because of its use for client reception.

3.6 The exceptions of shared rooms
Along with the evolution of the role of the *chef*, in relation to the system of modular defined individual offices, one must speak specifically about parallel and connected changes which can be specifically associated with cultural roles of gender. When exceptions to the individual room standard occur, people sharing those rooms tend to be women. From the conscious point of view of the employee, whether male or female, the reason behind all spatial layouts of Swedish offices is function. The fact existed, at least in 1974, that 65% of employees were women who, like in other

117

countries, did not hold a like percentage of administrative positions but did fill a disproportionate proportion of the small number of really "routine" work positions (Ordets Makt 1974:31). Functional reasons concluded that routine workers like typists (now word processors) needed to be in the same space, and these employees were virtually always women.

In spite of computer technology and general increased worker responsibilities, there remain a few situations where functional work relationships require possibilities of immediate conversation with coworkers or a supervisor. As probably an exception to the gender rule, the cooperative trucking firm visited contained a dispatch room shared by four or five men, though as in more historical offices each sat by a window. The essential communication function of truck dispatch demands these workers to be within conversation range with each other.

Figure 3.7 Office of the secretary to the Posthuset *chef*

In the large state tax authority building, of the eighty-five employees in one section investigated, only two women receptionists shared a room. In a typical office today, the reception function may be one of the last remaining areas where common rooms are felt to be necessary. The earlier exceptions to the individual room standard, the typist pool or *skrivcentralen* described in the late 1960's (Uggelberg 1975:5, 32) appears largely to have disappeared due to the personal computers now found in each office. All secretaries unanimously are said to require, and do have, their own room, again for functional reasons. In the historic central post office building in Malmö, the director's secretary has a room (figure 3.7) almost as large as that of the man with whom she works. Partially because recent remodeling did not wish to further subdivide the generally large rooms (originally that floor had been apartments), the designed plan was to have an additional person in the room with the secretary. Without pointing to any major political or personal confrontation, the other person, a woman who functions as an administrative assistant, described the process by which she very naturally was provided with her own office.

Today the only women other than receptionists who may tend to be found in shared rooms are those in which some sort of data entry, data access, or customer service function is involved. One middle-aged woman who is an administrative individual for an international construction firm and has her own office, described her earlier role as data supervisor in a computer room run by about seventeen women (this function has been radically decentralized by the p.c.). In what seems to be an initially unusual scenario for a shared office, she described no territoriality for office windows or other advantageous locations. Any new person always got the vacant desk. There was no major reshuffling among those with seniority. She herself did not have a window desk (perhaps being more centrally located) and did not ever desire an individual office. They all got along very well with each other. While statistically women participate fully in the now ubiquitous standard of "one person, one office", descriptions such as the above raise the possibility that in some situations, women may not be as prone to achieve or even desire their own space, particularly as an expression of an essentially patriarchal/individual status of *tjänsteman*. We recall the historical, predominantly male association with the patriarchal, either as master of the *by* farm, or early office worker.[19]

From the bibliography of Swedish lives and work one finds the following personal account of being a part of a female office group:

The best *kamratkrets* (circle of comrades) I experienced was at IRO in the 1970's. We sat four girls in one room and got along very well together. The one gladly helped the other, and even if we many times had a lot of work, it was fun. There was always someone who made jokes or lightened things up if it was needed. I remember that nobody wanted to stay home on account of sickness because they were afraid to miss some of the goings on. There was a work togetherness and comrade togetherness which was unique, but we understood that it couldn't go on forever. The foursome was broken up little by little, when someone had a child or a new person came to work.

Besides we four, who shared our room, there were eventually two or three other girls working with payroll, accounting, and the telephone switchboard. They also belonged to the *gäng*(gang). I know that we thought it was rare to have such work comrades *that one never heard anyone speak badly of another*. That was wonderful because then one could conclude that neither were they talking or gossiping about oneself behind the back (Bohman 1987:233).[20] (translation by author, italics emphasis added)

In one of the buildings investigated, the large central savings bank in Malmö, three such shared, though larger, data rooms still exist. Having from twelve to about twenty employees in each room, one room was entirely female, and the others predominantly so. Given the rare existence of shared rooms in other offices, all interviews in the bank were done with people from these spaces, two women and one man. Even though these rooms were recently remodeled and in their still linear form provided good exterior lighting, people with seniority gravitated to window positions. The male *chef* in one of the offices sat very territorially in the corner! Another male middle level supervisor in this same office felt that he needed a private office for his work. The female *chef* or supervisor in the all female room voiced no such need for an individual office, nor was her position in the room territorially significant. She felt that an all female group led to too many social difficulties and her present group was too large. Her ideal office situation was not an individual office for each, but a shared space of four to six people with a gender mix.

Figure 3.8 Rare shared data rooms: Sparbank Malmö

This woman had been the group supervisor prior to having taken a birth leave of several months. The new supervisor did not wish for her own room either. A great deal of the extensive social activity of this all female group seemed to involve traditional roles of women, i.e. marriage, birth, etc.. It would appear that some women prefer what really amounts to the older "family" relationship of the large office rooms, with men included, rather than the modernized, individual role made almost universally possible by the breakthrough. To a large extent these common data rooms were more a legacy of the functional, and perhaps social and cultural past. While the personnel director of the bank maintained that a functional need existed for the recent remodeling, the employees suggested that with their individual p.c.s, there was no need to be located near to common files and other data in the room.

Everything was in their personal computers. Immediate supervision was not that critical. In the room that received telephone data inquiries by customers, and complaints, the immediate presence of fellow workers was described as helpful, both functionally and emotionally.

3.7 Patriarchal views and women

Recent interviews done as part of this study contained no complaints by women about inappropriate male authority in space allocation or general work decisions. Yet in literature based on somewhat earlier conditions, though still during the emerging democratic period, one does find such evidence. The already cited ethnography of Swedish offices was done by a woman who had for several years worked as a middle level *chef* in different corporations. One of the sections of her book is entitled the *Patriarkaliska Aspekten* ("the patriarchal aspect", Holm-Löfgren 1980:149). Related to her frequent use of the family metaphor for office organization, she tells how some male bosses viewed female subordinates, particularly secretaries, receptionists and clerical personnel, from traditional family/gender points of view. Secretaries, for example were unable to get more responsibility and were often treated as opposite gender rather than "fellow" workers (ibid:157). In general the politically important norms for relationships were still essentially those traditionally conducted by males, yet still familial, rather than female, e.g. as might relate to roles of wife and homemaker (ibid:96). We have seen evidence that some female work groups in larger rooms appear to create a more female, but certainly less powerful, familial set of norms for office organization. While the democratic breakthrough has changed the patriarchal aspects of office life, shifting from an authoritative male patriarch to an accommodating "patron", in Holm-Löfgren's terms (ibid:191), male oriented values still exist (ibid:97).

In a related early 1970's article which specifically labels secretaries as the "housewife of the workplace", several other examples of more traditional, familial, male-female definitions are provided. There are differences in job ads: men are asked to be capable, striving to get ahead, with good prospects, while women are required to be cheerful, service oriented, to have a sense of order, and to be able to make coffee in pleasant environments (Ordets Makt 1974:32). Men are expected to be career oriented, women family oriented; women support and maintain much of men's work; and women who served at home at the turn of the century now serve men in the office (ibid:33-34). In a third and more recent study of female engineers, strong evidence of patriarchal structure still existed, especially in the relations between male *chef* and female subordinates (Lindgren 1985:135). These relationships could be perceived as either negative, where the subordinate felt that she was not given the same respect and responsibility as male subordinates, or positive, where the subordinate developed a strong familial loyalty toward the patriarchal boss (ibid:136).

This further clarifies the conflict a woman faced, perhaps mostly during the early democratic period, i.e. between being seen as an active and worthy co-participant in the modified hierarchical ladder of patriarchal *tjänsteman*, or playing the also traditionally and culturally based role of patriarchally related female. Such has certainly been an ambiguous experience for many women, particularly those in lower positions requiring less education and overall commitment. Most women, now a majority of today's office workers, undoubtedly see themselves as full participants in the redefined patriarchal, now really more "individual" definitions established by the breakthrough. Yet one cannot assume that all male coworkers will share that view. Particularly the older *tjänstemän* and *chef* have been shown at times to perpetuate older versions of the patriarchal. In one example, a female accountant could not travel with a male coworker simply because she was seen by her superiors in this older perspective (Ordets Makt 1974:30).

In the offices recently surveyed, very few spatial differences between men and women still exist. Virtually all women enjoy individual office definitions, suggesting that the emergent cultural definition of the familial/patriarchal/individual no longer uses sexual differences as any prominent aspect of its constitution. This somewhat begs the question, of why with such culturally legitimized participation of women in the hierarchical aspects of the system, more women are not found in higher administrative positions. In the territorial offices of the U.S., while the percentage of women in executive positions is about the same as in Sweden, it may be for different reasons. In the U.S., office organizations are perhaps the most challenging arenas in which to prove a woman's ability to compete with men. In Sweden, perhaps, today's office societies have radically diminished associations of individual competition and achievement. As we will see, the role of *chef* is to a far greater extent controlled and shaped by the needs of the collective. Still, residual "male" association cannot be totally eliminated as an influence in office society, perhaps particularly among executives. One cannot dismiss the history of ancient membership in Scandinavian collectives which was largely focused on organizing relationships between men.[21]

Is it true that for women neither the traditional cultural, nor territorial, nor the purely economic incentives are as strong? Furthermore, in spite of the suggested social competition between corporation as society and family as society, and in spite of the actual fragility of these groups, the family in Sweden has a much more positive cultural image and consequently receives far greater support from spouses, extended family, and certainly the government. Are women less tempted by a set of dazzling, more conscious third order images about ideal places to do battle with men and other women?

The often stated political goal of the Social Democratic party of a daycare place for every child in Sweden says much about the support the family receives.[22] Maternity leave may be taken by either parent, and a great deal of other leave and vacation time can be used to be with family members, etc.. There has actually recently been a minor baby boom of sorts in Sweden, partially because of the publicized decrease in population in the country, and perhaps also because of the new universal (rather than self-interested) freedom and opportunity achieved by truly democratic work.

It is also apparently true, from present indications, that for some of these same reasons, far fewer men covet the higher executive identities. While in the U.S. it is generally assumed that all men actively compete for higher and higher rank, in Sweden such demeanor becomes recognized by the larger work group as relatively unique, and even somewhat socially deviant. Such success is looked upon with jealousy (1983:32); status seeking behavior has a special term *karriärist* (Holm-Löfgren 1980:113), or phrase *dom som har gjort karriär* (Lindgren 1985:119) ("career opportunist", and "those who have made a career"). This certainly seems to be a clear byproduct of the democratic breakthrough, in contrast to the historical role of *tjänsteman* where making one's career was a positive norm.

Finally, one cannot leave the discussion of individual offices without commenting on the parallel phenomenon which occurs in the layout of restrooms. Here too, in all Swedish office and other institutional buildings, restrooms are not large, shared spaces but actual individual rooms as illustrated in figure 3.9. Usually linearly organized along some corridor or corridor coatroom space, each small and fully equipped facility (like any residential "half-bath") has its own door out into the public space. There is no need to designate rooms as either "male" or "female"; no urinals exist.

Some bathrooms are specially provisioned for the handicapped, and are so designated.

It may be cultural definitions of space versus the territorial that provides the differences between these individual rooms and the shared larger restrooms of U.S. offices and institutions where men at least are in either full or partial view of others. When compared to the private bathrooms of executives in the same building, these meanings appear to be related primarily to territorial rights and social status (Swedish individual restrooms can be just as efficiently cleaned as U.S. restrooms). The uses of bathrooms for social distinction occurs ubiquitously in third order building forms. In Sweden the perhaps culturally based system of identical, individual restrooms negates any territorial appropriation of restrooms for status. Special executive bathrooms do not exist. Research on comparisons

Figure 3.9 Individual restrooms typical of Swedish offices

between women's facilities in the U.S. and the unisex model in Sweden would undoubtedly be interesting as well. Women's use of larger common restrooms for socialization, in our relatively undesigned techno-economically determined offices, probably relates to gender differentiated office roles and the need for an expression of female solidarity.[23] While Swedish offices, as we will soon see, have many places specifically designed for "socialization", none carry special "male" or "female" connotations.

Notes

1 The actual term for office worker becomes *tjänstearbetare* (the combination of *tjänsteman* and *arbetare*) in at least one social science source on the changing definitions of office workers (Sandberg 1980:91).

2 Fieldwork was conducted in two phases which might for convenience be labeled "Smaller Offices" and "Larger Offices". The first portion of the first phase, Smaller Offices, began with the collection of typical floor plans for some ninety office buildings in the city of Lund (from the city's plan collection). This list was initially compiled from the city's register of businesses and spanned the entire cross section of organization and building types: public and private; the very small to the moderate sized (few of the very large organizations eventually investigated in phase two were in Lund); dense and sparse site

contexts; older and newer; historical and modern. In this partially Medieval city of about 60,000, ninety plans not only provides virtually all variations of offices, but actually represents most of the offices in the city. Once collected, the plan forms were analyzed and categorized. The overwhelming majority were variations of the linear scheme which is discussed more generally in the text. From the categorized linear schemes, and from the open landscape exceptions to the rule, some ten to twelve specific offices were chosen as organizations to be interviewed. Again, variation of type of organization and building form were considered in this selection. After a tour through the building, often with some executive or personnel director, one to two hour interviews were scheduled and conducted with an average of three employees with varied backgrounds. Photographs were taken during the tours, and all interviews were recorded. About ninety percent of all interviews were conducted in Swedish.

The intended second part of the work was to select from this more informal survey of offices, two or three on which to conduct a much more structured and detailed investigation. Sample questionnaires for three offices were prepared with the help of social science faculty in Architecture at the University of Lund. The intent of the questionnaires was to elicit a more precise personal history of employee's use of space in their respective offices. All three organizations felt the process would be too time consuming for their employees. There was probably also a sensitivity to any company-wide discussion of uses of space. As we will see, these organizations often undergo extreme amounts of participatory planning for their environments and are logically not want to open up this process after occupation. Space is a very sensitive issue for Swedish office workers, but the fact that they do *not* systematically do post-occupancy-evaluations, I believe, has less to do with any cover up of territorial realities--very little is shown to actually exist--than with the impracticality of doing extensive group participation in design issues for a second time. Once the issues have been decided during the planning stages, and the cultural ethos invariably has been permitted expression, Swedish office workers and administrators are as a rule very proud of their environments and very willing to talk about them, work time permitting.

Given the impossibility of completing the intended second phase, it was decided to do similar interviewing, but with the largest scale of organizations, many of which were in the larger city of Malmö. Using similar selection techniques, an initial tour of ten buildings was followed by a number of interviews, as many as would be permitted (usually about four of five). In addition to this informal fieldwork in the Malmö-Lund area of Southern Sweden (they are only about fifteen kilometers apart), several tours of offices in the Stockholm areas were conducted. Some of these, like at SAS, included quite detailed interviews with a key informant. Additionally, interviews were arranged with prominent scholars, architects and consultants in the field.

3   Susan Sontag's remark is often quoted, i.e. that for such a self-conscious people the Swedes are remarkably non-psychological in their interests (Daun & Forsman 1984:41).

4   The Swedes do place a great deal of emphasis on one's ability to independently and rationally approach work. The reason why an inability to do so causes

social ostracism can only be traced to the high participatory demands, in this case work and social skills, placed on the individual by the collective work group. Other cases are described where an individual is perceived by the group as expressing to much individuality, especially through dress, expensive dining, over-familiarity with an executive, etc. (Helmersson 1987:22) Here one might say that second order processes may be constraining third order expression.

5   The author is speaking here of more contemporary pubs. For a probable distinction between second and third order pubs (where the traditional is more ritually integrated into some localized community) see Hunt & Satterlee 1986.

6   In Daun's description of possible Swedish character, again, he cites other social scientists who have studied the socialization of Swedish children. There is a great emphasis on self-reliance, which eventually gives them their place in collectivity. He compares Swedes with Southern Europeans which actually try to inhibit the child's independence from the family (Daun 1989:93). Dependence is obviously on family rather than some other (collective) group in society.

7   Further investigation might establish a clearer relationship between modern uses of Lutheranism as the state religion, and essentially third order rhetoric for presentation of identity and status. Certainly these still quasi-sacred places of nominal contact with the other world cannot be said to be highly effective in any ritual or individually cognitive sense. The Church, does, however still retain control over particularly "patriarchal" or individual aspects of people's lives, e.g. the passage rites of baptism, confirmation, and death.

8   In spite of the many comparisons between the collective, consensus seeking behavior of Japanese corporations and that of the Swedes, Japanese office forms in no way resemble the evolutions in Sweden. Whether this is due to the extreme cost of space in Japanese cities, compared to elsewhere, or to other more expressive differences, remains to be seen in future research.

9   The source here is the *Arbetsmiljö* (Work Environments) handbook (1982). While general requirements of providing natural light for workers, both office and industrial, exist, no specific provision can be found which provides for the individual "ownership" of a window which occurs in private or individual offices.

10   The author is reminded of a student project which analyzed a stock brokerage firm here in Tucson, Arizona. While salaries were certainly not leveled, because each salesperson was totally on commission, there was no institutional linkage to earnings. In a sense, personal earnings were removed from any formal influence of the social and political organization of the group. What the company did use as incentive, was space. Having a private office with a window became the most recognizable and probably exaggerated means of expressing status. The example of the electronic "quality circles" office (figure 0.2 in the Introduction) provides another variation on this theme. In this case, space has been equalized as a commodity through the common landscape workstation (with conference rooms and a distant cafeteria facility). Differential salaries, however, exist very much as a separate and formal part of the institution. Americans, it would seem have attempted to keep the old

126

more hierarchical structure along side of the new horizontal team organization. Here one is probably financially rewarded for his or her participation in teams, while in Sweden the recognition comes from the socio-cultural aspects of the team itself.

11 Increasingly during the present period of individual rights in the U.S., one hears architects complaining about how specification has radically diminished one's ability to "design". The problem of course lies in the lack of ability for any client group of building users to come to a participatory agreement themselves about how their particular setting should be designed. In the absence of such participation, regulatory agencies have no alternative but to specify. Of course any truly participatory user process would alter the architect's role as designer as well.

12 The term "top-down" was Fritz Steele's and denotes exclusive decision making by a small number of individuals, usually executives (1973).

13 Did the third order patriarch refer to his space as *mitt kontor*, expressing the unusual rights of individual space, in comparison to the employees who would have called their shared space *kontor* as well? *"Mitt kontor"* could have been replaced by *"mitt rum"* because of the overly patriarchal connotations of the former.

14 The issue is somewhat analogous to the understanding of space and cultural processes in the so-called "peasant" societies. The anthropological term of "limited good", where one peasant's gain is another's loss, would seem to fit a territorial rather than cultural or expressive mode of space. Without reference to possible second order systems in such societies, the author's article on cultural space in Andalucia contains further discussion about distinctions between territorial and culturally determined kinds of space (Doxtater 1989).

15 It may be that the greater presence of family photographs in manager's or executive's offices relates to a more conscious metaphor of "family". Probably the meaning of the metaphor today is less that of "patriarch" than of "family member". Any such overt expression of traditional patriarchality on the part of either manager or typical employee would consciously offend virtually everybody, even though certain more subconscious expressions of individuality are obviously legitimate. As we will see middle level managers have had to actually play an advocacy role for an increased collective meaning and activity. The really third order rhetorical message of "family person" probably speaks to his or her conscious desire to promote group solidarity.

16 This may also explain the mistaken metaphor of associating office with family which occurs in the data. In the minds of modern Swedish office workers, the only comparable social institution where one has such institutionalized relationships, usually in contrast to friendship, is at least the image of "family". This however, could be only an exegetic or conscious explanation. Strong distinctions between collective and family groups exist at a more subconscious level of (second-order) practice. It would seem that third order expression is much more available to conscious understandings, and of course manipulation.

17 An interesting exception to the U.S. norm, where managers and executives are in corners, usually at a distance from the entrance, was discovered by one of my

design students during an analysis of an office building owned and occupied by the Girl Scouts. Included in a virtually all female cast of employees was the chief executive, who had decided that her office would be in an interior location, closest to the main entry. Whether this represents a kind of female territoriality--being in the center of things--or is more consciously social in motivation, remains to be seen.

18 The "linear" strategy of form appears to be a frequent pattern in the village layout of small egalitarian societies (Doxtater 1971). It is as yet, however, unclear how such patterns relate to the presence or absence of active first order expression. The question is whether or not the form is more related to a (first order) spatial scheme which provides thresholds of contact with the other world, at multiple scales, or whether the spatial structure of ritual (second order) oppositions is created by more local, behavioral, even folklore circumstances.

19 Consideration of the respective roles of men and women raise significant issues, far too extensive to be adequately included in the present work. One possible discussion may involve the general control, in very traditional societies, of culturally expressive systems by men as evident in Ortner's article on female associations with subordinate "nature" and male linkage to "culture" (Ortner 1974). If in fact second order systems such as those in Scandinavia are still highly expressive, then logically, they too may be used by or controlled more by men. Whether or not this is because of political dominance of males over females, as in Ortner, or alternatively that inherently men are more aggressive and therefore must set up expressive systems primarily to deal with their own relationships, as discussed further in Doxtater (1989), remains to be seen.

20 This description of the lack of "back" behavior so typical of rhetorical, third order society, lends weight to the probable hypothesis of its general absence in second order systems (even during the transitional period at the time of this ethnographic report).

21 In the old Norwegian farm culture, at least, the first order concept of space and symbolism used "male" and "female" labels and ritual sites to identify not so much men and women as such, but the distinction between two kinds of relationships possible among primarily males, i.e. as a hierarchical head of one's own farm ("female") or as a member of a collective group ("male") (Doxtater 1981). For a more general discussion of possible cross-cultural implications of the above, why much of the symbolism and ritual in traditional societies are "dominated" by men, see again Doxtater (1989).

22 The importance of daycare to Swedes is reflected in application of Bill Hillier's "space syntax" methods to actual facilities. In her architectural dissertation, Marjanna Berg (1987) seeks to evaluate whether or not the layout of the building actually supports the (largely discursive) goals of an open political relationship between child and staff.

23 Conradson mentions the use of bathrooms in patriarchal offices for boisterous, presumably group territorial behavior (1988:150). She does not have information about whether these groups were male or female, though such behavior was probably typical of both as it provided a unique place which could be controlled by otherwise illegal employee social groups.

128

4 Emerging work groups

4.1 *Mitt Arbetsgrupp*

According to the previous rationalist/patriarchal ideas, the earlier, large, shared work rooms expressed a sort of domestic work group, whose structure was conceptually functional and hierarchical. Nominally, each room would have originally been designed, and subsequently remodeled to fit those groups who actually worked together. The definition of family and functional group appears to have nicely overlapped, providing a patriarchal (cultural) basis to job relationships between employees, at least more so in earlier periods. What was the effect of the participatory manifestation of individual offices, which diminished remnant notions of family, as it were, to the scale of the individual? Would one expect some reformation of work group organization and expression to logically follow? Given the flexibility of moving people in and out of equal offices (among a majority of workers), the linear, prototypical form seemed to work well from a functional point of view. Certainly individuals had better task performance privacy, and work group adjacency could be more easily formed and reformed in terms of contiguous offices along either one or both sides of the corridor (depending upon the thickness of the linear core). Most linear buildings were and still are composed of such work group segments.

Unlike the previous large rooms where relationships between workers followed spatially asymmetrical expressions of status, the linear corridor of individual offices would eventually become part of a new more horizontal, egalitarian way of working. The basic conceptualization of work eventually shifted from an almost exclusively vertical notion to one which balanced the modular but limited notion of "patriarchy" with an essentially horizontal idea of work. This return to a much more cooperative concept of work, not

129

unlike that of the traditional *byar*, is hypothesized to have been a prior, cultural foundation of the actual democratization of work formalized as co-determination in the late 1970's Much literature exists on this general democratization of work in Sweden (e.g. Bradley, et. al. 1976:42 and elsewhere).

Unfortunately most of the literature about the democratization of Swedish work published elsewhere, concerns industrial organization and settings.   This literature compares horizontal industrial work in Sweden (and Norway) with Quality Circles organization in the U.S. and especially Japan (e.g. Cole 1989, Sandberg 1982). While illustrating the strong Scandinavian shift in thinking away from Tayloristic management practices, beginning in the 1960's, the basis for these changes is held to be less cultural than purely political. Cole, in fact states that: "the centralized Swedish model had a top-down quality and the various organizational instruments that were created were not mass organizations that ensured the involvement of large numbers of employees at all levels" (1989:271). Small group organization in industrial Sweden, and the U.S., is not seen as a pervasive, grass-roots cultural phenomenon, but something created more rationally by union and national executives. What these researchers have not looked at is the much more indigenous and widespread democratization of office work, paradoxically more inconspicuous precisely because of its non-discursive, more culturally or expressively based processes. These descriptions of the problematic nature of small groups in industrial settings, even in Sweden, emphasizes the unlikelihood of their having caused or created the recognized democratic breakthrough and general laws of co-determination.

In large scale vertical organization, whether empowered in part by traditional patriarchal values of Swedish culture, or the more economically   and   politically   immediate   power   of   U.S. organizations, conceptions of work emphasize the flow of information and authority from the top down. While smaller scale cooperative work is always possible *within* levels of the hierarchy, between those of equal status, Tayloristic systems emphasize vertical relationships as the primary key to maximum production, with recognition of such by differential salaries and third order statuses and identities. The democratic work organization which has emerged in Swedish offices recognizes the inherent functional need for some top-down initiative and planning, but places greatest conceptual value on cooperative sharing of information and authority in horizontal work groups. This kind of experience did not result from any conscious right won through collective

130

bargaining or topdown edict, but from a reemergence of the traditional second order expressive opposition between vertical and horizontal forms of social relationships. The standard of the individual office of the *smårumskontor*, the elimination of the large room "family" expression, and the following expression of individual and work group along sections of the corridors (as in figure 4.1), were hypothetical first steps.

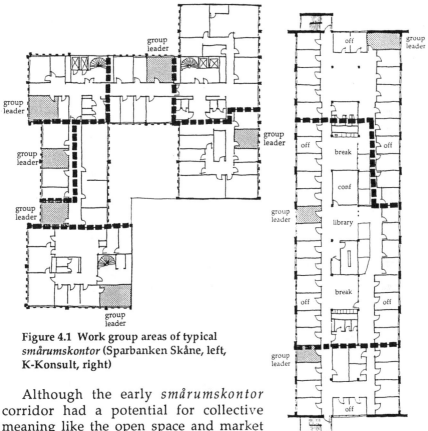

Figure 4.1 Work group areas of typical *smårumskontor* (Sparbanken Skåne, left, K-Konsult, right)

Although the early *smårumskontor* corridor had a potential for collective meaning like the open space and market of the old *by*, there were initially few actual collective social relationships by which to redefine the group, once larger familial meanings had declined. Democratic processes of actual work, the horizontal concept, could only occur between people who were socially and culturally defined as a group, *a priori*, as it were. The initial impulse of individual offices culturally defined only the revised patriarchal--now more "individual"--aspect of the eventual reemergence of second order ritual. The actual work relationships at first followed rationalist and hierarchical tradition. Formal means of address continued for a time in these new offices. One employee associated this formality with the closed doors and isolation of workers of the early sixties. Signal lights were common on all doors showing when the occupant was on the phone, or was otherwise not available. Indicative of the still reigning notions of traditional hierarchy, in one office at least, the highest *chef* could go directly into a subordinate's room without knocking (Holm-Löfgren 1980:54).

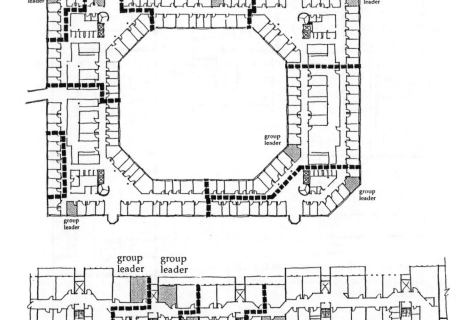

Figure 4.2 Work group areas of typical *smårumskontor* (Länsstyrelsen, top; ABV, below)

One has the distinct impression that during this first period of individual offices many employees became increasingly socially isolated, communicating with each other only as function demanded. The traditional patriarchal restaurants, usually spatially separate from work areas, may have been the locus of primarily

132

friendship rather than work group socialization (although aspects of formal, patriarchal dining may have continued here as well). Even from the interviews, one receives clear statements that socialization for the Swedish office person, or for any Swede for that matter, is not a natural thing where no social group is established. Strong tendencies exist for individuals to be highly solitary, even reclusive within their private office. The presence of equally strong needs to belong to a social group, however, would occur where such a group exists and is well defined (Lindgren 1985:141). This we take to be the legacy of second order tradition. The functional and balancing reality of horizontal work groups, would remain dependent upon the formation of well defined collective social groups.

Not unlike small group discourse in industry, though certainly less associated with union or governmental apparatus, were conscious perceptions of the second order need for a more active, well defined social basis of the formerly rationally based office work group. In one of the early seventies textbooks for high school students specializing in business, office workers are said to be obliged to: 1) show friendship, helpfulness and interest in others; 2) want to work together; 3) attempt to see things from others viewpoints; 4) think that one's own behavior influences the general spirit and joy of work (Skare 1967:14). Or in a contemporaneous piece of research about *samarbete på arbetsplatsen* (working together in the workplace), a study which details actual work experience in a late sixties administration department, repeated emphasis is placed on one's ability to *gå varandra till mötes*, an idiomatic expression which speaks about the need for individuals to be able to compromise in collective situations (Uggleberg 1975:4). While this need has obvious functional utility in the conduct of office business, a social basis for relationships apparently had to come first. From one of the major ethnographies of Swedish office work life, the author discusses: first, positions by the national union research office that work organizations must be created which make people more dependent upon each other (Holm-Löfgren 1980:54); second, processes by which the older (patriarchal) duty motive was replaced by motives of keeping strong (social) relationships with other workers and the company as a whole (ibid:57); and third the shift in concept of office organization from the "pyramid" to the "tent" (ibid:108), or from the vertical to the horizontal.

Information in more recent literature and interviews reflects a certain shift away from an awareness of the larger organizational need to reestablish the social basis of the work group, to the

133

recognition of the individual's need to participate once such definitions exist. Having "community" with the group is listed as one of three needs of workers, in addition to self-determination in everyday work decisions, and having interesting work (Bradley et. al. 1976:123). In the analysis of female engineers, several reported excessive work privacy as destructive. One had a "terribly great need to come into contact with other people" (Lindgren 1985:141). Similarly, a male traffic engineer in the Malmö city building, remembering the differences between earlier large rooms and present individual ones, said that "when in one's own room, one had to make an effort to go out and talk with others more".

In the offices of today's Sweden, the collective concept of work group is a cultural phenomenon. It is not evident from the present information whether earlier patriarchal offices even used the term *arbetsgrupp* (work group) to refer to the more family defined, vertically organized, consciously rational work relationships. Certainly the presently ubiquitous term for one's coworkers *arbetskamrater* (work comrades), with its obvious roots in the industrial worker's movement, would have been very unfashionable in earlier bourgeois and probably rationalized offices. The term appears to be less associated with functional, or even strictly political relationships than it is with the social essence of being a comrade, i.e. in a collectivity. Offices seldom have special union club rooms as one finds in industrial sites, and although all employees are members, participation for most is minimal. The use of the term, even by mid-level managers, and perhaps higher executives, illustrates the current established nature of well defined social groups, collective entities who then work together cooperatively.

U.S. organizations have no comparable terms, either *arbetsgrupp* or *arbetskamrater*, which express primarily collective social (and functional) relationships. Rather, most formal designations refer to hierarchical status relationships, while one does occasionally hear the term "team", especially in quality circle or management organization. Though some linkage with social and territorial meaning obviously occurs with "team" (less so in highly electronic offices), these terms ostensibly refer only to functional processes. The U.S. term which designates a somewhat horizontal social relation, but is not part of the work process and exists again only transiently, is "friend". The interviewed Swedish *tjänstemän* consistently made the distinction between social relations with work comrades and those with friends who usually were not coworkers. Even though one were doing things with coworkers which were similar to what one does with friends, e.g. having coffee together, these were *arbetskamrater*, not *venner* (friends).[1]

It is quite difficult for readers, and workers, from other cultures to fully appreciate the ubiquity of the term *arbetsgrupp* and its eventual depth of institutionalized, second order, cultural meaning. The Swedish employee is incredibly loyal to his or her work group. "One stays with the same company because of one's work comrades", responded one informant. Though the *grupp*, as it is often referred to, is not consciously felt to inhibit looking for work elsewhere, still Swedish *tjänstemän* are incredibly stable. In the cooperative agricultural office in Malmö, for example, the turnover among the several hundred employees is only about 5 to 6% a year, including those retiring. It should be noted that when interviewees were asked about whether they occasionally or frequently thought about looking elsewhere, they often responded with the established fact that *tjänstemän* jobs in Sweden are decreasing in number.[2] One could not be too adventurous, therefore, in thinking about other places.

To a certain extent, the concept of group may not in fact inhibit seeking work elsewhere, as much as does the general lack of extreme competition for hierarchical advancement and status. If, as is being maintained, the *arbetsgrupp* is really a second order cultural phenomenon, then membership is less specific to the particular corporation than it is to the larger Swedish society of which most offices seem to be a part. The previously cited ethnographic description of Swedish executives, provides perhaps the best reason why people are so reluctant to change offices. It simply takes so long to become fully part of the organization with its emphasis on collective, social participation. It takes at least a half year for the initial acclimatization, then a certain political period follows, and then after a couple of years, one's more natural and spontaneous approaches become restricted because of being in a certain net of relations with strong loyalty demands (Holm-Löfgren 1980:30).

Certainly the most vivid accounts of the strength of today's office group collectivity is found in the previously mentioned literature on adult *mobbning* (collective pressure and resulting ostracism). Many of the experiences detailed come from office settings, and particularly work group relationships. In one situation, two unmarried girls who do word processing for the group have to work more overtime than other girls who have families (Uggelberg 1975:19-23). While this may not be a functionally unusual problem, the effect is particularly Swedish. The two overworked employees complain not about the an unfair vertical relationship and the decisions of some superior, but about the rift which is caused in the work group. They use the term *okamratligt* (uncomradelike) to describe the relationships of the two married women to them. They say that *"det ar tråkigt att ve nu blir so osams"* (it is unpleasant that we now have become so "untogether").

In a second example, a man broke the collective bond of the work group, including its group leader, by complaining about the leader's extreme pettiness to higher authorities. He was set upon by his group, becoming socially isolated. He was called *kamratangivare* (comrade informant), even though the object had been the group leader. The worse it became, in terms of work relationships, personal economics and family life, the worse his fellow workers treated him (Uggelberg 1975:70). In this analysis, the individual was sacrificed repeatedly for the collectivity. Not surprisingly, in the choice between helping a member who is attacked by the collectivity and supporting the collectivity in its attempt to get rid of a fellow worker, union organization stands on the side of the collectivity (ibid:30). Given the fact that friends are not really recognized and aren't therefore politically effective in this cultural system, the individual in such cases can only retreat to the individual identity of his or her office, which as we will see will be given even more collective constraints.

In a third situation of adult *mobbning*, a highly qualified woman had to move to a central office because her branch office was phased out. No appropriate *chef* or *gruppledare* position was available, so she had to join a work group whose leader was younger and less experienced (ibid:23-28). While typically in the U.S., this sort of situation causes vertical difficulties between the manager and more experienced subordinate, the emphasis in the Swedish case was on the effect within the group. The younger group leader had responded negatively to the initial suggestion of the woman's being added to the group of five, saying that *"vi ar ett fint hopsvetsat gäng"* (we are a finely welded-together "gang"). After a year, she was described as still having not *"kommit in i arbetsgänget"* (come into the work "gang"). The reason given was because the others did not see her as *jämlike* (equal).

One of the general conclusions of Holm-Löfgren's office ethnography (1980:204), stresses the positive benefits of collective, horizontal work groups, e.g. that *samarbete* (cooperative work) leads to work satisfaction and gives a positive result for both employer and employee. She maintains that time together produces strong similarities in thinking among coworkers. One example is given of an individual who was too different and for that reason alone was asked to leave (ibid:112). Other positive examples of the fruits of like minded workers are given (ibid:133-134). The term *samarbetsovillig* applies to the exceptional individuals who are "unwilling to work together"(ibid:113). Within this same volume some other negative aspects of the power of the collectivity are given. In particular, established group employees can act as "breakers" inhibiting some of the beneficial attributes of younger, well trained, individuals who seek to implement new functional processes without the social consensus of the group (ibid:117-118). This sort of individual initiative may be one of the positive benefits of the more immediately political, territorial processes of U.S. offices, for example, as it is said to be in U.S. society generally.

As illustrated in some of the above examples, the role of the group leader appears at times ambiguous as to whether or not this person represents the patriarchal or collective pole (or both) of emerging second order ritual. While the mid-level managerial function will be more likely to carry greater "patriarchical" meaning than the universally individualized employee, collective meaning of being an *arbetskamrat* within the horizontal work group appears to be perhaps vitally important as well. Even a section *chef*, above the work group, will participate at times in this collective meaning.[3] Certainly this tendency for executives to express the "hierarchical" and the workers the "egalitarian", exists to one degree or another in particularly industrial organizations, cross-culturally. Again this relationship remains primarily political, a dialectic whose primary aim is control of the fruits of production. The culturally expressive integration of these essential ingredients in Swedish office organization, however, first establishes the two opposed aspects as social principles within the *same* group. All employees, whatever title, participate in both roles. The real world effect is primarily the control and sharing of decision making, with its broad ramifications, rather than only the equitable distribution of income or work conditions which to a large extent had been politically won earlier.

It is evident from the literature and interviews, that the emerging role of *gruppledare* has clear expressive meanings of mediation between patriarchal and collective ways of behaving. In the hierarchically much deeper, exclusively vertical relationships of U.S. offices, mid-level managers always have had to politically balance their split roles as both supervisor and subordinate. Difficult as this sometimes may be, these mid-level individuals still participate only in the hierarchically ordered system. The Swedish group leader, on the other hand, operates as a kind of vertical link to the executive *chef* level, but more importantly, unlike his or her U.S. counterpart, this person perhaps symbolizes the cultural opposition between principles. He or she must be a sort of corporate shaman of sorts! The job of being a group leader in Swedish offices is for this reason acknowledged to be extremely difficult (Bradley et. al. 1976:102). How can one be "vertical" in function, for example, when to an employee of the pharmaceutical head office there was no conceptual difference between the group leader and the other members of the work group. Perhaps no person more represents the social and symbolic paradox between the "individual" and the "collective" aspects of self which will eventually become ritually resolved on a daily and ceremonial basis.

The actual pressure to be perceived by the group as a member in good standing is vividly illustrated in several of the examples of *mobbning*. In one case a long standing member of a work group naturally became its leader when the position became vacant. After a year of some difficulty managing the new job, he was replaced by an outsider. The five employees of the work group eventually made the new person physically ill, and he finally quit (Uggelberg 1975:31). If a group leader were to become too much of a hierarchically minded boss, his or her life might also be made quite miserable. One such group leader who was a perfectionist to the extreme in his supervisory relationships to the rest of the group was placed (by higher executives) in a separated room and given little to do; eventually he too became sick and was given a medical retirement (ibid:34). A woman leader as well was extreme in her control over those "under" her and was subsequently ostracized by the group (ibid:35). A closer investigation of these middle level people would probably reveal many of these hierarchical extremes to be the legacy of the earlier, more exclusively patriarchal model of organization, particularly in older *tjänstemän*.

The culturally emerging meaning of the group leader appears to be in part dependent upon supporting architectural definition. As we recall in the discussion about the modular system of designating hierarchy, group leaders were reported in interviews to have a greater modular size than the typical group worker. In the analysis of actual plans for these buildings, such a case was really quite rare. The need for functional flexibility of work group formation and size along the corridor almost mandates similarity of *all* individual offices, given the practical difficulty of prolonged group discussions necessary when any physical change or remodeling is done. Yet the deeper meaning of equality of office size between leader and group might be best described as a necessary expression of the horizontal, collective relationship which must exist. But the group leader's office has to have the opposite, patriarchal expression as well. True to the cultural definition of "*chef* in the middle", group leaders, (sometimes also called *gruppchef)* are almost always located in the center of their group. This position also satisfies a real, communicational requirement between leader and group as explicitly defined for example in planning standards found in business education (Skare 1967:212). The central location is necessary for full knowledge of and participation in the work group, for both vertical and horizontal processes.

The concept of horizontal work group as it applies somewhat abstractly to the daily function of Swedish offices has been outlined. Having briefly demonstrated the primary association of group leader with his or her work comrades, rather than with the vertical flow of command, one can then draw comparisons of similarity between these cooperative work relationships and those of the traditional second order *byar.* Just as the farmers alternated between individual work on their own farm and cooperative work in the larger *by*--which was facilitated by an elected leader--so too does this pattern reemerge in Swedish offices during the democratic decades of the 60's and 70's. The initial facilitating aspect of these emergent office societies, i.e. the reappropriation of the cultural definition of the patriarchal or individual in terms of the individual room, has been identified. It is also maintained that an opposite expression of the collectivity, must occur *a priori,* or at least simultaneously to both the social and functional behavior of real work groups. These cultural definitions and activities establish the social order, on which the much more participatory, truly democratic actual work processes eventually are based.

4.2 The presumed cultural basis of cooperative work

The following description of formal collective aspects of office life will impress the reader with their uniqueness and extent, especially compared with third order or discursive offices in other countries. Within the evolution of Swedish culture, distinctions must be made between farm and office societies as to the way collective cultural expression links to work production. In the old first order Scandinavian farm society, with its spatially independent family farms, it is argued that the primary effect of expressive culture, particularly ritual, was to maintain an egalitarian distribution of scarce productive land. In Norway, cooperative work exchanges did exist (*dugnader*), but involved only a few immediate neighbors in comparison to the larger geographic and ritual group, the valley *bygd* or *bygdelag* (Doxtater 1981). The village like forms of second order *byar* of the Middle Ages, with their mosaics of tiny, individually owned parcels, greatly intensified cooperative work to the extended scale of the ritual or cultural *bygd* or *by*. Logically, the function of ritual in the Skånsk farm societies would seem to shift somewhat from the formerly more exclusive emphasis on equitable land distribution and wealth *per se*, to the provision of legitimacy for decision making processes of cooperative work.

Certainly the balanced power relationship between collective and patriarch, still expressed in second order ritual, continues to moderate the appetite for disproportionate shares of *by* wealth. Farms were passed on to only one heir, causing the wealth of the family to remain focused on one physical farm. Yet one senses a diminishing of territorial psychology given the fact that one's land was a hardly perceptible part of the mosaic, far different from the potential source of territorial pride and status in earlier and later "enclosed" farms. Furthermore, most of the decisions about how to farm these pieces were part of the cooperative way of working. While irrefutable evidence of how expression actually influences individuals acting in a socio-economic context is difficult if not impossible to establish, it seems that some of the effectiveness of expressive power shifted from land to decision making *per se*. One can speculate then, that second order culture continued to emotionally validate the proposition that the collective balances power with the individual, and that this effect facilitated the processes of *by* council and elected leader.

There are sizable differences between the nature of work and decision processes in the farm *byar* and in the emergent Swedish offices. Certainly less specialization existed. Knowledge about all aspects of farming was probably uniformly shared by most individual farmers. The biggest decisions undoubtedly had to do with the scheduling and manning of work and the allocation of shared resources such as pasturage or forest. Office organization, on the other hand, is totally preoccupied with the production of some good or service not immediately used by the workers. This may not in itself create such a difference since scheduling and allocation of personnel and production resources also require major decision making activities. It is perhaps primarily the specialization of tasks, and its segregation of work knowledge, which seems to demand, in purely functional terms, executive coordinators. Unlike the shift from land as wealth to decision making which occurred from first to second order societies, in office evolution, a specialized, functional, executive work organization was already in place as part of the preceding patriarchal/rationalist experience.

Given the initial individual office and the existing specialized organizational apparatus, the question is how do purely collective expressive activities emerge? How does this more balanced expression of the individual and collective lead to the actual changes in work process? How do coworkers increasingly participate in decision making which was earlier specialized and organized primarily by executives? Do we assume that the more specialized, rational apparatus was no longer felt to be legitimate or at least symbolically compensated for? Does a second order cultural "background" in Swedish office workers generate the demand for more equal distribution of power, i.e. that groups not individuals can organize and coordinate specialized functions?[4] Is there a demand for cultural expression establishing the balance between individual and collective, on which actual group decisions must be based?

Perhaps the establishment of individual rooms expressively culminated the demise of the patriarchal concept of corporation, limiting that aspect to the level of individual, and invoking associations with traditional second order culture. Once the family definition of the office had been limited, the larger social fabric of the corporation lost its expressive compensation as historically exaggerated form of the patriarchal. Becoming more like a traditional farm society of equal units, rather than one big family, associations with second order culture strongly suggested new political and expressive possibilities.

The essential proposition of both first and second order Scandinavian culture had always been the balance of collective and individual power applied to the realities of the economic and political world. The primary object of power, in the case of the emerging offices, was not the equitable distribution of wealth, because those issues had earlier been settled by largely political processes of the national social democratic movement. The issue of the "breakthrough" in offices was and is *participation* in decision making. The similarity of object between these offices and second order farm organization, i.e. decision making rather than raw land or wealth, has made the cultural association between the two all the more persuasive.

This scenario leads to the possibility that initially even when only the individual aspect (room) was being expressed, and a Tayloristic rational decision making apparatus was still in place,

141

even at that point the association with the traditional Scandinavian culture was strong enough in all *tjänstemän* to push for both greater expression of the collective aspect, and actual participation in decision making. One need not speculate about whether some more complete individual/collective opposition was in place before people began participating more democratically in decisions. For present purposes we assume them to be somewhat simultaneous but subsequent to the initial move to individual offices.

It must also be reemphasized that one of the first arenas of participatory decision making, prior to more daily work decisions, had been that of the physical work setting itself, again a prime factor in the choice of individual offices. Certainly as the veil of patriarchy lifted from the organization as a whole, the reconstruction of second order society must have been facilitated by a continued and intensified participation in the design of the physical setting. Expressively, the second order collective expression of the work group became represented by two rooms, the conference room and the break room, ubiquitously present and spatially opposed to the individual rooms.

4.3 The emergence of formal architectural oppositions

If we consider the initial expression of the individual room the smallest scale and first potential level of second order opposition, then one might speculate that the spatially adjacent corridor, with time, becomes the formal equivalent to the second order street in *by* society. This is not the contemporary tourist image of street as place for friends to recreate spontaneously or for the superficial gregariousness of which Philip Slater speaks (1970), nor the "neutral" zones of Korda (1975), rather it is more the immediately opposite expression of things in the organization which are under collective, not individual control. The linear corridors of these Swedish office buildings are potentially much more symbolic or expressive of the egalitarian relationship between rooms and the linkage to distinct collective places in which either group socialization or cooperative work occur. In a sense, the corridors which are becoming "collective" in meaning opposite from the "individual" of the universal office, are initially the byproducts of other building causes created primarily by the demand for individual offices with windows. The actual collective places as break rooms and restaurants must develop their own causality on the level of the expressive, i.e., as formal spatial opposition to individual rooms, particularly those of group leaders and *chef,* work group conference rooms, and larger corporate meeting places including board rooms.

Ideally within the scale of work group the tendency exists for an internal opposition between the individual and the collective. This same meaning may potentially be used to inform the oppositions *between* any two scales of organization, with the smaller being associated with the "individual" and the larger the "collective". The larger, collective must symbolically and ritually dominate the smaller and individual. This diagrammed structure of architectural and ritual meaning, very similar to that of the second order *by*, is here proposed as an ideal formal pattern of space and meaning in an evolutionary process still occurring during the late 1960's and early 1970's. Thus in the following tour through actual buildings, one looks as much for tendencies toward fulfillment of this pattern as for absolute conformity as might be more the case in traditional societies. Twenty years is a relatively short period of time for a somewhat independent subculture to produce ideal form, particularly considering the infrequency of rebuilding and the possible technical influence of the sophisticated Swedish construction industry.

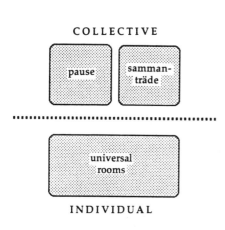

Figure 4.3 Developing second order opposition between collective and individual places at the scale of the horizontal *arbetsgrupp*

Evidence of the growing smallest scale expressive relationship between individual room and some sort of group space in the corridor might be found in the shift from closed doors and signal lights, to the custom of keeping one's door open. Virtually all of the offices visited had either an implicit or explicit open door policy, with very infrequent exceptions tending to occur either in the case of *chef* or very highly trained professions such as at the PhD or medical doctor level. Almost every interviewed *tjänsteman* was aware of the issue and could comment on those who might dare to close their doors and what this would mean in terms of their relationship to the work group or even corporation. There is clear evidence that in many cases the explicit demand for open doors comes from the group leader or higher *chef*. One could interpret this change as a response to a perceived need of middle level managers to visually control the work group. In one example from the research on *mobbning*, the right to have one's door closed became the rallying point of the work group against its unusually authoritarian leader (Leymann 1986:32). Certainly in such cases, open doors can provide greater, strictly territorial possibilities of supervision. The need for greater contact and communication between workers themselves is a much more frequent reason for open door policies given by Swedish *chef* and group leaders. This functional cause is given additional weight by taking into consideration the personal isolation created within the last decade by microcomputers.

A functional cause does not necessarily negate the simultaneous emergence of culturally expressive meaning in the same form. The author is reminded here of the egalitarian Andalucian village, in which an open door proscription exists between the parlor/dining room of the dwelling and the immediately contiguous street (Doxtater 1989). Whereas the opposition appears to be reversed in this Spanish case, with the dwelling representing more of a collective set of values and the street the individual, still, the open doorway would seem to be essential to the expression of these meanings. Thus, initially the individual rooms appeared primarily as a redefined patriarchal expression, or even sign of equal territoriality. As the larger architectural form became more associated with the oppositional contexts of Scandinavian second order culture, the tendency would exist to use the open door to express the opposition between room and collective corridor. The initially closed doors eventually created not only functional but social isolation as well. Second order culture does not provide many opportunities for individual social privacy, rather a culturally defined exercise of self, within the almost constant dominant or balancing relationship of the collectivity. We recall that much of the collective ritual in the *by* was performed as a sort of occupation of the individual farm dwelling. In the remnant courtyard farm structures of the *byar*, one sees powerful archway entrances, but no expressive gates between individual farm and collective street.

4.4 *Sammanträde*
If the national standard of the individual room strongly contrasts Swedish offices with those in other cultures, so too does the number of *designed* places for work groups to take breaks and

144

conduct their many participatory meetings. Immediately the reader may be thinking that these two activities probably take place in the same room, as often occurs in the U.S. with far fewer and more multipurpose "conference" rooms. Such is not the case. Within the fundamental work group level diagrammed in figure 4.2, both aspects of the collective received their own definition and as a pair are opposed to the individual office. In the period after initial decisions to create universal offices, Swedish organizations also begin to decide to have clearly designed and separate places for group meetings *(sammanträde)* and group breaks *(pause, kafferast, fica)* which are felt to be more purely social, as were the *fests* of the *byar*. After every collective work event in the *by*, a *fest* would follow!

Certainly the many group meetings in Swedish offices are more participatory than their counterparts in the U.S.. When compared to the more purely social and egalitarian character of the Swedish coffee break, group meetings are totally dedicated to work. How do we talk about this difference between the purely social and the purely instrumental in collective activities? At the largest scale, where the board room or executive conference room still in many cases has overtones of the traditional patriarchal, its members today can be shown to have considerable collective power within the largest scale of the organization. In today's Sweden, corporate boards also include fully participatory representation from the worker's unions.

Even at smaller scales, some patriarchal content seems evident. Middle level meetings of the work group are reportedly initiated by the group leader, one obvious source of vertical meaning. In our source ethnography of Swedish offices, again, Holm-Löfgren describes the power plays, particularly of men, in conference behavior (1980:64). However, one cannot imagine a great deal of such rhetorical positioning particularly among the often small numbers of work group members. We must remember that our source in this ethnography was herself an executive, and may have been reporting behavior in upper level conferences composed of group leaders and executives, where greater presentational power playing might be expected.

One must put the formal expression of some patriarchal/ individual aspect of the work group in perspective with the previously discussed, fundamentally horizontal work activity of the group. Like the break place and time, the specially designed group meeting place may only occasionally be used as a more formal expression of the limited, but functional vertical component of work groups. In the traditional *by* councils, the decorated staff was the symbol of the role of the elected leader. Probably, given the amount of informal cohesion evident and the often small size of the groups, there may be a tendency to use not even the more formal *sammanträde* rooms.

One might suggest that the work group conference room actively expresses the structural distinction between work and *fest* behavior. From an overall architectural point of view, we will see how functional causes of form (where actual meetings take place) often conflict with the purely social or ritual causes (the expression of different kinds of relationships potential among the group). The degree to which culture actually "recognizes" and expresses these inherent contradictions will be left to later chapters and the conclusion. We can at present be certain that the collective behaviors in the two kinds of places, *sammanträde* and *pause*, are very distinct. These expressive purposes of the conference rooms, along with the greater functional needs of larger horizontal work groups, together create the much larger number of smaller conference rooms in Swedish offices in comparison with offices in other countries. These meeting places are obviously responding to the far greater reality of horizontal participation than occurs in U.S. offices where primarily vertical decision making takes place more in private offices than internal conference rooms.

4.5 *Pause*

The expressive break place and behavior exhibit even more frequent, more formalized, institutionalization of use than its conference room complement, within the scale of the *arbetsgrupp*. One can begin to speak about purely ritual linkage of social order and expression. Activities exist independent of work but are crucial to the legitimization of work processes.[5] Categorically, Swedish *pause* ritual never takes place in conference rooms. During the last two decades, break behaviors in Sweden have moved from having one's coffee at one's desk, or an occasional informal and spontaneous gathering around a centrally located coffee maker, to highly proscribed and timed affairs where twice a day at predetermined times, all members of work groups are expected to assemble in specifically designed places. Earlier, even having coffee at one's desk would have been forbidden:

> To drink coffee during work time hasn't always been as taken for granted as it is today. Our supervisor was nice, but had decided that coffee was taboo. The result was that the gang[6] I belonged to

146

ordered coffee and rolls from the Sportscafe, which at that time would send out a girl with a basket. She was instructed to go to one of the upper floors to a janitor's closet, leave the basket there, and return in a half an hour to pick up the basket with the money. We stood there expectantly, drinking our coffee among cleaning utensils, brushes, and a not very clean sink. Heavens! An older gang with a lot of daring annexed quite simply one of the women's bathrooms, sat a table over one of the toilets, screwed out a light bulb and connected an electric hotplate, sending the scent of freshly brewed coffee seductively out into the corridor. But no man could go in to check it out, because it was *Damernas Egen* (Woman's Own, apparently a tradename) coffee that was brewing! (bibliographic account of a female office worker in Norrköpings courthouse, 1948: translation by author, Bohman 1987:205)

This image of forbidden coffee in the predemocratic workplace not only contrasts sharply to the coffee break today, but also to the institutionalized coffee ceremonies in residential and recreational contexts which began in the mid-nineteenth century in Scandinavia, e.g. as illustrated in figure 4.3. Originally an event associated with the upper classes, in many rural areas of Finland at least the coffee ceremony became one of the primary ritual expressions in the post-enclosure village. It maintained the balance between individual autonomy and community understood as different aspects of self (Roberts 1989). In old Finnish villages, no public space existed for this sort of collective activity, which Roberts similarly contrasts with street life in Southern Europe. Following the ancient Nordic pattern, the members of the community are invited into individual homes for coffee, presumably as a vestige of the ritual takeover of the patriarchal. The spatial locus for similar kinds of collective rites in Denmark is given more specific definition in Hansen's account of *hygge* (1976). Both a concept of place and behavior similar to that of the coffee ceremony (though much less formal in recent days in Denmark), its presence in the Danish home is consistent with other Scandinavian traditions. Thus in the present case, we may be seeing a shift of the traditional post-enclosure coffee ceremony from familial and rural contexts to modern groups working in office settings.

The degree of institutionalization and ritualization of today's *pause* in Swedish offices immediately strikes any foreign visitor. In talking with other visiting professors at the University of Lund, and having observed many of these buildings, one recognizes the ubiquitous pattern. Physically adjacent to all work groups are specially designed spaces for *pause* practices. A personal friend and Swedish professor of Anatomy described the elaborate coffee behavior which occurred precisely twice a day. Here the ten or so members of the department actually had two distinct rooms used exclusively for *pause*, one for morning, the other for afternoon. The number of such spaces in the faculty and staff areas of the Architecture building was equally impressive, perhaps a dozen or more, not counting the large cafeteria. These *pause* places were adjacent to each work group or department, generally five to ten individuals in number. The college of architecture building in which the author works, here in the U.S., though somewhat smaller has by contrast *no* single space for faculty, staff, or student break.

Figure 4.4 Non-work associated "coffee" group at a rural *gästgivargård* (inn), Sweden 1863 (Nordiska Museet)

Another initial example of the *pause* institution occurred while gathering office floor plans at the city planning office in Lund. The author happened to be talking with one of the planners as it became time for break. Invited to have a cup of coffee and pastry with the office, we went to a special *pause* room with several tables where virtually the entire office of some twenty or so created a vigorous conversational atmosphere. The communal, quasi-ritual character of these events strikes the foreign visitor as formal and institutional, in comparison to the much more spontaneous, unorganized, perhaps largely friendship (or "gang") based break experiences in the U.S., where they occur.

Conversation and behavior during *pause* can actually be quite formal, particularly if the group is large. Imagine ten to fifteen people sitting around a single table. This is particularly so if higher professional or executive titles, or variation in age, define the work group more formally. In the example mentioned above, a group of medical professors of varying rank and highly skilled technicians took *pause* together. While conversation was seldom specifically focused on work activities, still, deference had to be paid to the senior members of the group. From the literature one finds examples of such hierarchical influence in particularly *pause* groups with higher *chef* in them (Holm-Löfgren 1980:75). Examples are given of remnant male patriarchy which intimidate subordinate women during *pause* (Lindgren 1985: 135, 138). Tendencies appear to exist for higher executives and their immediate staff to function as a work group (Holm-Löfgren:75), though in several of the buildings visited, the higher *chef* only occasionally participated in *pause* ritual. Generally if the total organization is small *pause* participation of the executive will be more natural, since the institution as a whole is primarily related to the horizontal work group. As organizations grow in size, executive functions become less amenable to work group process; such individuals increasingly play specialized roles in relation to clients, corporate boards, and group leaders.

While most often somewhat formal, the atmosphere and conversational content of most pause ritual seems to focus not on work,[7] whether functional or political aspects, but on the sharing and discussion of things probably mostly related to values about Swedish culture at large. Given the lack of detailed observation and record of actual *pause* content one can only speculate at present about probable underlying themes. Pervasive second order values about historical or modern meanings of the individual/collective opposition in Sweden, would seem to be possible. From more formal personal social occasions with Swedish friends, and from having participated several times in actual break occasions, the subject of "Sweden", seems frequent. While one's status and purpose as a foreigner certainly will cause comparative discussions of culture, still, much in Swedish news, education and research illustrates a dialogue about Swedish culture in the broadest sense. Given the apparent inhibitions against overt vertical political manipulation of either work or friendship relationships during *pause*, it seems natural that conversation promotes the opposite associations probably linking back to some very traditional ethnic meanings, thus maintaining the "domain" content of the architectural place. In at least one example of a prevailing *pause* theme of collective equality, a female group leader gossips during break about other women not present; she is finally sanctioned by the group through being publicly embarrassed during *pause* conversation (Holm-Löfgren:70).

The Swedish *pause*, now institutional among all white collar workers,[8] has its primary purpose in the social and the cultural. It is true that the office break can provide psychological and physiological relief from work, yet according to such studies, sitting around a coffee table for fifteen to twenty minutes is not the best way to do it. Better are more frequent changes in work routine and motor activities. Even in the U.S. where more conscious Tayloristic philosophy justifies office break time as needed for greater individual productivity, still, social territorial forces are constantly at work. They attempt to form break groups and solidarity which counter the vertical social condition of work itself. The Tayloristic concept of break demands no architectural, spatial counterpart, usually assuming that break activities are supposed to be primarily individual, and for the most part can be carried on at one's workstation or in neutral circulation or multipurpose spaces. Designing a special place for employees to gather during break, which happens seldom in the U.S., demands that designers and executives admit to some more egalitarian social basis to relationships among workers. This is antithetical to beliefs about the legitimacy of vertical, third order social structure in work organization.

Yet these values are far less the product of processes at the level of culture, than a practical recognition of the inherent reality of *cultureless* means of organization. In the U.S., those lower, less professional, less mobile employees will have a correspondingly diminished belief in the validity of third order means, particularly given the breakdown of presentational symbolic capital by electronic media. It is among these workers primarily, that one finds interesting examples of *ad hoc* formation of break places within the often socially and culturally undesigned office setting--an expression of social solidarity of this group versus the vertical status system more available to the qualified.

150

In the analysis of U.S. offices, the author has seen examples of: a windowless room in a government parking garage having been turned, after the fact, into a break and lunch place; a janitorial closet on the top, presidential floor of a university administration building having been remodeled by female staff into a coffee/break room; departmental territories of female staff in this same building focused on the location of the coffee maker; a hallway adjacent to bathroom entrances being used by state agency employees for their breaks; a small utility room in a U.S. Forest Service office being fitted with odd tables and chairs for breaks; and one cannot mention all the entrances, corridors, bathrooms, copy rooms, storage rooms and conference rooms which may be used territorially by employee groups for breaks and lunch as they may.

Notes

1   This strong tendency against the formation of friendships within work organizations is further verified by research which shows, in a similar vein, the low frequency of friendship socialization with one's fellow employees after work (Daun 1989: 99).

2   Although the Swedish economy was essentially strong throughout the eighties, with minor deviations only, the number of white collar jobs is said by many to be decreasing (though probably nothing compared to the recession of the early nineties). While part of the cause of earlier sacrity of jobs might lie in the widespread adapation of computers in the late seventies and early eighties, the horizontal form of democratic work itself might also be a cause of increased efficiency of information flow and office production. When we arrive at the fully developed second order forms of offices, claims are often made that these organizations are more productive by significant percentages.

3   One middle level manager, a section head (the next scale above the work group) specifically informed the author of the term which he used for those in his section: *medarbetare* (coworkers). This is in distinction to the common practice elsewhere of referring to subordinates in the possessive, e.g. "my people", etc..

4   The key to quality circle success in industry, where it occurs, lies in the linkage or feedback between specialized knowledge and production. If as in typical top-down organization, specialized knowledge must flow first up through executives then down to production, then the process will be comparatively slow and unresponsive to real world "quality". In offices, the distinction between specialization and production is less sharp and computerization is increasingly making all forms of knowledge readily available to all longer term, well trained employees. Thus the computer may have made a common sharing of knowledge in contemporary Swedish offices more similar to the knowledge their farm ancestors shared. Such may be a necessary but insufficient condition for democratic co-determination. Tendencies will always exist for individuals to manipulate information for individual political ends,

especially in third order systems. Second order cultural definitions of social relationships not only enable decision making in an immediate political context, but also facilitate the general flow and sharing of knowledge.

5   The physical and symbolic distinction between these two spaces, both collective and both often spatially related to each other, suggests the one mechanism by which more purely ceremonial situations are associated with or linked to other situations more focused on actual cooperative work. This kind of second order process presumably replaces third order reliance upon more situationally external texts, including print "identities" which work in concert with more individually controlled, territorial processes of organization. First or second order "fusion" of situational realities (the effective association of cultural ethos to ecological realities) can only take place presumably where essentially symbolic and ritual conceptions of space are all-pervasive, whether at the potentially large scales of first order systems, or at small local scales of folk or second order groups.

6   We have seen several times already the use of the term *gang* (gang) to designate social groups in earlier offices. Given the territorial connotations of the term, presumably both in English and Swedish, one might expect this designation to change to *arbetsgrupp* as organizations move into second order forms.

7   According to Conradson, in the patriarchal/rational office of the post-war period, conversations at lunch definitely avoided work related topics. Neither did one talk about salary, politics, sex, union activities or religion (1988:150). She also believes, though apparently with less ethnographic evidence, that some of these topics were more easily approached during the later institutionalized but somehow also "informalized" *pauses*, this because the conversation would automatically break off in a short period of time.

8   Breaks have longer been institutionalized in industrial settings, though primarily for reasons of health and safety rather than social relationships. While the physical forms in these places are still caused largely by functional considerations, with much less socio-cultural expression possible, attempts are being made to more consciously create second order space (see Chapter Six). The author personally observed one example of an industrial *pause* space which did seem to have much of the expressive characteristics of those in offices. A small work group of four or five men were setting street pavers (by hand) in front of our apartment in Lund. The city had moved a small wood clad trailer to be adjacent to their work. It had windows, curtains, a table and chairs, and other amenities of any office *pause* space. This, including lunch, was of course its primary use.

5 The practice of break and conference

The following examples detail sixteen of the twenty office buildings which the author documented through visitation, interviews, photography and collection of other materials. In terms of *pause* and *sammanträde* spaces, the different types and sizes of the sixteen office buildings fall into groups which illustrate: 1) on-site offices for industrial companies, 2) earlier, larger exclusively office buildings which have been remodeled to accommodate these spaces, 3) newer, smaller office buildings with such spaces designed into them, 4) newer, larger buildings with *pause* and *sammanträde* places also as part of the original design, 5) and finally the response of the users in a unique example of a newer, larger office purposefully designed without these places. The remaining three or four offices of the study, together with other quite new offices in the Stockholm area, also contain ample provision for these activities. They will be discussed in following chapters.

The diagrams of figures 5.1 and 5.2 illustrate the places for break and work group conference for the office portions of the two smaller industrial companies. In both the facility for the wholesale bakery, Skogaholms, and that of the electronics applications company, ElectroSandberg, the break spaces are shared with the industrial workers of the contiguous plant portion of the site. As in many industrial settings, both in Sweden and the U.S., these break places are also lunch places and are labeled in Swedish *matsal* or dining room. While eating and other more obviously ceremonial activities will be discussed later, it should be pointed out here that these spaces provide break places for from ten to twenty office workers, the entire office in either case and a number which closely corresponds to the concept of "work group" *(arbetsgrupp)* in Swedish offices generally. In both examples, breaks are taken

153

collectively at established times. The collective character of the *pause*, seems not to bridge the apparent status gap between *tjänstemän* and *arbetare*, since the office work group(s) sit at their own tables, in distinction to groups of workers from the plant. The fact that white and blue collar workers share the same facility, may be more typical in Sweden than in other countries where separate facilities may be the norm.

5.1 Skogaholms
The organizational diagram of Skogaholm's bakery, figure 5.1, clearly illustrates the conceptual equality of office and plant workers at the highest decision making level. The highest executive, the *Platschef* (site superintendent) has a horizontal relationship with the information, decision making, and consulting group *(info- besluts- och samrådsgrupp)* which consists of equal participation by the chairpersons of the plant workers union (LO) and the industrial office workers union (SIF). From his dress in the photo in Chapter Three, figure 3.5, it appears that his role conceptually bridges the gap between white and blue collar worker. While the location of his room between plant and office (not in the territorial corner as commented on earlier) could be caused by a functional need for equal access, it also nicely expresses his dual role. Notice in the plan that a spatially formal opposition exists along the interior corridor between the plant superintendent (the patriarchal) and the large meeting room and *matsal* (the collective).

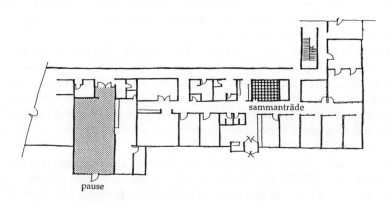

Figure 5.1 Locations of *pause* and *sammanträde* spaces in Skogaholm's bakery

154

5.2 ElectroSandberg

At ElectroSandberg, the fairly large *pause* space effects a quite formal association to the natural courtyard created in the expansion mentioned in Chapter Three. The bakery *matsal* as well has a strong relationship to the outside and its protruding form represents a sort of informal "collective", as opposed to "client", entry on the same side of the building. While the furnishings of both break/lunch spaces were probably done without professional interior design consultation, both are quite comfortable. Considering that the plant workers from the bakery, at least, can get quite dirty in their work, the visual quality of the lunchroom is very remarkable.

The separation and apparent territoriality which seems to exist between the two groups in the *matsal* might be less due to lingering status distinctions between *tjänstemän* and *arbetare*, than to the cultural need of work groups--regardless of the nature of the work-- to take *pause* together. We turn to our ethnographic source for an example of a group of industrial workers "kicking" a group of office executives out of a conference room when their time was up (Holm-Löfgren 1980:32). The plant workers felt their status was equal but perhaps just different, in their exercise of equal access to the space. Conference rooms are shared as well in the two examples being discussed, with apparently the same degree of equality of access. While the original, amply sized conference room was nicely centered to the office as work group, it also had direct and centralized access from the plant. Unfortunately for the present thesis, a quite formal cultural expression has given way to technical, functional needs since the entire office is now quite crowded. The

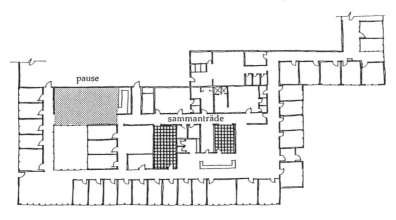

Figure 5.2 Locations of *pause* and *sammanträde* spaces in ElectoSandberg

155

room is presently filled with computer equipment. Meetings are therefore held in the larger conference room by the *matsal*, a place conceptually part of the largest scale of organization as we will see in later discussion.

The locations and meanings of the conference rooms at ElectroSandberg are similarly central to both office and plant groups. The two spaces, called the "Stora" (the large) and the "Lilla" (the small) *sammanträde* rooms, may tend to represent a larger all-corporate and a smaller work group level. The location of both serves for meetings with clients, adjacent as they are to the entry and as noted earlier to the *chef's* office. These spaces are well appointed, and offer state-of-the-art electronic equipment.

5.3 Åkerlund & Rausing

The third example of an office as part of a larger manufacturing site is Åkerlund & Rausing, a corporation which makes food and drink containers. Here, neither an older, linear office block (double-loaded) from the 1930's, nor the connected higher rise square block (with rooms surrounding a utility core) from the early 1950's has yet been remodeled to include special *pause* spaces. This represents a unique exception to the rest of the offices of the study, and to offices in Sweden generally. The greatest cause for this lack of collective space is the degree to which the older exaggerated patriarchal image still dominates the scene. The firm is one of the founding food related industries for which the Lund area is well known. Interviews disclosed the rich history of the original patriarch in the 1920's, an atmosphere still connected to the values and business orientation of the present organization. This is not to say that the national move toward workplace democracy has not influenced Åkerlund & Rausing. In the early eighties, the CEO (*V.D.* or *Verkställande Direktör*) declared that all employees should "take more responsibility", and this was reported to be not so much a radical change from what occurred before, but more an executive appreciation of it.

During the relatively brief interviews here, one had much more of a sense of an existing vertical way of work and a feeling that the horizontal concept of work group was far less developed in daily process. In a brief tour of this building[1], also conspicuously absent were the numerous small conference rooms one came to expect in more evolved offices. During the interviews, one became more aware of internal conference activities which occurred *within* the offices of executives or managers, behavior quite typical in U.S. offices, but seemingly rare in Sweden. The lack of formalized *pause*

156

groups clearly points as well to the absence of the essentially egalitarian work group. The concept of break, not unlike its industrial counterpart, is still primarily one of individual relief from work. In 1968, there was one centrally located coffee machine for the entire office of some fifty to one-hundred employees. A prohibition of other coffee makers in the building amounted to an effective proscription against the formation of coffee groups. Some movement toward the much more typical Swedish collective *pause* can be seen in the 1975 edict that individuals and groups could have their own coffee maker. Although even the *chef* is said to have taken his turn at making the daily coffee, still, no collective break times or places are presently sanctioned and organized, and most individuals drink their coffee at their desks.

5.4 Klockums

It appears that the design activities of engineering and architectural offices exert a greater purely functional influence on the spatial arrangement of individuals.   Open studios with rows of designer/draftsmen seem to be the norm in both the U.S. and Sweden. Closer evaluation of this particular kind of white collar setting may reveal strong social or even metaphorical reasons that people who design more or less symbiotically tend to be physically adjacent as they work.   More detailed studies may also reveal that newer Swedish design offices might provide designers with individual offices, as would conform to the norm for *tjänstemän* in Sweden. Two of the sites analyzed, the large construction firm, and the city building with its traffic division, showed a clear tendency for drafting to shift from larger shared rooms to individual ones as the firms moved from older to newer offices. Only one of the buildings of the present study, has engineering design as its primary function, and can only provide limited information for this special type of office. The plan and interviews of the large marine engineering firm in Malmö, called Klockums raises interesting questions about the evolution of this type of office in comparison with the others of the present research.

The plans of figure 5.3 show this office for a major Swedish shipyard in the Malmö harbor, the majority of its 500 to 800 office workers dedicating themselves to the engineering design of ships. Built in the mid-fifties, it remains one of the few highrise office structures in Malmö or even Southern Sweden. The somewhat unusual triangular plan, designed in part to control access for military and industrial security,[2] creates typical Swedish linear offices along its core, and open design studios at each of the three "prows"

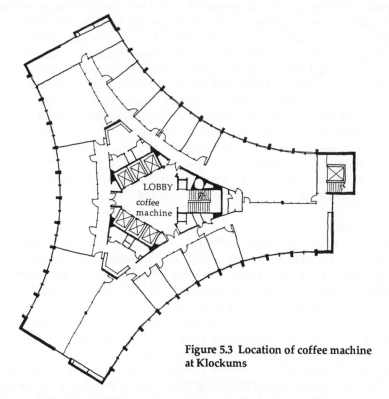

Figure 5.3 Location of coffee machine at Klockums

of the building. While most typically the prow space is open studio, it can be bisected to create either two smaller studios, or more linear offices on, for example, a purely administrative floor. From the limited information collected, it appears that the open studio produces little need for separate conference spaces, particularly since there is no client contact for most of these designers/draftspersons. No *pause* spaces were originally designed into the plan, nor have any been added through remodeling. Formalized collective breaks did not exist; individuals were only supposed to get coffee from the centralized coffee automat in the elevator lobby.

In practice all had their own thermos, secretly stashed away around their desk.[3] This prohibition of individual or area coffee sources was probably more consciously the desire to maintain a high level of rationalist productivity, and more subconsciously an attempt to limit the formation of socially collective, horizontal groups. Only within the past few years have area coffee pots begun to appear in corners of studio spaces, an apparent association with the work group. The frequent *ad hoc* coffee machines of U.S. offices, in contrast, tend to be located more incidentally in storage rooms, hallways, and even individual offices, as a sort of territorial control over those who use that particular coffee source. The long term archivist who worked on the 13th floor of the Klockums highrise indicated that people were beginning to gather around the coffee maker during specific break times, even though no formalized collective *pause* is recognized.

5.5 Posthuset
The Posthuset (central post office administration for the Malmö region) and Lundabygdens Sparbank (a major savings bank in Lund), figure 5.4, represent in the survey two larger buildings of historic significance. These have included multiple smaller *sammanträde* rooms and specific *pause* places in their remodeling over the last ten years. The Posthuset has also provided individual rooms for employees, at least in the section investigated. While information on the Lund savings bank comes only from two informal interviews and site visits,[4] one was left with a strong impression of multiple small conference areas and *pause* spaces associated with work group areas of the building. Similarly, and more specifically in the Posthuset, the two wings and the somewhat longer main segment of the linear building provide three architecturally definable areas, each of which tends to correspond to a work group. Perhaps partially because of the high demand for space in a building protected by historical registry, which highly constrained major additions, only one conference room, not three, appears on each floor. Across the hall a similarly singular *rökrum* (smokeroom) has been fashioned in the old stair tower which projects into the inner courtyard. This space is commonly referred to as the *torn rum* (tower room).

Originally the central post office building contained both administration and actual mail sorting and distribution processes. Probably quite early in the evolutionary scheme of offices in Sweden, the office portion of the building, and its *tjänstemän*, were given specific break times, undoubtedly because their more industrial counterparts on the lower floors had won the right for periodic relief from physical labor. In spite of the strong patriarchal, *tjänste* associations of the dining room on the highest, or sixth, floor, both groups of employees were expected to use this facility for breaks. While the use of the dining room by earlier letter carriers, for example, is not documented, one long term informant described their probable inhibitions in this regard. In the last twenty years, much of the physical processing of mail has been moved to larger, specialized sites elsewhere in the Malmö area, leaving the historic central post office for primarily administrative functions. While some of this old status distinction between *tjänstemän* and *arbetare* still exists between the upper and lower floors--the region *chef* sits on the sixth, for example--the dining room has been moved down to the fifth floor, making it at least more symbolically accessible to those below. This is still the place where *arbetsgrupper* are supposed to take their formal breaks twice a day. Yet obviously the presence of the tower room, more adjacent to the work groups which it represents, creates a contradiction to the traditional dining room rule. In practice, both dining room and tower rooms are used for *pause*. They may be called "smoke rooms" on the architectural plans, but they really represent the current national practice of designing special social/cultural spaces at the scale of the work group.

A vivid example of the social aspects of presently developed work groups in

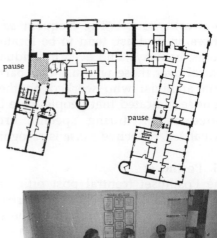

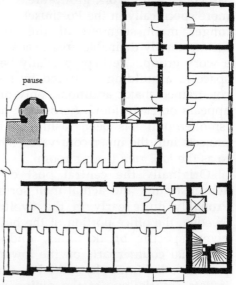

Figure 5.4 *Pause* and *sammanträde* in Sparbanken Lund (above) and Posthuset (below); pause group in historical building in Malmö, Wasa (middle)

160

the Posthuset was provided by a long term employee who functioned as part of the public relations work group. Because of remodeling due to space limitations in the old structure his group of seven individuals was temporarily housed in one large open room of an older office building in the Malmö central area. The inner portion of the room, without windows, became the coffee place where the group took *pause* and lunch together at specific times. At least four or five desks were crowded along the window wall. The informant's desk and probably the partitioned *chef's* office formed something of a middle element, between the row of desks and the coffee area. This work group formed strong social bonds, not only through daily *pause* and lunch, but by having numerous small parties and trips after-hours or on weekends. After a year and a half the group was split up, with several workers joining other groups in the remodeled Posthuset. They continued to have two or three outside *fests* together during the year, in addition to participating in their new work groups.

The second order opposition between work and socialization seems quite clear. All employees had individual offices before being in the temporary space, and all would have individual offices in the remodeled Posthuset. This, along with their position along the window wall, maintained the cultural balance between the individual and the collective; there is no hint of any territoriality in this open office space. From hearing about the apparent intensity of social relationships which occurred, particularly in the unusual after-hours activities of the group, one might speculate that the move to the shared space actually generated much of this behavior. Given the specifically social meanings of shared rooms used for *pause* and lunch, and even small conference rooms, the temporary, shared open office might today have such a meaning as its primary association. The great amount of time spent here would produce an intensity of positive social behavior in the context of Scandinavian second order culture.

5.6 Tre Skåne
Two also large, but newer office buildings, both in Malmö, provide additional examples of recent remodeling, especially to add *pause* spaces. Built primarily by a group of three cooperatives (dairy, meat and produce) in the early seventies, Tre Skåne chose the rare highrise form, placing the twelve story structure adjacent to a 1960's commercial center on the periphery of the city. The cooperative companies occupy space varying from a portion of one floor to several floors, with common facilities on two lower floors. The

present survey was confined to the Skånska Lantmännen (produce) and its "daughter" company Skånska Lantmännen Maskin (agricultural machinery). The parent company occupies the entire fifth and sixth floors and shares the fourth floor with its offspring. Originally designed and built with no special *pause* places, the single but generous conference rooms on each of the three floors have become *pause* places large enough to accommodate several work groups (see figure 5.5). One smaller break space has also been created by the Maskin company at the end of its western wing of the fourth floor. A remodeled space at the core of the fifth floor provides the only conference room for both parent and daughter companies.

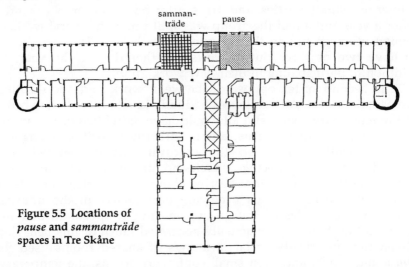

samman-   pause
träde

Figure 5.5 Locations of *pause* **and** *sammanträde* **spaces in Tre Skåne**

Swedish *pause* rooms are seldom if ever used for conferences, including the present example where a section *chef* characterized the break experience as "non-work" in relation to what happens in conferences. It is clear that the need for collective socialization has been given preference over the *sammanträde* function of the seventeen work groups within the three floors. The work group *sammanträde* room may be largely symbolic, rather than functional, particularly where the number of workers in any one group is small. In this sense, the layout of the fifth floor might be particularly expressive. Originally designed for other purposes, the south end of the main wing has become the locus for the director and an adjacent board room.[5] This more patriarchal aspect of the organization is formally opposed to the more collective meanings of the horizontal work group. At the north end of the main wing, subsequent remodeling produced the symbolic pair of work group places, *pause* and *sammanträde* rooms.[6]

5.7 Sparbanken Skåne

Constructed also in the late sixties or early seventies, the seven story Sparbanken Skåne building edges a central Malmö plaza. Diagramming the many work groups of the four and a half floors of non-public offices, figure 5.6, along with very recent remodeling, gives further illustration of our theme. Floors one and two have typical banking facilities for the public, while the seventh and top floor provide common meeting and education rooms for the entire building. Within the office floors three through six, the fifth is occupied by the *V.D.* and staff (the *chef* in the middle again), and the bank's restaurant used of course only by employees. Remodeling has produced two *pause* spaces on each of primary office floors (three, four, and six). One of the spaces on the third floor is considerably larger than the others, because of its adjacency to the rare larger shared offices

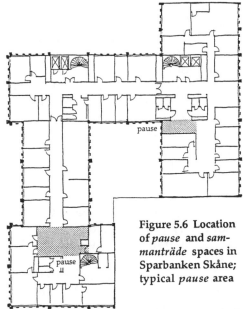

Figure 5.6 Location of *pause* and *sammanträde* spaces in Sparbanken Skåne; typical *pause* area

mentioned in Chapter Three. A generous coffee place also exists on the seventh or "meeting room" floor. The executive offices on the fifth floor have no separate *pause* space, but are again on the same floor as the restaurant. On the typical floors, two or three work groups are relatively adjacent to one of the two break places. The *pause* spaces are either large enough to accommodate all adjacent

163

groups, or some work groups will schedule their breaks at different times.

The all female data entry work group, with its large room, is interesting in that not unlike the temporary shared room experience of the Posthuset group, this Sparbank group of women seems also to have developed unusually strong social bonds.[7] The women of this group must always keep the greater portion of their number at their telephone stations and are therefore prohibited from taking *pause* and lunch as a total group. Their social bonding seems to have been expressed largely by organized non-calendrical, non-work hour *fests*, i.e. not associated with yearly events like Christmas held during work in the office. While it has been mentioned that such spontaneous, after-hour socialization is largely antithetical to the normal, institutionalized, events during work times, what is even more unusual in this case are the locations of these parties: in the individual homes of the women. At times they were organized by the female group leader, at other times initiated by the workers themselves. One might ask whether *fests* at home could only happen among women, recalling the possible tendency for more traditional female work groups to fall outside of the patriarchal/collective definitions of second order culture.

On the other hand we can also recall that in the agrarian *by*, the work group *fests* were also held in individual farm homes. An alternate interpretation would be that as long as all members of the work group are automatically invited to the party, then such behavior cannot be misinterpreted as the more rhetorical or third order friendship invitations to the home with which we in the U.S, for example, are more familiar. It could therefore conform to larger cultural traditions, though playing more directly off old family/community images. The difference between children's birthday parties in Sweden and the U.S. provides a convincing analogy. In the U.S. children are invited to the party, at the celebrant's home, according to the current friendship group or perhaps "click". In most Swedish situations, it seems, the birthday child must invite his or her entire school class, the child's primary non-family cultural group with whom he or she has been together from first through usually seventh grades.

Getting back to the larger consideration of the Sparbank, the somewhat unusual banking need for large educational spaces on the seventh floor, particularly for public contact functions at the central branch location, probably negates any functional demand for smaller *sammanträde* places more adjacent to the work groups. It is true that two of the new *pause* spaces were built in rooms originally designed as conference rooms. Two smaller conference rooms were spared during the remodeling, but do not have *arbetsgrupp* associations; one is next to the personnel *chef*, and the other part of the executive wing.

5.8 Lundafrakt

We now move to two smaller office buildings, built during the early seventies, in which *pause* and in particularly one case, multiple *sammanträde* spaces were part of the original design (see figures 5.7 and 5.8). Lundafrakt, the cooperative trucking organization headquartered in Lund, has a pair of these two kinds of rooms situated at one end of its linear form, similar to the remodeled form at Tre Skåne. However in this case the *chef*'s office is also at this

Figure 5.7 Locations of *pause* and *sammanträde* Lundafrakt; pause room

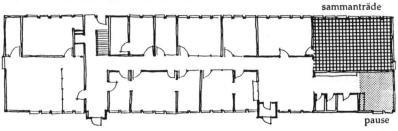

sammanträde

pause

end, directly across from the main entry, a traditional location. Perhaps this *chef* has less patriarchal association since he is elected by the individual truckers which in most cases own their own equipment (the cooperative does own some special service vehicles, such as garbage trucks); his location is therefore not as spatially opposite as in the case of Tre Skåne. One of the sources in this office was specifically asked if he felt uncomfortable having to walk by the "boss's office" on the way to the break room. The answer was emphatically negative, which also is understandable considering that the entire office, really a single work group, takes break together.

Looking at the overall plan of the building, it is true that the original intended position for the *chef's* office was at the opposite end from conference and break rooms. Subsequent remodeling moved the *chef* down to his present position, which in the original plan was labeled "vacant". The old office was used to create new space for the truck dispatchers. Thus this dispatch area really is not an integral part of the office work group; correspondingly it has its own *pentry* (wet bar) and small break room. As noted earlier the six or seven dispatchers must functionally share a workspace because of the need for immediate communication.

5.9 Kontorsutvekling
Kontorsutvekling, a computer/software sales and service firm in Lund, was originally built for a construction company with *pause* and *sammanträde* rooms. The issue of transferability appears, and can be related to the far fewer speculative buildings built in Sweden without an original owner/occupant. Speculative office buildings in the U.S. are designed primarily to techno-economic specifications. A low level of initial design for particular functional or social conditions exists, though the absence of such will eventually lead to tremendous territorial and even functional dialectics. One would think speculative buildings would be impossible in Sweden, given the large amount of employee participation in decisions, and the importance of physical layout to social and task performance activities. Yet because of the national character of the evolving Swedish office, one knows that these patterns of use will tend to be ethnically shared. It is therefore easier, from a more socio-culturally proactive design point of view, to design successful speculative office buildings in Sweden than the U.S.. We will see larger building examples in subsequent chapters.

The present building, originally designed for the construction firm, appears to nicely serve some of these national patterns needed by Kontorsutvekling. Yet this organization deals primarily with sales and is therefore somewhat different from more typical offices. It is also the only example which was non-union. The size of this office seems to be just on the borderline (around twenty plus) between the situation where the total office size corresponds with a typical work group, and that where several work groups exist. Unlike the somewhat smaller Lundafrakt, this one has its own

166

kitchen, which served a major midday meal to office and field employees of the construction firm. This original dining room at one end of the linear form, adjacent to the kitchen, now serves primarily as a conference and training space, but is sometimes used for dining during special occasions. A much smaller space, also adjacent to the kitchen is the present daily break and lunch room for the far smaller number of total employees in the computer firm.

In terms of purely functional definition of Kontorsutvekling, there exist four separate task designations, each consisting of four or five individuals. These seem not to function as horizontal work groups, given the fact that three of the designations are essentially for different kinds of sales activities (the

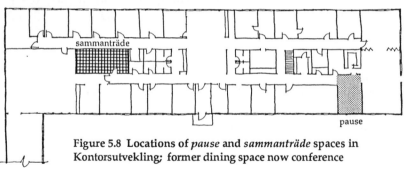

Figure 5.8 Locations of *pause* and *sammanträde* spaces in Kontorsutvekling; former dining space now conference

four technicians do sales part time). Most of these people work quite independently with their clients. Consequently no formalized break time or group is reported. Breaks tend to occur regularly about mid-morning and mid-afternoon among varying individuals who are not out with clients, and who are free from the constant client conversation and training which occurs on the site. The several conference/training spaces cannot be associated with any internal work group as such. They are used primarily by clients and salespeople. The original large conference room in the linear core, opposite from the kitchen end of the building, is used only for internal conferences and therefore associates with the office as work group. Its position opposite from dining and break spaces creates a formal pair between the collective social (dining/break) and the

167

collective meeting. Interestingly, and for reasons unknown, the original construction executive's position was adjacent to the kitchen, on the side opposite the break room. The *chef* for Kontorsutvekling located his office in the more typical position, in the middle of the building adjacent to the client entry.

5.10 ABV

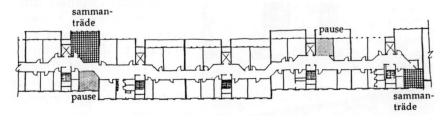

Figure 5.9 Locations of *pause* and *sammanträde* places in ABV

Projecting this standard linear form to multiple levels, we now consider two firms considerably larger in size. The Swedish construction firm of ABV works nationally and internationally and has several large offices in Sweden. One of these, the Malmö office, had recently moved into a portion of an immense structure, a nine story linear form called in Swedish the "Great Wall of China". It stretches several hundred feet along the edge of a "new town" portion of the city. As one of the few massive housing projects to be troubled by social and economic problems--a portion of its inhabitants were immigrants--the decision was made to convert to office space locating the inhabitants in other areas. ABV occupies about one third of the "wall", with city social services taking up most of the rest. A buffer zone of remodeled apartments exists between the two organizations and will serve for future expansion (an attribute of most linear forms). One of the executive assistants interviewed, a single woman, occupied one of these apartments. No interior access exists between offices and apartments, but the concept is a novel one, suggesting perhaps at least one solution to the mentioned ambiguity or tension between office as social group and family in a neighborhood or rural context.

While also a conversion of apartments to offices, this recent example differs radically from offices made from the prestigious and privileged apartments of the historic urban patriarchy. No such connotation existed with the "Great Wall of China". To the contrary, a certain negative meaning existed for the housing project.

Yet it must be noted that ethnic associations of housing areas or neighborhoods seems to be rare in the experience of most Swedes, and even in this large new town area, immigrants were probably not even the majority of occupants and were spatially interspersed with nationals. The decision to occupy the former housing structure carried no great stigma, as it might have in other countries with long histories of urban ethnic ghettos. The successful office tower of Tre Skåne was only a short distance away near the commercial center of the area. Furthermore, in terms of transportation, the site lies at the end of a major bus route, and is adjacent to an intersection with the city's ring road or freeway.

Finally, and perhaps most important among the factors behind the decision to move, was the fact that the linear form of the housing fit the internal space needs of the evolving democratic office. It was not a previously double loaded apartment scheme that had created the relatively shallow overall width, a dimension well suited to a corridor serving individual offices on either side. Rather it was the design of the apartment unit across the entire width, providing visual and climatic access to both exterior walls. These apartments were essentially two rooms and a circulation space wide, the spatial equivalent to the linear office with individual rooms. A separate elevator and stairway served only two units on each floor.

The section of the "wall" which ABV leases is about sixteen individual offices in length. The double loading along the corridor provides about thirty-two offices on each floor. The 1984 design, prior to moving in, shows two conference rooms and two *pause* spaces on each floor. This architectural, and evolving second order concept clearly attempts to create social groups composed of about sixteen individuals each, a number within the norm for Swedish work groups. The survey of the fifth floor occupied by ABV revealed that there had been some changes in conference and *pause* rooms, and that in functional reality the floor contained not two work groups but four: "Large Structures" (nine people), "Method Development" (six), "New Products" (five), and "Building Construction" (six). Although the more sizable Large Structures group had moved the originally designed *pause* space to a vacant room at the center of their group (a change in conference locations also occurred simultaneously), the number of *pause* and *sammanträde* rooms on the total floor remained at two each. This almost formal, dualistic tendency, a pair of social/meeting spaces at each end of the corridor, will appear in several other examples. The suggestion is of an increasingly second order, architectural definition of socio-cultural group which operates close to the size of the actual functional group and is associated with it, but yet is somewhat independent.

This formalistic tendency which increasingly appears to exist at the level of the cultural is further verified by the fact that the four work groups on the floor do not alternate their use of the break spaces, thus maintaining an exact correlation between functional and social aspects. In practice, all employees on this floor take *pause* at the same time. The largest work group is allowed to make its socialization coincident, by exclusively using the room centered in its area, but the other three groups jointly occupy the opposite *pause* space. The importance of this spatial expression is given additional weight by considering the way in which the Large Structures group took their break in the previous building. In actuality, this group on the fifth floor is only half of the total functional work group, the other portion being housed on the floor above. Previously, the entire group occupied a common space on one floor. There, all twenty of the work group took break together. It would have been possible to continue this practice in the new quarters, even though the group was split between floors. Yet spatial expression, the second order association with an adjacent social space, seems to have created the two separate social groups within the one functional entity. Still, the interviewed engineer of this group expressed some regret that the entire work group no longer took coffee together.

While the larger restaurant of ABV and other corporate offices will be addressed in a following chapter on the spaces and activities of the largest of office scales, one must mention a related phenomenon which undoubtedly belongs with the present work scale. Down on the lower floor, adjacent to the kitchen facilities, are found several small dining rooms separate from the main daily dining area. The example in figure 5.10 shows a considerable degree of care, and perhaps formality in the furnishing of these special spaces. Meals in these rooms are catered by the main kitchen for special events ordered by a particular *arbetsgrupp*. As explained by one ABV source, a work group might be just finishing or working late on a project. Such a situation calls for a special occasion. In the traditional *by* society the culmination of the cooperative work event was almost always a *fest*, the focus of which was food and spirits.

Seemingly similar tendencies also exist in other countries, even where work groups are primarily vertical in conception. A round of drinks or even dinner may follow particular work occasions. Yet seldom does one find on-site facilities which can be catered at no cost. There is no guarantee of participation by all. Certainly the

Figure 5.10 One of ABV's special dining rooms for *arbetsgrupper*

event will most often be spontaneous rather than well planned and even formal. The concept even during these after hour events may still be "vertical", as expressed by a boss who personally or corporately pays for drinks or food. In this sense, these occasions are more payment due than the expression of shared fruits of social solidarity as in the Swedish case. The fact that the work group dinner will admit only members of the group, and not spouses, and that the event may last quite late into the evening is also evidence of its cultural rather than spontaneous, third order basis.

Spontaneous after-hours activities in the U.S. and elsewhere probably will be seen as a conflict with the obligations to spouse and family, particularly if such events become real "nights-on-the-town" and spouses are not included. We will see many such occasions in Sweden where purely social activities of work groups and entire offices take place during prime after-hours times, and are apparently accepted as legitimate by both participants and uninvited spouses. Certainly the location of the *fest* as part of the second order social and work setting contributes greatly to this legitimacy, compared with spontaneous get-togethers in favorite pubs or restaurants.

171

5.11 K-Konsult

Similar in many ways to ABV is the Lund office of K-Konsult. Its size, linear form, and general function have much in common with ABV. The most interesting difference is that it is a new building of the early 80's, designed and built especially for this organization. K-Konsult performs a quasi-governmental planning and design role serving its almost exclusive clientele of Swedish *kommuner*(larger urban/rural districts roughly the equivalent of the U. S. "county"). As mentioned previously, they designed and supervised the construction of their own building. Although still quite new at the time of the present survey, the three story form of K-Konsult really represents the quintessential linear, individual office idea of the late sixties and seventies (see figure 5.11, and 6.1). Unlike earlier linear forms, but similar to other more recent linear offices, K-Konsult exhibits a subtle, but very significant evolution in its provisioning of *pause* and *sammanträde* spaces in its central core. While the thick core of the linear office had for some time been a common solution, it is only during the more recent phases of the breakthrough, when the communal spaces begin to balance individual offices, that the core has begun to take on greater associations of village street (larger level of organization beyond the work group). We will see this tendency receives far greater elaboration and scale in certain more architecturally novel, often very large offices in Sweden during the early eighties.

In K-Konsult the growing notion of communal core space exists within each floor primarily as an expression of work group. Like ABV, two *pause* spaces are provided, one at each end of the core. In the center of the core a single conference room and a library serve the entire floor. Since the number of people on each of the K-Konsult floors exceeds ABV's by about twenty, the two *pause* and one *sammanträde* rooms must also either be shared or alternately used by various work groups. Like ABV, the solution here is for the typically four or five designated work groups of each floor to take their scheduled break together, necessitating the sharing of one *pause* space by more than one work group. Unlike the conference room, which is scheduled to accommodate individual work groups, or portions of such, at unique times, there appears to be a pattern of having all personnel take their breaks at the same time. Is this a functional requirement, necessary so that fellow workers will know at which specific times others in the office will be unavailable for consultation? Perhaps not, in that the greatest need for collaboration will obviously occur within one's *arbetsgrupp*, and knowing where these others are is concomitantly solved by the

172

strong social need for the work group to take *pause* together at the same time.

Consider for the moment, in advance of its fuller discussion, the strong social tendency for the entire office to be together during the large Swedish meal which occurs around midday.[8] Here we begin to see the actual expression of scales larger than the work group. We will also see that expressively, in terms of the all-important architectural form, the larger scales may be easier to define than the smaller and more variable work group. As multiple work groups are assembled in portions of linear office floors, there may be a tendency for the formally defined halves of the floor to become the

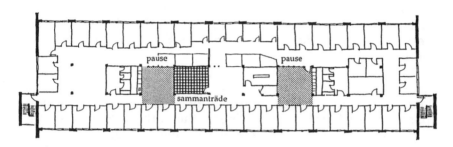

Figure 5.11 Locations of *pause* and *sammanträde* spaces in K-Konsult

expression of *"arbetsgrupp"*, in the absence of an ideal *pause* and conference space for each actual functional entity. Given the pervasive dualism of second order culture, it may be that each half of the floor must be related, or balanced, with the other. Entire floors take *pause* at the same time. The architectural tendency, because of the size of the building, is really to define some social/work group larger than the often quite small work group.

We must appreciate the evolutionary tension this situation creates. First, the initial linear impulse creates larger, relatively undifferentiated forms which have no recognition of the later work group. As the democratic work group concept evolves into these same settings, each group naturally seeks expression coincident with itself. Yet the older linear forms continue, with some designed number of break spaces occurring along the cores, a natural initial accommodation of the new demands. While serving to solidify the work group, the architectural sensitivity of second order belief may tend to try to recognize some group which is defined by dualistic *pause* spaces at the scale of the entire floor. While the numbers of individuals who take break together is within the work group scale, the intention is for the reader to recognize the expressive ambiguity which occurs in this phase of the historical process. Creating architectural expression of the small and more variable work group will eventually be a powerful motivation for major changes in the very linear *smårumskontor* form.

In actual practice on the K-Konsult floor, the number of workers who take break together everyday is in reality smaller and more like an *arbetsgrupp* than the fifty or so individual offices would suggest. At any given time the number of people who are away from the building is relatively large, so the institutionalized almost obligatory participation in *pause* will only produce about twelve to fifteen at each area. More than one work group will always be present in each. The more purely architectural expression of the total floor produces the reported tendency for work groups to take break at the most adjacent *pause* room--rather than with friends at another.

The problem of smoking in public places has provided a more functional basis for the dualistic expression at the scale of the entire floor. Although a decided minority of workers smoke, one break space is designated "smoking", the other "non-smoking". Compared with the social and expressive strength of the work group, smoking does not appear to create the strong social boundaries and actual territories in Sweden that it has more recently in the U.S. and perhaps elsewhere. To a certain extent the physical effect of smoking is less problematic in Swedish buildings where people generally can smoke in their individual offices, relying both on small scale mechanical devices and the ubiquitous operable window to exhaust the smoke. Usually no smoking is allowed in break areas. In the open plan offices of the U.S., designed with sometimes one but often no separate break spaces, smoking has quickly become a vital health and ultimately social issue within offices.[9]

5.12 Stadshuset
Pushing the size of the Swedish office building even higher, while at the same time shifting from private or quasi-private organizations to the governmental, we consider first the remarkably linear plan of the Stadshuset (City Building) for Malmö, see figure 5.12. Occupied in stages from 1985 to 1987, its potential 730 work places on five or seven floors, over ninety percent of which are individual offices, are divided up into several large departments, e.g. administration, personnel, planning and building safety, etc.. The source of the present interviews and analysis, the Gatukontoret

(literally the Street Office or department of transportation) was one of the largest departments, taking four floors of the rear addition, parts "B" and "C". These workers had recently moved in at the time of the survey. The entire building contains some fifty plus conference rooms integrated into the two rows of offices. The some-

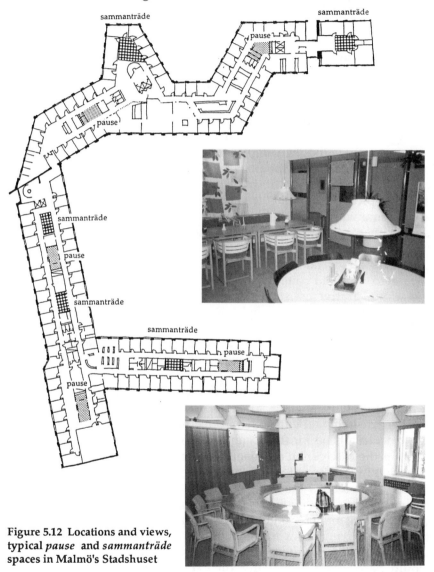

Figure 5.12 Locations and views, typical *pause* **and** *sammanträde* **spaces in Malmö's Stadshuset**

175

what thinner core, in comparison to K-Konsult, displays some forty specific *pause* spaces, and many other lounge like waiting areas, in addition to circulation, storage, and the like. The overall ratio of either *pause* or *sammanträde* spaces to workers is less than twenty to one. The pattern for work groups is similar to the two examples already discussed. Work groups tend to be only five to ten persons in number, and therefore must share *pause* spaces during the scheduled common break time.

The previously mentioned interview with the Gatukontoret's personnel director focused on the processes by which the workers participated in decisions about the design of the new building. Both employees and administration had been in full agreement about having individual offices. The content of the other interviews, a young male traffic engineer and a female administrative assistant about to retire, brought to light other things which probably had not been so predictable in the planning process. They had, since 1965, occupied a predemocratic building with the larger shared office spaces typical of the time. It is interesting that 1965 is also reported as the time when the *pause* was institutionalized in at least this city department. According to the engineer, a work group larger than his present one took breaks together in the old building. Speaking primarily about taking *pause*, he said it was *tyst*(sad) to become separated from old comrades in the new setting. The response from the administrative assistant also contained a negative feeling about becoming isolated from people one had been together with in the other building. In this case, however, the issue was not specifically directed at those one took break with, but more generally with a larger group of workers with which she maintained contact as part of her administrative position.

There seem to be at least two things happening here. First, the resulting very linear form spreads people out in space, diminishing the potential contact with others outside of one's work group. This is particularly true for the administrative assistant. It is not as clear why, in the case of the engineer, the earlier, larger work group was dissected in the move to the new facility. It may be that in the older building the size of the unit offices was neither appropriate for the individual nor the evolving work group. If these shared spaces contained a smaller number of workers, say from two to five as would be the norm for a higher rise core structure, then probably the emerging work group would initially be much larger. Perhaps it would be composed of many such rooms, thus his earlier breaks with a large "proto" work group. Even from the brief evidence of the Stadshuset, the new linear form allowed and perhaps even promoted redefinitions of work groups. They became smaller and perhaps more formalized. Given the extremely narrow form and the difficulty of communication along the length, any group larger than ten may be too large. Geometrically, if one takes a five office length of the double loaded *Stadshuset* corridor, ten workers in all, the shape of this form is closest to square.

It was too early in the occupation of this building to finally judge the initial negative effect of breaking up with one's former workmates. In Sweden, any movement of people is unanimously difficult because of even small changes in social group which often accompanies. This is true even if the move is within the same building. The extremely linear democratic forms present certain problems both in the second order definition and communicational function of some optimally sized work group. This low level ambiguity also characterizes the second example of a very large governmental entity, the federal tax agency building also in Malmö.

5.13 Länsstyrelsen

The Länsstyrelsen building shown in figure 5.13 is part of the "directorate" *(styrelsen)*, for the "federal region" *(läns)*, in Southern Sweden called Malmöhus. This facility for several tax related departments was designed in the early eighties by one of Sweden's best known architects, Carl Nyrén, and was subsequently published (Nyrén: 1981). Said by the architect to be a low cost work, its interior furnishing and detail appears unusually well designed in comparison to regional U.S. government buildings. It is really quite typical for Swedish offices, either public or private. In fact the basic double loaded plan concept, along with the level of design detail, is similar to the Stadshuset discussed above. The primary contribution of the architect to the Länsstyrelsen, and the reason for publication, is its exterior form and image in context with its historical urban Malmö setting. The large atrium space in the center was perhaps created as much by the exterior massing required of this urban context, as by the need for a major public open space within the building. Yet we will shortly see other "atrium" examples which suggest a positive, second order meaning to such spaces.

Each floor of the Länsstyrelsen contains four *pause* spaces and a varying but larger number of *sammanträde* rooms. The ratio of employees to break places is about double that of the Stadshuset, or about forty to one. In addition to the inherent ambiguity between more typically sized work groups as segments of the linear form, and some more or less adjacent break place, the sheer numbers

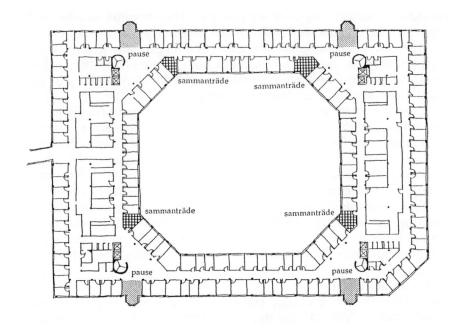

Figure 5.13 Locations and views of typical *pause* and *sammanträde* spaces in Länsstyrelsen, Malmö

of workers adds a unique element to Länsstyrelsen socialization. Since the *pause* spaces can only accommodate at a maximum the more ideal work group number of about sixteen, all employees cannot take *pause* at the same time. The solution is multiple scheduled break times for any particular space. In the earlier examples, architectural definitions of "floors" may have been a cause for the single break time for all workers on that floor. Even in the larger Stadshuset, each level was conceptually broken up into three "floors" of different building portions. One might speculate

178

in the case of the Länsstyrelsen structure, that the extreme length of the double loaded building floor, and the absence of clear architectural definitions of sub-areas, might diminish the tendency to associate oneself socially with this total group of about 120 people. This scale will actually be seen to relate to the communal atrium space more than to the four *pause* areas, although during the summer some work groups will take their afternoon *pause* in the atrium.

From the interviews it seems that the system of *omgånger* (shifts) for the break spaces may actually allow a greater architectural coincidence between work group size and adjacent *pause* space. Together with the variation provided by the two differently sized tables of each space, the availability of several time slots provides a greater ability to fit the work group to the architectural, or at least furniture form. In some of our previous examples, e.g. Skogaholms bakery and the Tre Skåne agricultural cooperative, larger break rooms were furnished with numerous smaller tables of a uniform size. Yet the clear tendency exists in most places to try to have one table per *arbetsgrupp*. One of the workers in the Länsstyrelsen told how his entire work group of fifteen to twenty crowded around the one larger break table, rather than have a portion sitting apart at the smaller table. It was also stated that the norm existed for each work group to take its break at the nearest, or most adjacent space. On one floor, the greater flexibility of *pause* times and table groupings, along with the diminished sense of relationship between break space and particular floor areas, as in the dualistic examples, has contributed to the take-over of at least one vacant space for *pause* purposes. More will be said shortly about this relatively rare phenomenon in the Swedish office.

Given the strength of the social solidarity developed within the work group by *sammanträde* and *pause* activities, among others, one of the questions posed during the interviews asked what happened in the event that for functional reasons one had to change work groups. In one case where an employee of one group became the group leader for another group, he continued to take *pause* with his original group. Another example in which the group leader did not take *pause* with his functional work group occurred with one of the people interviewed. A group of older workers, all who were group leaders had become a small separate break group. This seems to be the result of perhaps several changes of work groups over the years. It recognizes the impossibility of maintaining solidarity with original and subsequent groups over time. These individuals might as well still feel associated with older patriarchical forms of office groups.

The other group leader who was kind enough to spend time with this researcher was an unusually mobile, younger individual who during six years of work in the organization had been a member of six different work groups. When discussing the reality of changing break groups, he said it had become his practice to linger a few days, continuing to take break with the old group, and then switch. After the move to the new *pause* (work) group, it took several days, sometimes weeks to be accepted into the group. This group solidarity is sometimes felt to be too strong, particularly by younger employees. One such person had no reservations about always taking one's break with the same people, one's *arbetsgrupp*, but felt that the similar pressure to eat lunch together down in the larger restaurant precluded meeting new people.

The interviews with the two group leaders at Länsstyrelsen reinforced the idea that one of their principal aspects of this positional level is the actual promotion of the social and functional togetherness of the work group. If a new employee, for example, begins to keep the door closed while working in his or her individual office, the group leader will have a talk with that person, explaining how closed doors contribute to isolation. In all probability this isolation is put in terms of functional goals of increased communication, cooperation, and the like. An open door is also expressive of one's cultural and therefore social relationship to the others of the group. Just as the *sammanträde* and *pause* rooms are expressive, the ideal tendency also will be shown to exist for the grouping of individual rooms themselves to architecturally create a definition of the work group, similar to the way the individual farm dwellings created the overall *by* form.

The long linear office type of the initial phase of the democratic breakthrough largely precludes architectural definition of work group via the clustering of individual offices. Yet these forms do accommodate variation in the functional size and constitution of the work group. Both the functional and expressive definition of the work group must be seen as separate forces, each attempting to maximize its influence in the built form. Given the architectural limitations of clustering work groups, perhaps in deference to the functional, the national norm of having one's door open may be one of the few spatial means of work group expression available under the circumstances. The group leader recognized the inherent problem of creating greater communication among members of the work group located along the linear corridor. Open doors were felt to contribute to the solution, but stronger measures were also necessary.

A second example of the promotional role of the group *chef* or leader occurred as he recognized a general lack of cooperative spirit among the work group. The problem actually did not take place among the more typical work groups of the building, but among the small number of work groups who served the public on the first floor. The personnel manager had initially described these locations as the only ones in the building where because of functional reasons, individuals could not have separate window offices. He also described the difficulties they were having in making people satisfied with their interior, partitioned "landscape" workstations. Perhaps it is not coincidental that these are the areas where the group leader felt it necessary to take action. It is also true that some of the members of the *arbetsgrupp* tended to work more with the public than with each other.

Contrary to assumptions about greater cooperation in open plan offices, the reverse seems here at least to be the case. Individual offices may provide opportunities for isolation and introspection, but at the same time they are the basis of the political equality of the work group, a key component to the cultural foundation for cooperative work. The action taken in this case by the open plan group leader was the creation of a short play or skit about the nature of their work with the public. It required many hours of practice after work, and was performed in front of the rest of the department in the work group's actual setting. The three other similar work groups took turns with the performance in the following years. This quasi-ritual experience not only provided a vehicle for the expression of values about the work they did, but also provided the intended example of a cooperative work process. This enterprising group leader, not yet forty, had at the time of the interview moved up to being an assistant to the administrative *chef* for the entire building.

5.14 Draco

Our final example of a larger, linear office, also built in the early eighties, provides a unique and highly interesting contrast to the places discussed thus far. The pharmaceutical firm of Draco illustrated in figure 5.14 specifically designed its five storied, free-standing structure--part of a larger laboratory site--with multiple *sammanträde* rooms but no *pause* spaces. The occupants of this office building have a more extensive education than typical others. In this case the majority of people have higher academic and pro-

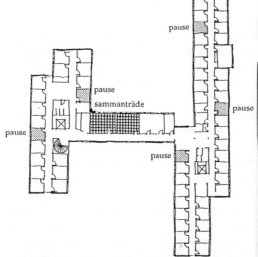

pause

pause

sammanträde

pause

pause

pause

pause

Figure 5. 14 Locations of *pause* and *sammanträde* spaces in Draco, Lund; individual office rooms appropriated by *arbetsgrupper* for their *pause*

fessional degrees, including medical doctors and PhDs in several medically related fields. In the company's earlier settings, the practice had been to have coffee making facilities available, but not to take breaks together. This may be understandable as a sort of lag phenomenon from pre-sixties periods when the *pause* was not institutionalized in Swedish offices. It also could be the result of the higher backgrounds of these individuals who may tend to work more independently of the horizontal work group concept. Yet the *arbetsgrupp* structure, including a group or section leader did exist at the time the participatory design decisions were made, though such may have been relatively recent. The new design appears to have continued earlier practices by placing a *pentry* (a wet or coffee bar) adjacent to the circulation focus of each floor. The building was built in two phases a short time apart. Each phase has its own circulation core and adjacent *pentry* on each floor.

What has happened since occupation is extremely revealing. About the time the second phase was completed, a number of individual offices were vacant, part of a designed intention for future expansion of the work force. Often adjacent to the functioning work groups, these spaces were considered for their potential as *pause* spaces. After the idea had spread among many work groups, the issue became a topic for formal participatory discussion among the office as a whole. This reportedly "major" discussion resulted in the decision to let each work group appropriate an adjacent individual office for its *pause*. The result provides one of the best fits between architectural *pause* space and actual work group, even though each *pause* room has no special,
formal architectural characteristics which distinguish it from other typical individual offices. Each pause space, however, is uniquely furnished by its respective work group, and thus has a strong expressive link with that group. Furthermore, break times are decided by the work groups themselves and will vary with others in the building. This provides additional associational linkage with the particular *arbetsgrupp*.

The need for highly trained individuals to form architecturally defined *pause* groups provides the clearest contrast with break behavior in other countries. In the U.S., it is especially these people who are least likely to participate in the usually unsanctioned, spontaneous breaks in the office. In this case, such groups and their places are due more to friendship formation or a territoriality of lower level employees. Higher level people either do not want to be seen as wasting time on purely social or friendship activities, or would not wish to be associated with territorial statements of lower level status. While friendship manipulation is a part of status seeking for the ambitious in U.S. offices, many of these activities tend to take place outside of the workplace. The fact that even the more highly trained and ambitious in Swedish offices have the need to form purely social, largely egalitarian community groups, clearly illustrates the cultural and emerging second order basis of this behavior. The author is reminded again of the previously described break ritual in the Anatomy Department at Lund University (described in Chapter 4.5). A group of eight to ten extremely well trained individuals, many medical doctors with Ph.Ds, met on schedule every morning and afternoon. They even had two different rooms used primarily for *pause*, one for each of the two daily break times.

Notes

1 Åkerlund & Rausing had been planned as one of the three sites on which to do much more intensive field work. The rejection of these research intentions also cut short other more informal interviews. The two women who were interviewed, the personnel director and another executive, were however, extremely cooperative.

2 Because of this security, no walk-through tour was permitted and the author could only interview two individuals at a location outside of the main office building.

3 The term for coffee hidden around one's desk or in the workplace was *smygkaffe* (slycoffee) in the insurance office studied by Conradson (1988:152).

4 This was another site, which after some very cooperative and informative interviews with a male executive and the bank's architect, could not ultimately be studied more intensively. The initial tour of this building was conducted by the bank's director himself.

5 While the location of the chief executive is conceptually again "in the middle" of the building, his position at the end of the wing is somewhat unusual in its possible connotations of territorial distance (typical means of impressing people in third order offices).

6 Given this alternative, structuralist, and second order interpretation of the location of the director/boardroom area, might one also dare to speculate that the ancient dominance of north over south, in Scandinavian ritual and myth, is here being subconsciously used to give subtle authority to the collective work group?

7 We have seen other examples of this strong family like bonding among women sharing a space, particularly during the 1940's and 50's; another informant from a construction company (ABV) recalled the similar social strength of her data entry group from this same period.

8 The term for the traditional large meal was *middag*, and as its composition suggests was held during the mid or middle portion of the day. The modern dictionary translation of *middag* is "dinner" or the large meal held in the

evening (at home). While the Danes eat more of a true lunch during work hours, many Norwegians and most Swedes in their corporate restaurants eat a large multi-course meal which they nevertheless call *lunch*. In many cases, both for Swedish school children and workers, *lunch* is the largest meal of the day. The author for some time had assumed that Swedes called this large mid-day meal by its traditional title *middag* (as it is in the rural areas of Norway), not only because of its size but its time. Not unlike the mentioned cultural meaning of the coffee celebration, this too may be an example of a formerly family and even elite custom moving into more collective contexts, i.e. the work place. The question is whether *lunch* with one's coworkers is more symbolically important than *middag* with the family?

9 In one such example here on the author's campus, the only possible place in the administration building to sneak a smoke was the restroom. As soon as one of the zealous non-smoking majority smelled the evidence of such clandestine activity, however, a memo was certain to be circulated.

6 Expression of the work group

In the previous *smårumskontor* examples of evolving second order expression, we have seen some formality in the positioning of opposite *pause* spaces on a linear office floor. Yet these may be almost self evident design solutions as architects add collective places to the already established linear form. Unquestionably it was the individual decision to have equal offices, not a collective need for break and conference spaces which was the primary force behind the linear form. The reemergence of a second order collective concept of *arbetsgrupp* creates a far more complicated design agenda. As the need for collective architectural expression becomes stronger, the potential exists for not one--the individual room--but two and eventually more architectural concepts which must be reconciled within a common form.

We have seen how remodeling or revisions within linear forms have left expressive ambiguities in terms of the collective. In these cases, where the linear idea remains dominant, the architects have contributed little, as yet, to the resolution of the expressive problem. This is one difference between a conscious design process and indigenous evolution of particularly second order settings. The tendency for designers to consciously focus on one idea, and let that concept be the primary determinant of form, contrasts to the fundamental second order processes which are much more embedded in actual social space or practice. This latter case probably more easily evolves through the opposed experiences of individuals and collective groups living in a common environment. A professional design process provides only secondary, yet necessary, contributions.

The role of the designer in the following major innovation in Swedish office layout seems more instrumental than in the earlier situation where each individual required his/her own office. A new phenomenon, the *kombi-kontor*(combination office) first produces built form in 1978. Yet a recent marketing publication by the electronics giant Ericsson includes a segment in which Ralph Erskine, a renown architect of British origin who has worked and lived mostly in Sweden, describes his conceptual evolution of the form in 1968. Erskine's sketches for the eventual office space for a large commercial bakery in Malmö must be prefaced by a reminder that this was exactly the time of the introduction in Sweden of the "office landscape" concept from Germany. Nominally the term *kombi-kontor* refers to the new form as a combination of open landscape and individual rooms of the *smårumskontor*. We will see that from an expressive point of view this term is not the most appropriate.

Swedish architects and researchers were very actively discussing the fashionable idea of the *kontorslandskap* (office landscape).[1] The reason the landscape office created such attention in Sweden, was that it presented a formal solution radically different than the emerging or already emerged linear form created by the demand for individual offices (see illustration of figure 6.1). While ostensibly the landscape idea was in part motivated by the desire for office democracy, at least in Germany, it has in retrospect become clear that primary purposes were

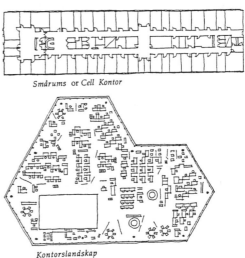

Smårums or *Cell Kontor*

Kontorslandskap

Figure 6.1 Contrast between the conventional cell or *smårums kontor* and the imported *kontorslandskap* (from Sonnenfeld & Ståldal, 1970)

more construction economics and functional or territorial flexibility. The landscape concept did not evolve indigenously as is the case with Swedish offices, but was essentially the product of decisions by management and designers. The difficulty of democratically determining the actual allocation of space in the open landscape has been mentioned earlier. This, along with the fact that the collective expression in offices does not evolve even in

Sweden until about the time true workplace democracy exists, some ten years later in the late 1970's, seems to suggest that the cultural meaning of the early landscape concept was more discursive promotional image than indigenous ethos. A few Swedish corporations actually built new landscape offices, influenced as they and their architects were by the promotion of the idea. The results as evidenced in the literature and in actual interviews were quite negative to the Swedes.

In Erskine's sketch process of 1968, it is not surprising that he first attempts to apply the new idea of the office landscape, figure 6.2. One can immediately discount the more typical economic motivation of the concept which attempts to provide the greatest space for the least construction cost. Erskine is working with a predetermined shape, an addition above a preexisting portion of a commercial bakery. While the only information presently available are the annotated sketches themselves, we may assume from both Erskine's reputation and the increasing participation in design programming at the time, that this progression of ideas emerges from an active relationship between prospective occupants and designer. The economics of construction aside, and assuming worker participation, the annotations of the first sketch seem to speak most about providing appropriate physical places for a rich variety of task activities, and the social implications of "community experience", which includes a double circled annotation that no (third order) symbols of hierarchy should exist. The motto included by Erskine at the top of the sketch says that: "Work is for, and a part of people. People do not exist for work." What is most inherently different in this Swedish landscape scheme from its counterparts elsewhere is the greater number of places for collective work or pure socialization. Individual work places tend to be arranged around the window walls, following Swedish tradition, with collective places located inside.

More commonly in landscape schemes of the time elsewhere, one sees an emphasis on the opportunities to flexibly group individual work stations according to functional interdependence. There are break places and shared facilities such as archives and conference spaces within these schemes, but they are fewer in number and more limited in terms of expressing group work. The interior and exterior of the open space have little of the potential formal opposition between collective (interior) and individual (exterior). Exterior window walls may be used for territorial status of executives or the location of conference or break spaces. It becomes evident that the primary intent of Erskine's scheme is to

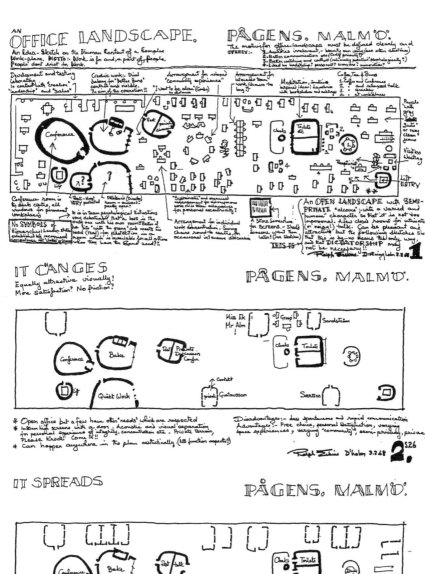

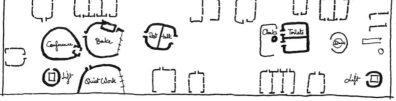

Figure 6.2 Sketches by Ralph Erskine, taken as prototypes for the *kombi* idea in Sweden (continued on next page)

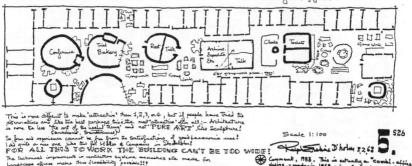

Figure 6.2 Sketches by Ralph Erskine, taken as prototypes for the *kombi* idea in Sweden (continued from previous page)

use the architectural form to express, consciously or subconsciously, the purely social relationships between individuals and the collective. True to the eventual second order reemergence of ritual practice in office form, social relationships and expression are primary, i.e. "work is for and a part of people; people do not exist to work". The horizontal concept of *arbetsgrupp* exists first in terms of second order cultural meaning (people), and then is linked to actual function activities of groups (work). The primary intent of other uses of the office landscape, however, remains at the level of functional work itself, particularly flexibility, in addition to other purely economic incentives.

The second, third, and fourth sketches are called respectively: "It changes", "It spreads", and "Many possibilities". The common theme in this sequence is the increasing recognition of the need for individual rooms, a need becoming standard among Swedish organizations at this time. Erskine's idea is more consciously functional and territorial than traditionally cultural. His intention is to accommodate an individual's possible desire for more privacy with the new flexibility of office landscape form. We do not know what the office situation was like for the employees involved in Erskine's programming sketches. Probably they worked in older office spaces with several people to a room. In this case acoustic privacy could have been a problem, similar to the concerns reported by interviewees who had worked in the short-lived office landscapes in Sweden. The architect intends for people to have access to private spaces for functional *(arbetstekniska skal)*, personal privacy *(känslomässiga skal)*, or status *(status skal)* reasons. Erskine uses the Swedish term for territory *revir* to include all of the above reasons for individual privacy. Perhaps such unlimited territoriality might work if those with more power did not have first choice of position within the overall layout, or if an infinite amount of space existed in which more or less equal spaces could spread.

But such territoriality, envisioned by Erskine in his three interim sketches, is probably impossible. Either a cultural, second order concept of egalitarian social relationships preexists, as it were, in the historical ethos of the society, or the ecological reality of organization power will appropriate space as signs of hierarchical, presentational territories--as is more typical in office landscapes and third order environments in general. We return to Stone and Luchetti's proposal (mentioned in the Introduction) for an ideal office layout which would eliminate the resulting wasteful plays of territoriality (1982). Each individual is given only the smallest of spaces, only a closet in reality, which he or she would call "home base". These have no windows nor territorial status in their position. The rest of the office space is open, with a variety of shared individual and team workstations for computing, conferencing in different numbers, doing archive work, etc. The basis of the concept is to simply eliminate any social or cultural use of space, again attempting to reduce office space to strictly functional purposes. All work spaces are shared, whether individual or team.

Such assumptions may be premature from an anthropological perspective. To assume that individuals with different ages, personalities, skills and incomes will not seek to politically manipulate shared, supposedly neutral areas is to either deny much of the historical function of expressive culture in smaller groups, to misconstrue the reaches of law, or to place too much credence in the power of altruistic rationalization. It seems that only through the manipulation of shared belief systems, either linked to or integrated with social rights and obligations, can political and relative material equality be maintained. In small economically or socially interdependent societies, where resources are limited and access and abilities are varied, equality is not a natural ecological or logical human condition. Perhaps only expressive culture can create such conditions. The force of law may provide for equality of opportunity but perhaps can never broadly legitimize true social and material equality. One may argue that corporate regulations may enforce equal access to shared resources, or work stations as in the present case, but without a common set of legitimizing beliefs the rules will be manipulated.

What Erskine's sequence of sketches appear to show us is how the fashionable idea of office landscape first of all consciously causes the architect in Sweden to abandon the dominant linear form. The planning of an architecturally undesigned open space creates opportunities for new expressive content to enter the design process, content which is largely subconscious, compared to considerations of task function and even implications of territoriality. The first scheme contains such a subconscious recognition of the developing opposition between individual (exterior) and collective (interior). More consciously then, considerations of individual privacy progress through schemes two, three and four until finally in the last sketch, almost all individuals have their own private rooms around the exterior, while the interior is left to collective socialization and work.

Erskine's comment in the Ericsson publication in 1983 is..."this is actually a 'combi-office' design, made in 1968 when the need could be thought out, but the suggestion aroused no interest! Even architects said 'not a proper landscape office.'" It is not clear who the disinterested decision making parties were, nor what the actual disposition of people was in the chosen office landscape plan approach. The basic concept of the unbuilt sketch five is quite similar, with at least one major difference, to the first *kombi-kontor* built ten years later in 1978. The similarity focuses on the provision of smaller individual offices around a common space, which is shared for socialization or work. The major distinction rests in Erskine's layout of the common space along a continuous linear core, not too unlike the concept of core in some of the later *smårumskontor* buildings. The built *kombi* forms of the late 70's and early 80's, as we will soon see, consist of discrete architectural clusters of about twenty individual rooms surrounding a common center. Whereas Erskine's final sketch contains the seeds of expressive opposition between individual and collective, collective meaning remains somewhat undifferentiated at scales smaller than the entire office.

Hypothetically, if the actual bakery organization and its existing environment was emerging from the patriarchal (or rational), and had not had the opportunity to first experience the right of individual offices, then we can assume that the need for horizontal work group expression either didn't exist or was in a very early stage. Erskine's proposal may have been prompted by the most initial indications of a desire for greater communication among employees, in addition to their desire for personal offices. Both in the literature and in actual interviews we hear this term frequently used to explain the advantages of the *kombi* form. As discussed earlier, virtually all the linear forms created by individual offices eventually developed a recognition of the need for greater communication, one result of which was the open door policies. Certainly this represents a real functional need as vertical concepts with their hierarchically channeled information are replaced by horizontal ones in which the *arbetsgrupp* must now share greater information by which to help make cooperative decisions. We see this tendency quite clearly in the Erskine scheme. From a purely functional or practical point of view, particularly in terms of work flexibility, the best solution is still the linear form with a continuous linear common core. Work groups may achieve the communication necessary across the common core, while movement of individuals and groups remains unhindered by any architectural definitions of those groups.

In this sense the creation of multiple office clusters which eventually appear as the built *kombi* form may be less inspired by purely functional or work needs for communication than by the need to architecturally express the other pole of the second order opposition, i.e. the *arbetsgrupp*. The horizontal work group concept was not at all well developed at the time of Erskine's sketch, although the opposition exists less formally stated between the individual room and the entire office, an expression with considerably less applicability to actual everyday work processes. It cannot be coincidence that the *kombi* form appears at the almost precise time that the participatory work group concept is well enough established to provide the basis for the co-determination laws of 1977.

It is not that the cultural expression of the work group does not precede its more formal emergence in law and architecture. Break spaces and conferences clearly accompany and expressively support the evolution of the work group. Rather, given the relatively immediate rejection of the office landscape idea in Sweden by employees and designers, it may have taken some time and circumstance before either the creative opportunity to break with the linear standard occurred, or people could positively consider something that looked like an office landscape. In any event, the *kombi* form appears to be an important expressive contribution, perhaps only made possible by the role of designers. The following examples of such offices, along with interviewed employees will diminish the purely communicational or functional source of the unique cluster form, emphasizing instead formal architectural contributions to the second order opposition between individual and work group. Such meaning exists primarily at the social and cultural level and is the foundation of actual office democracy in Sweden.

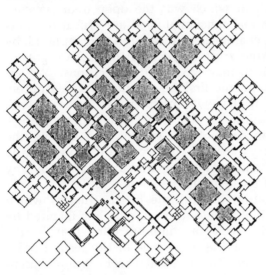

Three years before the *kombi* form appeared in Sweden, 1977-78, a very novel, seemingly proto-typical office building of modular clusters was built near Amsterdam, designed by the Dutch architect Herman Hertz-berger. The unusual de-centralized plan and experience of the insur-ance company building, figure 6.3, at first glance appears similar to the larger forms of connected Swedish clusters we will shortly see. Yet the far smaller scale of Hertz-berger's module is de-rived not from any evol-ving concept of horizon-tal work group, but from the size of a space needed to fit alternatively one, two, three, or four workstations. While a manager or executive may individually occupy an entire module, with or without walls, no pervasive concept exists to provide each employee with his or her own office. From the publications in architectural journals we cannot be certain how people are distributed within the amorphous grid layout, how communication between either vertical or horizontal work organization happens, how conference and coffee places relate to such organization, or where managers and executive are positioned. Yet these sources do tell us something of the architect's philosophy of design, which appears to be a stronger determinant than more indigenous socio-cultural evolution.

Figure 6.3 Plan of Hertzberger's Centraal Beheer, Apeldoorn, Netherlands (from Colquhoun 1974)

Hertzberger's conception of the design process is certainly sympathetic to the present thesis: "it is the user who plays the active role in a building, while the architect's role is rather to provide the framework that allows the user to choose his own behavior" (Colquhoun 1974:49). More specifically, the architect is said to interpret the building as a "small town", a "place where everyone would feel at home". There is a "sense of total community while at the same time suggesting islands of semi-privacy with which individuals and groups can identify" (ibid:50). The desire to create a non-hierarchical, non-discursive community is clear in Hertzberger's statement that..."the building is accessible at many points. There is no particular entrance with more pretension than any others" (ibid:50). Finally, this journal article suggests, but does not attempt to verify, that "managers are in tune with the libertarian ideals of the architect and know how to use the building as it was intended" (ibid:50). The emphasis on the intentionality of the architect in the origination of new form, rather than some more indigenous evolution, again seems to clearly distinguish this singular example from the Swedish *kombi*. Yet the question of whether an architect's well meaning innovation really works, socially and functionally, is seldom verified by architectural journals.

Is the small town really democratic? Who controls access to the best pieces of property? We return to the question of whether a more altruistically rational, or even corporately legal layout of space can be maintained over time? This is a set of meanings at a more conscious, rational level, even though largely metaphoric, in contrast to the long tradition and relative subconsciousness of second order expression. Given the parallel between smaller traditional societies and at least medium to larger office organizations, can true workplace democracy exist without a culturally derived set of definitions of basic social relations between individuals and groups? Hertzberger's metaphor of small town may intuitively be speaking to traditional second order values in rural Netherlands, yet its form has seemingly none of the formal, oppositional characteristics so intimate to the Swedish *byar* and ultimately offices. The difference between architectural intentions and more indigenous evolution (where the designer works essentially as a member of a participatory team or teams) is probably most striking in the different perceptions of these new forms in Sweden and Holland.

In the Dutch case, Hertzberger's more intentional design may have influenced other architects and perhaps corporations, both there and abroad, toward more altruistic conceptions of office design. Yet as influential as this example may have been, or continue to be--at least in architectural circles--it does not compare with the atmosphere which pervaded the initial *kombi* forms. In Sweden the much more indigenously, *arbetsgrupp* derived, *kombi* form becomes an almost institutionalized way of designing offices. Virtually identical forms are repeated in several new buildings in many different parts of the country. The form has a recognized name which quickly becomes known to designers and office workers alike. Although particular architects do specialize in such design and publicize their practice, and one can identify the first examples to be built and the offices which designed them, no individual designer is recognized as having created the new form (including Erskine).

The author's systematic search for office building examples in the Swedish architectural journals uncovered only one very brief account of Central Beheer. This one appears in the context of a larger article in Form, 1977, dedicated to work in the office place, specifically whether the changes that were happening within organizations were just a facade of democracy or true co-determination. In contrast to the above mentioned discussion of the project in the U.S. journal, the Swedish journal *begins* with an emphasis on the users right to help influence the form of their environment, rather than the mentioned emphasis on the discursive yet altruistic design contributions of the architect. In fact the first individual mentioned is not the architect, but the executive in charge of creating the project and choosing the architect, a man said to be more sociologist than technocrat (Christiansson 1977:10). The executive and architect, together with the employees, studied how their future office building would serve them best. Thus we are left with some confusion whether the "small town" metaphor was a philosophical label which evolved from the group process, or whether it was the invention of the architect?

In any event, the two page mostly photographic article in Form provides no plan of Central Beheer and no discussion of intentional spatial metaphors by the designer. In addition to description of worker amenities such as a daycare facility, a restaurant where parents and children can eat together, break places, conference places, small shops, a post office and bank, the Swedish article is also interested in the form and materials of the visual experience which the building creates. Given the standard linear form in Sweden at the time, it is understandable that to the Swedes the stacked unit form of Central Beheer creates a vision of some disorder. The title of the article is "Central Beheer--*trivsam myrstack*" (a flourishing anthill!). Essentially the article praises the social and functional amenities for the workers and the materials and furnishings which they either have chosen or may change. This lack of interest in some overall architectural intention of plan or larger concept is probably more typical in Sweden where much of the plan determination of office buildings evolves indigenously and subconsciously at the level of culture, rather than by individually created art or metaphor.

Central Beheer, therefore, was not seen as some major innovative architectural form to emulate. Within the rather copious volume of discussion in Swedish literature about the emerging co-determination processes at this time, ideas often focused on white collar workers and their settings. Yet there was apparently little new in the Dutch example, save for its anthill form. This form was not founded in any cultural tradition of second order space, as was already evolving in the formal opposition between individual offices and collective places which legitimized the horizontal work group. Based as it is upon cultural rather than philosophical intentions, the more socio-culturally developed *kombi-kontor* design makes its first published appearance as the finale of this same Form article. Its title, *"80-talets kontor--an ideskiss"* (the office of the '80s--an idea sketch) clearly shows the indigenous origin and independence of the *kombi* plan at this time. It is the expression of a collective pole of a cultural process in Sweden which had and probably continues to have no parallel abroad (though offices in the Netherlands need a closer look in this respect).[2]

6.1 The first *kombi*
The 1977 article in Form was written by Svante Sjöman, an architect and office interiors specialist working as a consultant to the historically well known Tengboms Architect's Office in Stockholm (Sjöman 1977). Though not a built project, the design of figure 6.4, really firms up the basic issues found earlier in Erskine's sketches. In this first published prototype of the *kombi*, the larger plan form is still a volume more typical of linear offices with thick utility and common cores. In spite of the larger linear form, and the ambiguity of whether the design was intended for a new building or a renovation, a segment of the core is defined in relation to sixteen employees, each, except for the receptionist, with his/her own office. These workers share the collective places which include copy machines, conference, typewriter station, computer station, archives, etc.. It is not clear from the information in the article whether a concept of *arbetsgrupp* consciously influenced this development of the "idea sketch for the 80's". We are not told

where *pause* would be taken or by whom. There is no specially designated place for *pause*, and the only group tables are labeled "conference" or "conversation".

In the discussion of this new but evolutionary Swedish design, the conscious emphasis is less on cultural expression than on combining the best functional aspects of the office landscape and ubiquitous Swedish linear *smårumskontor* forms, though the term *kombi-kontor* does not appear in this article. From the office landscape schemes are borrowed flexibility, communication, and better overall use of office space. From the *smårumskontor* one selects the better acoustic privacy and work performance as well as the better daylight and climate control available in the individual office.

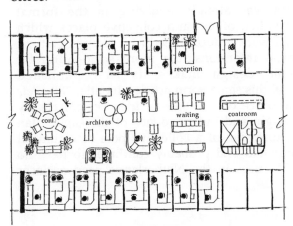

Figure 6.4 Sketch of *kombi* concept from Tengbolm's architectural firm, Stockholm (Sjöman 1977)

Extremely interesting in relation to the less conscious, second order expressive meanings which may underlie much of the above rationale, is Sjöman's statement that the advantages of the office landscape are promoted by management, while the benefits of individual rooms are championed by union representatives and the employees themselves. While one might interpret management's desire for office landscape schemes as primarily functional and economic in motivation, not unlike in the U.S., in Sweden, we have already seen several instances where particularly middle level work group leaders take a very active role in the promotion of what they call "communication". To a real extent, given the isolation of individuals which occurred when each was given an office in the linear form, one of the major roles of middle management was to facilitate the sharing of information necessary to make the participatory, horizontal system work. While consciously the term "communication" refers to the obvious functional benefits of sharing work information, more subconsciously, and culturally, the desire for better communication also and perhaps more fundamentally refers to the need to establish the social basis of the work group. Particularly on the level of the group leader, we see a good portion of his or her managerial skills being focused on the development and maintenance of collective and cooperative aspects of work. Such a role may not be that dissimilar to the elected council leader who organized both work and *fests* in the traditional *byar*. We must constantly remind ourselves that even the *pause* is less an individual right to relaxation than an obligation to maintain social relations with one's work comrades.

Because of the lack of expressive, architectural definition of work group along the linear form, the present scheme remains more a conscious, functional solution for the new horizontal work group concept. Like in Erskine's sketches, one might define the inside/outside relationships of the entire floor as an opposition between the patriarchal (becoming "individual") and the collective. Yet Sjöman's article continues to stress the more functional problems of both landscape and *smårumskontor* forms as rationale for the evolution of this new form. Because of the need for greater privacy in the office landscape, more and more screening was being added to original designs. Their flexibility had decreased dramatically (he does not mention additional difficulties created by the large amount of participatory time and effort required to make changes in employee settings). At the same time, the far more predominant linear forms created by universal individual offices are said to pose problems in using a standard bay or module for functions other than work stations (although this problem is solved very well by the space provided in a thick core of the linear form as in the recent city building in Malmö).

Another problem of the linear plan solved by the new form was the frequent dark corridor. The scheme developed by Tengbom's Office and Sjöman innovates the interior glass wall for the individual office. Light can pass through the offices to the collective space within. Yet while curtains are drawn on some of the individual offices, we will see from practice that this is seldom if ever an option for the occupant. Like the policies of keeping one's door open in the linear office buildings, in the *kombi* forms as well, one's wall must remain "open". In addition to the light provided by the interior window walls, they also help spatially extend the sense of individual office enclosure. The *kombi* scheme is based on a major trade of floor area between individual and cooperative spaces. *Kombi* individual offices are noticeably smaller than their predecessors in linear plans. This saved space has been allocated to the larger collective activities of the interior. These smaller *kombi* offices tend to be more carefully designed to still provide excellent control and use of the "four L's" as Sjöman calls them: light *(lus)*, sound *(ljud)*, air *(luft)*, and layout *(layout)*.[3]

These *kombi* advantages really do not require a major shift in overall plan form. As we have seen in both Erskine and Sjöman/Tengbom, a thick core linear form can accommodate all amenities mentioned in the 1977 *Form* article. In fact, although these are the issues most associated with the eventually built *kombi* forms, there is an interesting coincidence of the first use of the actual term *kombi* with a major change in architectural plan form. While certainly the origins of the term can be found in the Sjöman article as it speaks about "combining the best of the open landscape and the best of the cell office", the term may also have cultural meaning in its association with the new architectural expression of smaller socio-productive units more on the scale of the work group.

If it is true that these new clustering forms owe their origin not so much to functional combined advantages, but to a need to culturally express the primary work group opposition between individual office and collective place, then one should alter the meaning of the term. This will be even more reasonable if the following analysis reveals certain functional limitations to clustered forms in comparison to the more prototypical linear application of *kombi* ideas. For present purposes, at least, we will speak of the *kombi* as a concept, not a specific architectural form. In some respects it would be useful to have a Swedish term which was specific to the strictly architectural form of clustered offices.

One cannot use the term *arbetsgrupp* which, as described earlier, is the conventionally used term in Swedish offices. First of all, this term may have existed during the rational periods and perhaps even in the patriarchal. Its intention then was more purely functional and even socially hierarchical, in distinction to its present much more horizontal associations (again both social and functional). Secondly, while in some settings the term may be developing an architectural dimension to its multivalency, it remains difficult to use in the description of specific architectural aspects of its expressive, second order meaning. The search for a useful, specifically architectural term for the evolution of the Swedish office has its parallel in architectural studies of new socio-cultural forms for the industrial workplace.

200

This industrial research by Swedish architects underlines one of the principal themes of the present work. Because of the greater socio-cultural availability of architectural form in the office building, in contrast to the dominance of industrial engineering issues in industrial architecture, expressive changes in form happened in offices first. This led to or at least promoted true workplace democracy. Hired by Swedish Industry, architectural researchers such as Jan Hendriksson at the University of Stockholm have been attempting to create a socio-cultural equivalent to the *kombi* concept in industrial settings which because of the dominance of production engineering would probably not indigenously evolve.

Henriksson's and Lindqvist's publication of these more conscious design efforts occurs not coincidentally at this same time, 1977, when architectural expression of the work group as socio-cultural entity is finally materializing from its ten to fifteen years of evolutionary process. The title of their work, *Lägenheter på Verkstadsgolvet* (Apartments on the Workshop Floor) uses the Swedish term for "apartment" to capture their intentions of providing an architectural expression for the industrial equivalent of the socio-cultural work group (Henriksson and Lindquist 1977). In other more recent prototypical work for Volvo shown to me by Henriksson, one of my sponsors during this research, the attempt is to push industrial workplace democracy far beyond the earlier innovations of the Kalmar plant[4] where a work group could among themselves plan and execute a portion of the assembly process.

The "apartment" idea more recently being investigated for Volvo works under the proposition that an apartment work group would *totally* assemble a particular automobile. The larger factory, therefore, would contain no assembly lines or belts at all, only a large number of autonomous clusters served by an undoubtedly fantastic engineering process of parts supply. Certainly the architecturally defined apartment space will have considerable engineering determinants. Yet the architectural form is not immediately connected to increased production. Rather, the apartment helps create both socio-cultural symbolism and total autonomy of the participatory work group. Worker satisfaction and productivity increases occur as a result. As may already be apparent to the reader, the term "apartment" may be somewhat inappropriate because of its traditional association with the hierarchical, patriarchal, or family pole of the Scandinavian ethos. The best architectural metaphor for the horizontal, cooperative work group may be more appropriately *by*, or perhaps applied to modern settings, *arbetsby* (literally "work village").

6.2 Canon

In contrast to the less indigenous, more consciously designed, technically difficult industrial design attempts, a decade or more of actual built architectural evolution produces the first cluster like expression in Tengboms' 1977-78 office building for Canon in an outlying area of Stockholm. At first glance of the plan of figure 6.5, one sees a typical, square office landscape scheme, though with a small open courtyard in the center. Even portions of the second floor are actually laid out as an office landscape. Yet according to the text by Åke Bejne (1979:19), a member of the Tengbom design firm, this is the first built example of what they now call the *kombi-kontor*, the result, he says, of the firm's long experience with both landscape and small room linear forms. The benefits described are similar if not identical to Sjöman's earlier article. Given the larger scale of the square plan, it may not actually represent a major expressive difference from the essentially linear *kombi* sketches already discussed. This is really, again, an entire floor of some thirty to forty individuals, most of whom are provided with individual offices and an interior collective, cooperative space. Is the origin of the square form, limited as it is to floors of a single building rather than smaller and more numerous clusters, really a move toward the architectural expression of second order oppositions?

In a separate article of the same journal issue (1979:2), Bernt Sahlin compares the Canon office with three other new offices also published in the same volume, one of which is the linearly extreme IBM corporate center shown earlier in figure 3.1. An editorial introduction to Sahlin's article speaks of the *uttryckslösheten* (expressionless) character of the large linear office form, explaining its source as the demand for equal individual offices grouped along a single or double corridor, around an open yard, or stacked one on top of another. It continues with the recognition of the impact of the office landscape concept, not so much for its functional or social contribution, but for the way it forces architects to consider forms other than the extremely linear. The introduction says that the landscape idea *fick en kort blomstringstid* (bloomed for a short time) and that the architect's enthusiasm was strong and understandable while *dessvärre delades den aldrig av dem some skulle använda husen* (unfortunately the users of these new buildings never participated) (Hultin 1979). Thus again we see the idea that the small room office building was clearly the preference of the users, as they participated in design decisions, while the landscape schemes were more the product of top down executive and architect preferences. Yet these managerial motivations might promote both better building function (economy and flexibility as typical in the U.S.) and better communication with its underlying socio-cultural implications.

Thus it is with some interest that this issue of Arkitektur looks to the non-linear form created by Tengbom for Canon. It is not however, the *kombi* concept which is given credit for the square proto-cluster form, but a conscious or unconscious metaphor of building as camera (Canon of course). Design decision makers certainly recognized the advertising potential of the site, located as it is visibly adjacent to a major highway into Stockholm. With this in mind, according to Sahlin, it is

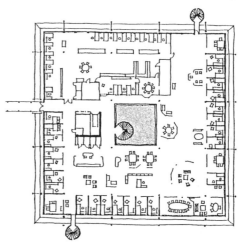

Figure 6.5 First floor plan of Canon office in Stockholm 1977 (Arkitektur h.4, 1979)

possible to speculate about the iconic expression of the building: the large atrium roof as a camera lens on the square body of the building; the circular exterior stairways as film cassettes; and even the dark background of glass and gray sheet metal as the camera eye. Certainly this kind of subtle play of imagery would not be unusual in Swedish commercial or public architecture. Yet the lack of association between the square form and *kombi* concept reinforces the notion that in its functional conception this building is essentially quite similar to those prototypical sketches where the *kombi* idea is applied to linear forms with thick cores. It is not until a year or so later when Sjöman is given the major consulting responsibility for the layout of Zander & Ingeström's corporate office in Stockholm (a daughter company of Alfa Laval), that the new cluster architectural form can be clearly associated with the *kombi* movement. According to the present thesis, this fulfills the particular need to express the horizontal *arbetsgrupp*.

6.3 Zander & Ingestrom

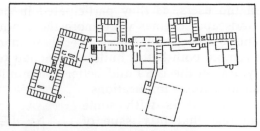

It is in Zander & Ingestroms building, that we can begin to use the term *kombi* (or ideally some other like *arbetsby)* to identify a purely expressive intention of a specific architectural form. Most significant to this definition is the smaller scale of the cluster form. The number of work comrades who belong to one *arbetsby* varies in Zander & Ingeström from a maximum of about twenty five to a minimum of about ten. In comparison to the numbers of employees on the entire floors of the prototypical *kombi* schemes, this smaller number clearly approximates the size of conceptual work

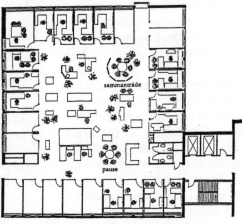

Figure 6.6 First (cluster) *kombi-kontor:* Zander & Ingström of Alfa Laval, Stockholm, 1979 (Arkitektur 3, 1980)

group. This number is similar to the number of farmers who might be members of a traditional Swedish *by,* hence some justification of our usage of the *arbetsby* term. Much of this meaning and the uniqueness of the *arbetsby* form was not consciously understood at the time. To the editors of Arkitektur, this was a *kombi-kontor* (Hultin 1980:14). Even though Svante Sjöman is given credit as a consultant, no mention is made of the origins, uniqueness, or meaning of the cluster form as *arbetsby.* Yet the cutting up of the linear form into architecturally discrete units is a major change in form! It does not seem to be consciously understood as an expressive phenomenon distinct from the more functional associations of the *kombi* concept, to which the small cluster form has come to be associated.[5]

The present thesis of *arbetsby* form as primarily socio-cultural in meaning is supported by several new expressive dimensions of the Zander & Ingeström design. Most significant, is the first architectural definition of the second order concept of work group.

204

The opposition of a smaller number of individual offices and collective space is extremely clear. Expressively there is no question which individual offices belong to the conceptual *arbetsby,* or what their relationship is to the communal center (even though we will see that actual work groups seldom exactly correspond). So well defined now is the collective space, that a term had to be coined apparently by the designer/consultant. The *vardagsrum,* as it has come to be known, is the term used for the most public space in the contemporary Swedish home. Contrasting sharply from earlier patriarchal associations of the parlor, *vardagsrum* translates as the "weekday", "workday", or "everyday" room. Perhaps more "family" than "living" room in American English, the implication is of a similar distinction between this space and the individuality of private places such as the bedrooms. Yet, not unlike the choice of *lägenheter* (apartment) for the work group concept in industrial settings, we see here a misappropriation of meaning from the traditionally opposite domain of family and hierarchy.

It is certainly not unusual for contemporary designers, in Sweden and elsewhere, to use the metaphor of family to refer to some ideal set of social relationships which transcends the more instrumental relationships of organization. It is also true that modern architects in Sweden, along with most educated others, will not consciously recognize the contribution which traditional second order practice makes to their life, nor concomitantly the ancient patriarchal/individual aspects of the Scandinavian family. In terms of a modern vocabulary of space, the term *vardagsrum* may be associationally the most appropriate. The recency of this term itself may preclude negative associational conflicts with traditional meanings of family and dwelling. In spite of the frequent contemporary use of the family metaphor as an ideal meaning of togetherness for some smaller social group, Swedish office workers themselves will seldom consciously make this analogy. One of the interview questions always asked concerned which other social group in Sweden was the work group or larger office most like? While some women occasionally did pick "family", this was by no means the most frequent answer. It was a difficult question for most, but more often than not elicited some sort of non-family group such as a "school class", "sports club", "neighborhood", and even once or twice the old farm *by.*

It seems part of the expressive meaning of the *arbetsby* that Zander & Ingeström's *vardagsrum* makes a clear distinction between *konferens* (conference) and *besökfica* (visitors/break). The fact that the furnishings of the two places are drawn identically suggests that functionally only one such place might be necessary, serving as is sometimes the U.S. case both conference and break activities. One could image actual conflicts for a single place particularly when the second order *arbetsby* form actually contains more than one functional work group. One group might wish to take their break while the other needs the space for conference. Nevertheless, similar to the clear distinction between conference and break place in remodeled or newer small room office buildings, with the *arbetsby* as well, the expressive distinction is apparently important.

The enlarged Zander & Ingeström *arbetsby* of figure 6.6 also illustrates one of the paradoxes of the new form. The extremely linear *smårumskontor* provided few architectural opportunities for territorially desirable corner offices. The square form of many *arbetsbyar* deviates from this condition by providing the potential for three to four corner offices per cluster. In the present example, one of the corners is enlarged to provide more interior space for either an executive or a middle level manager. The other three potential status positions are either negated by the placement of circulation links to other *arbetsbyar*, or are designed to have an interior identical to all the other offices. To a large degree the small room module system of allocating greater interior space for higher positions, while not distinguishing these spaces as seen from the corridor, still seems to be in effect with the early *arbetsby*. The single larger room is, from the *vardagsrum*, relatively undifferentiated, especially considering the fact that the other corners have no special meaning. Even the interior of this room with its three windows along one side is more module like than it might be with full fenestration on both sides as occurs often in offices with more territorial intentions. We will look in more detail at the question of whether the group leader is given a larger office, or whether these tend to be allocated only to executives. The Zander & Ingeström building is composed only of *arbetsbyar* forms, creating the necessity to house upper level executives among the expressively *arbetsgrupp* forms. Thus there appears to be little design intention to create separate areas for executives, managers and the like.

6.4 Skånska Brand / Wasa

It was fortuitous that one of the early *kombi* offices to use the *arbetsby* form had been built in Lund, the area of Southern Sweden, where two phases of fieldwork took place. Designed and constructed almost contemporaneously with Zander & Ingeström, in 1980-81, the *arbetsby* similarities to the Stockholm office building can be traced here as well to the consulting influence of Svante Sjöman. The author could not document the process by which this old Skåne firm (*Skånska*=Skåne region, *brand*=fire)[6] had included the architectural firm for which Sjöman was a consultant as one of the competition participants. One connection might be the fact that Zander & Ingeström is a daughter company of Alfa Laval, whose major manufacturing facilities are in Lund. Might one even speculate that the decisions to build the first *arbetsby* forms really came from Skåne, the area with perhaps the greatest *by* tradition? Our other *arbetsby/kombi* building visited is a more recent project also in Lund, and also a daughter company of Alfa Laval.

Figure 6.7 Historic Skånska Brand insurance building in the center of Lund

The history of Skånska Brand's traditional office building creates a fascinating and essential component of the decision to build the new office in *kombi* form. Founded in 1828, this insurance firm represented the quintessence of the third order meaning of *tjänsteman* and patriarchy, capturing as it did during this period the hierarchical pole of the ancient opposition. The building from which they moved in 1981-82 had been erected during the patriarchal period, 1910. Located prominently in the center of the traditionally religious and university city of Lund, just behind the cathedral and practically contiguous with the open air and historical museums, its rhetorical facade speaks clearly of the stylish, third order intentions of the time, figure 6.7. We will see in the next chapter that in 1980 there was still a great deal of affection for this building and its prestigious and convenient location in the *centrum*. It is clear that particularly the spatial layout did not fit emerging second order patterns. Growth in numbers of employees and needed archive space had been a constant fact of life from the 1940's, following the corresponding rise in white collar industry in Sweden; remodeling and additions were likewise continuous.

According to Skånska Brands own history of the old building, published after leaving in 1982,...*är det dock inte det gamla skalet, overfyllda arkiv, som tvingar oss ur stadens centrum* (...yet it isn't the old reason, overfilled archives, that requires us to leave the city center). *I stället är det en svarartad trängboddhet och besvärliga kommunikationer* (Instead, it is the malignant crowding of people and troublesome communication). This might translate into the need for individual offices and the functional, social aspects of cooperative "communication". Here was a Swedish organization whose evolving beliefs and ways of working were straining against the patriarchal image and layout of their physical environment. As much as the traditional *tjänsteman* and patriarch/individual in all of them might identify particularly with the facade image and central location, still, internally the old territoriality may have been a source of conflict. Relationships such as those between large rooms of the executives and crowded employee rooms was specifically given during the interviews as one of the principal reasons for the new building.

What could be more dramatically different then the *kombi* (*arbetsby*) form which Skånska Brand moved into in 1981-82, figure 6.8. There was a great deal of employee participation in the planning of their radically new form, facilitated again by Sjöman. There were no fewer than ten committee groups of about seven each who were involved in creating the program for the new building. Participants visited the Canon office in Stockholm and the similar Trygg-Hansa in Göteberg. On this basis, the *kombi* scheme was chosen over four others in an architectural competition. The fact that this was the first *kombi* office in Southern Sweden is well known among the organization members. In the four page pamphlet which describes the new structure to visitors, both clients and the architecturally curious, the first half page explains *Vad Är Ett Kombi-kontor?* (What is a *kombi-kontor?*). The list of attributes is outlined in these terms: 1) each individual gets an individual room; 2) all individual rooms have

208

glass walls facing into the common *vardagsrum* in the center; 3) the individual room is based on a module of 2 or 3 by 4 meters and equipped with furnishings which can be adapted to the needs of the individual and the room; 4) common activities occur in the *vardagsrum* whose furnishings will also vary according to the needs of particular departments; and 5) good internal communication will be achieved through short distance and quick contact (Other larger scale amenities of the building will be discussed in the following chapters).

It is no accident that the first issue listed above is that of having equally sized, individual rooms for practically all employees. This was reported to be a strong interest among the planning committees. Two of the female workers interviewed did not have their own office in the old central building. Both have been very happy in their spaces during the four years since the move. One said that she "felt at home" in her room (not unlike Conradson's data on individual rooms in her insurance company, Chapter Three). The other was equally emphatic about the pleasures of having one's own room, but added that many of those who had larger individual offices in the patriarchal building, mostly male managers or executives, complained about the small size of their new *kombi* offices. In spite of their small size, one can see from the photos of two such offices, that in addition to their primary second order meaning as "individual", these work spaces enhance many other kinds of environmental use.

Perhaps the large window is symbolic in its association with the spirituality of nature, as in the north view of the principal dwelling of the Skånsk *by* (the most prominent view away from the internal courtyard and towards the larger landscape). It also provides invaluable visual relief to the informationally overloaded work of the office, particularly this highly efficient, productive insurance organization. The ergonomics of working here is clearly superior to any office landscape scheme with its system furniture. A variety of work surfaces and light sources, both natural and artificial, provide a maximum of flexibility for individual preferences and task differences. Each individual exercises a high degree of control over ventilation, placement of many furnishing items, and personalization within the second order cultural framework. The items attached or placed in these Swedish offices are less the expression of individual interests and private family, as in the U.S., than they are of an individual appreciation of things which the larger Scandinavian culture deems aesthetic. Here works of contemporary art, photographs and objects of nature complement

209

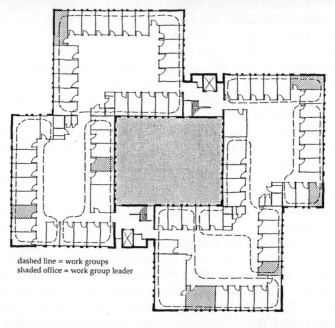

dashed line = work groups
shaded office = work group leader

Figure 6.8 *Arbetsbyar* of a typical floor at Skånska Brand (Wasa), Lund,
constructed 1981; views of individual rooms and collective spaces

the materials and textures of the collectively selected furniture.

In spite of the almost universal desire for the individual offices of the new building, and all the amenities which they provided, the *kombi* requirement of glass inner walls created skepticism among some. Probably all of the five competition schemes provided individual offices for each employee, but only the *kombi* scheme demanded transparency between individual room and community *vardagsrum*. We return again to the ubiquitous "open door" policies and the collective demand for expressive and functional communication between individual and group. It is not necessarily the individual who consciously wishes for this linkage, but really the *arbetsgrupp*.

The question of how social and functional communication is fostered by the *arbetsby* form and its glass threshold between opposites is crucial to any evaluation of the so called *kombi* offices. First of all one must make clear that although hypothetically the *arbetsby* form is primarily expressive in meaning, defining the opposition between individual and work group, in the work organization of Skånska Brand only one work group had exactly the same number (twenty-two) of members as *arbetsby* units have individual offices. The exact correspondence of the *Technique* group (actually called a "department" rather than a work group) is probably more than coincidental, where the architectural form actually influences the size of the group. Still, one immediately appreciates the practical difficulty of matching expressive form to functional group. The diagrams of figure 6.8. illustrate that functional work group sizes vary from as small as three or four to "departments" larger than twenty-two.

The coincidence of *arbetsby* form with actual social and functional groups is not consciously seen as a problem, even though hypothetically it is the underlying cause of the form. At the more conscious level, one of the original purposes of this *kombi* form was to provide the flexibility to move individuals and entire groups in and out of *arbetsbyar* as function demanded. Communication between individual and group would occur regardless of which particular *arbetsby* one was living in at the time. We must recall that in their traditional patriarchal building, it was said that people seldom were moved, in spite of the fact that functional organization constantly changed. One has the impression of quite permanent, long term "familial" associations, or at least quite stable territories, of individuals according to the more hierarchical layout of the architecture. The informants appear to be less conscious of the social obsolescence of the old building, focusing more on a perceived instrumental difficulty for people to adequately communicate in the new functional work groups.

If more horizontal *arbetsgrupper* were really forming in Skånska Brand, prior to the architectural change, then such would seem to contradict the thesis of simultaneous or even antecedent causality of architectural expression. One explanation consistent with the present hypothesis would rest on the relatively late date at which the rather abrupt evolution occurred. By the early 1980's, both the individual and collective expression of the *smårumskontor* forms had already thoroughly permeated Swedish corporate culture. It is not unlikely that Skånska Brand organization was aware of the new forms of work associated with those other kinds of settings. They may not have formed such groups prior to the new building, or were having difficulty establishing them, but their knowledge of them most certainly contributed to radical evolutionary change.

What the committees and designers could not foresee, was that not only would there be a tendency to make social and functional groups coincide with *arbetsbyar* form, but that contrary to the purpose of total flexibility, there would also be a tendency for work groups to attach themselves more permanently to particular *arbetsbyar*. Groups do express displeasure of forming associations, even decorating their *vardagsrum*, and then having to move to another. Just as individuals within offices have a maximum of control over their environment, so too do groups using the *vardagsrum*. Each group will decide when it will take its *pause*, whether it will be smoking or non-smoking, what particular furnishings it needs to function, when it will conference, etc. Where two or three work groups share an *arbetsby* the tendencies exist to more intensely use *vardagsrum* areas most adjacent to the work group, while still having access to the entire space. To a large extent, such multi-group use of the *vardagsrum* is facilitated by the fact that presently these spaces are somewhat functionally underutilized.

Even at their present size, reduced during the design process from something more like the Canon example, the intent at the time of construction was that one of the major common functional uses would be shared computer terminals. With the installation of personal computers only a couple of years after moving in, this major functional use of the *vardagsrum* was all but eliminated. One of the questions asked during the interviews attempted to get a feeling for just how much of the daily functional activity was spent out in the common area, vis-a-vis work done in the individual offices. Of the four people interviewed at Skånska Brand, they spent

212

from a minimum of about 5% to a maximum of about 30% of their work time out in the *vardagsrum*. Given the fact that most computer use and conferencing of two or three people takes place primarily within individual offices, the primary functional use of the *vardagsrum* is for larger conferences, usually of work groups. This activity, taken together with the other primary use, for *pause*, emphasizes the present socio-cultural hypothesis of the underlying expressive intentions of the *arbetsby* form. For its size, the Skånska Brand *arbetsby* is very much underutilized from a strictly functional or task performance point of view. Beyond function and expression we must continue to recognize the possible contribution of the *vardagsrum* space as a visual extension of the smaller *kombi* offices. Given the opportunity, individuals might well choose to close their curtains, thus sacrificing, perhaps, a visual aesthetic aspect for meanings much more social and cultural.

In the traditional Skånska Brand building there had been no specially designed and remodeled places for *pause*. This is not necessarily because the patriarchal ethos was too strong, administratively or architecturally. Just across the Cathedral square in central Lund one finds another very traditional, third order building still occupied by its long term owner, a savings bank. Only two administrators and a secretary were briefly interviewed here in preparation for the intended intensive second phase of the research. What the tours and plans of the central office of the savings bank revealed, was that rather than move from their prized historical building and location, they chose to decentralize aspects of their operation. During the same period in which Skånska Brand built its new facility, the savings bank was doing extensive remodeling. This included among other things several specifically designed *pause* and conference spaces (as partially illustrated in figure 5.6). Even with additional space created from decentralization of the central office, the original patriarchal form and structure of the building did not permit what may be the essential element in second order reemergence: individual offices for all (though not accurately surveyed, the impression of the remodeled floor plan, was that a greater number of individual spaces had been created).

One can certainly appreciate the difficulty of making the decision to move from the culturally and experientially loved Lund *centrum*. Had conditions permitted it would have been interesting to make a more specific comparison between these two processes and outcomes; Skånska Brand's *kombi-kontor* and the savings bank would have been two of three Lund offices studied at the proposed more intensive level. At what point in the decision making process about whether to remodel or move do the participatory worker committees come into the picture? At Skånska Brand, once the decision to construct a new facility was somehow made, employee preferences clearly emphasized the need for individual offices. It also seems probable, based upon present evidence, that the democratically felt need to alleviate "overcrowding" and create better "communication" must have been the basis of early decisions to move. What, therefore, was different in the process at the savings bank? Was this still a more ethnically patriarchal organization, where environmental decisions, though recognizing the already existing standard for break places, still were made more by executives than employee groups?

Such a comparative study would also probably show that it is overly simplistic to characterize one organization as "horizontal" (Skånska Brand) and the other still "vertical" (the savings bank). Even though decisions at Skånska Brand appear to have been more the result of newer democratic processes, still, transitions from older organizational meanings may not have been as complete as the form of the new building would suggest. The woman interviewed at Skånska Brand who had been part of the executive administrative staff, both in the old building and the new, revealed an unmistakable nostalgia, not only for the old location in the *centrum*, but for some of the purely social aspects of the former life as well. She missed the symbolic capital of old identities. The most interesting contrast here is the apparent shift in composition of social group which seems to have occurred in the move from old to new buildings. While no specially designated *pause* spaces existed in the old central *kontorshus*, this woman nonetheless did belong to a break group of sorts. About eight people, mostly longer term employees who had worked together for some time, would on a regular basis take break together at one place or another in the office. There were two men, including the *chef*, among the group.

In the interview, this group of people is *not* referred to as an *arbetsgrupp*, and one has the distinct impression that these people are related more according to long term friendship or perhaps a sort of familial bond within the patriarchal organization. After hours activities further distinguish the social basis of this group from more typical Swedish work group socialization and structure. At special coffee breaks on Friday afternoons, the group frequently planned a weekend outing, often a trip across the sound to Copenhagen. Although this woman definitely felt the new *kombi* office worked well in terms of task performance, she responded somewhat negatively when asked if the new building fostered stronger social relationships.

Two things appear to be happening here. First, is the possibility that groups composed of executives and staff (though not necessarily part of the same functional group) will be less "work group" like and more "familial", even well into the period of the democratic breakthrough. The other woman interviewed, who had not been part of an executive staff seemed to have a much more positive response to the new kinds of social group. In fact she complained that her actual work group of three or four people was really too small to be an effective social group. Second, and more related to the changes in architectural form, is the probability that for many of the particularly longer term employees of Skånska Brand, the socio-cultural meaning of the *arbetsby* opposition demands an essentially different form of social bond. For these people especially, the new *arbetsby* form of office demands a shift in social allegiance from long term familial groups to groups clearly linked to horizontal functional work as in the old cooperative *byar*. The personnel director's usage of the term *kultur folk* to refer to those who still had strong associations to the old building, also seems to capture the social essence of being the traditional *tjänsteman*. The symbolic capital of social position, good family and appreciation of "culture" may have formed the value basis of long term social groups in the older building. The intention of *arbetsby* expression, however, is to provide an expressive social basis to a work group whose members will fluctuate according to functional need.

One final note about the Skånska Brand *kombi* design involves the larger scale of office organization, the collection of *arbetsbyar* as the total corporate office. While this will be the topic of Chapter Eight, prototypical tendencies toward expression on this largest of scales appear in Skånska Brand and should be mentioned at this time. In the patriarchal office, often well appointed restaurants had long provided a strong third order image for the entire office organization. This extended family did not generally exclude lower classes as more common in dining facilities in other cultures, but included virtually all employees, although in a highly hierarchical pattern. Interestingly enough, it was the woman who had been part of the strong "cultural" group in the older building who felt that the new dining area, on the lower floor facing an outside terrace, was too large and impersonal. She missed the better contact with people in the smaller (more family like) dining room of the historical building. Though too small for all employees at one time, it still was accessible to all and presumably still provided that largest scale image of patriarchal family (see *fest* photo of this room in figure 7.7).

In addition to the socio-cultural tendency toward architectural definition of the *arbetsgrupp* and its individual offices, one finds similar second order tendencies at the larger scales as well. The patriarchal building may have contained a hierarchical ordering of individual statuses, which was reflected in the layout and location of the restaurant, but certainly no second order tendencies existed on this largest scale. There appears to be a shift in restaurant location from above to below as organizations become more democratic. A bottom level location is generally true of linear offices as well as in Skånska Brand's *kombi* office. As reflected in the employee's response, the traditional dining room has become less private, exclusive and familial and more public and collective.

In the case of the new Skånska Brand building, and others as we will see, the movement of restaurant from above to below also involves the shift from territorial third order position to something part of a second order opposition at the largest scale of organization. Penthouse like restaurants were an expression of the territorial status of being a *tjänsteman* in historical urban Sweden. These spatially exclusive locations were not ritually opposed to some larger "public" space. The urban street had few collective meanings ritually integrated with the life of the traditional office organization. To the contrary, the association of grand public spaces in traditional offices to the street, as clearly defined by Conradson (1988:118), was a sign of corporate status.

The exterior of the new *kombi* of Skånska Brand, figure 6.9, is certainly no expression of *tjänsteman* status. Obviously the initial design emphasis of the third order building will be on the meaning

Figure 6.9 Exterior of *kombi* offices: Skånska Brand (left), SattControl (right)

or expression of the exterior form. Second order architecture, in contrast, begins with the spatial and ritual oppositions *within* as the primary emphasis on the expressive level. As has been documented, the overwhelming design "intention" was the expression of work group as *arbetsby*. The exterior image and massing of the resulting building is simply the product of creating circulation links between four *arbetsbyar* on each floor. Even though the restaurant has been moved down to the ground level, adjacent to the main entry, there is as yet no larger scale design evolution of second order practice. We have as yet no clearly designed opposition between the collective restaurant or "village" street and the *arbetsby* units which will play the individual role at this largest scale of expression.

The arrangement of *arbetsbyar* creates an atrium or *gård* as it is called in the Skånska Brand plan. This layout, the relation between a center space and surrounding units, is formally identical to that created within the *arbetsby*. The potential exists, or existed during the design process, to expressively treat the atrium as a largest scale *vardagsrum*, something historically equivalent to the street, common or open space of the *by*. Yet spatial access to the atrium only occurs partially on the climatically enclosed ground floor, and only visually on the upper floors where the space is open to the elements and has no actual user access. Only a portion of the ground floor atrium form is open to the main entry and circulation spaces. Its "landscape" decor functions as a reception area and exhibit space. Furthermore, the focus of the restaurant is to the outside, not within to the atrium as we have seen in the federal tax building in Malmö, discussed in Chapter Four.

The only "ritual framework" of this potentially largest scale *vardagsrum* seems to be the large conference/meeting space which occupies a corner of the ground level atrium area. Particularly on the upper floors, Skånska Brand has no strong cognitive central space. Wayfinding orientation is difficult and second order expression incomplete. All four workers interviewed mentioned the difficulty of maintaining contact or relationships with others not part of one's work group or *arbetsby*. Apparently the historical office building had enabled better contact, or a feeling of third order identity at the largest scale of the organization. This was probably facilitated by strong circulation patterns associated with the hierarchical social layout of the spaces. In the longer term evolution of second order office architecture, Skånska Brand contributes greatly at the level of the *arbetsby*, but leaves the largest scale oppositions formally undeveloped.

217

6.5 SattControl

In 1986, about five years after Skånska Brand's innovative experiment built in the northern outskirts of Lund, the daughter company of Alfa Laval, SattControl, moved into its *kombi* office on the southern edge of the city. The electrical engineers and technicians who make up the large majority of this computer automation firm had previously worked in Alfa Laval office buildings built after the 1960's. Located at the major site in an older industrial portion of Lund, the layouts of these previous offices were either the *smårumskontor* or rare office landscape types. By the time of the design and construction of the SattControl facility, the *kombi* idea had become well known across Sweden. It was equally no novelty within the parent Alfa Laval, particularly since its other daughter company, Zander & Ingeström had early on consulted with Svante Sjöman to create the first *arbetsby* variation of the *kombi* idea in Stockholm. Although the specifics of the decision to use the *kombi* plan were not traced back through the planning offices of the parent company, one gathers from the interviews that this decision required much less deliberation than that accomplished five years earlier by Skånska Brand.

The decision to use the *kombi* form may have been easily reached by those involved, including the executives. After all, once the need for individual offices had become institutionalized, it was in executive interests to develop the "communicational" balance to office organization. In the introduction to SattControl's ten-page brochure which describes the new building, both for employees and visitors, the building's *"chef"* (his signature after this introduction has no title by it) describes the *bärande tänken* (the fundamental idea) behind the new building. He says that it has been partly to give everyone his/her own separate workplace, and partly to have common areas which promote and support working together. He concludes by thanking all who have worked with and contributed to the project's formulation and execution, a process which has been very free from friction. Thus we at least have some indication of a participatory programming process.

After the introduction and a Lund area map showing the location of SattControl, the architect of the project is given a page to explain the design intentions in more detail. On the facing page is a plan drawing, not of the overall building, but of a typical *arbetsby* almost identical to those of Skånska Brand, figure 6.10. This is not the continued professional contribution of Sjöman; rather it is evidence that the form belongs to Swedish office culture and can be emulated. Certainly it is not necessary for SattControl's architect

218

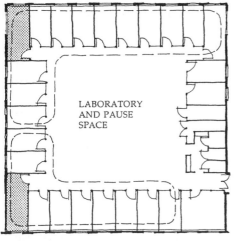

LABORATORY
AND PAUSE
SPACE

dashed line = work group
shaded office = work group leader

Figure 6.10 SattControl *arbetsby* plan, Lund; individual room and *pause* space

to make reference in his description of intentions to some original
(third order) "creator" of the type. Just as the original motivations
for the *arbetsby* form came primarily from the social exercise of the

219

traditional ethos, rather than from the designer as social "artist" *per se*, so too are later intentions of the *kombi* idea taken to be part of the shared cultural domain. After describing the overall form and usage of the project--two buildings of three floors (each building floor an *arbetsby*) connected by bridges--the architect informs us of his primary interpretation of *kombi* advantages, i.e. *flexibilitet* (flexibility). The idea for *SattControl* is to find an architectural form which facilitates their much more frequent recombination of work groups. Unlike the more constant work organization in Skånska Brand, for example, constantly varying engineering projects create parallel variation in work groups.

Again we find the term *vardagsrum* used to refer to the common space of the *arbetsby* form. The design program for SattControl, part of the effort to provide maximum flexibility, created shared laboratory space in the *vardagsrum*. Thus one would expect more work to occur in these common spaces than in those of Skånska Brand, for example. The final aspect of design intentions provided by the architectural firm in the brochure is called *Egen Profil* (one's own profile). This refers to either the architect's or client's perception of a need for overall identity, a problem mentioned above in the Skånska Brand example. The solution with SattControl, that of providing a "hi-tech" image or style, speaks more strongly of third order discourse than any conscious understanding of evolving second order processes. The architectural profession today is almost universally dominated by a preoccupation with third order expression, and Swedish architects are not uninfluenced by their foreign colleagues. Still, architects in Sweden do seem to march to a somewhat different drummer. Architectural students on fieldtrips through buildings sketch small details of the way the interiors are finished, or generally how things work. In the U.S., by contrast, students are clearly more interested in exterior facades and massing, for all their third order content.

All three of the engineers/technicians interviewed had worked in one of the three Alfa Laval landscape offices built during the early '70s. The space manager for these buildings, today a small portion of Alfa Laval's total office space in Lund, was interviewed as a preliminary part of the research. The reader will recall discussion about the difficulties of reaching participatory decisions concerning changes in locations of individual workstations and work groups. Where possible, these spaces are being converted to small individual rooms. Yet at the time of this research, major portions of at least two buildings were still being used as office landscapes. The interviews with two of these employees, very early in the study, solicited little negative response to the landscape scheme which they had lived with for ten to fifteen years. Still, remodeling processes were moving toward the national norm of the individual office, and at least the space manager was consciously aware of the new trends in some of Alfa Laval's more recent buildings. Once workers had moved from the landscape type to the *kombi*, they seemed more consciously aware of their new found amenities.

One electrical engineer recalled the "hype" which preceded Alfa Laval's first office landscape building in Lund. The idea seemed interesting and looked nice. There were about twenty to thirty members of his group in the new space. Whether this constitutes an early example of the horizontal work group, one cannot be certain without more intensive study. As a research idea, it may be logical to hypothesize that compared to the small room form, the early landscape offices in Sweden provided better architectural accommodation of emerging work groups. Certainly one of the early *Swedish* interests in the office landscapes, as in Erskine, was the architectural ability to create common or collective places.

Hypothetically, therefore, could not one see the office landscape as that aspect of office evolution which stood between the *smårumkontor* and the *kombi* schemes? First appeared individual offices, then collective spaces were developed in the open landscape, and finally the two become resolved in the *arbetsby*. More ethnographically correct is the probability that collective spaces were developing within the central corridor spaces of the *smårums-kontor* as we have seen, without any real influence from the few landscape schemes in the country. The prototypical *kombi* drawings were essentially linear schemes for widening the already collective spaces of the Swedish *smårumkontor*. The development of *arbetsby* form has far less to do with influence of the office landscape type than with the indigenous need to expressively oppose the individual with the collective.

More intensive research in the Swedish office landscape schemes would help explain why, according to two of the Alfa Laval engineers, as time went on in these spaces more and more screens would appear. From the author's visit to his former office, still in landscape form, it seemed that the screens were being used for both reasons eventually built into the *kombi* building, i.e. the provision of individual work space, and the definition of work group including *pause* and conference places. Given such an open space, one would expect a natural evolution into some sort of harmonious ethnic opposition between individual and group spaces. One of the primary reasons that no amount of participatory process can produce such a result in the office landscape, aside from the difficulty of having to constantly buy more and more screens, is that there was a third order, territorial status system already in place. Window space in the open landscape plan is limited and had at Alfa Laval become a sign of hierarchical status. Coupled with the remark that individuals were always trying to get the most screens possible, with managers perhaps also competing for screens to define the group vis-a-vis others, it is probable that the architectural layout and furnishings were working against the national reemergence of second order practice.

Two of the people interviewed strongly felt that the individual offices of their new *kombi* building were a welcome alternative to the acoustic and visual disruptions of the office landscape. The third, a technician who required a large drawing board had been unable to convince the planning committees that he needed a larger room of a module and a half, rather than the standard one module per person. As a result of this unrecorded planning process, he was essentially given his module and a half, but had to share a three module room with another person of similar technical need. Plans reveal no other such shared room in the facility. Either there were technical difficulties in positioning a wall in the center of a standard module, which appears from plan not to have been the case, or the individual office of a larger size would have run contrary to the limited, but effective status expression of the module system. Yet acoustically, because of excellent design consideration, either person of the shared studio office can have a telephone conversation without being overheard by the other occupant.

This individual was also convinced that no task performance reasons had even demanded that engineers or technicians be grouped in shared studio rooms. In addition to having worked in the office landscape, he had also shared older patriarchal or rational rooms with several other designer/draftspeople. One of these was for a short period after having worked for some time in a landscape space. By the time he left the landscape layout, enough screens had been commandeered to create a decent level of work privacy. By comparison, the shared room with its immediate wall and ceiling surfaces created huge acoustic problems. Finally, due to attrition of occupants of this particular building, he eventually was able to have an entire room of his own. It was the very positive memory of this more recent experience which had motivated his advocacy for an individual space in the new *kombi* office.

Alfa Laval is a large corporation, only recently decentralized into more autonomous units. Because of the international character of its business and many mid and upper level employees, its "hierarchical" tendencies may be somewhat more pronounced than in smaller, more indigenously Swedish corporations. Even though the latest *kombi* style of building is chosen by certain daughter companies, and perhaps by high level executives themselves, still, we see more of the modular system of patriarchal status in the SattControl example, than in Skånska Brand. The eventually negative decision of providing the interviewed technician with a module and a half appears to have been primarily one of status consideration, a carry over from earlier forms. The modular system of status within the *smårumkontor* was described as being conceptually within the patriarchal pole of the old second order opposition. If this limited form of status signage, seen primarily from within the rooms themselves, was in fact socially and culturally appropriate within the patriarchal, then what is appropriate for the *arbetsby* form?

Certainly with only two *kombi* examples studied in greater detail, it will be impossible to make any kind of definitive conclusion. From a strictly comparative posture, Skånska Brand very clearly spoke of the proposed plans as providing *equal* office space for each employee. Nor were corner positions strongly associated with different status. The pattern of use in SattControl, however, reveals much stronger tendencies to use both office size and location as status signs, see figure 6.10. Although the *arbetsby* plan is virtually identical to that at Skånska Brand, subtle differences have been designed in, and the flexibility of wall partitions has allowed other contrasts to occur. First, all the corner offices are about 20% to 30% larger than the standard module. It is a question whether this is simply the architect's solution to entering a corner space, creating a larger office rather than making a corridor to a standard sized one, or whether larger offices were intended for status reasons. In any event, the interviews clearly confirm that at SattControl, individuals know that managers and executives typically occupy corner offices. One such corner office was originally designed and subsequently used as a two and half module office for a department *chef*. Two other similarly sized corner spaces were being used as a larger conference space and a lab.

Given this partially designed, probably immediately available meaning of the corner position in SattControl, the above exceptions notwithstanding, these residual status conventions were headed for trouble in this *kombi* scheme. A few months after occupying the building, the automation firm acquired a small, technically related firm in Malmö. With the work groups from the assimilated company (who were given space in the SattControl building) also came several project leaders and the odd department *chef*. The overall organization became slightly top heavy by Swedish standards, and architecturally no corner positions were available for the newcomers.[7] They were given standard offices seemingly toward the center of the *arbetsby*. While functionally these spaces were adequate, as we have seen in Skånska Brand, a one module office simply was not appropriate in terms of the conventional status system. Within a short period from the move in to the time of the interviews, partitions had been taken down to create two module offices more compatible to managerial status.

It is perhaps too early to tell what the eventual effect of these more discursive, territorial uses of *arbetsby* space will have on the more second order potential of the form. Theoretically, the variation of interior modular space for purposes of status will have less of an effect than using spatial position of an office to express status or even control. Those interviewed did not consciously regard the corner position as a negative or intrusive meaning. When asked whether the project leader or *chef's* office in the corner created feelings of visual supervision or control, one engineer replied that..."if some boss came and told us how to behave, we would laugh at him", then he added that...."the boss must be part of the group". Still, it may be likely that any territorial usage of *arbetsby* space will negatively impact the collective control and usage of the second order opposition. The creation of latent third order corner positions in the *arbetsby* is essentially an incidental byproduct of the square carpentered form. The ideal form would be round, without corners. As we have seen in Skånska Brand, many of the effects of the square can be diminished or eliminated by careful design, assuming that such is the more or less conscious intent of both architect and client group.

Functionally, in comparison with the minimal usage of common space at Skånska Brand, these individual offices remain the primary place of work, in spite of the increased laboratory usage for portions of the *vardagsrum*. One of the engineers said he used the lab space from three to four times a week, for relatively small periods of time each. The other engineer estimated his total lab time at about 20%, with the rest spent in the individual office. The designer/technician was out in the lab more frequently, about five times a day, but for only a total of about 5% overall work time daily. The question of how much additional task performance time is spent in conferencing in the *vardagsrum* seems to relate to fundamental task differences between engineering (SattControl) and service (Skånska Brand) functions. Based on the initial survey visit, four or five hours of interviews, and a full day on site including the midday dinner, there seemed to be less emphasis on the conference aspect of work group decision making.

It would seem that the constant reformation of work groups around actual engineering projects, the facilitation of which was the primary design intention of this *kombi* scheme, creates an even greater contradiction to the formation of parallel socio-cultural and functional work groups. The shifting engineering projects, which after all create strong functional relationships among definite groups, are really quite similar to the various forms of work groups in the traditional *by* society. Largely unconstrained by the technically dominant layouts of industrial workplaces, both ecological situations demand a continued reformation of cooperative work groups of varying sizes and functions. The physical basis of the product of the work in itself would appear to create a strong identity of sorts among the participants, more so perhaps than with the more abstract informational product of an insurance firm, for example. Yet from the perspective of the quasi-independent cultural system of meaning, these varied and real groups must be expressed as the collective entity of this scale.

At SattControl, given the fact that people are constantly reorganized according to the natural ecology of engineering projects, how is the cultural concept of *arbetsgrupp* actually associated with real individuals? It appears, from the limited evidence, that the *arbetsby* form tends to function almost independently. In other words, instead of being able to move people in and out of *arbetsbyar* according to the constant reformation of projects, individuals seem to form groups socially similar to work groups, but firmly associated with particular individual offices and their opposed *vardagsrum* spaces. From the interviews it appears that these supra-ecological groups are not unlike the friendship formations we see more commonly in U. S. offices and perhaps blue collar workers generally, i.e. groups largely independent of some expressive space. A closer look at the diagrams of spatial locations of these "friends", figure 6.10, reveals to the contrary that they are in fact spatially and here culturally constituted.

It is also true that ideally, definitions of the actual work group tend to coincide with second order expressions in the democratic Swedish office building. Actual work groups establish regular *pause* and conference times, special work associated dinners, etc.. In the engineering organization of *SattControl*, on the other hand, the tendency to form somewhat separate socio-cultural groups, permanently located, has resulted in the spatial dispersion of the actual project or work group throughout the building. This conflict with the original design intentions was reported during the interviews.

These dispersed project groups must conference with at least some regularity and perhaps formality. In this conflict with the more purely cultural groups may lie the reason for diminished *vardagsrum* use for conferencing. Additionally there will be a project leader, labeled membership according to engineering specialization, and actual cooperative work. Nevertheless, when it comes to taking *pause*, the more ecologically determined definitions seem to take a back seat to taking *pause* in one's *arbetsby* space with one's spatially determined, socio-cultural comrades.

It is also not surprising that these localized breaks do not have the institutional scheduling one finds ubiquitously in service oriented offices. While it was reported that people tended to take two breaks a day, the timing was clearly much more spontaneous. The decision to take *pause* was determined essentially by either one member of the localized group having a free moment for a cup of coffee, thus being the first person present, or by seeing one of the group already at the *pause* table. One must certainly point out possible task performance reasons why at SattControl, the *pause* takes a more localized, spatially determined form. Dispersed as the members of the project group are in their individual offices, it may be more difficult for them to all be in one place at one time. Yet the project group could make the decision to have scheduled *pause* at particular times and places, but they do not. From a simple social territorial point of view, the constant reformation of project groups would necessitate a constant renewal of *pause* individuals. Such is a third order assumption and does not consider more traditionally based possibilities. According to the present hypothesis, therefore, it is such second order symbolic meaning of *arbetsby* spaces that positively creates its own representative groups, not based on friendship, but on reemerging Scandinavian practice.

Even though in the traditional *byar* cooperative groups would vary in size and function throughout the year, each participant expressively maintained second order relationships to others by virtue of the spatial pattern of individual farms and village layout. Thus, here too, we find a certain independence of the expressive to the ecological. Yet it is the effective strength of the spatial layout and associated rituals which in part provides the "belief" necessary

226

to maintain actual cooperative work. Expressive space creates ideal or representative individuals and collective groups--both as aspects of self. Even though the tendency may always exist for virtual coincidence between the expressive and the ecological, particularly in white collar service offices, the second order *arbetsby* forms will as well provide an expressive basis for engineering forms of work.

While we recognize that the largely independent socio-cultural group will have strong localization tendencies in particular *arbetsbyar*, still, the numbers in these groups appear to be smaller than the entire *arbetsby* form proposes, here something just over twenty. The *pause* groups observed and reported in the interviews were more like six to eight in number. One person felt this was an ideal size because of the naturally "shy" character of Swedes. He noted that if the group is larger, all sitting around one table as they will, people will be inhibited to converse, and silence may prevail. There appears to be a size limit to the number of people included on the basis of spatial contiguity.

Finally one must at least mention the apparent possibility of third order territoriality as smaller more purely socio-cultural groups occupy portions of a single *arbetsby*. A good example here is the contiguous portion of one *arbetsby* occupied by people from the absorbed firm in Malmö. Probably the largest reason that people from this other company were clustered together is, again, not that they formed a project group (their work is integrated into the SattControl organization) but that they knew one another and would naturally form one of these localized socio-cultural groups. On this floor the Malmö group took their *pause* together and had remained a separate entity. Is this not a source of territorial identity for this group, and why would not all localized portions of *arbetsbyar* be a source of such third order definition? It is simply because the second order patterns of the *arbetsbyar* effectively eliminate any possibility of status distinctions. No one portion of the *arbetsby* is different than any other. No presentational meaning exists, at least in the spatial, architectural form.

Even the non-hierarchical form of territoriality provided by simple separation is given no real spatial or architectural definition. Individual offices of one group merge indistinguishably with the others to form the overall exterior. No small socio-cultural group can stake out any portion of the *vardagsrum* as territory. *Pause* spaces must be time-shared. While the lab spaces in the *vardagsrum* were initially intended to serve immediately adjacent project groups, and therefore might be a source of territoriality, with time these have become more delocalized. One interviewed engineer's lab space was not immediately adjacent to his office, but diagonally across the *vardagsrum*.

Although the fit between expressive form and socio-cultural group is not ideal at SattControl, nevertheless it may be that second order *arbetsby* form does help legitimize participatory democracy in the actual project groups. The expressive intentions of the *arbetsby* form, in both Skånska Brand and SattControl, tends to be less consciously understood in terms of its role in the reemergence of second order space and practice. It is universally true that task performance concepts are easier for architects to conceptualize and consciously manipulate. Given our lack of traditional "ethos" in the U. S., for example, techno-economic third order aspects with some interior task performance will almost completely dominate the design process. But in Sweden, as we have seen, architects are managing to work with second order expressive content, albeit on a more intuitive level.

The result, as in both Skånska Brand and SattControl, has been a certain lack of resolution between the more conscious task-performance intentions of maximum flexibility and the more subconscious cultural desires to architecturally express the opposition between individual and collective. There appears to be a spatial or localized permanence required for the latter, a prerequisite which cannot yet be totally reconciled with frequent movement of individuals and groups for task performance purposes.[8] The problem may be somewhat similar to trying to move individual traditional farm families in and out of different dwelling units of the *by*, or even in and out of different *byar*--all according to some task performance need. Second order experience creates very strong feelings of and attachment to place.

Notes

1   The Swedish literature on the idea and implementation of the office landscape is quite extensive and if space permitted could be a substantial chapter or perhaps appendix to the present work. Since generally this type of office did not become the norm in Sweden as it did elsewhere, nor as we will see was it a true impetus to the *kombi-kontor* a more detailed discussion is not critical to our evolutionary, indigenous second order argument. Major articles which could be included in such an appendix might be: Office Landscape Report from Travel to Germany 1965 (*Kungl. Byggnadsstyrelsen* 1965); Some Work Psychology Viewpoints of Office Landscapes, Impressions from a Travel Study in Germany (Gustavsson 1966); A New Work Environment (Hjelm 1967); Don't Change Small Rooms into Large Ones (*Affärsekonomi* 1972); Only Dissatisfaction with the Office Landscape (Von Friesen 1976); The Office Landscape's Effect on

Well-Being and Effectivity (*Social-nytt* 1970); Are You Happy in the Office Landscape? (Christiansson 1970); Office Landscape or Not? (*Försäkrings-tidningen* 1970); Adjustments to Work in Office Landscapes (Rissler & Elgerot, 1980) (titles have been translated from the Swedish). To this brief list of the many articles collected during the present research should also be added Wolgers' book on the subject (Wolgers 1968) which quickly appeared during the first couple of years of the office landscape idea.

2   Currently popular "cohousing" studies point to prototypes in both Scandinavia and the Netherlands, without carefully distinguishing between the particular contributions of the two cultures. Comparisons between the architecture of coworking (offices) and cohousing should be an important next research project. The reader is reminded of the author's assertion that the coworking phenomenon is essentially much more pervasive than that of cohousing-- within Sweden at least.

3   The Swedish government has supported a good bit of research into converting pre-*kombi* linear forms into *kombi* offices with smaller offices and larger and more defined collective spaces, especially in state buildings (see for example the work of Jan Ahlin, Leif Carlsson, et. al. 1985).

4   The often publicized floorplans of the Volvo plant in Kalmar show the attempt to provide greater worker participation in and control of assembly line process. The respective wings of the plant are semi-autonomous where teams of workers decide at their own volition how to assemble portions of the vehicle. While some social meaning of this architectural change may certainly be discerned, the essential functional distribution of employees still remains dominant and relatively inflexible. This plan was not emulated in other Swedish plants.

5   In all the Swedish literature surveyed, the only explicit comparison made between *by* and *kontor* societies occurred in a four page segment of Holm-Löfgren's ethnography of offices (1980:102-105). Entitled *bysamhället-kontorsamhället* (farm society-office society), the emphasis is on the common functional abilities to work together, without any mention of ritual practice or architectural form.

6   The company was called Skånska Brand at the time it constructed its new *kombi-kontor*. This traditional Skånsk insurance company in 1986 merged with others to form a more national entity now called Wasa.

7   Even if the architect and clients intentionally created the corner positions for managers and executives--as happens so often in presentational forms elsewhere--they could not at the same time practically predict how many such positions would be needed over time.

8   This problem may be somewhat analogous to difficulties anthropologists have had in relating economic kinship groups to pan-cultural definitions of some more ideal group which plays this "individual" role in larger first or second-order processes. The difficulty of course, is determining what legitimizes membership in these fundamental "individual" units which must play both task performance and ritual roles. For years anthropologists have indulged themselves with elaborate kinship system analyses which many took to be the primary means of organizing the society. A first or second-order perspective of the larger ritual system of symbolism and spatial opposition, however, sees the

primary meanings of the expressive system as essentially affective and spatial, rather than specific as to real or fictive biology--or in the present case, functionally organic interdependence. Thus, to a large extent, these spaces exist independently of biological or ecological realities, though the role of symbolically elaborated kinship, for example, must be somewhere incorporated.

7 Major office *fests*

In our previous discussion of the fundamental horizontal work group and its eventual *arbetsby*, we saw glimpses of changing forms of larger groups such as a department or section, and particularly the entire occupancy of an office building as a whole. Briefly mentioned were the ways in which larger office "floors" included many work groups, how interior corridors tended to become "street" like as shared activities were added to the core of the *smårumskontor*, how restaurants tended to shift from more territorially or presentationally exclusive places above to more open locations below, and how at least some *kombi* schemes began to group their *arbetsbyar* around an atrium like space at the scale of the total office building.

Beyond the patriarchal farm in the traditional Skånska *by*, we recall the larger scale collective spaces including the street or village common, council meeting place and the special market and ceremonial place, the *torg*. While one can immediately begin to draw formal comparisons between these spaces and the above mentioned forms, still today in the process of evolution, it must be clear that many office organizations are much larger and in other ways different than *by* societies. First of all, while the scale and formal layout of the individual farm and courtyard, figure 1.10, is very similar to that of the office *arbetsby*, it would appear that both the numbers and social relationships of the two are different, i.e. the farm is "patriarchal" while the *arbetsby* is more "collective". While the number of family members (including hired hands) is about that of the ideal horizontal *arbetsgrupp*, the former is hierarchically ordered while the emphasis on the latter is on the cooperative. The scale of the office work group, particularly in the range of ten to fifteen members, seems more similar to the scale of the entire *by*

231

considering each farm head as a member. Yet we also know that actual cooperative work groups in the *by* could range from a small size of three or four, to a work force of perhaps thirty or forty.

The democratic Swedish office does not seek to resurrect the exact numbers and scale relationships of *by* social organization. It is a common spatial, structuralist logic of traditional second order practice which is being used to organize relationships between patriarchal/individual and collective entities. While the *by* farm is patriarchal in its relationship to the larger collective street or common, from *within*, its central courtyard may have similar collective meanings in opposition to the actual dwelling spaces for humans and animals around. In this sense the architectural forms which surround the courtyard spaces of both *gård* (family farm) and *arbetsby* share an association with the patriarchal, individual or hierarchical. The second order spatial logic of both farm and *arbetsby* may be quite similar. It is also true that this same logic extends to larger scales of *by* and leads to comparisons between the form of the office *arbetsby* and the way the farms as hierarchical units are arranged around the egalitarian street or common.

Hypothetically, it is this abstract spatial logic which resides in the larger Scandinavian ethos, rather than some actual visual image of an ideal *by* type which helps create *by*-like form in contemporary offices. Much of folk history and traditional activities must "contain" the opposition between individuals and groups, and still today leave a sizable impression in the minds of Scandinavians. Part of the definition and expression of these two ways of being--and the power relationships between the two--commonly involve cognitions of spatial opposition, whether from descriptions of ritualistic movement in folklore or the actual trip out to the summer *stuga* (principal farm dwelling or today summer cottage). Second order spatial opposition perhaps exists as a fundamental part of the ethos at large and likewise serves as an essential component of expression in actual localized, economically integrated organization. It is this principle, not any exact visual or ethnographic analogy to the *by*, which seeks form and practice at whatever scale of organization in the Swedish democratic office. Common spatial logic creates similar forms.

The sizes and numbers of organizational scales of offices will have greater variation than any traditional *by* society. Thus in addition to the abstract nature of the second order ethos, and the lack of clear traditional spatial pattern for democratic office to emulate--this is really a process of "re-evolution"--there will also be no clear precedent of how to architecturally integrate the greater variation of size and number of scales into one building form. We have seen in the *kombi (arbetsby)* schemes how larger scale expression was compromised by primary attention to form at the scale of the work group. In the following chapter the reader will see recent Swedish offices where, while also being derivative of the *smårumskontor* with its individual offices and linear corridors, the dominant formal concerns lie at the largest scale of total building. Then in Chapter Nine examples will be discussed where an accommodation of second order practice at two or more scales begins to characterize the most recent and innovative projects in Sweden. It is in these buildings that the architect plays an increasingly critical role in what appears to be the climax of the evolution of the democratic office workplace.

To each scale of second order organization in an office will correspond an extensive number of *fest*-like events which establish the social and symbolic basis of actual work on those scales. Similar to the cooperative *byar*, each work event of any size demands its own *fest*. Generally speaking, the larger the number of participants, the more formal and symbolic the nature of the event which also occurs at greater intervals of time. In the *by*, in addition to many kinds of smaller *fests* directly linked and timed by actual cooperative work and involving only a portion of the community, one found additional rites of passage and calendrical rituals celebrated by all members of the *by*. These were the events which ritually established the basic social disposition of either patriarchal or collective aspects of the self. In Swedish office life, particularly during the democratic evolution of the past thirty years, some of these largest of rites have come to express the largest of scales of organization. While it is true that the more traditionally formal and symbolic rites of an ethos, e.g. birth, marriage, death, winter and summer seasons, will always be recognized and perhaps celebrated to some degree by whatever group, many of these have become a highly institutionalized part of the second order process of office culture.

During the 1920's when the patriarchal images of the office were at their strongest, no employee *fests* existed in Conradson's insurance company, with the exception of a few special employees being invited to the director's summer place (Conradson 1988:111). The first large *fest* in this corporation took place in conjunction with a company meeting in 1926. While all employees were permitted to be present for a portion of the event, the primary participants were clients, executives and managers. At one party for the upper echelon at the Hotel Continental in 1931, even this

233

hierarchy was seated at tables according to rank (ibid). After the second world war, the patriarchal *fest* began to give way to what have come to be called *personalfester* (personnel parties). Far fewer in number than in today's organizations, and reported by many as *stela* (stiff) events, the content apparently focused more on the social disparities which still existed between employees and management. The lower level *tjänstemän* organized not only the overall events, but the poems and skits, many of which poked fun at the bosses (ibid). No mention is made in this source of special architectural places for these activities, or whether the traditional patriarchal dining room was used.

Across the present survey of Swedish offices, the institutionalization of *fest* activities and their relationship to architectural space is very clear at the smallest level of the powerful work group. It is also quite clear, as we will shortly see, in those cases where the entire office participates in major nationally recognized rites. While seldom if ever do we find an office, or even campus of buildings where the size is too great for all to participate, still there are size related tendencies for intermediate scales of organization, departments or sections, to duplicate these events in their own places. Seldom do we find an event exclusive to some intermediate scale. Conceptually the types of *fest* events, with a couple of exceptions, are limited to *pause* activities, the midday meal, some rites of passage, clubs, and major yearly celebrations. Except in the possible instance where a department or section occupies an entire floor, and they all take *pause* at the same time (but not the same place), the *pause* is the primary *fest* activity of the work group. The majority of other events, and the number is impressive, relates to larger scales, most often the largest.

7.1 Clubs
Swedish work organizations, particularly in the industrial sector, have a long and rich history of voluntary clubs (*klubb* in Swedish) which have served a variety of interests. In industrial settings not yet spatially grounded in second order meanings and practice, the unions created and continually promoted *kamrat klubb* (comrade clubs) representing the primary social expression of worker solidarity. Restricted as the functionally and patriarchally designed factory setting was from any expressive formation of horizontal work groups, clubs became a highly institutional and participatory part of the (discursive) expression of collectivity. They played an historically important role in the union movement and Social Democratic Party in Sweden. Clubs were dedicated to sports,

234

politics, education, culture and the like, though their underlying purpose was the foundation of worker solidarity.

Such voluntary social groups nominally cross-cut other groups based on kinship, actual work, or even ritual. The comrade clubs of industrial Sweden seem to vary somewhat from this usual definition. Since virtually all clubs were firmly associated with the workers' movement, social democracy, and the collective aspect of the traditional ethos, they were therefore conceptually quite related to each other, carrying strong associational commonalties to the larger cause. Very little cross-cutting occurred among different social groups. Only workers of the same class participated, both male and female. If one took all the different club activities together, conceptually they would differ only in surface content from the composite of group activities maintained in the *by*. Furthermore the need to practice many of these activities in some communal space, e.g. a folkpark or union locale, has been mentioned previously. In today's industrial workplaces in Sweden, most plants have a union office for members and their leadership which is most often called the *klubb*, probably as a reflection of its broader meaning of these kinds of activities. Though undoubtedly prominent in the cognitive maps workers have of their workplaces, the possibly territorial *klubb* does not yet represent the collective aspect in any more unified second order opposition involving the entire work organization.

Given the historical *tjänsteman's* status distinction from the *arbetare*, and the resulting lack of interest in the workers' movement and things associated with it, it also follows that pre-democratic offices seldom exhibited the overt club activity found in industrial settings. Yet once the majority of wage earners in Sweden worked in offices and unions at least nominally represented these workers as well, it seems logical to expect to see club activity here as well. Yet by now the reader surely recognizes that Swedish offices since the mid-sixties are not simply the product of (industrialized) union experience. Although virtually all office workers today are represented by one of a variety of *tjänsteman* unions, union activities and associations with the historic worker movement are extremely weak in comparison with their present or past industrial brethren. Of all the offices on which data of one sort or another was collected--well over one hundred examples from Lund building department archives, exploratory visits, actual surveys, published articles, etc.--no union *klubb* rooms were found in these white collar settings. The primary collective need has been satisfied with the second order practices.

235

On the larger scale of offices, beyond the work group, second order expression is less well developed. It may be at these larger scales that collective needs become translated into occasional *klubb* activity. While reference to participation in *klubbs* occurred in only four of the forty odd interviews, the unionization of office organizations did in fact create the structure for and limited manifestation of volunteer clubs. With two of the younger men interviewed, one at ABV, the other in the Malmö savings bank, the office sports club provided a very important source of comradeship. The term *idrott kamrat* (sports comrade) was used to refer to other members in the club with whom one played for example waterpolo or soccer. In these two offices at least, all voluntary activities available at the scale of the entire organization were subsumed under the title of *kamrat's klubb* (comrades club). Included under this umbrella organization at ABV are the activities of a "cultural" group interested in art and theater. They hold art lotteries for participating members and will organize excursions, often overnight to Copenhagen, to attend live theater performances and the like.

It is true that the *kamrat's klubb* structure exists in many of the particularly larger offices, even though it appears to have far fewer activities associated with it than in industrial organization. It is also probably true that some of these larger scale activities may occur as part of still evolving second order meanings. Sections or departments seem at times to also organize club like events, e.g. cultural trips or sporting events. Unlike the industrial setting, the tendency within the democratic office society is for all things to fall within these fundamental second order definitions. If these larger expressions and organization reach a fuller evolution, the question may be whether or not voluntary associations at the scale of the entire organization are needed to cross-cut the dominant structure of work groups, and sections or departments?

The purpose of the historical workers' movement was largely discursive or political (assuming that strong collective associations within these urban émigrés needed less development and maintenance). More recent club participation, especially those in offices, seems much more intent on the actual development of more purely social (collective) relationships; they seem to never have political overtones about discursive relationships between "them and us". Since most voluntary associations often have some socio-political agenda, one wonders about the Swedish office clubs. Is there a hidden political agenda to their activities? Do these compete with or otherwise contradict the mainstream political processes closely linked to second order space and expression? Are these more residual "family" or "patriarchal" groups? After all, voluntary associations seem to become more useful in traditional societies when first or second order institutions are breaking down. In the case of the Swedish office, therefore, the hypothesis of increasing second order practice suggests that the need for voluntary groups should be decreasing.

Perhaps closely related to the potential competition, the inherent differences, between voluntary clubs and institutionalized second order organization is the apparent fact that while second order expression is fundamentally spatial, one finds few if any places dedicated to clubs. The absence of a union *klubb* was mentioned, but one could also talk about other potentially available spaces in these buildings. We find no examples where *pause* or lobby areas have become associated with clubs or their activities, nor would such members apparently dare to sit together during the common midday meal. Perhaps the place seemingly most natural for such associations to develop would be the frequent exercise rooms of Swedish offices, often a lower or basement level facility. Yet in all the offices visited, one did not receive the impression, either through interviews or visual observation, that exercise rooms and shower facilities were very often used, not even as important places for club activities. In a tour of the very elaborate, architecturally recognized, national bank building in Stockholm the top floor contained not only restaurant-like facilities for the employees, but a large greenhouse with adjacent men's and women's saunas. During *fests* or after work, it was reported, people used the saunas. This association of saunas with major dining and *fest* space was unique among buildings surveyed (with the possible exception of Enator--see Chapter Eight). Normally saunas are included with showers and toilets adjacent to some sort of exercise space.

It is not entirely clear why the exercise rooms are not more popular, especially considering the general Swedish inclination for physical fitness. Certainly one reason could be the fact that rarely are these spaces given views or strong connections to exterior courtyards or landscape. Given the standard of an individual office and exterior window for each employee, it becomes difficult to rationalize view space for exercise, especially when basement space is generally available anyway. A more sociological or perhaps cultural reason might be that jogging or exercise is primarily an individual activity, or at least an activity done among a few friends. We return to the sense that solitary activities and friendship formation are largely antithetical to second order practice. Doing

237

things with friends, outside of the all important work groups, for example, seems to threaten the underlying social relationship of being an *arbetskamrat*.

These places do not seem appropriate for voluntary group activities which may compete with still evolving second order experience. It may be true that many voluntary activities occur, for this reason, away from the physical work setting. Sports groups often use public facilities elsewhere in the city; cultural clubs take trips; etc.. In sum, it could be that club activities in Swedish offices are in part a legacy of the workers' movement, processes more politically external to the social and functional organization of the actual work setting, and processes without their own internal "system" of second order spatial expression. With the evolution of the democratic office and built-in oppositions between the individual and collective, voluntary activities may be either antithetical or simply of little purpose, either social or political. It also may be that voluntary associations appear primarily under third order conditions, i.e. where some total socially based system of spatial expression is more the exception than the rule. The physical presence of the prevalent union *klubb* in Swedish industrial plants is probably territorial in its essence, standing as it at least used to (considering recent effects of co-determination laws) against the power of management. Logically, such territories cannot exist in second order places.

7.2 Individual rites of passage

In Scandinavian traditions or ethos,[1] individual changes in status were central to the definitions and continuity of the kinship based patriarchal farm. The passage of life, conceptually and ritually a movement from East to West in first order Norse cosmology (Doxtater 1981:124), began with the energy of the rising sun and birth, gathered most impact in the wedding at the center, and ended with ceremonies of death to the West. Much of this meaning continued into the second order *by* society, without perhaps the total ritual effect of consistent directional symbolism. Birth and marriage were strongly associated with the patriarchal family desire to maximize farm wealth through numbers of children and tacit alliance between other individual farms. Yet marriage was also the means of becoming a ritual member of the egalitarian community of farms. Death, while creating ancestors associated with particular farms, was more strongly significant in its effect of returning the mortal individual of the farm to the community of the all powerful other world. This is most evident in the communion rites where the body of the deceased was symbolically consumed by and reintegrated with community members. While the passage rituals of birth and marriage were also characteristically controlled by the community group, they nevertheless ultimately sanctioned these individual motivations essential to the maintenance of the farm and kinship group.

In many of the remote Norwegian valleys where first order meaning remained perhaps the longest, we have seen how the Reformation appears to have effectively moved these rituals from their ancient and highly symbolic setting of the domestic dwelling to the church site. It is not clear from existing studies if a similar phenomenon also occurred at the same time in the flatland *byar* which had much earlier become second order. In our discussion of the *fest* life of the Swedish *by*, we saw the strong folk association between the wedding and the major calendrical rite of *Midsommer*, a linkage also found in late accounts of first order Norwegian farm life. One suspects that this association was given much further emphasis in the closed, corporate second order communities. In many respects the wedding was the pivotal connection between the individual farm family and the collective community. Politically it was at the same time a means to family prosperity *and* community membership. When the major Norse calendrical and rites of passage were more or less fused with the life of Christ--in the church--two things were left out, the wedding (of Christ) and *Midsommer*. Thus, even though aspects of the *by* wedding would be held in the adjacent church, its ceremonial and associational link with exterior *by* spaces and *Midsommer* would naturally express indigenous second order ethos and practice. Baptism and funerals seem to have been more firmly located in the church, though vestiges of earlier dwelling ritual can be found in the folk culture of the *byar*.

During the period of industrialization and urbanization in Sweden, the wedding/*Midsommer* complex seems to have been associated with either the family (with its roots in some traditional farm place), or the *fest* activity of the workers' movement (which often took place in a *folk* park or open air museum). We find very little mention of these kinds of ritual activities in the context of either the historically patriarchal or the more recently democratic office society. A very strong tendency exists to celebrate *Midsommer* someplace else, preferably during vacation time with people from some common *by*-like setting, the location of one's *sommer stuga* (summer farmhouse). In today's urban Sweden, some weddings occur in churches, but a majority have no

239

significant ritual at all. People either live together in an institutionalized form of marriage called *sambo* (to live together), or they participate in a brief civil event. When Swedes discuss their religiosity they uniformly admit to a lack of general Church interest or attendance. When they explain the three times in one's life one does participate in such ritual--baptism, confirmation, and death-- the marriage rite is noticeably absent.

The only time during the interviews that individuals mentioned having some sort of a *fest* activity in association with either Church or kinship focused rites of passage was in the increasingly rare, small, totally female "family" groups of office workers. Two women, both relating experiences in data processing groups at the savings bank in Malmö and the construction firm of ABV, told about doing things similar to bridal or baby showers for girls in the office. When, for example the bride to be was dressed up in a comical costume and paraded through the streets, all members of the group were obliged to participate. None of these events, however, seem to have ever taken place *within* the increasingly second order office setting. Although it may be fairly common for fellow workers to "chip in" to buy a wedding present for one of their own, special *fests* within or outside of the office, or group attendance of church or civil rites, appears to happen infrequently, if at all.

Are there then, any, individual rites of passage which figure prominently in the *fest* life of Swedish offices? Are they controlled by the collective group? Unfortunately the existing records of the historical patriarchal office show little detail about the *fest* life of these family like groups. Were there stronger associations with actual Church and kinship rituals, such as in the above mentioned rites of passage? Or did the formal hierarchical structures of these offices create essentially new rites of passage to legitimize one's movement up the corporate ladder, a kind of emulation of the traditional patriarchal statuses celebrated in the farm family? One could imagine important rites associated with promotion to new levels of *tjänsteman* status. We see little evidence of any such separate *fests* in the patriarchal-become-individual aspects of today's second order setting. Such things may be less ceremoniously announced during some larger, perhaps annual corporate meeting. Though still including a traditional patriarchal aspect, the much more horizontal nature of the democratic office has diminished both the number of different statuses available, and their ceremonial importance as well. Exceptions still occur in an ongoing evolutionary process, e.g in the example of the thirty-year service *fest* at the home of one of the executives, figure 7.1.

It is probably true that the most important expression of the individual aspect of today's offices lies more in the personal office and its associated authority and responsibility than with any specific rites of passage. Within the larger Swedish society, the basic family unit and the church maintain basic responsibility for the more individually associated rites of passage. In this respect, along with the summer family celebration of *Midsommer*, the non-work sphere of society continues to be at least nominally associated with the traditional individual (family) aspects of Scandinavian culture. In contrast, at this largest scale of time and space, work places continue to increase their collective significance, especially considering the more recent democratization of white collar settings.

As office society becomes more and more complete, and includes and reintegrates both aspects of the ethos, it may tend to compete with or otherwise diminish the importance of domestic settings, as "family/patriarchical/individual" aspects in relation to collective work places, or as the sole successor to the historically complete *by* traditions.

Figure 7.1 *Fest* at *chef's* home for employees with thirty years of service, Länsstyrelsen

Some of this ambiguous tension between family and office spheres is felt in the one event, a kind of rite of passage, in which fellow workers of the normally very separate sphere of work actually go to an individual's home. While birthdays, particularly one's fiftieth, are strongly associated with the kinship side of things, they continue to be, or perhaps have more recently become the only rite of passage to be uniformly celebrated by Swedish offices. Some indication exists that in earlier patriarchal organizations, important *tjänsteman* birthdays were primary occasions for management to express their appreciation, usually in terms of some sort of gift. Yet we do not know the exact *fest* nature of such events, nor their relative importance. In virtually all of the contemporary offices interviewed, for one's fortieth and especially fiftieth, for example, donations for a sizable gift were solicited, often from the entire office. This suggests something of a shift in meaning of the gift, since it no longer expresses the employee's relationship with management, but with the office collectivity instead. We find some occasions in which the company still contributes. A bouquet of flowers seems to be a traditional gift from the company, and at the Lundafrakt trucking firm, the company invited the birthday person to cake and coffee.

Some work groups or smaller sections did recognize the common birthday years, usually with some sort of cake during the *pause*, as in the case of the small work group like situation at Lundafrakt. Yet there seems to be no *fest* activity within the building for major birthdays, even though the entire office may have contributed toward the gift. The pattern here is quite clear and probably revealing in terms of relationships between office and home. One stays home on one's fiftieth birthday! Someone from the office will then bring usually flowers and the gift to one's door. At Skogaholms bakery, one or two women make the delivery if the recipient was a woman, a couple of men if the birthday person was a man. Seldom is there any sort of *fest* to be celebrated within the individual's home, just as no major *fest* occurs within the office. It is almost as if the work sphere is recognizing two expressive aspects at the same time. The collection for the gift speaks of individual reward or "wealth" conferred through the collectivity; while the actual act of giving at the threshold of the home emphasizes or perhaps associates office patriarchality with the traditionally stronger patriarchality of the kin group. An interesting exception to this pattern occurred during the fortieth birthday of a woman in an *arbetsgrupp* at Länsstyrelsen. They bought a bottle of wine and took it to her house in the afternoon. In this case, all in the work group went, making a small *fest* of the occasion. The fact that the work group actually participated in a rare *fest* within the family dwelling may signify, in this case at least, a replacement of family group with office group, and again the ambiguous cultural tension between the two.

Somewhat similar to major birthdays, though with less patriarchal/individual significance, perhaps, are events associated with retirement, our final possible rite of passage to be considered. Was one's retirement an important *fest* occasion in the historical Swedish office, and how does one interpret the meaning of retirement in terms of evolving second order oppositions in today's offices? Earlier, meaning may have been more connected with the achievement of that last rung in the *tjänsteman* ladder, the recognition of years of dedication to the patriarchal group and the

242

sum of one's personal accomplishments. Even from our experience in other countries, one would here expect the usual gift as management's final reward for that ultimate status. Yet we do not specifically know what the actual *fest* activities were, where they took place, nor their significance to the larger patriarchal culture. In today's offices, much like major birthdays no large, formal *fest* occurs. The gift is now given by collecting donations from all the organization's employees. Like promotions, retirements will often be announced during annual business meetings.

Unlike major birthdays the gift is not taken to the individual's home. Thus when a person of long employment--and most are very long term members of these societies--we do find occasional small *fest*-like events held someplace in the building. At Skogaholm's bakery, a special table with cakes and flowers was set up in one of their large conference spaces. This "coffee" as it was called, was available for a couple of hours during the work day to employees on a drop-in basis. At the Malmö city building, Stadshuset, a somewhat larger *fest* event, including the major midday meal, was set up in a portion of the building restaurant. Only management personnel and the retiring employee were reported to be part of this event. This appears to be a remnant of strong patriarchal association. Given that many of the offices did not even have a small event such as these for one's retirement, suggests that what may have been an important earlier expression of the overall patriarchal office, has by now diminished considerably.

There has occurred what is probably an understandable shift in the nature of retirement celebration or activities. The new emphasis appears to be not the recognition of patriarchical/ individual status of retirement, but a much more collective social continuity with today's second order offices. In many of the organizations surveyed, retirement groups were found whose purpose was essentially the maintenance of horizontal social relations among the office's former employees. At the agricultural cooperative building of Tre Skåne, people began participating in these "club" activities at the age of fifty-five as a means of developing solidarity bonds which could be maintained after actual retirement as much as ten or more years later. The retirement club at the Malmö savings bank had as many as three or four *fests* during the year. In addition to their own club events, former employees are customarily invited to, and often given special seating places, at the major calendrical *fests* which will be discussed below. It is also logical, as was the case at the savings bank, that

243

these groups use the collective spaces of the office for their activities.

Retirement clubs are somewhat different than the other (voluntary) clubs in that their purpose more closely mirrors, and attempts to perpetuate, fundamental second order practice. Participation in retirement groups is voluntary, and not all are involved nor do all offices yet have such groups. Retirement clubs have no cross-cutting purposes. One participates not because of a special interest in sports or Culture, but because one wishes to continue to be a member of the social collectivity which underlies work organization. Again such purpose does not pose potential competition with mainstream second order patterns. These are not friendship groups ostensibly focused on special interests. It is simply the natural continuity of that purely social aspect of today's Swedish offices, and stands as good evidence of the essential independence of second order meaning from actual work activity, which nevertheless depends upon it.

7.3 *Middag* and the major *fests*

As in most societies, both traditional and contemporary, the sharing of food is a vital part of expressing one's membership in a particular group, whether the structure of the group is hierarchical or egalitarian. During traditional Scandinavian times, the principal meal at midday, was called the *middag*. This was the largest meal of the day, with lighter fare served during the early evening hours. *Middag* refers today to the family meal in the evening or any formal dinner, though in rural Norway, the term is still associated primarily with the midday meal. Yet in spite of this name shift, many Norwegian and Swedish schoolchildren and workers eat a very large meal at midday, which they now call *lunch*. Most of these meals are institutionally subsidized in one way or another.[2]

Stretching back to the early patriarchal offices, it has also always been the tradition for each localized office organization (building or buildings) to have its own restaurant for what more traditionally was called *middag* (as illustrated below in figure 7.2). The reader has already seen several examples in the offices thus far discussed. Two offices were found, ElectroSandberg and Lundafrakt, which were too small in number of employees to economically justify their own restaurants and staff. In virtually all offices, many times even when numbers are quite small, a very strong tradition exists to eat a large, major meal together as a total group at a place within the group's building or campus.[3]

244

Figure 7.2 Restaurants at Länsstyrelsen, Malmö (above), and SattControl, Lund (below)

245

The office restaurant, commonly called the *matsal* (dining room), appears to have moved during the democratic evolution from a position somewhere in the upper territorial reaches of the office building to a more open, internally "public" location. An additional aspect of the evolution of dining facilities was the relatively brief appearance of smaller, socially separate executive dining rooms. While exact data is unavailable for the early patriarchal buildings, the examples cited previously from Fredrik Bedoire (1979) and from surveyed buildings (Post Huset and Skånska Brand) suggests that at the time when *tjänsteman* status strongly characterized most office employees, no distinctions between executive and employee dining rooms were made. One fashionable dining room was used by all. Yet we know that as the numbers of office workers grew in Sweden, and the term *tjänsteman* became less and less exclusive during the twenty or thirty years prior to the beginning of the breakthrough, occasionally separate executive dining rooms were designed in some buildings.

Only one of the buildings in the present study had such an executive facility, the savings bank in Lund. Additionally, one of those interviewed at Tre Skåne remembered a dining room in a previous office building, prior to 1965, in which a portion of the large space was reserved for executives. They were served at their places, while the others ate cafeteria style. The rare executive dining room or other special treatment has become virtually extinct in Swedish offices built in the last twenty years. While smaller dining rooms in which to entertain special clients and guests exist today, no status distinctions are made as all levels of the organization commonly eat together, cafeteria style, in a usually large open *matsal* space. These are most often associated with the more "public", or as we will see second order and collective spaces of the building.

Although the costs of using the company restaurant are subsidized to a degree, eating a major meal together, often with most of the other workers, is clearly an institutionalized cultural event, a daily *fest* of sorts at the largest scale. Very few people ever eat quick sack lunches either alone in their offices, or with friends at one of the *pause* spaces. If, during the interview process, the author needed to continue after the dinner hour at midday, I would naturally be invited down to eat with those whom I happened to be with at the time. Like the institutionalized *pause fest*, the midday meal as well demands participation. This obligation, under possible threat of *mobbning* as mentioned earlier, would seem to be meaningful both on the scale of the entire office and that of the work group. The pattern is to sit with one's work group, or even larger localized group like a floor as section or department. One young office worker, just a couple of years out of school, felt that the compulsion to sit in work groups during *"lunch"* inhibited one from meeting new friends. This verifies that friendship formation is largely antithetical to institutionalized second order patterns.

Thus, if one were to meticulously map the seating patterns of Swedish office dining rooms through time, one would probably find a clear distinction between the patriarchal and the second order. During the patriarchal one probably sat, not so much with a work group, but with others of equal rank and tenure in the organization. In today's office restaurants, one sits with one's horizontal work group. Certainly eating the midday meal with one's closest *arbetskamrater* serves to promote the social solidarity so necessary to the actual democratic function of the work group. Yet compared to the two daily *pause fests*, as formally related to the work group offices as possible, the midday meal expression is certainly less explicit. The definition of work groups in the restaurant may have less to do with internal solidarity than of expressing the relation between the fundamental work groups and the total office organization. The large dining rooms, in this sense, become more explicitly macro-scale in their ability to express, better than any other place or event, the overall structure and solidarity of the organization. To this basic meaning of the Swedish office meal will be added other significance which comes from major *fest* activities in the restaurant and its spatial position relative to other spaces at this largest of scales.

7.4 Major yearly celebrations

Like the office meal, major yearly celebrations almost always involve a large collective *fest* dinner, often held in the same restaurant space. Architecturally such spaces are becoming more formally stated as part of the largest scale second order oppositions (between collective and individual entities). First, however, in considering the two major, traditionally opposed, Swedish rites of Christmas *(Jul)* and Midsummer *(Midsommer)* it becomes tempting to associate this scale of meaning with the largest scale relationship possible, i.e. that between the total office organization and the country of Sweden as an ethnic whole. In this scenario one can link the fact that the major office *fest* of the year is generally in the fall and/or winter with the mentioned reality that midsummer celebrations tend to occur apart, or perhaps even opposed, to the office at some country place with strong (second order) ethnic associations. Even though the same individuals do not participate in both rites, as would be the case in traditional first and second order societies, some such spatial logic may be actually effective at this largest scale of culture.

As the larger scale forms of contemporary office buildings in Sweden tend toward second order formality and practice, we will see the inclusion of major "exterior" spaces with which collective meanings are associated. We recall that following the probable historical second order internalization of natural ritual sites within the evolved *by* form, much of the collective rites, including *Midsommer*, then took place within the *by* itself--in spite of residual journeys out into the countryside during the celebrations. Today in Dalarna, for example, the *Majstång* (*Midsommer axis mundi*) stands permanently at a central open space within the *by* community. As these kinds of spaces develop in the office organization, will *Midsommer* events, even *Majstång* occur within the larger office complex as *"by"*? Will the present need for office workers to celebrate *Midsommer* out in the traditional country *by*-like place diminish correspondingly? Here it would seem that the traditional image of natural *Midsommer* setting, whether in city park or rural countryside, would have a powerful associational value, perhaps difficult for the new office buildings to match.

Today's midsummer rites are not the case of a family oriented summer event out in some *by*-like place opposed to the strictly work rite during the fall or winter in the city. Christmas (*Jul*) is still regarded as the primary calendrical event from a kinship point of view (Boholm 1983:157). In the old first and second order farm societies, *Jul* focused on the farm and hierarchical family while *Midsommer* expressed the collective association with the spirits at some natural site. One would logically expect a certain competition, at least during the patriarchal period of industrialization, between office and family dwelling. Both could be seen as expressively playing the hierarchical role, including a common emphasis on the winter events, in opposition to the collective summer rite out in the country. Since we have already mentioned accounts of present day competition between the family and office sphere, we might also suppose that both may still tend to be seen as opposed to the *Midsommer* experience.

We must remember that in the ancient Scandinavian scheme of things, the *Jul* rite was a kind of ritual death for the family and its master, with images of collective spirits invading the farm, displacing the occupants from the dwelling, and feasting at the ceremonial table. After Christianity finally managed to shift the

Figure 7.3 *Julbord* at 1800's farm exhibited in Skansen (Sjöquist 1964)

"death" ritual to Easter, at various periods of history in various parts of the North, what, then was the shift in meaning of the *Jul* rite which continued to have primary importance to the kinship group? We know of the new folklore which apparently accompanied the change, tales in which a hunter (a Christ figure perhaps) shoots the heathen spirits attempting to come down (invade) the chimney of the dwelling (Stigum 1971:178). The family is made safe from domination by ancient Norse collective spirits. But then what did the rite become? Was there a new meaning of *Jul* which undoubtedly became part of second order *by* practice? Probably not. We know that today *Jul* is still strongly associated with family, not collective meanings, as was the case in the second order *byar*. One only has to look at the rites as maintained in the open air museums, such as Skansen in Stockholm or Kulturen in Lund, to see that the wonderfully rich *Julfest* is focused on the family dwelling (see figure 7.3), while *Midsommer* takes place in the major outdoors space of the museum.

In second and third order times *Jul* has lost its effect as a kind of ritual death at the hands of the collectivity. It still at least represents the social bonds of the family vis-a-vis the community, though its ancient ritual effect of collective control is certainly gone. This representation may have been somewhat similar in the *by* and bourgeois city. With the intensity of daily life in the traditional *by*, and the frequent experience of expressive oppositions of the social and architectural form, one might think about the family

249

celebration of *Jul* as something which as much as anything identifies or reaffirms the patriarchal element in a very collectively controlled society. Rather than deflate the importance of the individual family, as occurred in first order *Jul* ritual at spatially distant farms, the effect in the *by* could have been much more of a strengthening of family definition. Such a provision of family identity and solidarity may also have been useful in the competitive arena of the urban bourgeois family. The patriarchal reaffirmation was perhaps not an attempt to maintain oneself in relation to the very strong collectivity, but to raise the power of the family to a level of greatest social, economic and political advantage over other families.

We can see the way in which the patriarchal Swedish office might have used *Jul* celebrations as such an affirmation of family (corporate) identity and competitive advantage.[4] Even in the more recently democratic organizations of today, the corporation competes on a daily and yearly basis with others. This could also be the emphasis of Christmas parties in corporations of other countries such as the U.S.. In Sweden one could see the *Jul* rites as primarily focused on the more traditional patriarchal meanings, whether this was in actual second order opposition to the Swedish *Midsommer* (a more uniquely Swedish experience), or more simply as a competitive response to others. In fact we will see aspects of both in the lengthy Advent Season which encompasses *Jul* celebrations in the office.

These large *fests* make logical sense at some larger scale, external to the actual office organization. Yet from within the corporation itself, and given the absence of *Midsommer* events internally, one would expect the largest scale *fest* to represent similarly the collectivity. This apparent paradox might be resolved by recognizing two, not one, kinds of *fest* which take place--though sometimes adjacent to one another--during the fall or winter period. In addition to the individual aspects of *Jul*, there often also appears the major, largest scale business meeting to which all are invited, as in the photo of figure 7.5. Though presently undocumented, it is likely that such gatherings of corporate members correspond to the democratization of office work. In still vertical corporations in the U. S., for example, while annual meetings of stock owners are institutional, it is difficult to find instances where the workers participate in such an event regardless of ownership.

If these yearly business meetings are in fact as they appear to be, more the expression of democratic participation than hierarchical

250

control, then we might again turn our associational process back to the second order Scandinavian society and the still well known annual meetings and ensuing *fest* of the cooperative farmers, discussed previously in Chapter One. Two of the offices surveyed, Lundafrakt (trucking) and Tre Skåne (agriculture), actually were cooperative organizations and therefore their annual meetings could be similar in meaning to those of the traditional *byar*, though certainly on a larger scale. Probably the large business meetings of the other offices visited tend toward this semantic as well.

Figure 7.4 Major business meeting, Wasa (Skånska Brand) Lund

According to the ethnographic record, the annual business meeting of the *by* farmers was held either in the spring or fall, with many of the Skånsk *byar* preferring the latter. Both temporal locations can make sense. The collective emphasis might either be associated with the collective Midsummer when both occur in the same timespace in Summer,[5] or might form a pair as a collective opposite to *Jul* in Winter, the timespace most associationally comfortable to offices in Sweden. In the interviews, at least one person from each office was asked to describe their major *fests*. All offices have at least two, and often three or more large events at the scale of the total organization. Of the calendrical *fests*, only one firm, Kontorsutvekling (computers), told of an annual *Midsommer*

251

fest out at some *gästgivargård* (a rural farm or manor house, historically an inn, which provides meals usually of a festive nature, as historically in figure 7.5). This group was particularly young, modern and small (about twenty). They not only had several annual *fests* but monthly events as well. All participated.

Figure. 7.5 Example of *gästgivargård* or traditional outdoors *fest* restaurant: "Rullan", Uppsala 1900 (Nordiska Museet)

In addition to yearly or calendrical *fests*, many will also hold large scale events for special anniversaries, introduction of new products, inauguration of new buildings, etc.. Skogaholms bakery, for example, had just celebrated their 60th anniversary at the Grand Hotel in Lund, perhaps *the* traditional *fest* hotel of the city center. People interviewed at the pharmaceutical firm of Draco told of their *fest* to announce a major new product. Held during the summer at a country park, the *fest* activities included dinner, games and other organized events. This appears to be a relatively rare occurrence of a major *fest* during the actual summer months. At the Ericcson electronics research laboratory in Lund--about which more will be said in Chapter Nine--when the two large project groups moved into the new building, one invited the other to an open house. The other group was to reciprocate the next year.

Påskkäring *fest* table at Draco

Figure 7.6 Examples of major *fests* in Swedish offices:Traditional Crawfish *fest* at Skånsk Brand (Wasa, above), Skånska Brand trip to Tivoli, Copenhagen (below)

Länsstyrelsen team: Malmö boat races

Figure 7.6 Examples of major *fests* (cont.): Skånska Brand *fest* in historic office dining room

While almost all other offices seemed reluctant to appropriate *Midsommer* many do find a way to hold some sort of large scale spring/summer event in addition of course to the typical business meeting and *Jul* in the opposite period. At the cooperative Lundafrakt, members (employees) participated in two yearly business meetings one in fall and spring. These would be held either at a restaurant or country inn (they have no large restaurant space of their own because of the small number of office workers and number of drivers not on site during midday). Here the greater cooperative functional need appears to require two rather than just one major meeting.

At K-Konsult (municipal or *kommun* design and engineering services) the entire building was invited and most participated in a spring excursion to Copenhagen. Also having a *fest* during the same season, and also going to Copenhagen, was a large section of the central post office in Malmö. This section of about fifty organized as well a spring dinner-dance. An engineering section of about eighty, and another mostly female computer group, both at ABV (national and international construction) also had their own major *fests*, one of which would be in the spring. The specific locations and types of events in this case would vary from year to year. Nevertheless, some major spring *fest* would be quite likely to occur, usually associated, as in other cases, with a trip away from the office building, or to a place with natural characteristics.

7.5 A "Winter" sequence of Business Meeting, *Lucia*, and *Jul Fests*

While the present research was not extensive enough to statistically document each *fest* for a significant number of offices, at least an intuitive pattern seemed to suggest a link between the fall business meeting and the traditional events of *Jul*, including Santa Lucia's Day. In a fluid and evolving context of largest second order office rites, such a pattern may not yet be at the level of even an ethnic ideal in the minds of office workers. Given the still externally strong definition of corporation as patriarchal-become-individual and the corresponding limitations of participation in *Midsommer* rites, the late fall and Christmas period probably statistically could be proven as the most frequent time for *the* major office *fest*. Within this larger constraint, really at the scale of overall Swedish society, the democratization of work has created an almost equally strong collective necessity to meet and celebrate at this same time of the year.

The case of ElectroSandberg (electronics applications) provides a somewhat special but perhaps illustrative example. Recall that some of the employees on site are white collar (*tjänstemän*), while others assemble products and might still be called in distinction blue collar *(arbetaren)*; both groups are well trained and probably paid about equally. Prior to a recent merger with another but smaller electronics firm, the *Jul* celebration for all employees was described as having been traditionally organized by the *arbetsgiver* (employer), in this case the long time founder and patriarch from whence came the firm's name. Both the retirement of the company founder and the merger had created a sensitive question about who or how the *Julfest* would be organized. To this ambiguity about the calendrical winter event, exists additional uncertainty about the other major *fest* which occurs a month or so earlier in the fall. People said that they would be having a *Jul Kaffe*. While *Jul* was strongly individual, the fall dinner dance was strongly collective in that this was, and ostensibly still is, the major event organized by the union or worker's *klubb*. Sometime also in the recent past, as the office employees became more democratic, these *tjänstemän* began to participate in this *klubb fest*, formerly for *arbetare* (perhaps in the absence of a true Fall Meeting).

Thus we see a recent evolution, not so much of the actual meaning of the individual *Jul* and collective Fall Meeting *fest*, but of the participants and the way in which the events are organized. One has the impression that the earlier *Jul* expressed very clearly the hierarchical relation between the patriarch and his "family"; whether this focused primarily on *tjänstemän*, not *arbetare*, one can only speculate. On the collective side of things, the earlier *klubb fest* may have been equally exclusive, expressing primarily the solidarity of worker vis-a-vis the company. At ElectroSandberg, what form will this evolution of calendrical ritual finally reach? One might predict that the patriarchal-become-individual aspects of *Jul* will not wither completely but reemerge. They will become an expression, not of hierarchical relationships between a family of *tjänstemän*, but of the company's competitive relationship and identity within the larger sphere of Swedish corporate culture. The collective Fall *fest*, on the other hand, may continue to move away from its historical union connotations to something more akin to the cooperative meeting/*fest*. The discursive distinctions between *tjänstemän* and *arbetare* will dissolve as all employees participate equally in both events. Connected by a relatively short time period, the two calendrical rites may form an effective pair, expressing both traditional aspects of second order society.

The pharmaceutical firm of Draco provides perhaps the best example of the way in which these two events, with their opposed meanings, can be paired together. Here both events, while occurring in different places, happen on the same day in Mid-December. At one o'clock in the afternoon all members of the large administration, research, and manufacturing site in Lund conduct a huge business meeting of four to five hundred people. The company leases an auditorium in an adjacent complex of the University of Lund. At three o'clock, after a short "coffee", all go home to prepare for the evening dinner dance which begins at seven. This event, referred to as the *Jul* dinner, takes place in Draco's own, new restaurant building, large enough to accommodate the midday meal for all members as well as the major calendrical rite of *Jul*. More will be said below about Draco's *Jul* event and its excellent *fest* facility. Presently, it might be noted that this apparently well evolved fusion of the collective and patriarchal may correspond to a longer period of assimilation of *tjänstemän* and *arbetare* among *Draco's* highly skilled employees or members. It may also be the case that in such situations of mixed membership, not unlike at ElectroSandberg, a clearer pattern evolves.

Finally, before leaving the Fall Meeting portion of what might become an ideal cultural pattern, one must mention situations in which no such cooperative business event occurs. From the interviews at the regional tax office, central post office, and city building (all in Malmö), it seems that public sector organizations may not be autonomous enough to make such general meetings meaningful. While conceptually the workers of these offices might associate themselves with the broader public or community they ultimately serve, in reality there always exists the structural separation between (bureaucratic) employees and elected decision makers, whether on city, regional or national scales. Thus it may be that public office places, though achieving second order expression on smaller particularly work group scales, really cannot create the elaborate, ideal larger scale expression one finds in private organization, at least in terms of the Fall Meeting.

In addition to structural separation between bureaucrat and elected representative, one also sees in the two federal functions an actual physical separation within the bureaucratic portion itself, i.e. some higher executive powers are of course located in Stockholm. Logically such a physical separation would impede some largest scale second order evolution, both in public and even private organization. Some branch or regional offices may be quite autonomous, such as in the example of the quasi-private K-Konsult where each regional office functions with considerable independence, especially when it comes to programming, designing, and building its own place. Though even here its quite recent *smårumskontor* form may represent a certain second order lag at the largest scales. Other examples may exist in which the parent office keeps the reigns comparatively tight, though such a case did not appear in the present research. In any more comprehensive and detailed study of our subject, one would certainly have to carefully consider the effect of physical separation on second order processes.

7.6 *Lucia*

The *Jul* or Christmas season begins formally in Sweden with the first Sunday of Advent early in December (four Sundays before the 25th). This is the time when homes, communities, and offices put up their decorations. Aside from the supposedly largest church attendance of the year, which certainly does not mean even any large minority of Swedes, the first event celebrated by most takes place on December 13th, St. Lucia's Day. This is the time of winter solstice as marked in the Middle Ages' Julian calendar. The shift to

257

our current Gregorian timetable corrected the solstice time to somewhere around the twenty-second which is more associated with today's celebration of Christ's birth. In spite of the 13th's dedication in the new Christian calendar to St. Lucia of Syracuse, Scandinavian folklore quickly reveals far greater indigenous Norse solstice meanings linked to this date, both during the Middle Ages and after. To a certain extent, after the calendrical correction moved the time of Christ's birth, the 13th became more exclusively indigenous, forming a clearer contrast with the Christian solstice date.

Figure 7.7 Lucia parade at Länsstyrelsen (left) and Lucia chorus for employees at Lund Sparbank (right)

While very little of the actual ritual effect of the ancient *Jul* invasion of the dwelling by the spirits remains, the symbolic death of hierarchical family mentioned earlier, today's events of *Lucia* contain the strongest echo of the Norse winter solstice. Not unlike the bringing of the natural *axis mundi* as fir tree into the architectural dwelling, Lucia as well involves the concept of a visit from Nature. Instead of an entourage of fearful spirits from the other world, sometime during the last centuries the characters changed dramatically. Today, partially due to a 1920's revitalization of this "new" form (which is known to have existed in the late eighteenth century), the object and leader of the visiting beings is a young girl, dressed in a white gown with a crown of candles in her hair. She is followed by similarly clad girls and boys, though without crowns. Sometimes boys will also play the part of *tomte* (elf) figures dressed like gingerbread men.

258

Some such visit occurs in virtually all Swedish homes, schools, clubs, etc., and especially for our present interests, in offices. At the historical Lund Sparbank in the city center, for example, the photographs of figure 7.7 represent the climax of the sequence in the visit by the young entourage. Lucia, in this case, was the daughter of one of the bank personnel; the rest of the group were her elementary school classmates. They costumed in one of the conference rooms, then paraded while singing into the main floor teller area. All transactions stopped in the large public space for fifteen or twenty minutes during which the children sang several songs, including the melodic St. Lucia itself. Then, singing traditional songs, they wove their way through the office spaces of the upper floors (which had been prestigious apartments during the first decades of the century). Of course personnel stopped and watched, then assembled in the restaurant dining room to hear the final numbers by the visitors. Afterwards, all shared in the traditionally made *Lucia Katter*, shaped saffron rolls, with coffee and other drinks for the children.

Virtually all of the other offices surveyed celebrated some such variation of this visit by Lucia. At Skogaholms bakery, of course, their "homemade" rolls were available all day long, in a kind of ongoing *Lucia Fest*. In one report, the personnel themselves dressed up in the appropriate costumes and paraded through the office. At SattControl the *Lucia* for the entire organization--both *kombi* wings included--was organized each year by new employee members hired the preceding year. In something of a pattern, the recent arrivals at Länsstyrelsen were responsible for the major *Jul* fest. The interviews clearly defined *Lucia* as one event which was exclusive to the largest of scales. No indication appeared that smaller sections or much less work groups might organize their own *Lucia* procession (can the visiting spirits only be ritually invoked by the largest scale of collectivity?). The research complex called Ideon (the plans of which will be discussed in Chapter Nine) provides an interesting example of just how far this concept of "one place, one *Lucia*" might be taken. Consisting of several large national and international research companies within a mall-like architectural setting near Lund University, the administration of Ideon organized one very large *Lucia* for all. Traditional food and drinks followed in the large, common restaurant.

In contrast to the ancient powerful ritual impact of the visit by spirits from the other world, today's *Lucia* evokes no such effect. It appears to be more of an indigenous Norse prelude to the much more lengthy, elaborate and socially significant *Jul Fest* itself. One might attempt to see patriarchal or familial overtones in that Lucia is traditionally the oldest daughter of the "family", who in a sense portrays herself. The chosen Lucia does not consciously represent any particular being from the spirit world (Lucia manifestations in older folklore express an opposite, negative, "black" meaning). It is however established that in the old folk culture, things associated with unmarried daughters (the "female", Eastern direction on the first order farm) were strongly connected with the farm's wealth and well-being, either through the symbolism of fertility or the reality of political alliance.

Dare one speculate, then, that the Lucia visit today captures some of that old ritual meaning which occurred as the bride moved in procession from her position in the East to the central place of the domestic dwelling to the West? Does the *Lucia* procession through the office evoke, at least minimally, feelings of "family" good fortune and alliance, just as during the folk wedding? It is interesting that the ritual return from the other world during the wedding--a kind of *Lucia*-like procession in white coming from nature--would have declined about the same time that Christianity was also displacing the significant visitation effect of the Norse *Jul*. Some such patriarchal or familial meaning might still underlie the widespread popularity of *Lucia* in its context of "individual" social places such as homes, schools, clubs, and offices.

7.7 *Jul*

Across Sweden, the composite *Jul* events of Advent, *Lucia*, *Julafton* (Christmas Eve), Christmas Day, and Knut's Day (a week after Twelfth Night) clearly form the most important major calendrical ritual node of the year. The same is true in offices, even excluding the cooperative business meeting. The total *fest* time and energy spent in Swedish organizations, in comparison to Christmas office parties in the U. S., for example, is large indeed! In addition to at least some sort of recognition of the other composite events just mentioned, virtually all Swedish offices celebrate the *Jul* event with an elaborate formal dinner *(middag)*, often including a dance. This largest scale office event is held within the workday calendar and does not openly compete with the family *Jul* celebration on the 24th and 25th. The separation between the two *Juls* is made more complete by the exclusivity of participation. Office friends are not brought home to be part of the family *Jul*, conforming perhaps with ancient meanings,[6] while at the same time spouses are rarely invited to the *Jul* dinner-dance of the office.

Besides this *fest* at the largest scale of membership, many sections or departments feel obliged to organize their own *middag/fest* event at some other time. It seems desirable for all *Jul fests*, at whatever scale, to take place within the corporate site itself. This remains consistent with the traditional *Jul* focus on the familial dwelling. If the office is too small, or an on-site facility is not available as in the case of Lundafrakt, the *Jul* event will be held at a commercial restaurant or *fest* locale.

The significance of *Jul* activities to office societies was made particularly vivid by the author's interviews at several different sites during this special time of the year. The description of the *Lucia* visit at the Lunds Sparbank came from a particular arrangement to be present for the event. At Skogaholm's commercial bakery, two delightful women were interviewed in the middle of their planning and decorating for the *Jul Fest*. With Advent candles and wreaths already placed throughout, we sat in the more senior woman's office (she was the personnel director) eating cakes and drinking coffee as we talked. With enthusiasm and pride they described the traditional *Jul Bord* (Christmas Table) to be set up in the center of the company dinning room. All the traditional *Jul* foods create the *smörgåsbord* which includes among many other items, hams, jellied pig's feet, marinated fish, special breads and drinks. In addition to the smaller tables, a special long table for retired members of the organization presides over one side of the space. My informant said that, "all the retired workers come". Together again with their work "family", both present and past members were said to *gå til bords* (literally "go to the table" or generally to participate in a *middag* or *fest*).

At the much larger Åkerlund & Rausing (manufacturing of packaging) the author was invited to participate in a similar *Jul* dinner, also in their on-site dining facility. Unlike the somewhat more formal event at Skogaholms, here the *Jul* dinner took place at the same time of the normal midday meal, with people participating as they typically would. The primary difference was the traditional *smörgåsbord* food and drink on specially set up tables. The typical distribution of tables, size of the space, and normal variance of particular employee's meal times precluded any speeches or other formalities, which is surprising considering that at any formal Swedish meal, speeches, usually including a *tacktal* or thank you speech, are always in order. Nor was this the case at the smaller Skogaholms affair, where speeches were kept to a minimum. It is interesting that at both of these sites, where the

261

Jul coffee in administration *arbetsgrupp*

Jul Fest

Jul Dance in lobby of Länsstyrelsen building

Figure 7.8 Scenes from Jul celebrations at the federal tax building, Länsstyrelsen, Malmöhus Läns.

much more numerous plant or *arbetare* portion is still somewhat less skilled and "blue collar" than in other higher tech industries, that the *Jul* dinner is still essentially a *middag* (as it is Christmas day among the family) rather than an evening dinner-dance. Yet the more elaborate and perhaps bourgeois simulation of "the grand ball" is not limited to or even ubiquitous in all purely white collar organizations.

The pharmaceutical firm of Draco provided both the fourth opportunity to observe these events first hand, and an example of a composite organization (of both office and plant) which creates a very elaborate dinner-dance event. In this case the *fest* may have actually been influenced by the recent construction of an independent on-site restaurant/collective place. The first indication of this probable second order relationship between space and ritual-like events, is the common understanding of Draco membership that the new building was a *Jul* gift for having worked so well. It was to this place, after the afternoon business meeting at an adjacent university site that some two-hundred-ninety spouseless members came for dinner and dancing that evening. Only about one-fourth of the total number of personnel, four hundred, did not participate.

By comparison to the *middag* (midday meal) event at Åkerlund & Rausing, this was indeed a formal affair. After a lottery process determined who would sit at each of the eight-person tables throughout the large space, one person was designated "host" for each table. Thus the normal work group pattern of eating the midday meal together in this same facility was broken up. During the serving, the duty of the host was to make certain that all were well taken care of in terms of food and wine. A conscious attempt was made to distribute men and women as equally as possible at each table. Perhaps because of a larger overall number of women than men, when the seating lottery created a group which was predominantly women, these were placed at the smaller round tables in the center of the dining space. Male executives or *chef* were then selected to join these groups, one per table. One of the single women interviewed in this organization remarked that she thought it was a very good idea not to invite spouses; she felt the single girls in particular would be left out otherwise.

The lack of invitation of spouses to the *Jul* rite at Draco might at first appear to be (symbolically) logical considering the patriarchal meanings of the event in Sweden. These dinner-dance relationships between men and women are not part of the second order oppositions which found the daily work life, but seem to want to create a kind of fictive kinship or family image *within* the office. Yet this behavior is not exclusive to *Jul*, as spouses stay home from many other events with similar kinds of connotations. The only possible explanation, it would seem, lies in the demonstrated probability that more traditional male-female distinctions are still quite strong in Sweden. Together with this family based meaning is the additional probability that much of the old second order expression occurred primarily within an exclusively male arena. Thus while second order organization has hypothetically reappeared in Swedish office societies, traditional male-female meanings among mixed personnel remain somewhat enigmatic. More highly educated and career oriented women seem to be more or less fully participating in these reemergent second order systems, playing strong roles of individuals and at least group leaders. At the same time more family oriented women with less background may still evoke more traditional male-female images, both within themselves and the men with whom they work. It may be that many of the women at the special Draco *Jul* tables fall under this latter characterization, though the present study cannot pretend to suggest firm answers here.

The "male-female" aspects of the Draco evening were by no means the dominant impression of the total event. Even though the tables were mixed, both in terms of daily work groups and sex, it appears to have been more of a "family" atmosphere with little if any emphasis on particular couples. While actual romantic affairs happen in Swedish offices as well as anywhere else, even the dancing seldom would show indications of special relationships between particular pairs. The intention is to dance with everybody. Place this atmosphere together with short speeches during dinner, and a performance by the Draco women's choir (a seemingly rare *klubb* activity in the organization), and the overall *Jul Fest* falls into its proper perspective. A minor male-female aspect nicely fuses with the larger patriarchal, "cultural" (bourgeois) connotations of the night.

Elaborate as the Draco dinner-dance was, it still does not conclude the larger *Jul* season in the office which also has included the Advent decorations, the visit by Lucia, and the business meeting, not to mention many smaller scale *Jul* fests in sections or departments. The final event in which all members are invited, interestingly enough, specifically includes both spouses and children. Immediately after people return to work after the actual calendrical *Jul* (25th), the firm re-creates the traditional taking down of the tree (*Julgran plundering*) as a *fest*, again in the community building. The focus of this event is on the children, with most of the activities especially designed for their enjoyment. Drinks, coffee and cakes complete the affair.

Although this has only been a limited example of how a few offices celebrate *Jul*, the visitor is left with the clear impression that the composite Christmas is not only a major event in Sweden, but in these work organizations as well. Taken together with all the other *fest* activities of the year, beyond the extensive daily expressions of *arbetsgrupp pause* and larger midday meal, one is truly impressed with the importance Swedish organizations place on the purely socio-cultural basis of their work life. Recalling one senior woman's remark that few *fests* were held in the older, exclusively patriarchal offices of her father's time, the impression is that much of today's behavior is directly linked to the recent second order re-establishment of a more complete, *by*-like society in these organizations. Both the individual and collective seem to be again reaching a fuller and more balanced practice. Our remaining task is to show how particularly the larger scale rituals may be expressively framed by recent evolutions of architectural form.

Notes

1. The author admits to a degree of ambiguity in the use of the term "ethos". On the one hand the central argument centers on the necessity of spatial setting as expressive "frame" for actual ritual practice, yet on the other one must allude to symbolic meanings which exist more generally in non-localized, non-practice forms in this modern yet traditional society. It may be that a kind of "cosmic dust" exists in the debris of very ancient first and even second order expressive space (remnants of the "big bang" of modernization). These symbolic remnants will have inherent spatial connotations, but remain essentially unorganized into actual, effective ritual systems. Their meanings become available to third order or discursive processes at non-localized scales. Clearly these meanings are still generally effective in terms of actual behavior, as evident in Daun's description of national character (1989). The fact that Daun does not mention any spatial basis to these still effective expressive processes raises many questions for future research. The largest one is whether in fact spatial connotations exist in national or non-localized "character".

2. Offices will either have their own restaurants, where meals are discounted, or primarily in cases where organizations are too small to afford their own facilities, they will issue reduced price coupons for employees to eat in public restaurants. This system is managed by the (federal?) government! It appears that companies are given tax credits for providing meals themselves, and that the coupons are similarly subsidized by the government. Private restaurants will display small decals on their windows communicating that they will accept these coupons. Virtually all do.

3. In one small Icelandic office of only thirty to forty employees situated in the center of Reykjavik, an entire floor of the small tower like five story building was dedicated to their restaurant and what was for many the major meal of the day. Iceland was not systematically included in the survey, but staying in Reykjavik three days during a trip back to the U.S., the author had the opportunity to visit this office.

4. Yet a woman close to retirement at the Malmö central post office--reinforcing Conradson's previously cited evidence--said that there weren't many *fests* in the time of her *tjänsteman* father. Whether this included *Jul* or not was not specified.

5. According to the ancient first order conceptions of space and time, during the month of April the seasons shifted from Winter to Summer. Each season's apex lay with the major solstice rites, respectively *Jul* and *Midsommer*. First order dwelling orientation was keenly associated with the East-West direction. The old Icelandic month corresponding to April was called the "cuckoo month", i.e. when the cuckoos returned from the South. In terms of the Icelandic and probable Viking spatial conception of the months of the year, the cuckoo month

was located directly East (also with associations of birth, renewal, etc.). The top most log of the gable ends of first order Norwegian dwellings, which gave the roof peak its East-West orientation, was called *gauken* (the cuckoo). Cuckoo clocks are undoubtedly a legacy of this important ritual meaning associated with dwelling orientation.

6   It was specifically prohibited to *fest* beyond the family scale in the old folk *Jul*. If one was caught out journeying to another's farm for such a non-family *fest*, he or she would be in imminent danger of being taken to the other world by the entourage of northern spirits, who were themselves visiting the farms. Or when King Olav of the saga periods was making his way across Sweden during *Jul*, he was refused lodging at a farm presumably for the same reason (see Doxtater 1981:184).

8 Largest Scale Oppositions

8.1 "Collective" Restaurant : "Individual" Office Building

When Draco's membership goes to its restaurant daily for the midday meal or yearly for *Jul* and other events, they do not simply take the nearest most task efficient route to a central location within the office structure itself, as may have been the case in patriarchal and early democratic buildings.   They leave one kind of architectural domain and clearly go to another.   Were it not for several other examples of Swedish office restaurants being sited separate from the actual office spaces, one might simply argue that Draco's separate building (the Christmas gift to the membership) is so because it serves not only office workers, but also a larger number from other buildings with laboratory/plant functions.   It is suggested here that this plan separation, not unlike the evolution of the *arbetsby* form, creates a much greater expression of the largest scale opposition between individual *smårumskontor* and the collective *restaurang*. If the primary purpose of formally separating the two architectural aspects is expressive, then one would suppose a heightened ritual like effect as people move, rather formally, from the one kind of space to the other.

This presumably effective architectural articulation of second order principles might as yet be too simple to fully express all aspects of large scale work and *fest* activity. At the scale of the work group we saw the clear need to establish not one but two spaces expressive of collective aspects of the group, *sammanträde* and *pause* places. In spite of the fact that the *arbetsby* form somewhat diminishes the formal spatial and architectural distinctions between the two, cooperative work needs to be distinguished from collective socialization. Do similar distinctions want to occur at the largest second order scales of Swedish offices? The yearly business meet-

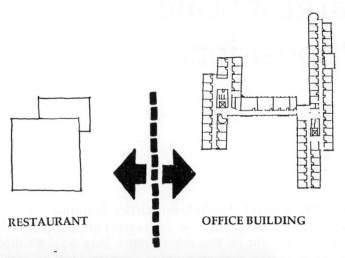

RESTAURANT   OFFICE BUILDING

Figure 8.1 Draco office
building and restaurant
(above), with interior
view of restaurant
building

ing at Draco was not held in its new collective restaurant/recreation facility. It is true that the university auditorium really was more efficient for the meeting. Yet it also may be that such activity would not associationally fit in the restaurant setting which clearly has much more social activities as its primary expressive purpose. The yearly business meeting in the traditional *by* took place outdoors, in the *by* common, while many of the smaller collective *fests* occurred inside one of the member farms. The large Midsummer rite was of course held in the central, "natural" space of the *by*.

In the present architectural examples, while we are beginning to see interesting and effective second order practice, the process may either not be complete or perhaps possible in the layout of

268

contemporary offices. How difficult is it to find an example in which the firm has built two collective spaces at the largest of scales, one for business, the other for *fests* or social ritual? While daily usage of the restaurant largely legitimates its costs, any major meeting space is more difficult to justify by its much more infrequent use. Yet from a more symbolic than functional point of view, we might begin to look at the separation of restaurant from *smårumskontor* as not just the creation of one kind of collective space, but perhaps also a tendency toward a second as illustrated in figure 8.2. It may not be just separation providing expressive meaning, but also association of the collective with exterior, natural environments or spaces. As these restaurants and some meeting spaces pull themselves apart from the linear office blocks, they also create much stronger links with Scandinavian meanings of Nature. While one cannot envision any sort of large scale collective meetings being held today in some outside space, one can find historical precedents (see again figure 2.6).

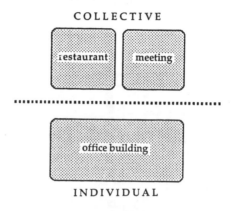

Figure 8.2 Spatial logic of largest scale second order opposition between paired collective entities (Fest and Meeting) and "individual" office building

Within this collective pole at present, there may be certain ambiguities over just what kinds of events belong. The daily midday meal stands as the large scale equivalent to the work group *pause*, with similar formal overtones of ritual practice. But what about *Jul*, with its patriarchal/individual associations? The traditional *middag* itself could traditionally either be expressive of the patriarchal, e.g. during family meals including *Jul*, or of the collective, e.g. during meals shared by member farmers of the *by*. While some of the major collective *fests* were held outside, especially *Midsommer*, others took place within the farmsteads. Is it likely that when one sits down to eat the daily meal in the large office restaurant, that the informal layout of tables maintains the collective, egalitarian expression? During *Jul*, to the contrary, the common sometimes nighttime orientation to a "front" speaker-entertainment area may create the opposite hierarchical sentiment. Would the midday orientation to exterior spaces also contrast to the nighttime focus on the interior and front of the architectural space, providing greater associational distinction to these two kinds of events? Are these indications that within the largest collective space on the site one may begin to look for architectural and landscape manifestation of both kinds of *fests*?

The opposition of K-Konsult's linear office block to its separate collective building, figure 8.3, provides a second example, but for a somewhat smaller, totally white collar organization. This formalism is clearly stated as one enters the enclosed space between the two very different domains. To the west is the office portion with its reception area. Spatially opposed to the east lies the collective functions. While the dining space does face a large natural portion of the suburban site, through a glass wall to the south, the formally defined collective form is clearly the building itself, not some exterior space. What is very interesting here, however, is the division of the collective building into two aspects, the restaurant and a large conference room for up to 110 people (about the size of office membership). Not unlike the formal distinctions be-

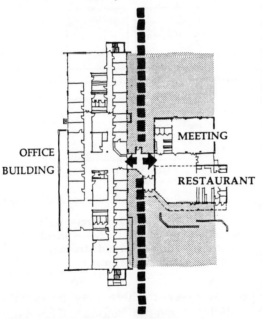

Figure 8.3 Second order oppositions between office building and restaurant/meeting: K-Konsult, Lund

tween *sammanträde* and *pause* rooms on each floor of the office building, we thus find a largest scale, second order equivalent *within* the collective entity. In the case of K-Konsult, the economics of the large meeting space is justified by renting the room periodically to Lund's Kommun (the city/county administrative unit) for educational purposes.

270

Formally very similar, two large offices in outlying areas of Stockholm provide an even greater drama of a separate collective place in association with the natural setting. Return to the striking linear form of IBM's (1978) executive building in the industrial park of Kista, Stockholm's "silicon valley" (figure 8.4 below and figure 3.1 earlier). One approaches the complex through the quintessential Stockholm landscape of fir trees and gigantically sculpted rock outcroppings. The vehicular and primary pedestrian entry is almost identical to that of the much more modest K-Konsult, though the visitor does not actually enter the internally used "ritual" bridge between individual linear offices and collective unitary restaurant/meeting.

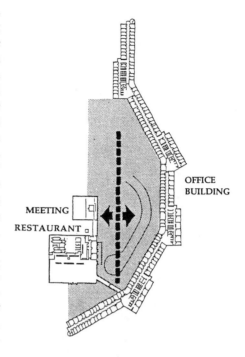

Figure 8.4 Opposition between office building and restaurant/meeting domains at IBM, Stockholm (plan redrawn from Arkitektur 79:4, pg.16)

While the restaurant is strongly in the natural landscape of the site, the focus is still on the architectural form of the collective place. At IBM one has a much stronger impression of going "through" nature to get to the restaurant. The curved linear form, along with the glass enclosed bridge, creates this expressive contribution to the opposition. The low profile of the collective building lies very much at the human scale of the underforest, while the five story office form weaves through the tree foliage above. In the collective place, we again see a rather formal subdivision into two entities, more like Draco this time, as restaurant and recreation.

In another new outlying area of Stockholm, Rissne i Sundbyberg, we see a fine opposition in an office complex very similar to IBM in scale and even layout. Its name is taken after the new neighborhood designation in which it is located, Lädmakaren, see figure 8.5. The restaurant, which can accommodate 750, lies similarly separated by a strip of nature which runs between it and the linear, six-story *smårumskontor* building. The Lädmakaren complex built in 1983 appears to create a more formal exterior space between the two opposed places. It is, however, primarily a parking area (the upper level of three). The views from the restaurant face not into this parking lot, nicely landscaped though it may be, but out to the other side and the larger valley below. Thus the pattern remains quite similar to the examples mentioned above. The focus is on the collective building itself, not the exterior space, though restaurant lies strongly *within* Nature. This primarily architectural opposition between the two places is further confirmed by the contrasting images of both. The horizontal window bands of the seven story office structure speak of rows of individual rooms inside. The pitched roof forms of the single story collective restaurant resemble more the integrated landscape form of dwelling or other farm building.

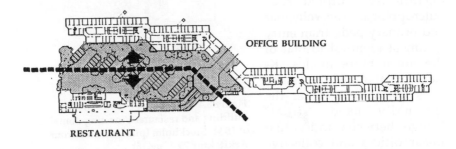

OFFICE BUILDING

RESTAURANT

Figure 8.5 Separate and opposed restaurant and office building, Lädmakaren (from Arkitektur 84:1: pg. 29)

In addition to the clear oppositional pattern which Lädmakaren gives us at the largest of second order scales, it also provides an important case in point to the present research. Lädmakaren, unlike most of the other examples of this book, is a speculative enterprise, not built to be owned by the occupants. Its complete conformity of layout to second order practice in Swedish offices--at both work group and largest scales--is in itself verification of the pervasiveness, the ethnicity, of the pattern. Across private, public, owner occupied and even speculative situations, the evolution of second order form remains essentially a Swedish phenomenon, not the unique invention of particular corporations or even designers.

8.2 Exterior *gård* (atria)

In the four examples just discussed, the formal play between linear office and restaurant-in-the-landscape depends upon the precondition of a generous site. In more constraining urban conditions, the mandate for individual window rooms tends to create, in the larger linear form, one or more exterior atria-like spaces (as we have seen in some of the offices of Chapter Five). In many cases one does not know, from the form itself, whether these are *de facto* atria, or whether such represent the actual expressive formation of largest scale second order space. One indication may be the relationship between restaurant and defined exterior space. If the view from the dining space focuses on the atrium or atrium-like exterior, then we begin to see a more purposeful association of collective meaning.

The tightly composed plans of figure 8.6 might be taken to be a definition of work groups, not unlike the *kombi (arbetsby)* form. Yet looking closer, one recognizes that the collective center spaces really are not functionally or expressively useful. These small exterior atria are essentially the byproduct of what the designer must do to maintain the *smårums* principle without creating a building a mile long. Internally, the concept is that of any typical *smårumskontor*. The dates of these offices just precede or are coterminous (1978-80) with the development of the *kombi* idea and *arbetsby* form. These *de facto* atria neither create expressively positive spaces at smaller scales, nor in two of the cases at least, VBB and Oxen Större, is there any visual relationship between restaurant and any particular atrium. Of course both offices exist in a very tight urban context, one in Göteborg (VBB), the other in Stockholm (Oxen Större). In both situations, the *smårums* configuration is applied to upper levels of the structure, leaving lower street levels for parking, storage, shops, and in both cases, the office restaurant. Exterior atria spaces only occur above. Originally the zoning for the Oxen Större site allowed and assumed that a multi-level open landscape office would fill in this vacant space in the Stockholm inner core. In the mid 1970's, however, the Salén corporation actually replanned its proposal to reflect the more current *smårum* idea (Landberg, et. al. 1979:2).

Strange as it may seem, the upper example, though even more tightly composed in plan than these other two, actually was laid out on a generous suburban site. There are only two levels to this office building for Swedish Geological Research (Uppsala). Inside, the continuous linearity receives little articulation as to work group or even simple wayfinding orientation. Although the central corridor has special *pause* spaces along it with views directly into the atria (on the first floor only), it is still just one of the many corridor spaces in the building. One finds no major two story articulation of

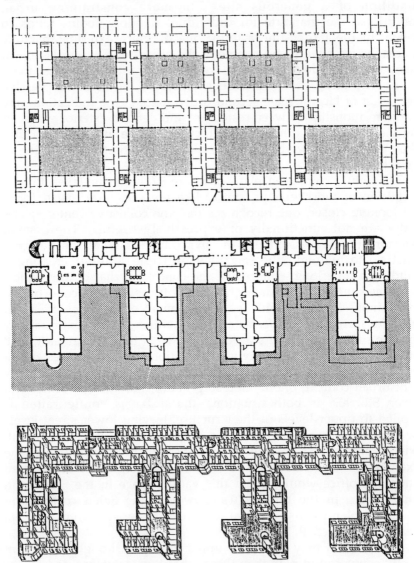

Figure 8.6 *Smårumskontor* on limited sites which create atria: SGU (top, from Arkitektur 79:4, pg.9), VBB (middle, from Arkitektur 82:8, pg.29), Oxen Större (below, from Arkitektur 79:1, pg.7)

any largest scale common area. The restaurant is given a place of some prominence in its association with one of the typical atrium spaces, opened up to create the building's major entry. Yet from the perspective of the daily use of the interior spaces, the restaurant expresses no strong expressive opposition to the rest of the building.

At the Stadshuset in Malmö (discussed previously in Chapter Five, figure 5.12) the facilities executive himself proudly showed the author through the recently completed building. As a person with interior design background, he had played a particularly involved role in the design of spaces and furnishings. The very nicely appointed restaurant was given a prominent ground floor association with the large exterior *gård* (literally translated again as "yard, farmyard or courtyard", in addition to its more traditional meaning of "farm").

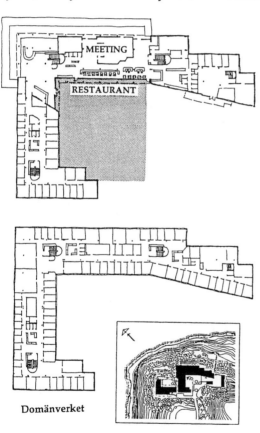

Figure 8.7 Domänverket (from Arkitektur 80:7)

From the plan of the total site, one tends to view this atrium space as being only partly expressive, while also a *de facto* response to the relatively tight urban Malmö site. Accessibility to, and any expressive value of the large exterior space tends to be focused on only one portion of the *gård*, the location of the restaurant. Otherwise the area is treated largely as a kind of park which provides visual interest to the individual offices surrounding the atrium, even on most of the ground level. Little collective association is created in these portions since the *pause* spaces are in the interior corridor space and do not expressively link to the atrium.

275

The relationship between restaurant and exterior courtyard appears to be of greater strength in the smaller, two-story Domänverket office in Falun, figure 8.7. An abundant natural site, a point on a lake, has allowed the architect to use *smårum* form (in 1977) to clearly define the major exterior space which serves as both entry and restaurant terrace. Spatially one's eye travels from this partially formed atrium, through the first floor glassed reception, restaurant and conference areas, out the other side to the building's terraced prow and lake view. The larger landscape form, slope, shore and water, which passes through the opposing architectural form, probably still has strong connotations of collectivity.

The published account of this Swedish office, which relatively early shows clear intentionality at the largest scale of second order meaning, concludes with a quote from the architect concerning the advantages of *samarbete* (working together). He/she describes how the client organization, Domänverket, created a special *arbetsgrupp* consisting of representatives from *verksledning* (work leadership) and *personal* (personnel) to actively participate in programming and design. This participatory process was felt by the architects to be very effective in providing support to the actual designers (Miskar 1980:37). It is no accident that the ethnic oppositions of individual and collective are nicely balanced in the final solution.

Referring to figure 8.8, we spend a moment with the more recent IBM *smårumskontor* (1985), their client/sales/education facility, also at Kista. Like many of the other new office buildings in this rapidly growing silicon suburb of Stockholm, IBM Forum as well has had to adapt to a more constrained, less generously natural site. The site is still large enough, by comparison to central city locations, to allow considerable variation in overall *smårums* layout. In this researcher's opinion at least, both the fully enclosed and partially enclosed *gård* spaces are evidence of quite formal design purpose at the largest second order scale. We even have another example of two meaningful aspects *within* the collective activities associated with the atria. In the innermost, cloister-like space, one finds quite formally and architecturally articulated activities associated with "meeting" at the largest of scales, i.e. library and auditorium. The *fest* activities of the collectivity, on the other hand, are located quite formally and conceptually as a separate place at the center of the partial *gård* with its one side open to the at least partially natural landscape. A spacious, glassed loggia penetrates both spaces symmetrically from entry in the front to primary vertical circulation at the back. The materials and detail of the place certainly measure up or even exceed the Scandinavian norm.

From only a two hour tour and midday meal one certainly felt the almost ritual effectiveness of moving from *smårums* corridor to the paired *gårdar* with their complementary oppositions of meeting and *fest*. The office portions of the complex were themselves interesting-- aside from the mentioned wayfinding problems the symmetrical form created--in that a comparatively small number of *pause* spaces had been originally provided. The thinking by the Swedish design teams had been that since most of the occupants were primarily involved in IBM sales, usually with actual clients, that contrary to the typical Swedish pattern, work would be much more individual than group oriented. In

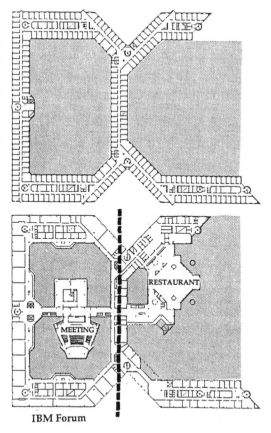

IBM Forum

Figure 8.8 IBM Forum (from Arkitektur 86:2, pg.22)

the corridors of Forum, relatively infrequent *pentry* (coffee bars) were predicted sufficient to accommodate the primarily individual need to fill his/her coffee cup, at whatever time of day. As we were walking through the office spaces a year or so after occupation, one saw and heard evidence that, contrary to expectations, small work groups were in fact forming. These groups were physically creating their own permanent *pause* spaces, just as had been the case at Draco. The organization was in the process of providing more space and furnishings for the practice. If it is still true that most of these people do not actually work that much together as a group, then we may be witnessing a fundamental socio-cultural need that is so pervasive by now in Sweden that it demands expression "before" and in spite of actual work processes.[1]

277

While IBM appears to have allowed the indigenous second order processes in Sweden to take their course, at least in terms of the *smårums* concept and larger scale second order oppositions, the same would seem to be less the case with Volvo's new head office in Göteborg, figure 8.9. In spite of the fact that Volvo is the most imageable Swedish multinational, some group of executive decision makers, perhaps Gyllenhammar himself, decided that Swedish designers (and even the participatory process as well) were not quite up to the task of designing such a world prestigious headquarters. Instead, the American-Italian Romaldo Giurgola created the villa-like image and layout on a natural prominence overlooking the city. The solution, and its obvious acceptance by at least Volvo executives sets up an immediate paradox. Volvo, after all, has been one of the prime innovators of new architectural forms and processes of industrial work, even including the work group concept of the "apartment" (see discussion in Chapter Six). It is almost as if consciously, these concerns have remained most strongly associated with the industrial setting, while office environments are, by contrast and even opposition, still more patriarchal (though one speaks here of only one of Volvo's offices).

Giurgola's villa plan creates a strong atrium, but the space has far less to do with collective associations than with the Beaux-Arts intensification of the visual link between major entry and the grand, colonnaded executive conference room at the terminus of the axis. Taken from a more discursive, third order perspective, the complex forms two hierarchically ordered spaces. The transverse axis which crosses the major entry/atrium/conference axis creates two territories, one for executives at the prominent view side, the other for ordinary office workers at the interior of the site. The atrium organizes the executive territory (labeled *Koncernledning* or "organizational leadership") and thus communicates not collectivity, but rhetorical authority. Gyllenhammer's own office forms the dominant power corner of the executive arena, complete with balcony overlooking greater Göteborg. Both the executive in the corner, and the architectural definition of separate executive suites or wings of offices are, as we have seen, highly uncharacteristic of recent buildings in Sweden. On the "other side of the tracks", in this Volvo villa of sorts, the more typically Swedish and here subordinate territory includes a *smårums* portion (*Kontorsflygel* or "office wing") and a separate conference/restaurant entity (*Konferensflygel* or "conference wing"). The large meeting spaces occupy

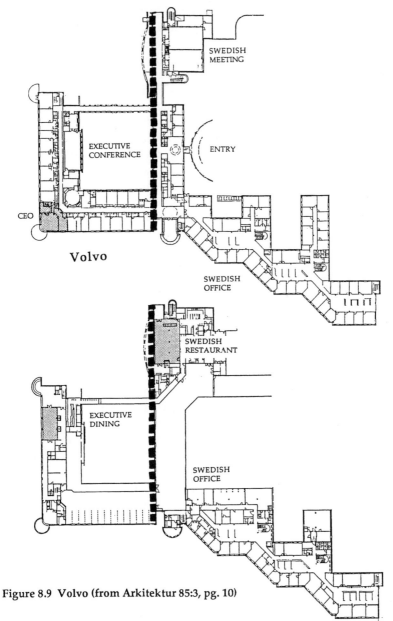

Figure 8.9 Volvo (from Arkitektur 85:3, pg. 10)

the top floor with the restaurant below. A smaller *Direktions Matsal* (executive dining room) similarly lies below the conference space in the executive territory.

Thus at the largest scale of the complex, one speaks not of more indigenous, second order oppositions, but third order presentational definitions of status and authority. This is not a ritual relationship between two aspects of meaning which all participate in alternatively, i.e. as balanced selves of the same individual. One lives on one side of the tracks or the other. The architectural cross axis establishes the preference of one portion of the site over another. This is a process of associating differential status with different kinds of people. The medium of architecture functions more semiologically, to communicate, much as any commercial sign rhetorically attempts to associate one thing with another. While at this largest scale one finds no evidence of ritual usage involving the spatial layout, *within* the ordinary office side of the villa, things may conform to typical second order Swedish practice. Even the separate collective domain is formally articulated into complementary oppositions between meeting and *fest*. Is a discursive statement being made in the overall building and site about the dominance of international concerns *(Koncernledning)* over Swedish considerations *(Kontors & Konferensflygelen)?* After all, Volvo sells far more vehicles abroad than at home, and has recently become partners with Renault. This makes sense in terms of the paradox between manufacturing and office architecture. The first is essentially Swedish while the concerns of the other are more international.

From the third order Volvo villa, we turn to two examples of exterior *gårdar* which clearly express more indigenous second order meanings at the largest scale, figure 8.10. In the far north city of Skellefteå, the square shape of the central city site was logically combined with the universal *smårums* standard. Because of glass interior walls to the individual offices, and because it was designed by Tengbom's office in 1978, the scheme is referred to as a *kombi* office. "Brinkenhuset", as it is called, thus forms a very simple, but formal statement with its large office courtyard. The building on the outside is three-hundred feet long. On the first floor of the five-story structure, focusing into the *gård* along one of its sides, is found the major public space, the *galleria*, with adjoining largest scale conference and meeting rooms. The restaurant, almost diagonally opposite from the *galleria*, surprisingly enough does not face the interior yard as one would expect--as a nice complementary statement between *fest* and meeting spaces, both focused on the major collective space.

There is an expressively logical reason that the restaurant was located on the outside corner of the building. An even larger collective natural space, Skellefteå's city park lies directly in front of Brinkenhuset and its exterior facing dining facilities. Not only is it expressively logical to associate the collective activities of the restaurant with the major park of the city, but the street which runs

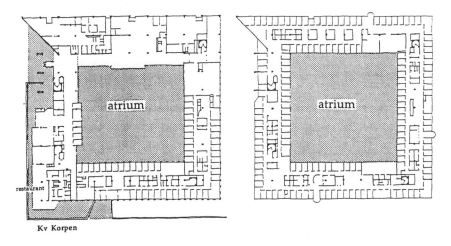

Kv Korpen

Figure 8.10 Kv Korpen (from Byggnadskonst 4:83, pg. 61)

between park and major building facade, including entrance and restaurant, is called *Trädgårdsgatan* (garden or landscape street). Diagrammatically, the relationship between the two *gårdar* is very similar to the plan layout at IBM Forum, where business meetings were associated with an architectural atrium or courtyard, while the restaurant focused out to a more park-like public natural space. This opposed complementary relationship is very nicely (though perhaps not that consciously) expressed in the office in Skellefteå. The building is semantically divided along one courtyard diagonal into collective and office portions, on the first floor only. One enters at the front corner symmetrically, on the other diagonal, between a meeting wing on the left and a *fest* wing on the right. It is also true that the spatial relationship between each of these interior functions and their adjacent exterior spaces is formally identical.

Thus we begin to find formal relationships among large scale components of Swedish offices which can primarily be understood in terms of evolving second order expression. In the example of figure 8.11, the Länsstyrelsen office in Malmö of which we have already spoken (Chapter Five), one also finds quite diagrammatically logical relationships. Though not unlike the formality of

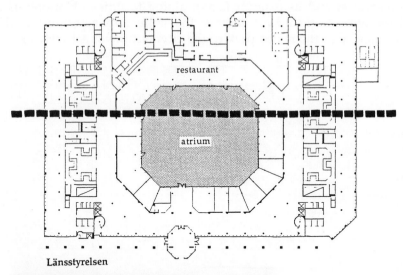

Länsstyrelsen

shared *pause* spaces on the upper five office floors, one sees an even more complete social/ritual correspondence in the large scale expression of the almost symmetrical ground level *gård*. In Länsstyrelsen, the design process has clustered all the primary collective spaces around the natural *gård* on this entry level, with a continuous exterior wall of full height glass dramatically associating inside with outside. Within this strong expression of the collective we find complementary oppositions between meeting and *fest* spaces. The longitudinal cross axis through the *gård* appears to articulate meeting places on the entrance side and the large, wonderfully detailed restaurant on the opposite other.

8.3 Interior *ljusgårder* (glassed atria)

We have seen the shift in location of the restaurant from its more patriarchal position up within the familial reaches of the office building to its present collective location on the main "ground" or "entry" level. In the previous examples, the restaurant and often large conference space are strongly associated with some natural landscape or exterior atrium. In spite of the radical change in meaning between these collective spaces and those in the now largely historical patriarchal offices, it appears that the restaurant/conference association with a natural space may not be the total meaning possible at this largest scale of second order practice. Returning to the traditional image of the Swedish *by*, one immediately recognizes that the largest scale collective spaces are not only "natural" in association--particularly in the linkage with first order associations--but are also the locus of much daily and ceremonial activity. As of yet in the Swedish office buildings of the late 70's and early 80's, most of this kind of second order activity, particularly *fests*, takes place *within* the restaurant or meeting spaces.

The movement of these places to the ground level, and their association with natural landscapes, verifies second order meaning developing at these scales in Swedish offices. It may be that this association remains primarily a third order semiotic, essentially a rhetorical attempt to link traditional collective connotations of nature with spaces which by virtue of their architectural "interiority" still have patriarchal-become-individual overtones. While such expression undoubtedly has its effect, it may be less powerful than a re-establishment of actual second order practice in street-like places with associations to nature. The fairly recent evolution of interior atria or streets in Swedish offices may be in part caused by this second order need to recreate the ritual *bygata* (*by* street).

Earlier examples of the *smårum* form, usually applied to more limited sites, often created exterior atria which could have easily been glassed over if collective activities in these places had been desired, programmed, or otherwise envisioned. It probably is true that the earlier *de facto* atria forms, caused primarily by the simpler provisioning of individual rooms, were necessary prototypical images. These forms suggested or made imaginable the next phase in second order evolution, even though the *de facto* office atria were not intended for a great deal of collective activity (and even their association with natural landscape was often minimal). In addition to the suggestive images of Swedish offices with exterior atria, there also existed in both historical and contemporary architecture examples of glassed atria or "streets" for collective activities in shopping arcades, hotel lobbies, government buildings, and the like. In spite of prototypical images and built examples in other types of architecture, the actual application of the glassed collective street to the Swedish office--a novelty in this building type--must also have depended upon the second order readiness of particular office societies themselves. There is an important distinction to be made here.

It is no accident that the scene for the development of the office *ljusgård* (glassed atrium) appears to have been the Swedish silicon suburb called Kista (including the neighboring area of Solna), on the north side of Stockholm. Here, large office organizations perhaps most aware of their internal communicational or social need have teamed with cutting edge architectural groups to produce what must be the finest office buildings in the world. They are not at all identical to the new envisioned electronic offices of the U.S. described in this book's introduction. The first of these Swedish places with large interior atria, or *ljusgårdar*, consciously intended for collective activity, was a pair buildings for two data firms JCC and Sperry (figure 8.12). Built between 1983 and 1985, the design process for both was facilitated by the largest architectural firm in Sweden, FFNS. It was not the size of the firm, *per se*, which perhaps allowed it to generate intentional prototype examples of second order, enclosed atria offices. In reading the firm's own brochure, where the *ljusgård* offices provide the cover image and much of the content within, and in interviewing one of the principals, Johannes Olivegren, it becomes very clear that the firm understands much of the second order issues of the day. Its own group organization serves to maximally facilitate the link between client and designer.[2]

The lead article in this issue of *FFNSnu* is written by Olivegren under the title: *Konsten att formge ett kontorsliv* (the art of designing office life). He gives a brief history of the office in Sweden, the isolation of individual offices in the *smårumskontor*, the Swedish rejection of the office landscape, the *kombi-kontor* by Erskine and Tengbom, and then proceeds to present reasons behind the latest examples, particularly in Kista. He says that architects traditionally have paid attention to things like function, comfort and the like, while often lacking critical knowledge of how the shape of the building influences social relationships in the workplace (ibid:3). From the following discussion of the specifics of social organization, it becomes clear that such is seen as the primary cause for the form of these *katedraler for kontorsfolket* (cathedrals for office societies). The workplace is essential as a meeting place for people; environments which promote opportunities to meet and discuss stimulate both people and ideas.

Olivegren then specifically identifies the major collective space, which he calls *bygata* (*by* street) or *strög* (thoroughfare), as a vital *sociala huvudrum* (central social space). Associated with restaurant, large meeting rooms, and other large scale facilities, such central spaces are said to have been found in earlier epochs of building--though not specified--and express the organization's themes and feelings of worker commonalty (ibid:4). Suggesting that these present examples of atrium spaces may still be evolutionarily incomplete, he mentions the *interna bygata* (internal *by* street) concept for the new SAS building. This design competition had just been completed at the time of Olivegren's article. Also predictive of this future SAS environment is Olivegren's description of smaller scales of groups which must also be architecturally expressed, his *enheter* (entities), *avdelningar* (departments), and *grupper* (work groups). He recognizes the inherent conflicts between the social aspects of form and the need for functional flexibility. From personal conversation with Olivegren, it appeared that their designers were attempting to find an architectural solution in which frequently reformed functional groups could actually themselves create--via architectural form--expression of themselves as social groups as well (not at all unlike the phenomenon at Draco, Chapter Five).

FFNS's discussion of the art of designing offices is essentially a summary of past experience and suggestions for the future, particularly in the case of SAS. The JCC-Huset in Kista (figure 8.12), again one of their first, is really only a partial example of the full potential expressed by Olivegren. Its major innovation is the glassed atrium or *ljusgård* (in this case a pair of atria), as central social spaces for the data corporation. Associated are the restaurant, meeting rooms and the like. What is missing in JCC-Huset is an articulation of smaller scale entities. Probably for circulation reasons alone, the length of the building is divided symmetrically. At the smallest scale of individual office, the traditional *smårums* corridor allows for little expression of the *arbetsgrupp*. While the Sperry building in adjacent Solna (same figure) uses the interior atrium to express largest scale collectivity and eliminate the double-loaded *smårums* corridor, it allows for little definition of the work group, though the asymmetrical divisions along the building length may relate to departmental or sectional entities. Yet the perceptual

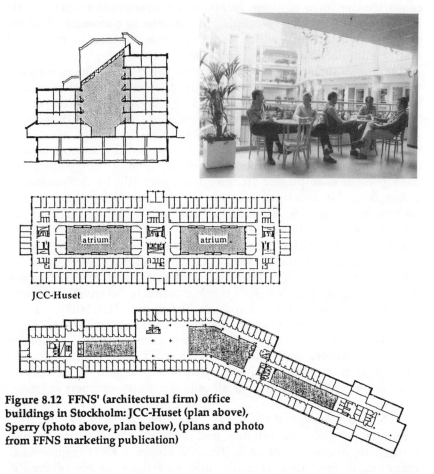

Figure 8.12 FFNS' (architectural firm) office buildings in Stockholm: JCC-Huset (plan above), Sperry (photo above, plan below), (plans and photo from FFNS marketing publication)

and social impact of the *ljusgård* spaces in both of these buildings represents a major evolutionary shift in the experience of the Swedish office.

More prominently featured in the FFNS publication, yet designed during this same period, is the international construction firm ABV's headquarters, also in Solna (fig. 8.13).[3] Featured on the cover, and the first building to be discussed after Olivegren's article, ABV comes closer to developing smaller scale expression of work groups, sections, and departments--in addition to its glassed-over central social space. It seems as if the break up of individual office segments in plan was useful in expressing work groups focused on *pause* spaces. Without more detailed information about the distribution of entities, one can at least see ABV as an early example

286

of the experimentation with some total second order solution, an attempt to satisfactorily express all scales of organization.

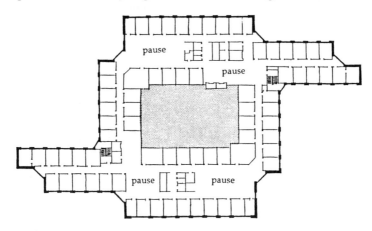

Figure 8.13
Headquarters office, ABV (from FFNS marketing publication)

It is not entirely clear from these three examples alone, what the total extent of activities in the central social space is. Aside from the major circulation to office floors, restaurant, meeting rooms, etc., and somewhat discursive presentation of corporate images which occur in the atria, the only activity which actually occurs in the large space is the coffee shop. While this use may be more intense at JCC and Sperry, where no *pause* spaces are provided in the *smårum* areas, it seems to be redundant at ABV where break areas exist in abundance. Given the immediate adjacency of the atrium coffee shop to the restaurant, part of the enclosed space surrounding the *ljusgård*, its most frequent usage may be for coffee after the midday meal, as one passes from the restaurant through the atrium space. The social meaning of this space may be dependent upon whether circulation on upper office floors is visually and expressively associated with the atrium. At both JCC and ABV, for example, *smårum* circulation is not visually connected to the *ljusgård*, while at Sperry, when one walks back and forth between offices, one is *in* the central social space. Yet this may work against expression at the smaller scales.

The most perceptually spectacular *ljusgård*, the visual themes of which extend through the surrounding work places, was created by the data and management consulting firm called Enator, also located in Kista (figure 8.14). A twenty-four page marketing description of Enator and its design process not only does full-color justice to the perceptual experience of its interior materials and furnishings, but clearly describes again a team process of design. The primary team responsible for "architecture, environment, furnishing and artistic creation" consisted of nineteen individuals from three separate design organizations: the architect's office (Lennart Bergstroms Arkitektkontor), an interiors firm (Svenska Rum Arkitektkontor), and a group of environmental artists (Ahlsén och Lindström AB). The process additionally included a project management team of five individuals and eight others acting as consultants in construction, heating-water-sanitation, electricity, lighting and acoustics. Enator itself was represented by an individual whose actual title is not given in the publication, but appears to be the *V.D.* (chief executive officer).

As visually exciting as this atrium space is, with its unusual floor mosaic, it remains relatively small by comparison and serves no other activities than circulation and the subtle expression of corporate theme. The atrium metaphor of ground as sky generates the impression of constant change, as the movement of cloud forms. Together with the extensive use of glass partitions and other smaller scale examples of the metaphor, i.e. the patterns on table surfaces reflecting those on the floors piercing through the partitions, these create the sought after expression of continuous creativity. This metaphor is the conscious expression of what the firm does in its data/management consultation at the highest levels of client organization. One perhaps might argue that in this case the *ljusgård* functions less as the (second order) central social room than a kind of third order attempt to rhetorically influence both workers and clients. The more typical associations of nature with collective space in other buildings might be second order because they are participating in the development and maintenance of oppositional meaning in the ritual layout of space. At Enator its

atrium and theme of creativity participate less in establishment of ritually effective social/spatial oppositions. Here, the semiotic theme intentionally pervades the entire building, attempting perhaps to even break down anything as structured as second order space.

To what degree is the Enator design team conscious of pervasive second order processes in Swedish office buildings? Are they intentionally saying that second order organization may not be optimal in terms of creativity? Or is this an example of conscious third order intentions superimposed over the larger, more subconscious second order ethic? The building has many of the standard second order features: central atrium, conference and *pause* spaces at several scales, and several banks of *smårum* individual offices with of course glass partitions in a

Figure 8.14 Environmental art and architecture of Enator's atrium

configuration similar to the *kombi*. Yet many things in the building are exceptions to the Swedish rule of the day.

First, more than half of the employees appear to not have their own office, sitting in open landscape spaces with only glass partitions around work group numbers of about six. From the brief tour (no survey or interviews), it was said that some of the people without offices were involved in sales and spent more work time outside of the building. Secondly, what appear to be *pause* spaces, really are not. The two "bar" areas on each floor are intended to be used for spontaneous, creative encounters, not as institutionalized places for breaks where entire work groups sit down across a common table. The form is therefore different. Similarly, the multiple conference rooms on each floor may say less about the opposition between group meeting and group socialization, than about accessibility for creative brain-storming in groups. Perhaps the best indication of the deemphasis of more institutionalized (second order) practice is the absence of the large common restaurant and the midday meal, casting further doubt on the collective meaning of the *ljusgård*. Somewhat more reminiscent of patriarchal organization, one finds on the top floors very nicely appointed places to be used primarily by board members and clients, who again are primarily upper level management. A small dining room for about fifteen people, board room and larger meeting space for about fifty to sixty comprise a more structured portion with spontaneous bar spaces and a generous pool/sauna/relaxation/ entertainment area adjacent. These spaces have little visual relationship to the building's atrium.

As patriarchal as the top floor may seem, the larger meeting room and spontaneous "inspiration" areas are specifically intended to be used by all in the building. Whether or not everyone will at some time or another use the dining room, catered by a professional chef, is another question. On the whole, the intentions of the building's common spaces appear to be less concerned with the establishment of an *a priori* second order social structure than the encouragement of more spontaneous individual and group creativity. To do this they use rhetorical third order images, e.g. "ground as sky", "tropical spa", "nightclub". How this office is and will be used can only be answered by a more detailed investigation.

More information is also needed on the design process itself. Usually a strong participatory contribution of the actual workers generates the essential pattern of ethnic practice. In the present case, one is not certain of the extent of this contribution to the overall process of team design. In spite of a sizable design team, *per se*, the actual office organization was said to be represented by only one person, the company's *V.D.*. If the formal elements of second order offices are so pervasive within the vocabulary of the design professions themselves, then much of this building could be subconsciously or latently structured in accordance with the larger ethos. In spite of more conscious intentions, use could evolve similarly to many others. Enator may provide us with an interesting case study of the effectiveness of executive, discursive, third order imagery vs. participatory, second order ritual.

Notes

1   In a smaller, extremely handsome *kombi* office shown to me by Svante Sjöman (the main office for a chemical exterminating company in Stockholm) one *arbetsby* portion of one floor was dedicated to salespeople who spent most of their time out of the office. In this case each employee was not given his or her own window and office since functionally there was very little need; each had a minimal desk tightly contiguous in a common space. This group was however given the typical meeting and *pause* amenities of other *kombi vardagsrum* (common spaces) in the office, suggesting again, that socio-cultural aspects will occur in spite of limited functional interdependence.

2   Tragically, Johannes Olivegren died in the interim between the fieldwork interview and the present publication. As probably the architect most quoted in connection with the human amenities of Swedish office buildings, his was obviously a mission of designing for the user. Other work on housing, connected with his university faculty work in Göteborg, showed the degree to which the users could be given participatory responsibility for the physical environment. His detailed description of these processes, carried out as the basis for an actual housing project, appears in *Brukarplanering* (User Planning) (Olivegren 1975). Here one sees how a cooperatively working group of land owners, with the assistance of design professionals, push the decision making process to new heights. No scale of design is too large or too small to be acted upon in this process. Much of Olivegren's interest in offices was less from a historical or anthropological perspective, as in the present case, then in creating design process and forms which would allow the maximum of user participation. Such decision making is of course central to our thesis of second order evolution of form.

3   This is the main ABV office in Sweden, and has under its organizational structure the branch office of the same name in Malmö, discussed in Chapter Five.

9 Resolution of Second Order Scales

9.1 Ideon

In the fall of 1982, regional authorities and Lund University began planning in earnest for a new research complex to be built adjacent to the existing campus. It was to be called "Ideon", or "place of ideas". The first *kombi* offices had just appeared in Stockholm and Lund, and largest scale atria offices were also in the early planning stages. While this "ethnic" background had its influence over the design solution, developed by the Anshelm Architectural Group, there was much indigenous to the program that demanded a more conscious resolution of second order expression. The rational motivation behind the project was to foster the participation of private, hi-tech research industries in the technical portion of Lund University. This not only meant physical adjacency but more importantly an emphasis on the advantages of common or collective relationships between all players, including both research corporations and university departments (*Arkitektur* 1986:14). Sited as it was on the edge of the University and Lund with a view of the traditional Skånsk *by* landscape, this future place with both clearly distinctive individual elements and conscious collective intentions was most naturally called a *forskningsby* (research *by*)--possibly the first such Swedish label association of an office structure with the second order concept of *by*.

Not only do we find the term *by* being used, but also *gata* (way or street). Just as the *bygata* created the foundation for largest scale, second order architecture and activity in the traditional Skånsk village, we find an analogous function of the enclosed, linear street of the Ideon layout. The *gata*, of course, is the primary vehicle for the collective, cooperative intentions of the planners. As illustrated in figure 9.1, Ideon's streets of its three phases run linearly along the

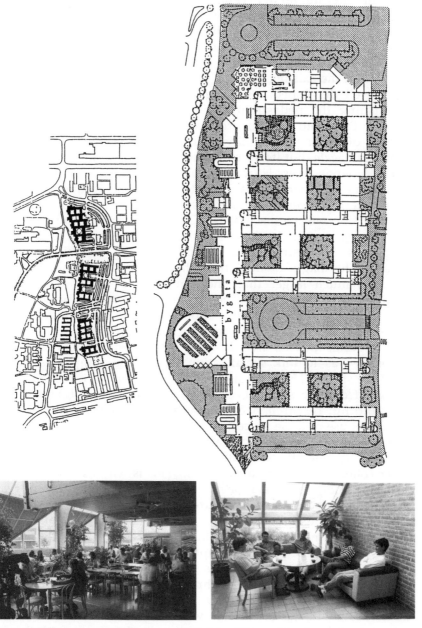

Figure 9.1 Site plans of Ideon (from Arkitektur 86:2, pg. 16), views of restaurant and coffee gatherings in *bygata*

293

edge of the university (Phase One was complete in 1986). Expressively, the intention was to link the row of technical departments and buildings on the campus side of the new *gata* with the research corporations on the other. Unfortunately, as pointed out in a critical review of the project (Edman 1986:19), physical access from the existing backs of the university's technical buildings is not well developed. Existing parking lots were left, severely diminishing the pedestrian or urban quality of the connecting spaces. From our second order vantage point, it is not the site concept of linking university with research corporation, via the *forsknings bygata*, but its execution which might be less than ideal.

Hindered as access is from the university side, these people also use Ideon's *gata*, particularly its restaurant at the northern terminus of the interior street (the possible symbolic and ritual meanings of this direction will be discussed). Conference rooms, coffee spaces, and the auditorium in the *gata* are used mostly by the research companies. The street is most active during the midday meal period. The length of the *gata*, whether in Phase One, Two, or Three, is much larger than the sum total of social or meeting activities actually require. The smaller *pause* spaces provided on balconies overlooking the *gata* appear to be seldom used. Strong tendencies exist here as well to associate the *pause* space with the smaller scale, internal *arbetsby* form. The design intention of the balconies was to link socialization within the companies to the collective street. The vertical separation and lack of direct access to balcony from the street, because of the relatively tight security surrounding research work groups, may contribute to the infrequent use of these spaces.

Yet the real reason for lack of use may be that they are expressively out of scale with the *gata*. The street relates to the larger collective entity of Ideon itself. This is why its major activity occurs at midday, in relation to the restaurant, not during break times. The photograph of figure 9.1, however, illustrates how smaller groups use the break-like places of the *gata* to take coffee after the large meal. Similar to the underutilized atria or *ljusgårder* we have seen in the previous chapter, Ideon's *gata* tends to function differently than the spontaneous shopping or recreational streets which have become popular throughout Europe and the U.S.. Swedish architects may too have shared this largely metaphoric urban design image of "street" when thinking about these new office forms--being less conscious of the now apparent evolution of second order practice. Yet the *gata* may in reality have a greater tendency toward more formalized social and cultural activities. In

Latin societies, for example, urban spaces such as church plazas appear to be used for both ritual events *and* spontaneously sitting or promenading around with family or friends. This latter use of public or collective spaces has traditionally been far less characteristic of Scandinavia.

Here a personal incident comes to mind. After eating the midday meal at a restaurant in a new urban shopping/community center in Malmö, the author looked for a place in the interior mall to spontaneously sit to smoke a small cigar and simply watch people. There were virtually no benches! I sat down on the steps of a small platform intended for more formal events. Within a few minutes a pair of security officers informed me that people were not allowed to sit there, and for that matter were discouraged from sitting anywhere else! One does find benches in exterior public spaces in Sweden, and walking streets have now been developed in many cities. The incident in Malmö involved a particular group of inhabitants of high rise apartments surrounding the shopping/community center, specifically, a large number of workers and their families from Southern Europe. Public street life was a much more traditional part of these cultures, particularly for men. It is not clear exactly why the authorities had decided to actively discourage their age old customs in this Malmö new-town center.

Why in Malmö, where new walking streets and annual outdoor urban festivals have recently begun to compete with street life across the sound in Copenhagen, was similar behavior seemingly taboo in that particular locale? Were these people spending too much time in the mall, somehow inhibiting others from using the place, particularly for shopping? Was it simple prejudice; a way to reduce the strong public image of foreigners in the area? Or is there something inherently different in Swedish culture about an indoor *gata*, in comparison to outdoor urban walking streets. Is spontaneous, sometimes territorial behavior appropriate in larger, urban settings, while second order or architectonically defined interior places still have strong expressive connotations of particularly Swedish collective groups and responsibilities. From this perspective it is easy to see how the prominent, more extensive use of such spaces by foreigners would not set well with the Swedes. They had difficulty associating collectively with these groups and therefore with the expressive expectations of the *gata* space. The reader must know that this center, though primarily used for shopping, contained local collective and/or governmental activities. One might argue that exterior walking streets too will at times possess these associations.

This line of reasoning is given further weight in the fact that relatively few interior shopping malls are built in Scandinavia compared with other countries, especially the U.S.. On the surface, it seems that Swedes are more willing to use atria or interior street spaces in offices than shopping centers, where because of the social indeterminacy of the users, perhaps, collective expression and activities cannot achieve strong levels of second order effect. It certainly would be interesting to study in greater detail two different kinds of "street" activities in Scandinavia, i.e. the urban scale, exterior *gågata* (walking street) and the interior, second order scale *bygata*. Again, one would hypothesize almost opposite kinds of activities for each.

The *gågata* allows more spontaneous and less socially controlled behavior of individuals, friends, lovers and perhaps voluntary associations and even family members. In addition to the general seeing and being seen, in all sorts of attire, we find music and other artistic performances, political speeches, preaching, selling, etc.. Of all the effects possible in such milieu, little appears to be focused on the maintenance and organization of more institutional or culturally defined social groups. Socially, these are recreational, even tourist opportunities, neutral or free territories in the midst of surrounding third order rhetoric, with its ubiquitous private and authoritative discourse. When huge numbers of people throng to the renown *gågata* in Copenhagen for the new Carnival, fashioned after its namesake in Brazil, the effect only superficially compares with the ritual reversal of social roles and places where it occurs indigenously. When several hundred thousand Danes do the Samba, certainly there is a social effect of release or escape from the everyday and everyplace. Little rubs off to the actual workings of important socio-political organizations in the Danish daily life.[1]

To achieve such ends, and thereby be distinguished from these walking streets, second order *gata* must be much smaller and involve not recreational others but fellow workers. The activities in these places are more socially controlled, less voluntary, and otherwise more institutionally integrated into the entire "society", the office organization as best example. We might more properly speak about ritual practice with all its anthropological connotations of traditional symbolism, proscriptive participation and specific social effect. In the novel second order *gata* of Ideon, for example, one is not going to see much if any of the spontaneous recreation, political agitation or religious proselytization common to the public walking street. Instead, as the second order organization continues to evolve, one would expect to see other events of a more ritualistic nature, in addition to the mentioned activities of the midday meal. During the author's visit to this site in early December, they were organizing a Lucia *fest* for all Ideon in the restaurant portion of the *gata*. True to the ancient association of *Jul* with the smaller patriarchal-become-individual entities, the particular research companies were to have their own *Jul fests* within their respective places.

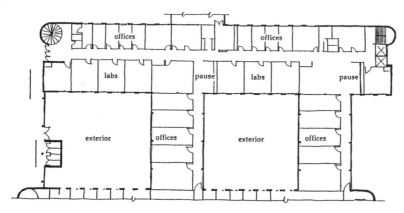

Figure 9.2 Typical *arbetsby* for Ericcson at Ideon

The largest tenant of the first phase of Ideon, about two-thirds of the office/lab space, was Ericcson Radio Systems, a subdivision of the Swedish communications giant, Ericcson. Because of very tight industrial security, it was only possible to interview one person, though in some depth. As part of the interview, this external affairs person included a tour through one of their typical floors, see plan of figure 9.2. During the planning stages Ericcson was known to be the first and largest participant. It is not therefore unlikely that they were consulted about the layout of their prospective spaces. The corporation had physically been part of Stockholm's silicon suburb, Kista, where much innovation and evolution in office design had taken place. The newest Ericcson offices in Kista had the *kombi* form. The informant, though in no way especially associated with Ericcson's planning and design processes, was very knowledgeable about the shared Swedish ethic of office design. He knew about both *kombi* and new *ljusgård* (atria) forms.

In part because of Ericcson's previous experience, in addition to the undoubted ethnic awareness of the actual designers, the primary form of the research space is an entity at the scale of fifteen to twenty persons, again an almost standard architectural expression of the *arbetsby*. These obvious units of horizontal work group may be linked together in a variety of combinations both on the same floor and between floors. Each *arbetsby* was originally designed to provide on an average of five individual *(kombi)* offices, one larger office for the group leader, four two-person lab spaces, and one large multi-use space. Each work group also has its own *pause* room. The assembled spaces form an "L", defining one half of a small exterior atrium. It is probably the desire for natural light in the lab spaces which has effectively replaced the actual collective activities at the center of the more typical *arbetsby* with the natural collective associations of an exterior atrium. A good comparison here would be the frequent electronics lab spaces which are set up in the collective "living room" spaces at Alfa Laval's SattControl (see figure 6.10). The necessary solid partitions of the lab activities in part defeat the intentions of providing natural light to these spaces via the glassed walls of individual offices. The quality of natural light in the Ericcson labs is superior.

The reason everyone was not given a separate office in the Ideon scheme lies in the distinction between more theoretical work, generally done by those with university education in engineering, and laboratory application done by technicians. From a functional point of view, Ericcson has a tradition of working in pairs in lab spaces as a means of providing greater safety while using high voltages. From the socio-cultural point of view, it is antithetical to the second order ethos to provide individual office expression for some members of the horizontal work group and not others. How powerful is this ethos, compared with functional intentions? Just months after occupation, Ericcson had begun filling in the large multipurpose spaces of the "L" with individual offices! In some *arbetsbyar* the *kombi*-like offices were deep enough to include individual lab spaces as well. From the interview, it was clear that already a consensus existed. Individuals did not like to share lab space, and each wanted his/her own office space.

For reasons of both functional communication and expressive membership, Ericcson consciously attempted to tailor its project groups to the architectural *arbetsby* form, i.e. about fifteen to twenty people. There were exceptions as one might imagine. On one floor a particular research group required twice the normal number of workers. It occupied two adjacent modules. When they took *pause* they still attempted to use only one common break space, as the ritual practice of their group would demand. Executives were also aware of the way in which the *arbetsbyar* forms tended to isolate these groups within the total Radio Systems organization at Ideon, limiting "communication" in this of all companies. It has been mentioned that the individual company balconies of the *gata* did not apparently accommodate this need, yet certainly the midday meal might be a positive example, though perhaps more purely social than functional.

Does one speak of the prospects of some intermediate scaled collective space *within* the organization confines of individual research companies? It is readily apparent from the plan that the internal corridors and stairways between the *arbetsbyar* leave little opportunity for either functional communication or ritual activities at this scale. Christmas decorations were being put up throughout all *arbetsbyar* the day of my tour. But there was no major *Jul fest* for the entire organization as would be the case in other offices, only the departmental or divisional parties, presumably held in a selected *arbetsby*. Other indications suggest a somewhat stronger departmental identity here than elsewhere. When a new division from Malmö joined the Radio Systems group at Ideon they invited all to an open house. Next year some other division was to reciprocate. Is this in part because of the lack of architectural expression of the total organization? To a large extent the color-coded architectural wings of Ideon, described as "ships" by the architects, are more to the scale of departments, sections, or divisions, at least in the case of Ericcson.

9.2 Norrviksstrand and Televerket Radio

About the same time that Ideon was first occupied, early 1986, the development/construction firm of Convector Byggnads sponsored a competition for a new office city near Sollentuna, a new-town node of Stockholm adjacent to Kista. The solution recommended by the jury, "Norrviksstrand" (figure 9.3), is quite comparable to Ideon in its expression of three distinct scales of organization: work group, section or department, and total corporation. The structures of this hypothetical new city of 4,000 to 5,000 contain no laboratory spaces, only typical *smårums* and *kombi* offices, according to the specific instructions of the competition guidelines (Medfoljer AT:1987). The universality of the Swedish office ethic, here specifically individual offices and collective spaces, is apparent in this proscription for speculative offices. At this point in the evolution, no actual participatory organization is necessary to program or otherwise institutionalize these requirements! Designers of Norrviksstrand, from the firm of Rosenberg and Stål, have created a basic "Z" floor module of two *arbetsbyar* of about sixteen persons each. A short run of double loaded corridor connects the two and

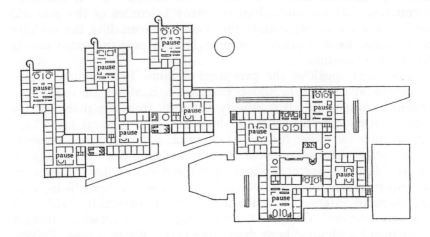

Figure 9.3 Competition entry "Norrviksstrand" (from Medfoljer AT:1987)

presumably allows for some functional flexibility of membership in the two groups, assuming an ideal of two *arbetsgrupper* per floor. The reality of the situation, were these offices to be built and occupied, might rather be four or five smaller work groups on each floor. Whether the total "Z" shape of each floor would tend to correspond to a section or department, a second scale of expression, is difficult to speculate on because of the greater variability of organizational size beyond the work group. Intuitively the scale of the typical Norrviksstrand floor seems to fit some sectional or departmental size.

At the largest scale of organization, the floors of the "Z" blocks are minimally connected at each level, thereby focusing on the interior *gata* space on the ground floor as the major expression of the whole, in this case a linear string of three "Z"s. Just as an expressive predetermination of section size was difficult without actual corporate structures in mind, at this largest of levels it becomes impossible to precisely express just what the "whole" is. The overall Norrviksstrand scheme (only partially shown in figure 9.3) has three entities of three blocks each, two with two blocks, and one unusual central form, with four conventionally defined *arbetsby* spaces clustered to create a large *ljushall* (in the architects terms) or *ljusgård*.

This precise expression in the central structure of just the two scales, work group and company, suggests perhaps a less conscious intention for the apparent section scales of the "Z" forms. The

300

primary reason for the configuration of "Z" forms may be the desire to emulate the central *ljushall* for any given foursome of *arbetsbyar* on the same level. Pairs of "Z"s create their exterior *gård* in symbolic association perhaps with the atrium of the central core of the office city. In terms of actual second order activities, it is the interior *gata*, running in front of the groups of "Z" blocks and unconnected with their *gård*, which probably would carry the greatest association to the central atrium.

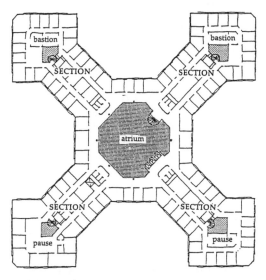

Figure 9.4 FFNS' plan for the Televerket office building (from ABV marketing brochure:1987)

The idea of the central *ljusgård* appears in perhaps its most monumental extent in FFNS's proposal for Televerket Radio about this same time (figure 9.4). Picking up where their solution for ABV left off a couple of years earlier (figure 8.13), Olivegren and group continue to emphasize the *socialt huvudrum* (central social space), as they refer to it (ABV:1987). New in the Televerket plan is the attempt to more clearly articulate expression on smaller scales. While seeming for all the world in plan like some classical or renaissance discourse on the (ancient) sacred, the cardinally directed wings more accurately reflect the design awareness at FFNS of state of the art second order needs. Particularly novel is the conscious design of collective spaces at the intermediate scale of the *sektion* (section). The wedge-like spaces at the end of the wings are intended to express organization at this scale, not the work group. The designers have invented a special term here: *bastionera* or *sektionens sociala huvudrum* ("bastion", presumably after its fortress like shape, or "section's central social space"). One of the features which allows for variation in section size is the ability to open up the collective "bastion" areas to one or more other floors, creating a vertical "living room" at the section scale.

Their conceptions of the scales of space to be included in any office are extremely clear in the brochure. Under the introductory rubric of *arbetsmiljö* (work environment), four sub-categories of scale are discussed: 1) the atrium (*socialt huvudrum och social huvudplusåder*), 2) the bastions (*sektionernas sociala rum*), 3) work groups (*mindre gruppenheter*), and 4) individual offices (*arbetsrum med synkontakt*). The apparent lessening of expression of the work group, compared to atrium and bastion, is quite intentional on the part of the architects. It is in recognition of the functional need to frequently reorganize work groups that it was decided to use a more flexible, linear collective space for *pause,* conference, and other activities at this scale, not unlike the earliest, linear *kombi* forms (see Chapter Six). Even considering the fact that the individual offices form a linear "wrap" around *all* three kinds of spaces-- atrium, corridor *kombi,* and bastion--the work groups focus their collective activities as need arises along that length of *kombi corridor*. One cannot predict just how flexible these spaces would actually be in practice. This intentional flexibility relates to Olivegren, et. al. mentioned interest in maximum user particiption in creating social, cultural settings.

From a functional point of view, it is true that sections will be more permanent than work groups. One could thereby justify the architecturally permanent expression of company sections. Even more permanent is the atrium as associated with the whole. It is also probably true that the concept of flexible collective work group spaces will not solve the continuous problem of linking place of ritual practice with functional group. The social activities of the *pause* space, for example, are still relatively separate from work activities, whether in individual offices or at conference places. In all likelihood, once *pause* spaces are set up in the *kombi* corridors, they will become relatively permanent. Newly formed *arbets- grupper* will not be able to spontaneously create new practice places adjacent to their offices, due to the same reasons this was impossible in the office landscape schemes. Every work group would have to be participant in difficult, protracted, decision making processes. Given the reality that the greatest need of second order organization in Sweden is the horizontal *arbetsgrupp,* it might always justify greater architectural expression than in this case the section, even if permanent and shared with other work groups. The idea of allowing work groups to spontaneously create expressively effective places, associated with changes in functional work group composition, is still an interesting second order ambition!

9.3 The architectural competition for SAS

Sometime before the announcement for the competition in July 1984, a planning team of the Scandinavian Airlines System (SAS) had determined that it would be financially feasible to assemble fourteen-hundred people from thirty separate offices into one location. The site chosen lay in a portion of Frösundavik, a park-like area of Solna, one of the new-town areas adjacent to Stockholm's silicon suburb Kista. Not only was the new structure to be in the vicinity of many of the newest and most evolved of Sweden's large office buildings, but two of them, ABV and Sperry (figures 8.12 and 8.13) were actually visible neighbors.

While felt to be the decision of SAS's highly successful and charismatic CEO, Jan Carlzon, the architectural competition was inevitable. As a consortium of three national airlines from Denmark, Norway and Sweden, SAS could not have practically found any other means of choosing an architect, obviously from only one of the countries. As one of the most prominent representatives of Scandinavia, with its relative cultural homogeneity of inhabitants, the corporation must live up to these ethnic values, both in its public relations and internal organization. SAS at times serves as a source of enculturation of aspects of the Scandinavian ethos. Though in part a response to efficiency needs, it has, for example, eliminated class distinctions of seating on all flights within the member countries.

One-hundred-thirty-one architectural offices communicated their interest in designing the new SAS headquarters. According to Olof Hultin, editor of the architectural journal Arkitektur, this represented a mobilization of architectural expertise in a manner perhaps unequaled by other corporations (Hultin 1985:16). Of this number then, ten were chosen through an anonymous competition phase. The selection represented the best, the "cream", of Scandinavian architects, not including Finland (ibid). The program given these ten, to be designed for the park-like Frösundavik site, was to provide for "rational activities"; it should be "changeable" and have minimal floor area and operating cost. Important also was the site's natural beauty. Not the least consideration was to have been the expression of SAS's philosophy. In terms of this last, one could expect decentralization, democracy and similar concepts to be applied to the architecture (ibid). It was Neils Torp's office from Oslo which the jury felt best satisfied the requirements of the program, considering the "landscape treatment, architectonic form, economy, organization, work environment, and flexibility" (ibid).

Criticism of the other nine submissions, including one by Ralph Erskine, had most to do with the way in which the architectural massing fit the largely natural landscape site in Solna. Many of these forms were judged to be unnecessarily dramatic, either in their simple height as office towers, or as more literal attempts to rhetorically advertise for SAS. Some were criticized for their impression of "royalty" which came not only from tower portions, but from historically nostalgic Beaux-Arts layout of plans as evident in the Larsen scheme shown in figure 9.5. One finds substantial pieces of the evolving second order logic in at least the three non-premiated submissions published with the winning entry (Hultin 1985:22-24), e.g. *smårums* form, *kombi* units, and large atria. It is Torp's scheme which best turns several scales including the interior *gata* into an evolutionarily novel, integrated example of office architecture. Much of this content remains at the ethnically subconscious level in Sweden.

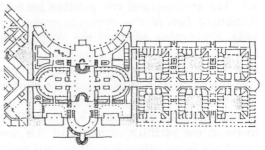

Henning Larsens Tegnstue - Copenhagen

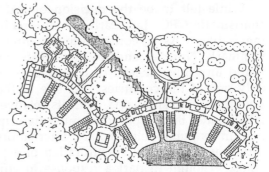

Carl Nyrén Arkitektkontor - Stockholm

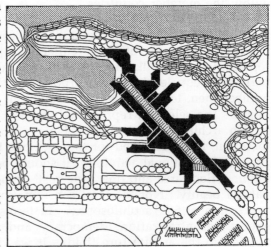

Niels Torp A/S - Oslo

Figure 9.5 Entries to the SAS competition: Niels Torp's winning solution below, (from Arkitektur 85:3, pg. 19)

One assumes that the jury intuitively felt the same, in spite of the lack of verbal articulation of these characteristics. It is somewhat ironic that the Swedish firm perhaps most conscious of the ethic in office architecture--FFNS--was apparently not invited to submit as part of the final ten.

Recall the forms of the traditional *byar* in Southern Sweden and Denmark (Chapter One), again the penultimate second order examples. Compared to the other entries, Torp's scheme, also shown in figure 9.5, is clearly most analogous. As Torp is said to have remarked about the size of the SAS headquarters during the competition, "fourteen-hundred people in Norway is not an office, but a *by!*" (personal conversation with SAS informant). Even considering that in Norwegian the term *by* is a general one applied to any architectural settlement, whether rural village *(bygdby)* or city (Oslo *by)*, it still carries a predominantly small scale connotation as it does more exclusively in Sweden.[2]

Just how literal was the image of the Norwegian *gårdstun* or more southern *by* in the minds of the designers in Torp's architectural office (see again diagram of figure 0.1 in the Introduction)? It is impossible to speculate whether these people were influenced by actual images of the past, or whether in a more likely scenario they intuitively understood all the more abstract elements of reemerging second order practice in recent Scandinavian, particularly Swedish, offices.[3] In this latter case, then, the designers can be seen to have made a greater creative contribution to the evolutionary process than in the simple emulation of historical forms. Nevertheless, it is highly probable that most of the designers had walked through several of *gårdstun* which still exist as museums along the fjords and valleys in Norway. Although very few southern *byar* survived the enclosure acts, much of this form certainly has been experienced in the folk museums of Oslo, Copenhagen, Stockholm, Lund, and many other places in Scandinavia.

Pursuing this more literal, third order possibility a bit further, one can compare the winning scheme with the most *by*-like Swedish proposal by Carl Nyrén (figure 9.5). Not unlike the innovations at Ideon being built at the same time, a linear, multi-level collective interior street links together *smårum* wings approximately at the scale of work groups. We also see the formal separation and opposition of the restaurant at the center of the interior *gata*. Even compared to the impending Swedish developments elsewhere, Nyrén's scheme does not create a glassed street, nor fully integrate the restaurant into this space. What is most Swedish, in terms of reflections of historical form, is the measured cadence of the relationships between work group wings and prototypical *gata*. The *byar* of Skåne and elsewhere were much more formal than their later second order counterparts, the *gårdstun*, in Norway (see again figure 1.7).

What the Torp group seems to have done, somehow as part of the largely subconscious design process, is to unify the restaurant in the most fully glassed *gata* to date. This best emulates the outdoor *gata* of the second order villages, while at the same time modifying the formality of the units which create it. The jagged informality of the actual building entities, along with an association of *gata* to sea, perhaps reminiscent of the irregular fjord *gårdstun*, provide the most distinctive Norwegian overtones in the production. Although from birdseye view one can see this angular character as an appropriate metaphor of (SAS) flight, perhaps, still from the actual users vantage point this association largely disappears. Others see the "hi-tech" use of materials as a major (third order) design intention and effect, along with other interior details of airline equipment. This was not, however, any primary determinant of overall form.

9.4 Patron or ethos?

Much has been said in the forgoing chapters about the essential role of participatory processes in instigating and maintaining the evolution of second order office form. The emphasis has been on a more natural cultural evolution rather than on either political legislation or the importance of individual change agents. Evidence seems quite conclusive that both office workers and architects in Sweden today share a truly ethnic set of values about expressive practice in white collar environments. This remains central to the present thesis, that one of the first things Scandinavians do when given the right to participate in design decisions is to architecturally and ritually establish the traditional socio-ethnic balance between individual and group. Architectural form is not only critical to the development of this cultural reality in the work place, but logically either simultaneous with or even prior to the democratic function of actual work groups. While at all scales of organization we have seen examples in which managers or executives facilitate the administrative process of architectural change, they cannot be given the major credit for the underlying impetus.

In the case of SAS, Jan Carlzon speaks of the new building as "something of a revolution" (SAS Corporate Communications 1988:4), which could either imply significant individual contribution or the unique achievement of some larger group--or both. As elsewhere in Sweden, many individuals are naturally not fully conscious of the larger ethnic evolution in which they are immersed. Neither particular individuals nor unique organizations can be said to effectively create themselves the architectural and organizational changes which they enjoy. In spite of often retrospective description of executive or organizational motivations, e.g. to reduce hierarchy, engender creativity, foster communication, or simply to get together (ibid:4, 5), it is clear that these are the byproducts of now widely held, but less conscious, second order convictions about the shape of Swedish offices. Yet participatory committees were not formed until after the selection of the Torp scheme. This suggests not so much that the winning design resulted primarily from executive initiative, but that by the mid-eighties the ethic was in fact reaching something of a climax. A set of values were so widespread that the Pan-Scandinavian competition format was, in itself, capable of allowing the expression evident in SAS.

Thus it appears to be a third order assumption to give primary emphasis to Carlzon's role, no matter how important his personal inspiration, patriarchal image, and actual executive contribution has been to the prosperity of SAS.[4] This, however, will naturally be the view not only of those immersed within the ethos in Sweden, but to those in other countries more accustomed to reporting the "top-down" power of executives in making decisions about office environments. The story of the SAS building in Britain's Architectural Review begins with the statement that..."Carlzon is the key to understanding the new SAS headquarters" (Duffy 1989: 43). They suggest furthermore that SAS is one of a very few and unique examples of a particular kind of corporate architecture in Western Countries, attributing this success to the rarity of enlightened executives. One of the comparisons is to the relation of Hertzberger to the brilliant head of the insurance company Central Beheer in the Netherlands, a relationship detailed earlier in Chapter Six. They conclude that..."the SAS building--envisaged by Carlzon and crafted by Neils Torp--belongs to this noble but brief list of honor". On the contrary, the list of honor is by now quite extensive, but the vast majority remains somewhat anonymously concealed beneath the quiet and evolutionary processes of daily Scandinavian practice. In spite of the major emphasis on executive as benefactor in this British architectural journal, in the following discussion about how the place actually works, there is specific but unexplained recognition of second order practice.

307

9.5 Daily life at SAS: *"mitt rum"*

Even compared with examples of enlightened offices in other countries, "what makes SAS even more different is the Scandinavian rigor with which the heretical proposition of 'user first' has been worked out". A bit further on the article states that.."what this vision represents is not only a higher level of understanding of what complex office work involves...but also a huge difference in the standard of the working environment compared with what office workers tolerate in Britain and the U.S." (Duffy 1989:44). But it is when the Architectural Review begins to speak about the specific, smaller scale layout that our present theme becomes most immediately recognizable:

> Practically everyone working in this very large building for 1500 people has his own individual daylit room of approximately 13.5 m. Each of these rooms is totally private....On the other side of each individual's private door there is always a common group space, a kind of living room, where each group of 20 or so office staff shares common equipment, meeting spaces, and group filing. Needless to say--*this is Scandinavia*--each such small group enjoys its own beautifully equipped kitchen. (italics added, ibid:45)

Given the determination of the basic architectural form by the combination of Pan-Scandinavian design competition, and the critical initiation and facilitation by SAS executives, the subsequent participatory user groups at least determined the furnishings of the huge number of private offices. *All* members of the organization had the opportunity to visit the site in the summer of 1987, prior to move-in. They could see a typical office--all are virtually the same size with the exception of less than ten highest executive spaces-- and could chose furniture from a list pre-selected by committee, e.g. three kinds of desks, five different chairs, and various lamps (Boëthius n.d. pg. 3) The photograph of figure 9.6 gives the reader a good impression of the excellent resulting amenities, and continued choice available to every individual worker.

The large three by four meter size of the rooms, unusual in terms of the typically smaller individual spaces of other *arbetsby* forms, may create an added measure of patriarchical-become-individual character. For one of the interior designers from the firm Plan 5 Arkitekter AB, the association with the familial dwelling is quite conscious: "We have designed interiors with a touch of home". As an example of such detail, "the desk is a bit like

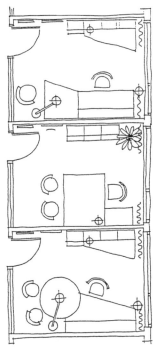

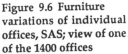

Figure 9.6 Furniture variations of individual offices, SAS; view of one of the 1400 offices

an old-fashioned writing desk with pigeonholes" (SAS Corporate Communications 1988:19).   Thus at SAS, these rooms become perhaps more to the scale and image of "den" spaces found in more contemporary dwellings. Each room has the generous capacity to entertain two or three visitors and to have available wall and horizontal surfaces personally decorated as one would a semi-public space in the home. The overall effect is one not necessarily of being a patriarch in the most historical meaning of the term, but of having a recognizable sense of individual worth.

This aspect of the self and the potential for absolute privacy remains moderated by the typical glassed inner wall of the Swedish *arbetsby*, together with the almost perpetually open door, now designed to be a lockable coat closet when in that position (an innovation we saw earlier at Enator).   Notice here the subtle disappearance of the collective coat room often adjacent to the bank of individual restrooms in the *smårumskontor*. The presence of a coat closet behind the open door provides additional association of individual office to dwelling. One final element of the expression of the individual lies in the office "owners" name on the inner glass wall adjacent to the door. No titles, just first and last name directly communicate both a horizontal relationship to others in the *arbetsby* and an ultimate source of individual affect, one's family name.

Just as at home one is free to come and go, so too at SAS, as well as in many other Swedish organizations, the office worker controls his or her own time. *Flextid* (flex-time), or the ability to decide when one wants to be in the office, is one of the important ingredients to the SAS concept of "freedom under responsibility" (Boëthius n.d.:1). This freedom seems to have a complementary association to the architectural aspects of the large individual office. An important part of being in almost total control of one's *rum* is the ability to decide when to actually be there.

The functional mechanics of this reality is facilitated by a networked computer system by which locations and expected timetables of individuals are tracked by the reception/information desk. Information about any particular worker's momentary whereabouts or overall work pattern, including all the potential vacation and other off time, is available to all employees through the network, not just the information center. Significantly this information is reported *not* to be systematically used by accounting or other managerial departments as a means of verifying the amount of time actually spent in the office. Such flex-time systems are common in the second order Swedish office. This is an expressively more important kind of flexibility than the half hour or hour variability, often to facilitate traffic problems of getting to or from work, possible in some organizations in other countries. Some people at SAS, though not a large number, choose to work very irregular hours, many evenings, even late into the night. It appears to be relatively easy to integrate individual work into the larger needs of the horizontal group. Yet the work group concept at SAS varies somewhat from the norm.

In that virtually all individual offices, save for those of the few major executives, were designed to be equivalent, the location of middle level managers was not preordained. Notice here among the more recent second order offices in Sweden that the earlier modular presentation of status (using numbers of modules as signs of hierarchical level in the *smårumskontor)*, is becoming less and less evident on the level of middle manager or work group leader. From the overall plan layout of spatial entities at SAS, either at *arbetsgrupp* or larger *avdelning* (department) scales, one can see that the architects consciously avoided giving leaders larger offices. Neither were conspicuous "power-corner" opportunities for certain office locations created. This may not have been such an easy task, considering the enormous variation of plan form. Special places occur on the ends of most projecting wings. They may in part be the more simple visual necessity of terminating the tighter, *smårums* portion of the wing with some larger, interesting "destination". Or as we will see below, they may be part of the institutional second order opposition between *sammanträde* (wing tip) and *pause* (inner portion of collective space).

A brief analysis was made of one of the SAS *avdelninger* or departments, "Route Sector Sweden" (the minicompany, 50% owned nationally, which manages aircraft and services for flights wholly within Sweden). The locations of two of the four *sektion chefs* (section leaders) revealed a preference to be as far out on the wing as possible, see figure 9.7. This seems to be a clear pattern given that this department only has two "wing tips" at its disposal. The other two *chefs* have appropriated first one of the rare corner positions, which may not be unexpected for an accounting *sektion* where perhaps the idea of hierarchy is more pronounced. The

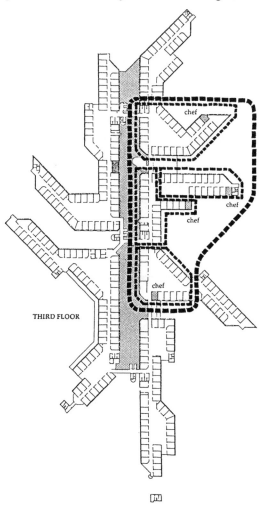

THIRD FLOOR

Figure 9.7 **Plan of SAS office floor; diagram of "Route Sector Sweden" department, section or work group areas, and locations of section** *chefs*

311

second occupies an office immediately adjacent to one of the department entrances. This position may be associated with the more public or external nature of what this advertising and promotion *sektion* does. Only in this last case does the *chef*'s location seem to correspond to the earlier mentioned axiom of being in the center of one's group and being more immediately adjacent to where the visitor will enter.

Are we to interpret the distance from entry to *chef's* location on the wing tip as a sign of territorial power, as such distance often is in offices in other countries? Is it perhaps the case that these people do not use their office to entertain important clients, using instead one of the many other amenities of the larger office. Alternatively, it may be that they participate in major decision making primarily in conjunction with higher level executives, perhaps in some less adjacent location in the SAS building? If so, how is one to explain the preference for this seemingly territorial location? The departmental *chef* of Route Sector Sweden had in fact just "taken over" the conference room which had been adjacent to his office. The conscious reason had to do with a negative task performance relationship between the two spaces in the previous arrangement. The noise of voices during conferencing disturbed the *chef* in his office, of course with the door open. Yet the decision to move the *chef* to the existing conference space, and create a new conference room near the entry, was not a top down, territorial take over. It was made by the total administrative group which occupies that wing.

More than likely it was not only acoustic privacy at the root of the move, but the implication of supervision by a *chef* being so close to the "horizontal" *sammanträde* place. Why then would not the *chef* be moved inward away from the conference room? In this case the *chef* would become more associated with, or perhaps even have strong visual supervision over the larger collective space in the center of the wing. It was reported that the only supervision necessary was the odd walk through the wing on the way to activities on the outside, e.g. the restroom, etc.. This was more to keep some current notion about who is potentially available at any given time in the office, and to make him or herself available, rather than to supervise actual work. The decision of the collective group to locate the *chef* at the tip may have been largely a second order response, one which wants to more strongly associate the *sammanträde* space with *pause* in the larger "living-room". Assuming that the wing tip location for the *chef* does not in fact function to territorially heighten the respect and even anxiety of

312

employees and visitors, we can see this alternatively as a nice cultural expression. It is an opposition between the most visible patriarchal-become-individual room and the major interior space of the collectivity.

What of the office of Jan Carlzon? From the interior photograph of figure 9.8, one quickly recognizes from the size, furnishings and unique shape that this is a special place. While everyone in the building has an immediate view to at least some natural landscape, this office, because of its position at the top-floor "prow" of the administrative *avdelning*, (department) commands a 180 degree overlook of the entire site and fjord. To achieve this effect, it is true that Carlzon's office and administrative *avdelning* had to have been placed on the highest floor, at least from where one stands in that portion of the building. The potential hierarchical and territorial implications of this position is moderated by several aspects of the design. First, there exist *avdelninger* or department floors at the entry portion which act-

Figure 9.8 Bridge to administration department (above), entry to office (middle), CEO's office (below)

313

ually are higher, given the way the building steps down to the lake below. Conceptually, according to second order practice, the *V.D.'s* (CEO) office and administrative *avdelning* is located at the mid-point of street and overall layout, though on the seventh floor. A second moderation of potential externally visible hierarchy is the lack of any distinguishing features of the administrative *avdelning* as one enters from street bridge, as seen in the photo of figure 9.8.

Even after one enters this typical *avdelning* door, the reception area makes no unusual discursive statement, compared with the uniformly high standards of furnishings throughout the building. A third aspect of the design which specifically moderates potential hierarchy, possibly a conscious statement by designer, is the glass partition and door which actually leads to Carlzon's inner office. In spite of the size and amenities of the office interior, the glass entry partition is virtually the same size as a typical individual *rum*. The treatment of the name on the glass panel next to the door is standard: no variation in size or material, and no title.

In addition to Carlzon's office, the administrative *avdelning* contains a small number of individual offices for the SAS vice presidents. These are all a common size, about double that of the typical *rum* elsewhere. Aside from the size, their glassed inner walls, views, furnishings appear very similar to all other offices. The SAS board room occupies the central portion of the *avdelning* running along an exterior wall typically used for individual offices on other floors. It was consciously designed without any presentational (third order) status images, e.g. portraits of previous board members, corporate logos, display cases, etc.. Centrally adjacent to the "living room" formed by the individual offices of this typical *arbetsby* form--used here as a lounge or *pause* space--the board room is simply a somewhat larger *sammanträde* space, presumably reflecting the second order work group concept even at this level of organization.

9.6 *Arbetsgrupp*
The small number of occupants of the administrative group approximates a typical Swedish work group. Yet the formally defined *avdelninger* of the building and organization contain many more members, perhaps from 40 to 80, and will break down into several *sektioner* (sections). If we return to the *avdelning* called Route Sector Sweden, for which we have information, one finds four identifiable *sektioner* which turn out to be about the size of the norm for a typical *arbetsgrupp*, i.e. from about fifteen to twenty persons. It appears from the layout of Route Sector Sweden, at least

(see figure 9.7), that the seemingly aesthetically motivated variations of the SAS plan lend themselves very well to the architectural definition of these smaller, all-important horizontal work groups.

In this second order sense the *sektion* may be seen as the *kombi*-like expression or *arbetsby*. In a few cases sections which occupy only a portion of the linear wing, e.g. Domestic Sweden or the small section called "Route Sector Cargo", might have less of the now almost standard second order opposition between individual office and collective "living room". Even here one finds at least one end of the wing which opens up as part of the various configurations of the central shared space. One cannot question the overall conceptual importance of *arbetsby* expression to the architectural SAS scheme. Questions can be asked about the traditions and current function of work groups in this particular organization. SAS does not work in quite the same way as most other corporations in Sweden.

First of all the label of *sektion* is somewhat unique and more formal than would usually characterize a typical work group. One can find other examples of similarly sized, formally labeled sub-groups within departments in Sweden, but then one would also find smaller groups actually serving as the primaryhorizontal *arbetsgrupp*. These appear to be absent in SAS daily practice. No mention was made of such functional groups. No labels like "group leader" exist. SAS has never had institutionalized *pause* times for such groups. Does this mean that in terms of participatory decision making that SAS is actually less democratic than several other corporations where the work group is more clearly visible? Or could it be that here the section is essentially just a larger work group which manages to effectively link its social expression with participatory decision making at this scale? We have seen work groups almost this large in other organizations.

The answer to this question may lie in understanding the degree to which the "ethos" has influenced corporations in other Scandinavian countries. Given the limitations of the present study, one can say that there seems to be less consistent architectural evidence of second order expression in Norway and Denmark (Iceland is not part of SAS). One can find examples of virtually all architectural components we have discussed in these countries. Participatory decision making in office organization may be less institutionalized in those countries. Even though the *lingua franca* at SAS is essentially Swedish, we must remember that of the 1400 workers at this site, about thirty-five to forty percent of the total are *not* Swedish; Danes and Norwegians each comprise about twenty percent of the whole.

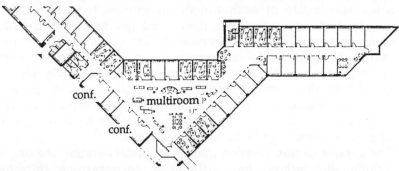

Figure 9.9 Plan and photo of typical *arbetsby* or "multiroom"

To a certain extent the *arbetsby* form at SAS may be something of an imposition from the larger second order ethic now widely extant, at least in Sweden. The administration at SAS talks about the organization of scales of groups in the building only in functional terms. Given the lack of set times or groups with which to take *pause*, both the living rooms with their adjacent mini-kitchens and *bygata* with its shops and restaurants are more consciously seen as places where individuals can spontaneously and creatively "get together", a concept not unlike that at Enator. The form of SAS, however, carries such powerful expression of second order meaning at several scales that it is difficult to imagine such content being not institutionally effective. True, administration talks about a building plan which breaks down the formation of separate groups, alluding to the functional difficulties caused primarily by social ties. They also talk about being able to move people around strictly according to functional need. In the same breath they also admit the difficulty of doing so, describing how individuals become attached to their particular view or office location. This in all probability is in fact a reluctance to leave one's second order social group, referring not to membership in smaller work groups but to the more formalized sections.

Not only are the sections architecturally expressed, as earlier described, but whenever one frequently sees a group socializing in the multiroom, it is a section group celebrating someone's birthday or otherwise cementing their strictly social bonds. Presumably all the institutional obligations of the Swedish *arbetsgrupp* also tend to be in effect here. Such events probably occur fairly regularly and one really must attend. Such ritualized behavior is probably a continuation of practices in their previously more autonomous locales, prior to the consolidation into the present site. In fact, while the SAS multirooms contain some shared work resources such as copiers, their primary meaning is the practice of the social collectivity of the section. Unlike other *vardagsrum* of the Swedish *kombi* or *arbetsby* form, at SAS the conference spaces are not part of this collective center space. The move of one such conference room was mentioned earlier, perhaps to be more associated with the multiroom space. The new conference space was created out of a portion of the glass partitioned space around the collective area. Given the emphasis on the section scale of organization, as the fundamental group entity, one can understand the need for a larger, more formal conference space, adjacent to but more formally distinguished from the purely ritual area of the collectivity.

In addition to the clear architectural expression of the section, or basic work group, possibilities also exist on the *avdelning* or department scale. If we recall FFNS's emphasis on the definition of some level larger than the *arbetsby*, (see again the plans for Televerket in figure 9.4), we recognize the true social complexity of the SAS scheme. While at Televerket the *vardagsrum* expression existed primarily at the larger departmental scale with little or no definition of the work group, at SAS both levels are possible. From the layout of the building, figure 9.7, we see that each departmental entity, i.e. those parts clearly separated by courtyards and coded by separate color schemes, contain two multirooms each. One recalls the frequent dualism evident in smaller scale egalitarian societies, expressed as part of first or second order symbolism. The anthropologist might be quick to point out such potential in this pattern of dual collective spaces within the *avdelning*. More cannot be said because one has far too little evidence about the existing use of this office, and the setting had not been occupied long enough at the time of the interviews.

In the present brief evaluation of the Route Sector Sweden department, together with cursory information about some other departments on the same floor, one cannot even report a conscious association of particular *avdelninger* with the departmental expression of the architecture. One has no record of any intention of such on the part of the designers. Remember that the intent of SAS administration is to break down separate departments in the interest of creating a maximum of "togetherness". This is but another example of how the second order practice in Swedish office buildings often exists more sub-consciously and again recognizes the essential separation of and often contradiction between socio-cultural expression and the organization of actual work.

The split of Route Sector Sweden between two adjacent departmental units of the architecture speaks either to the functional difficulty of fitting every *avdelning* into its own expressive entity, or to the actual lack of need for second order expression at this scale. Some departments actually fit or have been made to fit wholly within a particular architectural unit, e.g. that of the SAS Training Center illustrated in the overall plan of figure 9.7. More time of occupation may be needed before the pre-existing work organization can take full advantage of the second order potential at multiple scales. It is not only the existing ethnic function of the SAS architecture, but its potential as well which is so interesting.

9.7 The SAS "Gata"

Duffy's article on SAS pays particular attention to the *gata*:

> The whole building is predicated on the idea of the street. It would be a sad understatement to call this street an atrium-- connotations of dullness, cricked necks, lifelessness would immediately be conjured up. Instead SAS enjoys a real street which is sometimes full of sunlight and at other times sparkles with beautifully designed, magical, artificial light. There are two

318

major changes of level (not to mention waterfalls), groups of trees, both long and short vistas, bridges across. The internal elevations are varied, complex, interesting. The scale feels absolutely right--never more than seven stories, sometimes four. But above all the street is full of life. People move in and out of major meeting and conference rooms, stroll down to the restaurant at the far end by the lake, take a turn in the sauna or the swimming pool, or most importantly carry out their primary mission of talking to one another, sometimes meeting by chance on the way to somewhere else, or at times by design, sitting at one of the

Figure 9.10 Office announcement of events to take place in the *Gatan*

many little seats or cafe tables. What Niels Torp has done is to capture the best features of the most common of all urban forms, the street, to allow SAS, through the Street's symbolic meaning as well as its utility, to bind 1500 people (and all their thousands of visitors) together in a completely natural and unforgettable way. (Duffy 1989:44)

Clearly the visual aesthetics of the SAS street do all these things, and better than many of the atrium offices mentioned earlier (see plan of figure 9.11). No one can doubt the importance of some such visual relief from the information intensity and often overload which occurs during office work, particularly considering the generally high level of responsibility given to most Scandinavians. The views, however, from the upper level offices facing the street may be less visually interesting than views to the exterior landscape

319

from the more numerous perimeter offices. The primary importance of the street or *Gatan*, as it is called, is of course socio-cultural. While the Architectural Review briefly mentions the symbolic "togetherness" which the architectural form of the street seems to provide, the article places most emphasis on the typical function of a successful urban street. Again we have the more conscious view, not only by architect and reviewer, but by client as well. The image is identical to the new pedestrian streets, mentioned previously, in major cities of Scandinavia. Not unlike the concept behind Enator and perhaps the electronic offices of the U. S., the notion is that streetscape opportunities will provide the locus for a spontaneous and productive "getting together".

It is also true that the amenities provided on the SAS street generate a more frequent usage beyond the midday meal, a greater overall frequency than the interior street at Ideon, for example. From the plan one can locate along the street a money exchange, clothing shop, bank/travel agency, clinic, sports hall, gym room, swimming pool, saunas, clubroom, cafe/deli, conference rooms, auditorium, library, and dining places. This street setting, perhaps even more than the multiroom spaces at the scale of the sections, was consciously intended to provide one of the primary means of what Carlzon has called "something of a cultural revolution" (SAS Corporate Communications 1988:4). But this really is not the second order form of expressive practice presently hypothesized. The more conscious image on the part of the SAS executive officer, the architects, and again the reviewers, is for a kind of territorial neutral place--the European urban street--where third order hierarchical distinctions disappear and spontaneous creativity leads to new solutions for work. More specifically, Carlzon says that:

> We need to become comfortable with a different perspective on our work. Growth results from encounters and dialogue. Sitting at your desk does not necessarily mean being productive. Meeting a colleague from another department over a cup of coffee is not the same as shirking your duties (ibid:5).

Unfortunately we have no data at present as to whether or to what degree the street is actually used for this ideal image of creative work. Nor can one easily establish the "symbolic" effect of a central atrium in an office building.[5] In second order architecture, forms are not in themselves the primary source of symbolism, but are rather structural and cognitive "containers" for other meaning, e.g. the individual or collective in Scandinavian tradition. In third

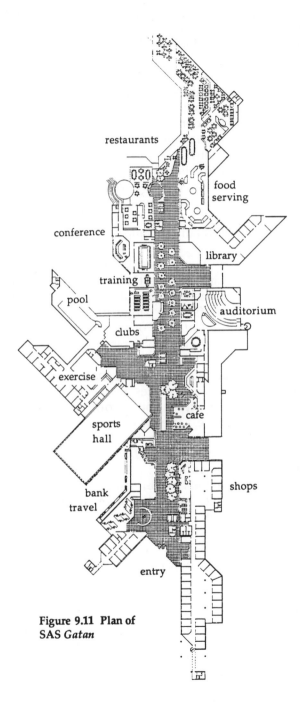

restaurants

food
serving

conference

library

training

pool

auditorium

clubs

exercise

cafe

sports
hall

bank
travel

shops

entry

**Figure 9.11 Plan of
SAS *Gatan***

order groups (often functioning through a less socially integrated manipulation of such traditional or heavily associational meanings) one often finds the frequent assertion that territorially neutral public spaces connote "togetherness" among a usually loosely connected group. Yet the actual usage of such places, most pedestrian streets included, appears as mentioned before to be "superficial gregariousness" (Slater 1970), minimally evocative communication of perhaps only vague recollections of community. At the very least such places function positively as neutral territories with at least some feeling of group identity. They can be visually and socially interesting, and entertaining. They are really "signs" not symbols of "togetherness".

Much of this open territoriality, social spontaneity and the like is inimical to a larger part of Swedish office experience where if possible, second order practices are preferred as a means of relieving and better controlling the necessity of hierarchy, distribution of power, and the like. The new urban streets in Scandinavia provide the kind of territorial release which Slater speaks ill of, with a presumed effect in a still third order and territorial urban milieu. The overwhelming evidence gathered in other office settings again suggests a greater and fundamentally different set of meanings attached to these spaces. In all likelihood the SAS *Gatan* will have far less meaning as a place to do creative work or to casually socialize as a sign of togetherness, than it will as a place to practice second order ritual. Individual or friendship use of spaces contradicts the effects of fully institutionalized collective events in these same places.

We do not need to look very far for first indications of the importance of second order meanings of the *Gatan*. First of all, it is *not* open to the public. One enters a carefully controlled initial visitors area, and must have a confirming badge attached before being allowed to enter and use the *Gatan*. For most employees, and visitors, it seems, the street is not primarily a place for more casual activities of individuals or small groups of spontaneously interacting people. While it may metaphorically look like an urban street with shopping and occasional places to meet or stop and watch people, the three or four actual shops form only the first portion of the street at the entrance. The two major changes in *gata* level create in effect a set of thresholds between three distinct domains. Following the diagram of figure 9.12 one can describe a possible recognition of the inherent distinction or even contradiction between spontaneous urban street and collective places for second order practice. Whether entering from one's private car, shopping briefly, banking, or buying one's air ticket, all these things may be associated with individual experience of the profane third order environment. Even the location of the small clinic may express the modern value of personal health rather than collective participation.

It would be tempting to attach the second order label of "individual" to this first, entry, or Street portion of the sequence, forming a symmetrical opposition with the collective portion associated with restaurants and lake. Such an interpretation suggests that urban streets in Scandinavian can in fact be considered not just as kinds of free or neutral territories, but as deeper construc-

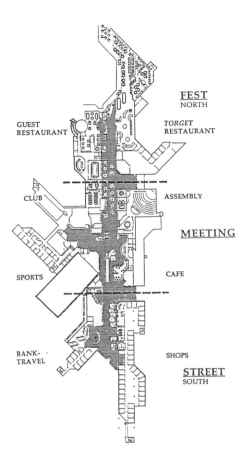

FEST
NORTH

GUEST
RESTAURANT

TORGET
RESTAURANT

CLUB

ASSEMBLY

MEETING

SPORTS

CAFE

BANK-
TRAVEL

SHOPS

STREET
SOUTH

Figure 9.12 Major domains of the SAS
Gatan; photos of the two threshold
positions

tions of meaning at the level of second order culture. The proof lies in being able to identify aspects of the Street area which provide clear association with the familial, patriarchal, individual meanings of the Scandinavian past. Returning to the primary source of this meaning, the individual/family space, one finds very few of these kinds of associations in the shopping atmosphere of the first portion of the *gata*. More convincing is the fact that because of the stepped configuration of the building the vast majority of employees actually use this first portion as the primary access to their individual offices. People tend not to walk down the major stairs between first and second portions, or much less the additional stairs between second and third portions, just to go *up* again in the elevators located in these particular sections. The primary entry to "individual" departments (at this largest of scales), sections, or rooms is the set of elevators immediately adjacent to the front parking lot entry. With only a few exceptions, one goes first vertically to the appropriate level, then horizontally *within* the "individual" areas--*not the Gatan*. Even though the design intention was to create as much street-like access and activity in the circulation plan, other things, perhaps site topography and more subconscious second order needs, have created almost the opposite effect.

In terms of the present proposition, a reduction of spontaneous street activity in a modern Scandinavian office building is not seen as a negative, but in fact part of a positive effect in developing and maintaining second order meaning at the largest scale of organization. We might call the first portion "Street" in its strong association with the individual entities which are accessed here. This spatial sequence is conceptually very similar to the separation between a portion of the building with office spaces and the formally separate collective spaces which were discussed in the preceding chapter. The significant ritual effect is the trip from one opposed space to the other. At SAS one enters the office spaces from the Street portion, both vertically and horizontally, but then one uses other circulation to enter the second and third portions, i.e. the elevators or associated stairs in those sections (not the major longitudinal *gata* stairs). The trip to the collective spaces of SAS, it may be argued, is conceptually not the spontaneous street experience one might at first have expected, but a definite and positive ritual procession to architecturally distinct collective places.

The articulations between the three levels are in this sense more than visually interesting sequences of vertical circulation. Rather than broad terraces which would speak more to a "public", neutral territorial interpretation of the street sequence, the passage between first and second sections is somewhat constricted by typical urban standards. The more ceremonial stairway, along with the transitional symbolism of the very linear water course parallel to it, provokes a much greater sense of ritual threshold. Apparently used less for functional circulation than for cultural effect, this threshold is more pronounced than that between the second and third portions. This may be an important expression of the major, largest scale opposition between the Street portion of the building, and domains where particularly collective events occur. Not only are these spaces not "public" in the true sense of the word, but within the organization as well one will tend to use these places in a more organized, institutionalized manner, i.e. at particular times with particular social others.

It is interesting that in the *Gatan* the only apparent sidewalk cafe, that hallmark of urban street life, occurs as part of the level change of this first major threshold. To a certain degree it exists liminally poised *between* the definitions of individual office and collective place. The only actual place in the everyday experience of the *Gatan* for the more spontaneous, creative togetherness envisioned by the design image of street, the cafe may actually function in this way, particularly for certain people who may in one way or another fall outside of spheres of localized practice. Though when compared to the more organized creativity of much more numerous second order *fest* occasions which take place elsewhere, at various scales, one may question the effectiveness of the small cafe in relation to the overall scale of the organization. This kind of liminal place, more typical of Latin urban culture perhaps, simply does not appear to be part of the more totally defined, *by*-like, concepts of space in traditional Scandinavia, particularly where some social group has control over the total setting.

9.8 "Meeting"
We have discussed the importance of the Street level as the largest scale threshold between office portions of the buildings and collective spaces. This latter portion of the opposition, composed of the second and third levels of the *Gatan*, can then be seen as itself internally divided into two aspects of collective practice. Like the previously discussed opposition in other large office buildings one finds the distinction between "Meeting" and "Fest" at the largest of scales clearly evident in SAS as well. The reader will also recall the expression of this same distinction at several levels of organization, especially at that of the work group with their *pause* and *sammanträde* spaces. Many of the activities of the upper portion of the collective domain--the middle level of the *Gatan*---are clearly more functionally purposeful, including the group *möte* (meeting). In a bit of additional association, the large auditorium with its electronic linkage to national television networks, a kind of extension of SAS group to this largest scale of membership, lies directly below the office of Jan Carlzon and other executives. Given the lack of hierarchical expression of vertical office location, mentioned above, this relationship represents more the typical

opposition of *any* individual office above and largest scale collective places below. The formal positioning of Carlzon's office in relation to the electronic auditorium is specifically representative.

Within the Meeting aspect of the collective, a further distinction is made in the *gata*. The clearly preponderant usage of the side opposite from the large auditorium is that of sports, including the multi-purpose gym, exercise facility, and swimming pool. A fourth space here is called the "clubroom". Returning to previous discussion of these general recreation activities in Swedish offices, we revisit the proposition that the greatest usage of these spaces is by organized groups, not individuals, who are institutionally linked with other second order definitions of the corporation, i.e. sections, departments, or the SAS as a whole. While no detailed analysis of these users was possible, many indications of the organized nature of SAS sports, such as schedules or lists of team memberships, were evident to the visitor. Lap swimming would certainly be the exception here, as would jogging or other strictly individual exercise.

The shared, organized activities represent as well a form of purposeful collective experience, one distinct from those of the *fest* and consistent with the Meeting portion of the *Gatan*. In Sweden, good physical health is very much part of the collective social consciousness. It is in the collective best interests of SAS to encourage and even enforce, through required examination, the health of its members. In addition to this association between collective participation and physical well-being, one finds the possibility that organized sports represent a significant arena of culturally acceptable competition. While consensus is the goal of most meeting activities in the Scandinavian offices, perhaps most symbolized in the auditorium at SAS, the other side of the *gata* may actually provide a kind of ritual relief of potentially disruptive, overly competitive desires. The primary second order vehicle in this regard is of course the *fest* which forms a natural sequence of most Meeting activities.

A more logical emphasis of organized sports activity would probably be the collective effect of working together as members of teams. Yet it would be inappropriate to lay too much importance on the contribution of sports to the horizontal basis of the typical Swedish office organization. Such is an integral part of second order process at virtually all levels of daily and ceremonial practice and would seem not to depend to any significant degree upon extracurricular events such as sports. The presence of cross-cutting clubs, as at least made possible by the clubroom, do not appear to be important sources of social solidarity or political power. The place called "club room" in plan was not even mentioned on the author's tour, nor was there any indication near its minimally expressed *gata* entry of any activity such as club meetings, events, and the like. Advertisements for athletic participation, on the other hand, were clearly to be seen in front of those respective areas.

The middle or Meeting level of the *Gatan*, as the largest of the three sections, is itself an important, perhaps the most important, assembly place for the largest number of members of the SAS society. Recall the traditional meeting of the *by* council in the

Danish National Day

Norwegian National Day

Swedish National Day

New route to the Far East

Figure 9.13 Events focused in central Meeting domain of SAS *Gatan*

center of the village open space. Similarly, during certain SAS events speeches by Jan Carlzon and others will be made to those standing in this middle level, and on the multi-leveled bridges on each side of this space. The natural podium for speeches as well as other more festive aspects of events here, such as choral groups, is the principal stair/waterfall threshold overlooking the meeting domain. Both conceptually and physically, many events, including Santa Lucia, the highly prominent celebrations of the three national days of Denmark, Norway, and Sweden, and more purely promotional expressions, for example the opening of a new air route to some part of the world, all appear to originate at this threshold point in the *Gatan* (see images of figure 9.13)

In addition to the business or sports consensus which is reached during more purposeful activities in the meeting portion of the *gata*, one may also speak of more thematic events. These also occur in this major portion of the SAS setting, as distinct from the actual communitas acts of eating and drinking together which occur in the climax of the *Gatan*.[6] Most thematic are practices expressing Scandinavian nationalism such as the national day celebrations and uses of the electronic auditorium, Santa Lucia, and even SAS business relations. Most provide the emotional content, which when associated with the purposeful activities of Meeting, perhaps facilitates the formation of consensus.

9.9 "Fest"

The second order, opposed frameworks created by the architectural forms at different scales provide the cognitive structure for the mentioned contents or associations of the ethos--maintained and invoked by ritual practice. The architectural medium is in effect largely limited, in second order space, to this abstract structural contribution. It appears inhibited from important imageable or presentational content. We see no architectural or graphic images which are special to any particular domain, e.g. no permanent images are associated with domain themes like Meeting. Interestingly enough, the same is not true of the landscape where office buildings or parts thereof are oriented expressly toward traditional Scandinavian meanings of Nature. It is no accident at SAS that the ritual procession begun at the major threshold culminates with the powerful fusion of restaurant/*fest* area and natural fjord. The Fest domain is not only separated from the Meeting domain by a lessor threshold with stairs and again water (both domains being part of the "collective") but its natural associations achieve an almost spiritual level of meaning distinct

328

Figure 9.14 View of "fjord" from Fest domain

perhaps from the thematic meeting or organizational content of the central portion of the *Gatan*.[7]

As has been described in the architectural journals, the lowest and culminating area of the *Gatan* is simply a very interesting visual setting for the midday escape from the stress of office work. The well landscaped artificial lake nicely simulates the original design intention of terminating the axis on the actual fjord, which for technical reasons could not be built. As constructed, the lake almost reaches the natural water of the sound, lying only a few meters above. Facing the lake are two separate dining facilities, one on each side of the *gata*. The smaller more intimate, and more expensive restaurant is called the *gästmatsal* (guest dining room) and is used for guests and other special occasions. The much larger restaurant whose seating areas wrap graciously along the other side of the lake is referred to as the *personalmatsal* (personnel dining room). The generous and visually delightful serving area of this typical cafeteria style facility (the guest dining room follows this general pattern as well) has been labeled the *serveringstorg* (food market). A sign in the *gata*, *"Torget"* (the

329

market) hangs by the entrance. Like all other members of SAS, Jan Carlzon and other *chef* most regularly eat their midday meal in the *Torget*, using the smaller restaurant for guest and other special occasions, sometimes with executives only.

In addition to and certainly more significant than the visual aesthetics of this portion of the street, remains the Scandinavian meaning of *fest* as one participates in what for many may be the major meal of the day. Recalling all the institutionalized aspects of this daily collective experience at the largest of scales, the walk to this lower portion of the *Gatan* should be seen for the ritual practice which it is. Whether coming from the office portions of the building or from a thematic event in the Meeting domain, one moves to an associationally distinct and opposed place. Here members eat and drink together in an associationally "natural" setting, not unlike the primarily collective Scandinavian ritual of *Midsommer* where the emphasis is on the *fest* at the natural site of the *by*. Even the term *torget* as used to designate the large dining place has traditional meaning. The major collective ritual (*Midsommer*) was held at the identically named market place, usually as part of the *bygata*. In earlier first order times, these ritual sites were out in the larger landscape and strongly associated with the gods and spirituality. They were always conceptually and at times geographically "north" of human and architectural forms. The SAS *Gatan* orients exactly north and south, with the *fest/ natur/torg* climax to the north. Recall the same ancient symbolism in the location of the restaurant at the northern focus of the *gata* at Ideon.[8]

How speculative is it that modern Scandinavians still associate that highest of spiritual power with the direction of north?[9] Much in known folklore and tradition remains permeated with the old Norse directional symbolism, though it apparently has no active use such as one finds in the case of geomancy in aspects of modern Chinese building practice. Yet Swedes still use Middle Ages churches, many of which maintain their unusual primary south/north entrances. Still one can only speculate about such a possible associational meaning to be added to other aspects of the Fest domain at SAS. A closer look at the actual ceremonial activities of this domain may, however, provide additional definition of the "spiritual".

It is here, not in the upper, street-like portion of the *gata* that frequent "pub nights" are organized. Usually Friday after work, tables are moved into the *gata* between the two major restaurant *fest* spaces. No detailed information is available about just which groups meet at this time for a round or two of beer or wine. Are these cross-cutting groups of friends, or is this another occasion for expression of the more purely social aspects of work groups? The brief survey did not allow details about who was dining with whom during the midday meal. We can only infer from the widespread pattern in other Swedish corporations that here too, such *fest* activity usually focuses on somewhat obligatory relationships between work comrades. The Danish and Norwegian aspects of the SAS society might have some influence on the Swedish norm.

What, one might ask, associates drinking with the proposed "spirituality" of the northern or Fest domain? Aside from the now distant but frequent references to transformational symbolism of

Figure 9.15 "Pub Night" in the Fest domain of the SAS *Gatan*

drink and *mead* in Norse mythology or folklore, one still finds drinking at many major Swedish *fests*, and probably especially during more nature associated events such as *Midsommer*. Alcoholic drink is a principal means of entering into a state of communitas with one's others. This expression of pure "I-thou" relationships, in Turner's terms (1968), is then associated with the spiritual world or North, vesting the egalitarian community with the ultimate symbolic and ritual power. Second order expression is politically and practically inhibited from using the most ritually effective first order devices of actual contact, i.e., places where people believe the spirits actually enter their world. Yet much of the very ancient symbolic associations, even at times including directional meanings, may subtly persevere though with obviously less emotional effect.

One cannot today at SAS speak about a fully logical ceremonial cycle of events, which as in first order time and space opposed both summer and winter solstice events. As discussed earlier, one finds little overt *Midsommer* celebration by corporate organizations, though some tendencies may be exerting themselves more recently to balance the very visible winter celebrations in virtually all offices. Compared with the hundreds of years of occupation in either the traditional first or second order communities, one particular building, even SAS, can only capture some portion of the greater Scandinavian ethnic repertoire--in spite of the twenty or so years of modern second order evolution. Contradictions and major changes may occur, either through the creative process of design or influence by other non-expressive causes of form. The sequence of the Santa Lucia procession at SAS is a case in point.

Figure 9.16 *Lucia* parade moving through SAS *Gatan*

In what must be a wonderfully evocative scene--the candles of the Lucia procession after dark--the second order ritual actually moves through the *Gatan* in the wrong direction, at least according to traditional ritual and folklore. Traditionally, the Norse winter solstice was that time when the spirits come out of the mountains in the north and visited individual family farms. This was in temporal and spatial opposition to the community which moved to the natural site in the North at *Midsommer*. Visits from the other world such as in the *Lucia* procession always conceptually moved from nature to architecture as it were, from outside to in. Yet here at SAS, and perhaps elsewhere, the parade moves from the major threshold towards the place with the greatest nature or spiritual association, the fjord in the North. The procession and brief speeches in the meeting domain ultimately culminate with food and drink again in the Fest domain, like all others.

One might chose to interpret this as a ritual change consistent with the absence of the *Midsommer* rite in the corporate calendar. The major office ritual at winter cannot only be an expression of the dominance of collective spirits over the individual. It might also include the opposed meaning of the summer rite. If the procession were to actually begin in the entry, or even outside, then move to the first portion, and then to the center for the customary speech, this would then mimic only the winter ritual. The spirits come to visit the familial-become-individual domains. The movement from center to Fest domain could subsequently represent the *Midsommer* linkage of collectivity with nature and north. This collapsed meaning of the *Gatan* sequence is presumably effective in many events, though perhaps most strongly expressed in such purely ritual occasions such as Santa Lucia.

The Northern domain is the highest expression of the linkage of pure egalitarian communitas with pure associations of spirit or more generally of Scandinavian "culture". Whereas the thematic associations of the central, meeting domain appear to refer more to actual social, political manifestations of collectivity, i.e. the emphasis on Scandinavian nationalism or sports, the contents of the North refer more to things essentially unapproachable on the plane of political reality. It attempts a fusion of pure, unapproachable cultural essence or power with the fundamental feeling of communitas, the essence of the traditional *Midsommer*. It is as well in the Fest area of the *Gatan* (between the two restaurants) that renowned musicians perform as part of a continuous program of cultural events. In the present context the collective appreciation of music adds to the associational depth of things which transcend the physical or the political. Both music and art displays of the Northern portion of the *Gatan* emphasize for the Swedish office workers not the importance of discursive creativity as they often do in (third order) forms in other places, but the presence of a shared emotional response with no immediate connotations of actual social or political collectivities, a pure spirituality perhaps. With time these meanings become associated with or otherwise legitimize both social and meeting relationships at all scales of the organization.

The location of the SAS library directly above the *Torget*, even though entered from above, may also express a certain kind of cultural knowledge, even spirit. This must exist independently of the thematic references to actual social groups while at the same time being firmly linked with the social feeling of communitas. Yet would this be more true of public or community libraries than those used for more immediately functional corporate purposes? The impossibility of an in-depth ethnography of multiple office buildings, including SAS, has prohibited detailed information about how many spaces are actually used.

Second order ritual in the *Gatan* will continue to develop as the organization further appropriates the inherent symbolic potential of these spatial sequences. A year or two of occupation is still a relatively limited time frame for a corporation in a new physical and organizational setting, even in Sweden. Although a good portion of the second order content of SAS may have emerged through more collective, perhaps less fully conscious, truly ethnic processes of design competition and development, still the post-occupancy development of *Gatan* events, at least, owes its success in no small degree to conscious decisions by the corporation. In part because of the lack of ritual traditions of this previously dispersed organization, and in part perhaps because of the marvelously new second order potential of the SAS environment, the decision was made to create a "street manager". The sole responsibility of this person has been the development and execution of *Gatan* activities. Thus many of the events discussed above were either created anew or adapted to the new setting by a kind of ritual coordinator, presently a female executive apparently very popular with the SAS community.[10]

The rational management of cultural events at this largest of scales also seems to reinforce the present interpretation of the SAS *Gatan* as primarily a second order phenomenon, in contrast to more widely held images of typical urban street. Aspects of street activities in places like Copenhagen will at times be organized by local agencies, whether public or private. Yet the essence of the successful urban street is not its organized events, but its territorial freedom and spontaneity. While almost totally organized events of the SAS *Gatan* are nominally voluntary, still a great deal of the obligation towards participating in *fests* with one's work comrades must exist on the largest scale as well. There exists a great deal of collective control over the associational content and ritual usage of this spatial sequence. It has a far greater formality and ritual potential than any piece of today's urban landscape. The involvement of Swedish executives in the fostering of collective culture has been seen throughout the second order evolution. Part of the individual decision making responsibility of the patriarchal-become-individual has during these last twenty or thirty years been focused on creating socio-cultural foundations of horizontal work patterns. Today when one plays managerial roles in these organizations one very consciously recognizes that efficient production depends critically upon the effectiveness of collective ritual practice. Managers too have dual aspects of self!

Notes

1   David Gilmore, in his article about a traditional city in Spain (1977), provides a good description but not really theoretical basis of what might be second order space at this larger scale. Instead of the Scandinavian opposition between individual and collectivity, the concentric layout of this city and its cemetery express the social opposition between the aristocracy in the center, and common laborers on the periphery. The reason why such a spatial disposition isn't simple territoriality lies in the ritual movements of respective actors *between* domains. One such ritual, Carnival, is the ritual reversal where masquerading workers from the periphery commune in the city center with the upper class. An opposite event, at an opposite time of the year, finds the aristocracy moving to the periphery. Most likely the associational, symbolic meanings of center and periphery are far more integrated with socio-political history in Spain or Brazil, for example, than in Copenhagen. While doing Carnival in Copenhagen may involve going to the central *gågata* for many, it undoubtedly does not serve to expressively legitimatize a hierarchical relationship between dominant and subordinate groups. For further discussion, see (Doxtater 1984).

2   While the Swedes use the term *stad* almost exclusively for "city", the Norwegians will use this term as well as *by*. Remember that when the Norwegian farms began clustering into second order forms, later perhaps than in Denmark and Southern Sweden, the term *by* in Norway was probably already associated with settlement forms primarily in those two other countries, whether village or city. The indigenous term for the newer clustering of farms particularly in Western Norway was simply an extension of the old term for house cluster or core of individual farms, i.e. *tun*. The second order village-like entity became the *gårdstun* (cluster of farms).

335

3   The reader is reminded of one of the basic theoretical tenets of the present argument, i.e. that more conscious image or metaphor manipulation in the design process usually will not be associated with any deeper level understanding of second order symbols and processes (unusual artistic contributions notwithstanding). More conscious attachment of meanings to architectural form tends to be the primary contribution of architects to expression in third order contexts.

4   Carlzon's role in the economic salvation and prosperity of SAS is documented in a book of his own experiences, *Moments of Truth* (1987). The original title in Swedish was *Riv Pyramidin* (Tear Down the Pyramid), which may have been judged too radical of a title to sell to larger markets outside of Sweden. Apparently written before the SAS building was constructed, it describes many of the organizational changes which occurred during this breakthrough period in Sweden. In addition to the natural focus on executive leadership, particularly in reversing the role of middle level managers to support "front line" people rather than supervise from above, Carlzon does give credit to wider influences happening across the country, e.g. the positive use of *MBL* (again, the co-determination law of 1977). Most interesting is his description of the new direction of the corporation in 1984, two or three years after it became solvent again. This movement he calls the "second-wave". While the description of these intentions concerns primarily new levels of productivity, it is also true that this is precisely the time when SAS is making the decision to create in effect the ritual basis for its new organizational forms, i.e. the consolidation of many groups into the large headquarters site in Stockholm. Is "second-wave" really "second order"?

5   Design students, particularly in the hot climate of the Southwest, frequently create atria spaces within their buildings. The conscious intention is to provide visual and climatic amenities adjacent to interior spaces. Yet most often these intentions cannot become reality because of limited natural landscape within an overly architectural container, and because of the lack of "prospect and refuge" (being personally and socially uncomfortable with someone looking at your back from some portion of the building). Most designers probably intuitively sense this behavioral reality of many such spaces, but persist in using the atrium primarily from a less conscious motivation to communicate some sort of socio-cultural "togetherness" to the occupants. The historical Hispanic/Moorish image is also influential in this region of the Americas. Nevertheless one questions the effectiveness of using either historical or metaphoric images of atria, especially when compared to the ritual power of similar spaces when part of more associationally deep, structurally opposed second order practice.

6   See again discussion of Turner's notion of structure and anti-structure discussed briefly in Chapter 2.3, specifically footnote four.

7   One could view the two aspects of the collective portion of the *gata* as similar to Victor Turner's distinction between "physiological" and "normative" symbols (1969), or Joseph Cambell's difference between "Kama" and "Dharma" (1969). Here the emotional content of symbolism is felt to come from affect associated with basic physiological fears and pleasures; these are then linked through expressive means with some ideological message--itself inherently devoid of affective power--which the society deems important. Given the ritual

sequence of meeting and following *fest*, one might interpret the thematic contents of the meeting as the "ideological" which is then given its affective power through linkage with more "physiological" contents in the *fest*, here connotations of death and spirituality--if they still exist. For a more extended discussion with respect these notions in first order Scandinavian practice, see again Doxtater (1981:204).

8   In assembling the plans of *byar* and offices for figure 0.1 (in the introduction), the author became aware of the north-south orientation of the *bygata* of these plans. While this is probably a coincidence, the issue deserves more study. This orientation is opposite from the traditional east-west pattern of the community road which went through the first order, autonomous Norwegian farm.

9   The author recalls a discussion after a seminar in which first order symbolism of Norwegian "folk" farms was presented to a group of Swedish professors of architecture. Rather than assume that all of the original directional symbolism had by now disappeared from Scandinavian architecture, they seriously proposed the likelihood that some such meaning might still be found.

10 At the time of publication, SAS has had to terminate this position because of financial problems associated with the recession in Sweden. The possibility also exists that at some time after occupation, these rites might have become institutionalized and essentially self-managed, thus eliminating the need for an actual manager.

10 Final discussion

10.1 Evolution of architectural expression in Scandinavia

What began in the sixties and is culminating in the late eighties and early nineties represents a reenactment of the aboriginal second order concept of *by*, though in a much more condensed period of time. The use of the terms *arbetsby* or even *"kontorsby"*, as one might refer to largest scale second order expression (office village), suggests not so much the direct and more rational emulation of earlier forms than a less conscious, cultural phenomenon at the national scale. Though management and designers contribute significantly to the process, they are but a portion of a much larger, essentially participatory phenomenon. Just as in the Middle Ages *byar* of Scandinavia, it is hypothesized that in offices as well two symbolic meanings have been essential to the realization of second order practice. First, a large set of associations, stretching back to ancient first order times, must be attached to the basic social conditions of hierarchy (the "familial/patriarchal/individual") and equality (the "collective"). Secondly, these concepts must be ritually operationalized in terms of real participatory actors and semantically opposed places. In the historical absence of first order systems of sacred axes, direction and the like, the expression of opposed concepts and associated social groups relies heavily upon architectural form.

In first order Scandinavian expression, oppositions between family and community were strongly associated with and structured by systems of sacred space connecting and influencing all scales of social experience: dwelling, settlement, region, larger natural landscape, etc.. It has been assumed that these environmental meanings were essentially "pre-textual", not in the modern rhetorical meaning of the term, but as socially and spatially derived systems of expression relatively independent of or at least more fundamental than medial texts of myth or folklore. Whether at the scale of the local marriage ceremony or that of the Icelandic All-Thing, these meanings provided the frameworks for all ritual practice.

Second order uses of space and architectural expression are also assumed to be essentially pre-textual. Both first and second order forms have been contrasted with modern "discursive" uses of architecture. This is a distinction between expression founded in ritual practice and that more influenced by the systems of discourse surrounding certain elite and other self-interested groups. The contrast is between "localized" and "non-localized" processes of expressive practice. Complementary to our first assumption about the pre-textual basis of first and second order expression, third order discourse is much more dependent upon the use of media and text. The use of architecture for the communication of style, philosophy and other aspects of discursive groups, contrasts radically with its use in sacred (first order) and collective (second order) examples. Given the relative absence of territoriality in societies where ritual practices predominate (at least within the localized entity), and its frequent presence in modern rhetorical or discursive processes, one assumes a causal linkage in the latter case.

The distinction between pre-textual and textual practice will certainly complicate thinking about structuration, or the way complex, often socially diverse historical or modern societies are somehow influenced by expressive culture, i.e. the linkage between expressive experience and larger institutional forms. Previously, all expression was essentially assumed by most scholars to stem in one way or another from speech or language based social experience. Structuration problems were cast in terms of how culture "medially" amplifies or distributes "talking" as societies evolve from simple personally known entities to complex institutionally organized nations and even worlds.

The idea that sacred and so-called peasant societies were not influenced primarily by speech experience *per se*, but by the environmentally derived frameworks of ritual practice, forces one to theoretically understand the contributions of natural and architectural form in processes of structuration. One must distinguish these aspects from effects of language and language media. Such is essential to any true theory of architecture, and a more accurate evolutionary grounding to structuration theory. Social commentators like Giddens and Meyrowitz accurately describe the effects of language media on modern society, in relation to territorial uses of space. Yet they cannot explain or incorporate either the ancient sacred cosmologies nor the localized villages. While it is not really problematic in their case, interested as they primarily are in modern or modernizing processes, it omits some very interesting contemporary phenomena. One speaks here of localized co-working or co-living societies. Whether or not these spatially based forms of social organization will become widely used alternatives to discursive processes, and what their organizational limits will be only time will tell.

What a pre-textual understanding also provides for the first time is a structuration focus on the actual process by which ancient sacred systems are modified by diversifying historical processes. Pred's mentioned study of the breakup of Danish and Southern Swedish villages assumed to be highlighting evolutionarily initial problems as socio-cultural processes went from small to much larger and more complex entities. It was not an investigation into how the spatially sacred transformed into the discursive modern. What is just as interesting is the way in which the villages formed in the first place as an expressive reaction to disruptions in sacred systems of practice. More significant is the possibly that these changes represent a unique form of (non-sacred) ritual practice.

In spite of the overt prohibitions by Christianity of much of the indigenous Norse calendrical ritual, and the ritual usage of many sacred spaces, it is argued that aspects of this symbolism became covertly reconstituted in the new forms of the second order *byar*. Ritual oppositions and practice, now framed much more subtly and yet uniquely by architectural form, still operated more pre-textually than textually (though folklore undoubtedly begins to play a larger role). We saw the probable symbolic internalization of the sacred tree in the farm courtyard, or the maypole or other symbol of *axis mundi* within the larger open space of the *by*. Aspects of symbolic orientation continued in the placement of the dwelling portion of the farm complex of buildings. Some calendrical rituals such as *Midsommer* appear to have shifted almost intact to the new spatial layout.

Fests occurred along with every work event in these cooperative villages, something which existed with communal labor in first order societies but with far less frequency. This heightened form of ritual practice may signify a shift in the way a more architectonically based and systematically limited ritual effect operates. To a certain extent there appears to be a greater experiential need to frequently associate real groups of family and community with formally structured architectural spaces. This contrasts with the first order emphasis on essentially fictive relationships between humans and spirits. Sacred practices are dependent upon symbolically more powerful but also more abstract conceptions of space. History has shown us that it is possible for first order participation to be circumscribed by specialists or priests as these abstract systems become more complex. Ultimately it will be a theocratic figure alone who may make contact with or play the role of the gods.[1] In second order experience calendrical ritual continues, but in a more subtle form with a greater emphasis on village space *per se*. This tends to associationally substitute the power of ancient gods with the power of an actual collective group.

In sacred societies the symbolic effect of major calendrical rites becomes associated with lessor ritual practices at smaller scales of organization and setting. Associational strategies of "homologue" link the most sacred power to all levels of expressive experience. In second order practice, smaller scale rites and experience can as well be associated with larger rituals. Yet this linkage appears to be severely limited by the necessity for individuals to actually participate in all levels of practice. It is almost as if in first order societies, power flows ritually and spatially from some most sacred locus. In second order experience power may flow in essentially the opposite direction. Based more on the differing social realities of equal and hierarchical selves--stripped as they have been of their sacred symbolism--power relationships are more fundamentally established at the smallest and most participatory levels of society. The more frequent daily practice of working and festing together becomes the foundation upon which limited extensions to larger scales occur. These limits may be characterized by the need to fully participate with, or socially know, all others, and by the need for all architectural frameworks of practice to be intimately known or experientially contiguous.

To a certain extent, second order experience is more presentational than the sacred, given its emphasis on aspects of the self rather than on more abstract relationships between humans and spirits. Territorially based expression existed *between* localized *byar*, and one distinguished between one's own village and other villages or the discursively known outside world. Yet *within* the small Scandinavian *by*, how conscious was the presentation of the two aspects of the same self? In many respects the image of "master of the farm" seems consciously over-expressed in relation to any images of self as a participant in the collectivity. Probably much of the patriarchical imagery of the male farm head appeared late in the *by* period, at a time when bourgeois discourse was making its way into the countryside.

More pervasively we should recognize the lack of Goffman's "front" and "back" regions in second order villages. The frequent ritual practice of inviting co-workers into the family dwelling for a *fest* clearly confirms the ultimate collective control over these settings with their high presentational potential. Probably it is only after the introduction of the "fine room" that the individual family itself begins to initiate front and back behavior in the dwelling. Prior to modernization in the rural areas, it is possible that the only way any collective group could establish egalitarian relationships between individuals and the group--as aspects of the same self--was through non-discursive, localized, highly participatory ritual practice. It was this power which inhibited presentational behavior as most of us in modern organizations experience it.

Given the present emphasis on the spatial basis of traditional *by* culture in Scandinavia, indeed that such cooperative relationships could not have existed without architectural expression, one can now look with a new perspective on the physical breakup of the *byar* during the first half of the nineteenth century. Motivated by third order economics and politics of Swedish Nationalism, European Commercialism, and Luthernism, the enclosure acts attempted to radically alter or even destroy the foundation of an operationalized Scandinavian ethos, i.e. its shared, participatory ritual practices and architectural frameworks. A good part of what follows in the new milieu of Swedish industrialization and urbanization is suggested as having been influenced by aspects of the old second order culture. A "de-localization" of the traditional opposition between family and farm community appears to have created two separate urban groups: the white collar *tjänstemän* and the blue collar *arbetare*. The former assumes the primary meaning of the traditional "familial/patriarchal" and the latter the "collective".

These were more purely political, territorial, or presentational phenomena which created exclusive social and political entities. Symbolism formerly intimately associated with structurally opposed architectural spaces was now available for discursive manipulation in text and territory. Gone were traditional second order systems in which members wore both hats, as it were. Both patriarchal and collective meanings worked effectively in the same mind and ultimately served to make politically legitimate some total social organization. The settings and scale of modernizing Sweden precluded any such second order reality. These two groups

342

shared neither living nor working space. A balanced socio-cultural system, based upon shared architectural frameworks for ritual practice, was impossible during this period.

Social groups become spatially and systematically removed from prior second order contexts, whether the post-enclosure wealthy farmers or their urban cousins as either blue or white collar workers. The term "third order" has been used to describe unique discursive functions of architectural expression. Once aspects of the society became territorially exclusive, the more imageable, object-like potentials of architecture became available to presentationally tout the political statuses and identities of owners. It may be useful to think of third order architectural meaning as that usage which tends to occur *between* individuals or groups which have no operationalized ritual relationships. It remains to be seen to what degree such largely antithetical meaning may exist in the architectural medium in first order or cosmic societies.[2]

Second order societies, as we have seen in Scandinavia, by definition tend to be small in physical scale and in degree of organizational complexity. Within these highly internalized, architecturally expressed evolutions of earlier first order systems, things are anything but territorial. People did not just happen to form villages *(byar)* because of defensive purposes or because they rather suddenly just wanted to live close to each other. In such tight, expressively founded communities, third order uses of architectural form are inimical to more fundamental second order meanings. Taboos existed about how one could decorate or design even one's own architecture of the family farm, prior to the enclosure acts and modernization.

10.2 The historical opportunity of office settings in Sweden

The rational views of the Modern Movement in the period prior to the Second World War may have shifted third order meanings of offices from historical to modern styles, but few significant changes in essential office organization or "patriarchal" meaning occurred. Even immediately after the war, into the late fifties and early sixties, Swedish offices were still extremely formal places. In spite of minor advances in office technology and the growing number of office workers, the original cultural concept of *tjänsteman* was still largely dominant. The basic layout of office architecture had not changed dramatically from very early periods. Executives still had unique private offices and most employees shared space in rooms whose sizes varied according to function and territorial control. The only quasi-collective space, the dining facility, often was found in some upper portion of the building and had specific patriarchical or hierarchical rules about its usage.

It has not been uncommon for the radical changes in office form which began in the sixties to be thought of as the product of the overall Swedish ability to make very rational decisions in groups. This has been the perceived source of the "Swedish Model" and eventually the "Democratic Breakthrough" of the late seventies and eighties. The logic of being logical is almost self-evident. When given the right of participation in design processes, people naturally chose first to have their own office. Then, aided by the rational recognition of managers and designers, these same organizations logically decided that workers needed more communication, hence the other kinds of shared, collective spaces described herein. Certainly it is also true that most of these decisions emerged from the logical conclusions of many *sammanträde* (meetings).

Swedish ethnographers describe this general participatory and egalitarian propensity in Swedish culture which has resulted in the ability of work organizations to create consensus. They see the larger social and economic conditions of post-war Europe as an enabling context for these Swedish abilities to plan. To a certain extent, the reason that the democratic breakthrough had not occurred in the century prior to World War II, appears to be the previous dominance of the more typically European class system.[3] The general breakdown of class thinking, along with an opening of the economic system which followed the war seems to be sufficient cause, for most, to have provided the opportunity for the emergence of truly democratic institutions. The present work has tried to document this conventional wisdom which Swedes themselves have of these radical changes of the past twenty years.

Conradson's diachronic ethnography of a Stockholm insurance company, cited many times, has provided important verification to the description of the earlier "patriarchal" and "rational" office. It has also illustrated the broader cloak of rationalism which so frequently defines more recent forms and processes of office organization. While much of her work focused on the pre-democratic periods, she returned to her site in the early 80's. At the time of her return, the company was just beginning an extensive remodel of its historical building in central Stockholm. The renovations, appear *not* to have been extensively designed along many of the second order principles which contemporaneously were being built across much of corporate Sweden. Thus what Conradson observed was largely a continuation of the still

344

patriarchal and rational organization more widespread, say twenty years ago.

The major shift in organizational structure and meaning, for Conradson, is not any truly democratic way of working, but a rather imageable shift away from the formality of earlier times, coupled with a more hidden, increased administrative dominance of work via computers. The new informality of Swedish offices is felt to be "family-like", while organization and technology has gone in the opposite direction (1988:211). Earlier, social control was founded in (third order) physical settings, while more recently work control has been integrated in institutional arrangements. Individuals experience freedom concerning socializing, conversation, clothing, and time but have become more subject to greater bureaucracy and increased computer manipulation. From this perspective, she says that social rules in the past gave personal freedom to organize one's job, a strong source of satisfaction. Conradson supports this view of the new office, i.e. that the control of work is hidden under superficial freedoms, by referencing similar views of a well known ethnographer whose writing deals more generally with work in Sweden (Ehn 1981).

Conradson's approach echoes much of Meyrowitz's, especially in a common recognition of the decline of importance of physical space for presentational purposes. Unlike Meyrowitz, she sees informality as somehow reproducing family-like relationships, something Meyrowitz says is breaking down as well, especially in terms of traditional male-female, and child-adult relationships (1985). Their account of the effect of computers is consistent in a common recognition of the corresponding breakdown of the need for presentational space, yet Conradson and Ehn both see a negative, hidden structure of bureaucratic control which replaces traditional, presentational uses of space. Meyrowitz's alternative description of this new world is of a return to small "oral hunting and gathering" organizations already evident in the workings of some electronics corporations.

The issue of computer effect, a negative side of rationalization, needs greater attention than has been presently possible in this volume. It seems likely that early computer usage in the 1960's initially created many of the effects mentioned by Conradson. Given the still patriarchal flow of information of most offices at this time, the use of these new machines to further control and rationalize work processes seems quite logical. Considering the lack of second order expressive evolution in Conradson's particular office--recall the much more radical evolution at the insurance

345

company Skånska Brand at this same time--it is completely understandable that the existing, still largely third order power structure would use any tool at its disposal, especially computers, to further its own ends.

Yet it is difficult for the author to imagine as much personal control over one's job in earlier offices as is maintained by Conradson. More likely, a hierarchical supervision of work occurred in both patriarchal and rational organizations; early computer use simply shifted this control from territorial individuals to machines, perhaps themselves presentationally located. In this particular office the new images of informality and freedom are essentially just new forms of presentational symbolic capital which compensate for this lack of control, just as earlier *tjänsteman* symbolism did. Much of the spatial presentation of earlier times still exists, in spite of, or integrated with limited new signs of informality. Theoretically, while one finds these same outward signs of informality in second order organizations, they do not function so much as compensatory signs, but are actually the result of prohibitions of traditional third order expression in such settings.

This widespread and dramatic shift from formal to informal behavior has not escaped the notice of one of Sweden's founding ethnographers, Orvar Löfgren. In his anthology about the informalization of Sweden, Löfgren's introductory article articulates the theme:

> Informalization can be analyzed both as a symbolic message and a concrete, practical agenda. Symbolic function can express the world as equality, togetherness and closeness, while the practical application can provide support for working together and common understanding of decisions. This suggests that informalization even has its aspects of scale. It is easier to create freedom from rules and formlessness in small, well defined social systems than in large ones. The informal interactions within the little, knowledge sharing group can function as a symbolic border device towards the larger world, and it can also provide many practical advantages (1988:16).

This view, not unlike what Conradson found in her insurance office, seems to look at the overt symbols of informality as capital to be used in the really still third order expression of individual or group *distinctions*. Thus it is small, essentially minority, groups where such symbols can function as a "border" device (considering the less powerful, more informally dressed employees of the office as a political minority). This perspective receives again more detailed discussion in Fyrkman's contribution to the same volume (1988). Using Turner's ideas of structure and anti-structure more broadly to refer to an entire national society, Fyrkman describes the essentially political, anti-structural advantages to being informal, in contradiction to structural norms. He uses the dress of university professors as a central example of this "strategic game".

Such third order, even territorially based, approaches to the recent informality of Sweden differs fundamentally to Meyrowitz's view of informality as essentially the reduction of presentational contrasts *per se*. They also vary somewhat with the present hypothesis and reference to these same ideas of Turner. If one uses Turner's work as it relates to small, egalitarian societies, then the distinction between structure and anti-structure or communitas is *not* really one between socially separate formal and informal groups, but between principles of social relationships among individuals common to one group or society.

There may be two forms of Turner's model, one in which these experiences act as aspects of the same self (the Scandinavian village tradition) and the other more discursive case where selves become politically available to individual agency. In the former or second order case the symbolism of communitas ritual has much more to do with the associational linkage between the principle of equality and spiritual affect, as in the calendrical SAS ritual. This is distinguished from the expression of a political contradiction to some other group not present, or with some creative, new alternative to that other structure. In the usage of Turner's concept in more primitive societies, communitas often associates with the collective, which in turn dominates the structural or hierarchical pole, usually as some family group.

Even though workers in second order offices may appear to be manipulating the symbols of informality, they do not make any such third order statement which distinguishes them from some political other. They are, after all not only the majority, but also do effectively control the political character of their organizations. This researcher believes the evidence of the power of the horizontal *arbetsgrupp* (work group) is so persuasive that one must accept the alternative explanation, i.e. that they *are* the collectivity and actually dominate not absent and territorially exclusive others, but aspects of their *own* patriarchality-become-individuality.

Though insufficient background has been presented, it is possible that once these expressive systems were firmly in place, and the personal computer had decentralized the computing function to individuals, that the collectivity will control the information flow in today's offices (not the programmer, executive, etc.). In spite of what outsiders take to be informal behavior and dress on the part of Swedish office workers, their participation in communitas ritual exhibits a great deal of formality. Times, seating arrangements, architectural opposition, all speak of systematic practice. These are not spontaneous, consciously or politically motivated, sign appropriating events. How much structural creativity can emerge if they do not even talk about work.[4] Images of informality in the second order office are not used in the third order fashion which may occur in "minority" situations elsewhere.

10.3 The second order effect of architectural form

Much of the scholarly rejection of more overt influence of the traditional *by* culture in the democratic breakthrough lies in the inability to trace expressive forms to some modern manifestation. This goes back to the assumptions of verbal or textual priorities, and the lack of theoretical understanding of spatially founded processes of ritual practice. Both first order Viking and subsequent folk communities are more frequently interpreted in functional rather than expressive terms. While some literature exists about the influence of spatial symbolism in Viking organization, it remains based upon mythic rather than archaeological evidence and hence some distance from actual localized social organization. The hypothesis that *by* architecture was a primary symbolic and ritual vehicle of expression in portions of Post-Viking Scandinavia would of course be anathema to most folk historians in these countries. The overwhelming interpretation of folk architecture in the literature and in museums is as a technical vehicle for very physical (and logical) performance of some task. Thus if *by* architecture were in fact *the* founding framework of ritual practice and cooperative work, and this fact were generally unknown, then one can easily understand the difficulty of scholars in conceptualizing an expressive basis to the recent "breakthrough".

The present work cannot claim to have definitively put to rest the potential argument between emphases on Macro-European causes and those of an indigenous, enabling expressive phenomenon of architecture. In the first place, the idea of second order architectural form, and its importance to *by* society, occurred only recently, as part of the present attempt to theoretically understand a potential expressive contribution of Swedish offices.[5] Much historical study and perhaps even actual fieldwork in extant

Scandinavian (second order) communities needs to be done to firmly establish that architectural form critically supports non-sacred forms of ritual practice. Secondly, the present preoccupation with architectural form has left little time or space for the proper establishment of the symbolic associations of the Scandinavian ethos as it exists pervasively in the culture, prior to any ritual operationalization. Particularly important here may be the question of whether clear definitions of "patriarchal-become-individual" and "collective" can be found, and whether strong notions of spatial opposition tend to accompany. Such evidence would give additional strength to the many architectural forms which have here been interpreted along these dimensions.[6]

As an architect-anthropologist the author is accustomed to seeing the powerful expressive contributions of architecture cross-culturally, especially in first order Scandinavia. Architecturally the present examples of form in Swedish offices cannot be explained by references to European influences, the purely political ability to make decisions in groups, or the new informality. The only change in architectural form which *might* be attributed to these causes could have been the initial decision to create huge numbers of individual universal offices *(smårumskontor)*. This can be seen as the combination of the external political movement of industrial workers to gain control over their environment, nominally for health and safety. Subsequently Swedish office workers borrow this right to make decisions about actual design layouts of their settings. Though the enabling cause of this most significant evolutionary change in office form came from external influences, the actual decision for individual offices speaks not to functional but cultural needs. It is still true that the best functional office form of this period, and still today elsewhere, was the office landscape, given the eventual control of visual and auditory problems. Although the standardization of common offices solved the practical problem of making group decisions about any movement of personnel, remodeling, or design of new facilities, it did much that was illogical in terms of the overall performance of functional work groups.

Nor were changes in office form the response to informalization as described in Meyrowitz. The architectural effect was the opposite of the new electronic U. S. office. In the mid to late sixties, Swedes were making decisions to create more, not fewer, private offices! In an unusual extension of Gidden's interpretation of the presentational private office as a communication of "trust" (1987:159), one could see the universal provisioning of individual rooms as a sort of universal trust. This interpretation seems too dependent upon the operation of strong collective values at a time when offices were still quite patriarchal, rational, and still largely passive to union participation. Most probably, the individual decisions to have one's own office came from a combination of traditional association of each individual with the old ideals of being a strong "individual" Scandinavian entity, and still presentational desires for *tjänsteman* identity and status. The effect of the radical new forms created by universal individual offices was largely opposite from individual motivations. While more consciously motivated by these values, the primary architectural sources of presentational effect, and certainly most territoriality, had been effectively constrained. Now a framework for ritual practice could evolve. These more conscious motivations created an essential equality of space as resource.

Initially, much of the rational contribution of managers and executives sought to redress the poor communication among walled off employees, prior to the development of true horizontal work groups. Even though some of these contributions such as the open door policies and pressures for shared collective spaces ultimately became expressive, from the manager's point of view his or her rational motivations were very much focused on better work performance of the organization. Even though such agents, including the architects, contributed rationally to the evolution, these more conscious motivations in no way explain the purely social and expressive (second order) practice which eventually develops. Most revealing in this regard is the emergence of the *arbetsby* or *kombi* form. Contrary to most interpretations of the *kombi* as the product of very functional rational goals by managers and designers, it has here been shown that the actual enclosed cluster form can *only* be explained in expressive terms.

From a purely rational motivation of communication and movement of personnel, the earlier linear forms of *kombi* actually worked better. This all gives weight to the thesis that second order expressive form is in many ways independent from a purely functional uses of architecture. Much of the present work reveals the constant conflict between the two causes of form, and design attempts both subconscious and rational to resolve them in the single manifestation called "building".[7] In the second order *by*, much work took place away from physical settings used ritually, though the same actors participated in both. It is not yet clear whether such is possible in contemporary work settings, particularly considering the apparent maxim of being able to move people for functional reasons.

350

This book has argued that much of the purely expressive form of second order office organization intimately accompanied, and even preceded, the emergence of the horizontal *arbetsgrupp* with its separate task needs for form. Not only were these expressive forms *not* primarily the result of rational, functional decision making processes, but they actually had to expressively establish the nature of group relationships *before* any truly democratic work could be done. Though the design decisions for new and expressive forms of *pause* and *sammanträde* spaces, for example, did emerge from participatory processes between users and designers, such was seldom rationalized in terms of its expressive function. The national scale of this evolutionary arena may have contributed greatly to the acceptance and proliferation of new forms.

Although virtually all office organizations were going through similar decision making processes, when either functional or social needs for new space made themselves felt, they were not choosing new forms in a vacuum. The tracing of the *kombi* form, once nudged into prototypical being by an individual or small group of architects, revealed the amazing transmission through the culture of Swedish offices. A pronounced propensity to share information in Sweden--part of participatory democratic process itself--has accompanied the country's general commitment to education and research. Corporate and design arenas appear to readily share in knowledge processes, thus facilitating in this case the dissemination of culturally meaningful form. An excellent and accompanying example is the way in which Sweden as a nation investigated and responded, in no uncertain terms at this national level, to the introduction of the office landscape. An easy transmission of information does not in itself mean that decision processes are purely rational. Given a shared set of architectural forms circulating both in corporate and architectural circles, much of their adoption probably relied as much on the subconscious expressive meanings of the architectural forms, than on more conscious understandings of task performance.

Not only did *pause* and *sammanträde* spaces become remarkably pervasive across Sweden, but as new buildings appeared, larger scales of second order meaning came into practice. Moved to the ground or major collective level of the building, the restaurants often play part of architecturally formal oppositions. The site of the collective ritual of the midday meal, the dining space either itself or in collaboration with a large meeting place, forms the "collective" component opposed to the "individual" office block at this the largest of scales. Within the collective, the smaller scale opposition

351

of restaurant and meeting space parallel the collective meanings of *pause* and *sammanträde* places in *arbetsbyar*. In addition to the purely expressive formality of many offices at the largest scale, one finds recurrent Nature symbolism, with its ancient Scandinavian expression of spirituality and the collective, associated with the restaurant/meeting domain.

Within tighter, more urban contexts, aspects of this symbolism combine with a larger scale expression of the collective--the atrium. This form is similar in intent to the shape of the collective core of the *arbetsby*. Together with its semantic of nature and spirituality the larger scale collective spaces of office buildings also began to resemble and associate with the character of the *bygata* (street/market) spaces of the traditional *by* itself. Ultimately the resolution of the formal necessities of multiple scales of second order organization develops in more recent works like Ideon and SAS. While no quantified evidence has been included, enough information has been provided to suggest that a marked increase in ritual practice, at all scales, has intimately accompanied these evolutions of architectural form. One sees not only ritual such as the *pause* closely associated with the actual work of the horizontal group, but many rites especially at larger often calendrical scales and times. As an extension of second order expression to the largest scales of the physical place, calendrical rituals take place within the same known architectural framework as smaller scale, everyday events. The smaller scale work group and larger aspects of the organization are thus both associationally and effectively linked.

Particularly at larger scales, both the expressive clarity of architectural form and the increase of accompanying ritual create even more convincing evidence of powerful expressive forces separate from the logical processes of making decisions in Swedish groups. These "other" processes by which ethnic content becomes expressed architecturally and practiced ritually almost uniformly across an entire country, cannot be explained in conventional terms. It comes neither from a general Scandinavian personality, nor from conscious decisions to socio-culturally support work relationships by having a lot of parties, nor from the simple influence of an informal electronic society. It seems much more probable that an active portion of Swedish office organization has, over the past twenty years, sought its own expressive means and ends. This is a rekindled desire to live by a legitimate set of definitions of the relationship between hierarchy and equality, a process which never reaches the level of full consciousness or rationality, in spite of all the business meetings of groups.

If in fact architectural form is the prime cognitive organizer and ritual facilitator of second order culture, then it is to the processes of architectural decision making themselves, not work decision making, that one must find the possibilities of second order realization and evolution. Again what is perceived by the participants as primarily functional or technical in motivation, as for example the lengthy decision process about whether to have individual offices or not, turns out have extremely significant social and cultural consequences. It is difficult to verbally or rationally capture either the expressive content, or the social implications of architectural form. Such meaning is still there and in a cultural and information context like Sweden it will be intuitively understood by most. Once the office members had the right to participate in the processes of design, and in spite of the perceived functional nature of that process, no decision about any form could be made without implicit agreement about its social-cultural meaning as well.

Thus one can speak at least tentatively about the causal contribution of architectural form to the eventual democratic breakthrough. Historically in Sweden one might be persuaded to see both the period of modernization as well as the breakthrough itself in more cultural terms. The breakup of the farms, industrialization, and urbanization was not the total substitution of the modern for the traditional. The ethos existed pervasively at the scale of the nation, but in a more latent, ritually inoperable form, at the disposal of discursive interests. What had been the powerful ritual oppositions of the family (patriarchal) and the community (collective), became the third order identities of the territorially exclusive groups of *tjänstemän* and *arbetare*. While the historical forces which caused the shift from second to third order societies were certainly intrusive or external to any localized society, those which initiated and maintained the evolutionary return were certainly less so. To a large extent, all that was needed for a ritual reemergence of second order practice, was the political right of design participation by all, and the simple fact of occupation of a localized space by both of the opposed ethnic themes or groups.

Given the relative independence of functional causes of form in office buildings, as distinct from the industrial workplace, white collar settings became the loci for the renaissance of fully ritualized Scandinavian second order culture. Highly coincident to this process were the large numbers of office workers, a majority, who undoubtedly facilitated the rapid transmission of new forms, both within offices themselves, and then to adjacent spheres. Were any major settings in Swedish life, with the possible exception of the residential,[8] immune from the impact of new office forms? Whether government agencies or industry, the second order experiences of executives and related employees could perhaps not help but influence their perspectives of broader national issues or the nature of blue collar work. The mentioned effort of Volvo to find the industrial equivalent to the *arbetsby* provides convincing evidence, at least in this latter sphere.

10.4 Territoriality in the discursive, rhetorical, or presentational

The original thesis of this work, and the basis of funding by the National Endowment for the Arts (US), was that culturally defined spaces in Swedish offices would inhibit or outright prohibit the kind of overt territoriality or presentation of self we see in modern offices elsewhere. The idea assumed from the start that one of the major uses of office form in either case, again de-emphasizing the actual role of task performance, had something to do with the social relationships in these organizations. Had one been permitted to carry out the more detailed portion of the fieldwork, it might have been possible to even statistically establish that second order practice effectively eliminates most third order use of space as we know it. The overwhelming conclusion from the revised method of fieldwork is that the second order definition of space and social relations in Swedish offices is so legitimate that virtually no individual would dream of manipulating space for personal reasons of territorial identity, status, and the like.

The initially proposed contrast between "cultural or expressive space" and "territoriality", has now been theoretically incorporated into present ideas. The shift from simple territoriality to the discursive/rhetorical/presentational enables us to integrate the existing literature on offices elsewhere. These explanations make frequent reference to corporate "symbols" and "culture" which paradoxically are involved in more territorial uses of space. The introduction of ideas about first, second, and third order expression allow us to begin to ask much more specific questions about the general role of culture in corporate societies. We wish to know under what conditions second order processes can develop and be sustained to provide the legitimacy for work organization. We can begin to investigate with perhaps more clarity the apparent fact that fully operationalized second order processes can support only democratic, egalitarian and collective forms of organization, while third order uses of symbolism seem much more associated with vertical models of information flow and work.

354

Returning briefly to the pre-breakthrough period in Sweden, we recall the more competitive, vertical structure of the *tjänsteman* concept and the offices in which they worked. To a certain extent one saw a lesser amount of overt territoriality, at least in earlier times, in these settings than in modern offices in the U.S., for example. Did the patriarchal concept, somewhat inflated but still part of the ancient ethos, provide a certain legitimacy or at least *stability* to the hierarchical/territorial structure in the organization? Recall Conradson's description of early Swedish office personnel who were distinguished from the worker class by their abilities to work with written texts (1984:85). What is the contribution of print media in this case? Is the third order history of Swedish offices something of a special case, theoretically interim between second order processes and fully modern organizations in heterogenous cultures?

How satisfying in fact was the identity and status of the Swedish *tjänsteman?* Did one actually feel more powerful than the collectivity of *arbetare*, spatially separated both domestically and economically? How legitimate was the abnormally large office "family" of which he was a part? Could one be satisfied by always playing the role of subordinate to some great patriarchal figure? While obviously much more ethnographic information is needed to answer such questions at present, it seems quite possible that the need for strong third order images of *tjänsteman* status and Swedish family actually reflected the lack of essential legitimacy within the organization itself. How could one refer to only patriarchal aspects of the ethos without at least invoking contradictory messages about collective participation and the like? Though perhaps repressed, the collective portion of the ancient ethos still existed in various medial forms. The comparatively exaggerated forms of Swedish patriarchality may be explained an a kind of over-compensation for the loss of the collective.

In comparison to the powerful ritual effects of second order practice, the meaning of the spatial layout of patriarchal offices seems far less legitimate. The building facade and dining room existed as an aspect of the constant battle to ameliorate one's feelings of political subordination within the office. One used these discursive vehicles in imaging one's perceived superiority over *arbetare*. The hierarchical spatial layout of the office might well have been taken negatively by the working majority in common rooms. Their lack of territory was a sign of subordination. For these people it was access to Conradson's "symbolic capital" of being a *tjänsteman* and a member of a good Swedish "family"--clothing,

355

building facade, dining room, etc.--that along with clean work and some economic stability compensated for the unusual hierarchy of the internal organization.

Tentatively, one can interpret the spatial layout of these traditional offices as primarily an attempt by executive powers to control--by discursively manipulating both traditional symbolism and new class distinctions. In spite of general symbolic linkage of the office to the patriarchal meanings of the traditional Swedish family and dwelling, the internal layout did not completely emulate the second order meaning of that smaller scale setting. It is perhaps axiomatic in first and second order practice that any setting will internally contain both contents of the major symbolic opposition, i.e. the patriarchal and collective, even though externally at a larger scale, a setting may express only one domain meaning in relation to some opposite.[9] The layout of the patriarchal office does not contain both aspects, nor is it the setting for ritual movement between such opposed places.

One assumes that the territorially and presentationally created definition of social organization in the patriarchal office is more coercive than legitimate. There is no ancient balancing of symbolic and social oppositions. Its power to operate comes from the recognition of the actual economic and territorial power of the patriarch. For most in the office, its territoriality must have had negative connotations. Rather than being the source of legitimacy to the organization, it communicated the true nature of power and the way the organization was structured. This reality could only be compensated by *tjänsteman-familj* images of class superiority-- trading, as it were, a subordinate territorial reality of self for a dominant discursive one.

There is little spatial structuring of symbolic content into clear and powerfully affective domains in traditional offices. Associational meanings in third order offices seem much less intuitive and emotional in character, than conventional as simpler communication.[10] To be intuitively and emotionally deep, as a spatially symbolic "domain", requires a much more extensive cultural and environmental experience, particularly if these less conscious meanings are to be shared. The more communicational signs in traditional third order offices come primarily from point sources of power. These are not the results of a social group developing or incorporating a shared set of ritually effective meanings over long periods of environmental experience, living and working together in the same place. Third order "culture" may consist largely of signs of status and identity which originate or are appropriated less and less in the social body as a whole, than in the pronouncements and behavior of those who control property.

The major difference between traditional offices, such as in Sweden, and modern ones in the U.S., for example, seems to lie only in the availability of traditional symbols by which to compensate for the negative signs of essentially illegitimate social and economic authority. The primary commonalty between both, and the basis for the mutual designation of "third order" is their use of discursively defined status signs to compensate for often quite negative territorial realities. In both cases, it is primarily executives who essentially decide what the symbolic capital will be!

10.5 Tentative third order definitions in the U.S.

Certainly the most comprehensive and referred to evaluation of American office settings is the Bosti work: *Using Office Design to Increase Productivity* (Brill, et. al 1984). Without getting into the overall causes of form in these usually large office buildings, we can summarize aspects of this study and its recommendations as they include or exclude particularly social and cultural uses of environmental form. The results in Volume II list the following major headings: The Workspace (Physical Enclosure, Floor Area, Layout, Furniture, Windows); Ambient Conditions (Temperature and Air Quality, Lighting, Noise); Psychophysical Constructs (Privacy, Communication, Pathfinding, Comfort, Display and Personalization, Status Communication, Appearance); and Facilities Design and Management (Participation, Flexibility, Occupancy, Workgroup Types as "independent", "sequential", "team"). The following excerpts from Bosti's own introductory overview of these results provides the reader with a good impression of how the vast majority of American offices differ from those in Sweden (1984:15-22; excerpt numbers added):

1.) Physical proximity to coworkers and face-to-face communications are still preferred for many. Managers want to "see" body language and facial expression, to have many short meetings and engage in their finely honed and effective networking behavior; professionals require peer discussions and co-examination of materials, including complex, manipulable electronic displays; clerical workers derive much job satisfaction from relationships with peers, work accomplished and satisfied superiors. All this implies that electronic "distancing" is not desirable for many. It is also widely felt that being "around" and being "known" are still requisites for advancement in most organizations.

2.) There seem to be fewer professional workers than we thought and more managers and clerical workers. The diagram of our work force really looks more like an hourglass than a pyramid.

3.) The unit of work will, even more so than now, be the individual's workspace--with more limited emphasis on the workgroup. Distributed intelligence, integrated software, universal terminals and good on-line data can reduce dependence on the information held by others and increase spatial autonomy. There is much research based evidence for the need for privacy and for individual enclosure.

4.) While we still move more than a third of the people around in the office each year, there seems to be a slow trend toward fewer physical relocations as organizations develop more effective strategies for reducing their "churn" rate. There will still be a substantial relocation rate, but the *pattern* of relocations may change.

5.) The office has always been a highly constrained esthetic opportunity for designers and workers alike. The forces that act on office design tend to impoverish the esthetic repertoire that even skilled designers bring to this problem. We see few fundamental changes in these forces or the opportunities for much richer esthetic experiences in the office of the future. What are these forces, and how have they constrained office esthetics?

Most esthetic variety in the office comes from designers' desires for unique interpretations of place or from sensitivity to and symbolic expression of organizational culture. When substantial esthetic variation occurs, it is most frequently expressed in public and group spaces, and far less in the day-to-day work interiors. This is unfortunate, for our findings show an employee preference for being in an overall office interior visually distinct from those in other organizations.

The size and shape of an office building is determined more by the economics of its location and its allowable bulk than by designer choice. The same economics make its interiors into flat, nine-foot-high "sandwiches" of space with little opportunity for any spatial verticality. The trend toward larger floors has reduced visual access to windows and reduced the sense of spatial definition that a closer relationship between the perimeter wall and the core might bring. Status concerns have obscured natural light in the interiors by giving the window wall over to a small number of private offices.

There is a sameness of office interiors both across buildings and within buildings. Since the office tends to house large numbers of people, many doing similar jobs, the economics of mass production and the problems of facility management conspire toward uniformity and interchangeability of workspaces and the furniture they contain. Natural variation is suppressed. The democratic need to satisfy (or at least not to offend) the large numbers of office workers has narrowed the band of colors and materials and, as well, reduced the use of other artistic means of enhancing environments.

Systems furniture, increasingly found in work interiors, has many manufacturers but only a limited range of appearances--and those few which do appear "radically" different tend to be stylistically rather than functionally different. Recent experiments have generated office buildings composed entirely of same-size private offices on double-loaded corridors. These are attempts to reduce the problems of relocation while providing high levels of privacy (response to computer, not social). Even with several choices among furniture sets, these buildings further reduce variety. (parentheses added)

6.) While there will be continued experimentation and change in automated systems for handling information and communications, much evidence points to not much major physical change in the office. Some evidence that little fundamental physical change is expected is that pictures and designs of "the office of the future" are notoriously absent from our design magazines.

Most striking about this comparison of American offices with their Swedish counterparts, is the apparent lack of importance of expressive symbols or ceremony, as would effect the physical form of these buildings. The above excerpts very clearly illustrate that the major causal forces in building form are not even socio-cultural (whether second or third order), but are dedicated to maximize primarily economic aspects of production. Given the causal primacy of socio-cultural needs in the evolution of democratic

Swedish buildings, economically and technologically formed American office settings cannot for these reasons alone be likely candidates for second order expression. In spite of non-social architectural forces, how do existing socio-cultural possibilities fall into the presently proposed definition of "third order"? The reader should be aware of how territorial the Bosti conclusions are, and how utterly absent much of this behavior is in Swedish settings.

In the first excerpt, for example, face to face communication is seen primarily in terms of spatially effective managerial control, while the status distinctions between clerical workers and professional-managers are clearly expressed spatially. This coincides with the image of organizational structure in excerpt two. The focus of the third quote is on the computer generated functional need for individual, acoustically and visually private offices--"with a more limited emphasis on the (functional) workgroup" (parentheses added). While it is unlikely that most managers will allow the breakup of territorial control which individual offices imply, the fact that offices move in this direction for purely instrumental reasons is particularly revealing. To suggest parenthetically that work group spaces will simultaneously decline in importance obviously stresses only functional relationships among employees. Recall the discussion about those, including Meyrowitz, who paint a similar picture. The total lack of purely social meaning attached to any group spaces, probably means that employee groups have few such legitimate territories of their own in the overall scheme of spatial authority.

While the number of people moved every year in American offices is more than a third, according to excerpt four, the statistic for Swedish settings is estimated by the author as something under five percent, if that.[11] Given the equal sizes of the standard Swedish office *rum*, it is easier both functionally and socially to move people, and indeed this is one of the major tenets of the *kombi* office. The relative lack of movement under these Swedish conditions, means again that the second order use of space is dominating functional and outright prohibiting personal territorial causes. What percentage of the large number of American moves is due to function and what percentage to due to territorial or discursive reasons? Such work in American offices is extremely time consuming for the organization and very sensitive because of the typical denial of territorial processes, hiding always behind the front of instrumentality. After much exposure to American offices through the teaching of design studios, it is this researchers opinion that the most frequent motivation, not only for moving, but remodeling as well, is simply the territorial and discursive play for identity.

The overall tenor of the large fifth excerpt of the Bosti study is territorial. Such spatial phenomena are almost non-existent in second order Swedish offices. The primary role of the designer, given the huge dominance of techno-economic forces on building form, is to provide "esthetic variation". One might otherwise interpret the meanings of visual aesthetics as a source of relief from the informational and even social stress which can occur in office work. The findings that people are using visual aesthetics to be distinct from other organizations is a clear confirmation of this artifactual use as presentational signs (perhaps in the absence of a legacy of traditional familial or class symbolism to choose from). More in terms of the internal organization itself, limited window space of these large non-linear floor areas is always an important status sign for a small number of managers and executives. The only use of the term "democracy" does not even refer to any spatial, territorial right, but to a limited usage of color and materials of furnishings as compensatory signs available to employees. A second mention of "recent experiments with same-size private offices on double-loaded corridors"--to reduce problems of relocation and increase functional privacy--is seen less in terms of its potential social, and eventual cultural, possibilities than as an actual detriment to visual variety.

The Bosti work concludes with examples of ideal American offices, sketches from well known architectural firms based on the above mentioned conclusions of Volume II. The primary concern in all schemes is a means of accommodating the three types of work: independent, sequential, and team. A technologically and economically determined (non-linear) exterior building shell is assumed in all solutions as a given. Exterior windows do not figure strongly in the proposed layouts, either for functional or social purposes. All schemes not only eliminate the possibility of any socio-cultural causality in terms of overall building form, but also wish to minimize such causality on the interior, where totally instrumental concepts of work flow dominate the layout of workstations.

Yet while the location of managers follows the functional logic of their higher need for communication and/or supervision, in many solutions their special locations along with larger spaces give an immediate impression of territorial dominance. This fact, couples with the political reality that all of these landscape solutions will be decided by the same managers and their executive superiors.

If built, these spaces would lead to fairly negative territorial realities for most employees. The average worker would be given certain amenities, primarily in terms of the "aesthetic variety" of material furnishings and personalization of individual workstations. Yet this "symbolic" compensation will certainly not have the strength of, for example, the more traditional patriarchal or even class images in Sweden. Thus in the American settings, one would expect much more overt territorial play by the majority of the employees as they attempt to counter the social meaning of the instrumental layout designed by managers and designers. Would such layouts really function well, or is instrumentality again essentially a myth to mask socio-political power. Perhaps considering the larger third order predisposition of American society, these schemes might be the most productive, all things considered. They may not be as productive as second order practice in Sweden.

The Bosti absence of an emphasis on existing or potential role of "corporate culture" in the physical setting of offices is understandable given its *de facto* acceptance of territorial and presentational practices, always consciously subordinate to instrumentality. The particular absence of importance in this study of not only "corporate culture", but more specifically symbolism, may be misleading. Given the lack of traditional ethnic symbols from which to borrow, some research does exist which not only finds much "symbolism" present in American corporations, but also considers it to be influential.

Very little of this literature on "symbols of identity", one of the three kinds of research interests identified in Wineman's survey,[12] rests on a deeper, more anthropologically based ethnographic method. The Bosti study, like most others here, relies primarily on questionnaires and either methodologically avoids or is politically prohibited from getting information on the social reality of these places. This has only been relatively easy in Sweden because of the larger social meaning of office form itself, one of the primary sources of data. In non-socially formed American offices, where the overall form has little "indigenous" meaning, the true social and possibly cultural nature of these groups is much more difficult to investigate. No one wants to talk publicly about the constant use of territoriality and its "symbols" for political ends. One recent dissertation attempts to place these questions about American corporate symbols in the context of a limited, but much more intimately understood, ethnographic context.

This investigation of corporate head offices in the Boston area (Mazumdar 1988), first of all reinforces a conscious or perhaps mythic belief in both contemporary Swedish and American offices, i.e. that instrumentality is a primary cause of doing things. The overriding belief in functional motivations is defined essentially as a rhetorical mask for some very important social and cultural phenomena. What Mazumdar finds, penetrating behind these screens of functionality, is a constant communication or "environmental reading" of Goffmanesque identities, "socio-physical congregation and distancing", "environmental embarrassment", and "environmental deprivation" (ibid:265). It is clear that much of this content is expressed through the manipulation of limited presentational/territorial resources, given the non-social causes of these building forms as well. Goffman's notion of "front" and "back" zones are referenced, for example, while a key concept behind environmental deprivation is what Mazumdar calls "take-aways", the status loss incurred when employee territories or expressions of such are reduced or otherwise altered negatively by management.

One of the most interesting questions raised by this work is not necessarily whether elaborate status/territorial signs or symbols exist in most American offices--this we all can intuitively confirm from working in these places--but whether such in fact constitute the truly cultural, expressive phenomenon that the current interest in corporate culture suggests. In the present discussion, is there a spectrum from the traditionally discursive to the more purely territorial in modern organization, both as aspects of third order space? Is there a system of operating symbols which in a Durkheimian sense legitimizes or otherwise reinforces social structure? What is such a symbol systems' relationship to ubiquitous territoriality? Mazumdar describes these physical attributes of offices in terms of "rules and norms", suggesting a degree of institutionalization of meaning, though he mentions as well the probable limitations of such "systems" by the scale and diversity of the corporate landscape in America. The dissertation does not attempt to solve the thorny problem of distinguishing between conventional, communicational usage of signs and a more truly traditional usage of symbolism for less discursive, more expressive purposes.

The admitted spatial bias of the present argument has left out any contribution of print to the efficacy of at least pre-electronic modern organizations. It may be that this paramount medium of texts does in fact causally participate in the shifting from sacred (first order) to discursive (third order) forms. Intuitively, this may be the distinction between earlier modern offices where forms of presentation are more deeply associational, formalized and informed to some degree by print specialization of the actors, and more recent corporate settings where electronic informality has, perhaps, unleashed a more primitive form of pure territoriality. In any event, there seems to be basic territorial bases to all aspects of third order space. The presence or absence of presentational "symbolic capital" may have more to do with coping with a form of cognitive dissonance between selves than actual experiential reality, this especially in earlier offices. In the more territorially overt offices current in countries like the U.S., on the other hand, there may be no internal compensation for absence of participatory power. Thus in these societies, there may be increasing pressures to spatially escape to isolated family and recreational experience. It may well be that much of Meyrowitz's reemerged hunting and gathering society has, in fact, also returned to more primitive forms of territoriality.

10.6 Architectural language and metaphor as third order forms

Part of the present hypothesis suggests that the architectural medium is too socially constrained in first and second order examples to play a language-like or perhaps communicational role, where signs attached to territories are more freely used according to the agency of individuals or self-interested groups. We saw in the Swedish case how the use of building style became important both for the new upper class farmers and virtually all groups in the growing cities. Without getting into the history of architectural languages, the meaning of classical orders for example, one can associate more current uses of style in office buildings to territorial processes. One of the best examples of aspects or images of office buildings as territorial signs was a recent conference presentation of ongoing work by Kim Dovey, of the University of Melbourne (1992). His study of the marketing imagery to sell large high rise towers in Melbourne revealed status implications of territorial location, views, or height--an obvious "penis" competition in the words of one well known environmental psychologist in the audience. One is left with the question of whether the power of third order expression comes from the discursive background, in this case the meaning of the architectural style, or an apparent territoriality? In everyday experience today, seldom is a philosophical intention perceived by the user, rather one tends to read the image as an emotionally neutral sign whose persuasiveness must ultimately come from the immediate association with territorial might.

While much more work remains to be done, initially, most of today's "linguistic" content of architectural style seems to be strongly related to territorial processes and the present definition of third order. How actual office organizations use this content, once the dotted line has been signed by some executive, and the otherwise very techno-economic form is occupied, remains also an object for future inquiry. Does this strong "external" notion of territorial and social superiority function similarly to the use of more traditional patriarchal, and class images in early Swedish offices? Does it somehow compensate in terms of personal identity for the territorially subordinate roles most employees must invariably play within these buildings?

As the Bosti report so clearly identified, the interiors of techno-economically caused American office form, in comparison to the mentioned exterior images, have far less "design content". While some stylistic meaning may be possible in terms of materials, furnishings and the like on the interior, the architectural medium itself far less frequently participates as a language inside the building. There are cases in which not only the facade but the internal form itself is said to be "symbolic" though less in stylistic than metaphoric ways. Already discussed in Chapter Six is an example in which the architectural form of an insurance office building in the Netherlands, Central Beheer, was used to metaphorically mean "small town" (see 6.1). Such larger, more inclusive uses of the overall building form are relatively rare, compared to techno-economic form and its superficial territorial signage. The *intentions* of using form metaphorically to create or reflect socio-cultural values shared by all can either come from enlightened executives, existing collectively shared beliefs, and of course the designers themselves.

When the two organizational researchers, Berg and Kreiner attempt to define the positive ways symbolism can be used to influence organization, they primarily talk about the metaphoric images which their selected buildings communicate to the occupants (1990). Showing a birdseye view of the SAS building, for example, they comment on the management idea of "horizontality" as apparently the primary meaning or effect on those who use the setting. They quote Carlzon and otherwise similarly discuss the assumed influence of the metaphor much like the journal treatment of Central Beheer. One of the major conscious goals of the SAS metaphor is "creative stimulation", not unlike the efforts of the unusual Enator environment discussed in Chapter Eight. This notion of collective creativity as one of the primary products of

Scandinavian office architecture is also used by Berg and Kreiner to interpret the meaning of spontaneous atria spaces like that at ABV. The present discussion of these collective spaces emphasized not the liminal spontaneity which is assumed to occur in these metaphorical urban streets--in fact some tend not to be used spontaneously and sit mostly empty much of the time--but the evolving ritual meaning related to second order Scandinavian practice.

It is interesting that on the page opposite the SAS image, in Berg and Kreiner, one finds an exterior view of the well known German office shaped like one half of a pyramid, an accurate and intentional metaphor of organization within. Mentioned as contrasting corporate images, one might ask more specifically about the sources of affect in these expressions. The pyramid seems much more an obvious territorial sign whose emotional "punch" comes from the reality of the actual occupation of space rather than the metaphor *per se*. There could, for example, be a communal space on top rather than the CEO. Ignoring our second order definition of SAS for the moment, the horizontal image of the airline's building would seem not to derive its impact from territorial signage. A horizontal building in most other countries provides no guarantee of territorial equality (if such a thing as "territorial" equality can actually exist as a result of purely territorial processes). Instead, like Central Beheer in the Netherlands, it is somehow the associational linkage of such a large "billboard" with the *idea* of horizontal work which presumably makes the expression effective. The function of metaphor is exactly this associational linkage between two concepts, images or ideas, the one being given properties or being understood in terms of the other. Perhaps, one might argue, the more metaphysical idea is given greater expressive validity by the concreteness of the architectural portion of the metaphor. One might admit a limited contribution of the visual, not territorial, image of the horizontal building.

Other corporations not in Sweden can be found which really do seem to have some set of collectively shared symbols or values. The author can think of several examples locally which students have discovered in their search for a "real client" on which to base their hypothetical designs. Both the Girl Scout headquarters and the regional Forest Service office, for example, are rich in "cultural" themes or propositions. Yet both are housed in highly techno-economic structures, totally eliminating any larger metaphoric content in the architectural form. Someone should try to study in ethnographic depth the architecture of IBM and other more affluent organizations said to have greater degrees of corporate culture.[13]

What one would eventually find, as discussed earlier in reference to Central Beheer, might be a far less effective form of expression than we have seen in second order examples. In spite of the good intentions of using office architecture metaphorically, a single more conscious image, as metaphor, is probably far less socially persuasive than more indigenously evolved and largely subconscious second order ritual processes. Whether the use of metaphor wants to be included in the general language-like production of images in the third order concept, or is really some special "artistic" or "performative" form of cultural expression, is a question for future discussion.[14] One can distinguish, perhaps, metaphoric images from other signs on the basis of source of affect, i.e. whether from associationally deep cultural themes, propositions, philosophies, etc., or from territorial realities. The fundamental reality of much contemporary third order experience, is both a proliferation of images in multiple often electronic media *and* a heightened territoriality. As a linguistic and metaphoric vehicle, architecture is just one of many media, and perhaps even a less effective or flexible medium at that

Metaphoric architecture suggests a greater degree of user participation in design processes than certainly territorial signs. Still it must be recognized that even metaphoric images come primarily from individual minds, probably most often those of executives or designers. But all this needs far greater data and explanation than is possible in this conclusion. There is no existing, coherent, commonly understood theory of the human use of space, particularly as it relates to architectural expression in primitive to modern societies. This is not only true across the broad spectrum from the more environmental psychological uses of space to highly symbolic, cultural examples, but within the cultural or expressive field itself.[15] When researchers focus on the contribution of physical form in office settings, in the present case, not only much new fieldwork is required but also many theoretical threads will be left dangling. In their admittedly introductory article, Berg and Kreiner attempt only to show that: "the relationship between the building as such and what it is meant to signify in the life of the organization or in society is not only a largely unexplored empirical field, but also a highly problematic theoretical territory" (1990:43).

One of the most specific recent attempts to form a theoretical introduction to the meanings of the "symbolic environment" to corporate organization is Pasquale Gagliardi's frontpiece to his anthology on the subject (1990). His intricate and thorough response to the anthology articles, considered from his background in organizational research and consulting, provides a greater philosophical context to many of the issues dealt with here in the present conclusion. His piece traces the veil of instrumentality, for example, beyond the exegetic responses of both American and Swedish office workers to a more pervasive "primacy of reason in Western thought" (the historical, philosophical basis of third order society) particularly in the motivations of social science or organizational researchers themselves.[16] One result cited by Gagliardi is the total lack of empirical studies in traditional organization research which organically examine the connection between the distinctive culture of the organization and properties of the work environment (ibid:5). The central theme of this article really goes much further. Once people begin to take "organizational artifacts" seriously, they will discover that much social science theory of cognitive classification and symbolism will have to be abandoned. Typical preoccupation with "actions and words" will not capture the unique informational and experiential nature of this "alternative universe".

To Gagliardi such a universe perhaps does not include much of the immediate territoriality found especially in American offices, but does contain more metaphorical, "spatially symbolic" kinds of meaning. His "pathways of action" are artifacts which:

> ...constitute a concrete element in the social structure: actors daily create and recreate the reality of their own identity and of the mutual relationships within bounds which are the result of previous choices, made by other actors or by themselves at different moments (ibid:14).

Taken at face value, this Goffman-like definition seems to span the symbolic range from third order identities to the highly participatory processes of second order ritual and space. Gagliardi includes both the "symbolic potency of artifacts", a la Geertz, and a sequential section dedicated to more spatial meaning as "cognitive maps, sensory maps, and fourth level controls" (a fourth kind of organizational control exerted via the sensory, artifactual setting). To a large extent this section focuses more on non-expressive than ritual meanings of form. But it is when he talks about "root-metaphors, concrete images and organizational order" that the nature of his alternate universe becomes more clearly relevant to our present purposes.

He believes that "at the heart of tacit or informal knowledge, what are to be found are concrete images, rather than philosophies" (ibid:26). This at least suggests the importance of metaphor, if not "deeper" associational processes of first and second order space. He goes on to quote several anthropologists in defining this approach as one which attempts "to interpret the cultural order on the basis of a dominant drive or an integrating theme which can be stored in synthesizing symbols" (ibid:27). More specifically, "the root metaphor incorporated and transmitted by the artifactual setting tends to be a concrete multi-sensory image which simultaneously activates self-consistent patterns of association and reaction" (ibid:33). One finds a general absence of reference to the phenomenon of structural space, i.e. cognitive and ritual oppositions, not only universal in first and second order expression, but often the basis of meaning otherwise expressed as root-metaphors (Doxtater 1984). Does this absence, together with the focal use of the term "image" suggest something like indigenous metaphor rather than participatory, spatially structured ritual domains as the basis of sensory concreteness? Can images or root-metaphors also have ritual implications as "pathways of action". We need more specific definition of the actual shapes and locations of the artifacts in relation to movement within, something obviously beyond an introductory article by the editor.

In time we may find an important distinction between the metaphorical use of architectural artifacts, for example, something which really may not belong so cleanly to this alternate universe, and the kinds of meanings which possibly began with simple territoriality and evolved into powerful ritual processes. There is something very "linguistic" or even "discursive" about the use of the term "metaphor", or even "image" for that matter. But such is the fundamental expressive process of the day. This is the way one thinks in third order experience.

The spatial settings of first and second order societies have the structuralist capacity to organize massive symbolic (cognitive) association and then produce affective change through ritual practice. While many anthropologists probably would not agree, it seems that these spatially and architecturally derived meanings are in many ways "expressively prior" to the use of metaphor (and metonym) or other more communicational "texts". This could be so because of the structural, cognitive and social primacy of spatial meanings, embedded as they are in immediate (localized) experience. Traditional expressive texts, which may rely more on the structuring properties of metaphor and metonym, may, however, be largely derived from core meanings of the ritual environment.

Gagliardi captures much of this special expressive character of the artifactual/spatial aspects of culture. It is just the terminology which may prove problematic in the future. What if, for example, the spatial structuralism of first and second order experience really is expressively prior to other and secondary processes of symbolic manipulation like metaphor. If history denies the essential "dwelling" origins of these primary spatial forms of expression, then processes like metaphor, image, and the like will become even more dominant. We will need to be very specific about evolutionary differences in the way societies are able effectively use symbolic expression. The well intentioned but essentially third order interpretation of SAS by Berg and Kreiner, using terms like image, symbol, and metaphor, may actually deny understanding and potential emulation of a process rarely captured in many of our highly mobile, electronic societies. We need to sort out differences between artifacts as metaphors and as territorial signs, both of which seem to fall within the Gagliardi's "alternate universe" and both of which seem to belong to third order or at least non-ritual processes in most contemporary societies.

10.7 Second order possibilities in third order society

Our final thoughts leave the dangling threads of theory and jump paradoxically to actual application of some of these ideas to the design process of new office buildings in places like the U.S.. This adventure comes not so much from the results of the present Swedish ethnography, but from the mentioned years of teaching students to analyze and design offices in third order milieu. It was an article describing the novelty of such a "ritual" approach which caught the eye of Pasquale Gagliardi who included it in his anthology (Doxtater 1990). In addition to a student example of a hypothetical design using a actual client organization, the author's own analysis of another organization is also included (Doxtater 1981b). Very much in the context of an alternate symbolic universe, but much more attentive to structured patterns of space, we have found tantalizing indications of things like second order space in many ordinary white collar workplaces. The possible territorial origins of these meanings expressed formally in the layout of the buildings has been briefly discussed in previous articles (Doxtater 1984, 1989). These are in no way metaphoric or imageable expres-

370

sions, but evolutions of environmental meaning which occur through the socio-political action of more situational "practice", in usually small scale, less formally hierarchical organizations.

Inasmuch as it appears that these meaningful layouts do not yet fully function as ritual settings, they may not even be yet prototypical. If and when these settings become full blown second order processes (the term did not exist at the time of this article) will possibly depend upon both the degree of political participation in design decisions and perhaps the availability of symbolic content to inform the structured domains. One of the key ingredients which made the Swedish phenomenon possible was the preexistent ethos symbolism of "patriarchal" and "collective" which could be operationalized in architectural form and ritual practice. The symbolism of the collective was still emotionally dominant, creating the essential political basis of social office organization, again prior to actual work. In the author's analysis example in Gagliardi's anthology, the power axis between dominant and subordinate places is still very territorial. The window wall is the dominant location of professionals and executives, "opposed" to an interior wall where subordinate, more collective-like activities occur. Aside from professional identities expressed along the other axis of the office form, this organization shows only minimal indications of any extensive corporate "ethos".

For a more thorough discussion of such patterns the reader is invited again to see Doxtater (1984), where other examples suggest somewhat greater second order similarity in contemporary organizational settings. In these cases greater participation, symbolism and ritual practice occur and the dominant symbolic domain belongs to the social group as a whole, rather than executive or professional individuals. The question remains whether in a social and culturally diverse country like the U.S., corporations themselves can generate first the political right of design participation, and second the symbolic density necessary for ultimate ritual practice. In Sweden, as we have seen, both these aspects were largely *external* to particular office organizations.

The student's design solution, which provides the major focus of the article in Gagliardi's anthology, represents what a small scale, local, U.S. office might look like given processes presently described as second order. Unfortunately the meanings of the structuralist layout were never discussed with any participatory client group. This academic project assumed a collective set of purely social practices which paired with instrumental, horizontal decision making processes. No discussion was possible about either the

371

symbolic meanings of these opposed domains or how ritual practice might effectively link the two fundamentally different experiences.

What is clear from this very hypothetical experience, an initial look at second order possibilities at small scales in the U. S., is that much more ethnographic analysis needs to be done on existing organizational settings. We must look for both prototypical and functioning second order expression, all the while attempting to distinguish antecedent territorial meanings of these spaces. It will also be necessary to find an organization interested in emulating the social and productive success of the Swedes, and try to create the process. Unquestionably a great deal of indigenous and historical contribution will have to be replaced by motivated and knowledgeable specialists in what must be a highly participatory process. Assuming the quasi-independent necessity of architectural (ritual) expression in establishing a politically appropriate social order--prior to actual work--the essential first step will be the right to *co-determine* the design of the office. This achieved, corporate, managerial, and architectural specialists will have to guide the organization membership toward their ultimate goal of second order practice. Perhaps other portions of our third order milieu will then be used to express more the balance of collective and individual aspects of the same self, than the increasingly territorial competition between multitudinous "others".

Notes

1   This corresponds to Foucault's description of crime against the personal figure of the monarch, and by extension the gods (as an example of the distinction between sacred and discursive practice). Most related torture seems also intent on some sort of sacred or contact symbolism, e.g. cruxificion where one dies on the universal first order symbol of axial contact, the cross.

2   Certainly one can quickly think of situations where groups of a particular people become disenfranchised from the participation in first order systems of ritual, whether by powerful priests, military rulers, or purely ecological circumstance. In such cases, space becomes again territorial or presentational, and the efficacy of the architectural message between groups comes more from status and identity images than from the structuralist, cognitive effects of ritual practice. Though in most first order or sacred societies, no matter how highly organized, most architecture still promotes ritual rather than territorial ends.

3   Conradson makes this point (1988:12), agreeing in turn with Frykman & Löfgren's ideas that the fight against bourgeois culture during the 1930's prepared the way for "modern, rational thinking men" (1985:14).

4   It would be the author's guess that creativity does of course flow from the positive aspects of one's individual self, but that its fruition would depend upon the activities of the *sammanträde* (meeting) rather than the more purely expressive *pause*.

5   During the preparation of the manuscript for the present work, this theory of three "orders" of architectural media has been the subject of annual seminars in architecture and of a very short article (Doxtater 1990). The orders were here originally labeled "cosmic" (first-order), "architectonic" (second-order), and "semiotic" (third-order). This piece, extremely restricted by the length limitations of the conference proceedings of which it was a part, outlines the essential ideas of the theory, not using Scandinavian content as examples, but sources from the Pueblo cultures of the American Southwest. A much more detailed work on the author's first order analysis of the Chacoan Anasazi (Pueblo ancestors) can be found in Grøn, Engelstad and Lindblom (eds) (1991). Presently, the labels of "sacred" (first order), "non-sacred or collective" (second order), and "discursive or rhetorical" (third order) forms of architectural expression are proving more usable.

6   The idea here is that fundamental symbolic oppositions in first and second order expression have evolved indigenously, "on-the-ground" as it were, fundamentally prior to influences of media texts. This of course can only be an ideal situation, since external historical power will often and perhaps early create "delocalizing", discursive influences. It still may nevertheless be assumed that the object of such textualization will be symbolic domain contents--now despatialized and destructuralized in terms of ritual practice-- which can now be more rhetorically manipulated. It has been suggested in this work that these more discursively manipulated remnants of "cosmos" may contain spatial associations for some time, at least in Scandinavia, e.g. collective meanings with natural settings and symbolism, individual meanings with architectural settings and symbolism.

7   Rather than think of a "building" as some ultimate wholistic experience, we should think of multiple experiences by multiple actors. Our architectural research should be focused, not on metaphoric assumptions of wholism, but on theoretically separate layers of meaning potential in any physical setting. Ultimately we need to develop data and explanation about how or if such potentially independent spheres are linked, whether from a more experiential, psychological point of view, or from one more culturally ecological as in the present case where task-performance needs of form are different from but linked to expressive uses of form.

8   Some of the very recent "co-housing" projects in Denmark and Sweden, where economically and socially cooperative groups usually plan and otherwise control their residential environment, are certainly "structurally" similar to second order phenomena in offices, as well as traditional *byar*. Would investigation of this parallel phenomena reveal an initial influence from the white-collar arena, i.e. that the ethos became revitalized here first? White collar co-working is a far more pervasive phenomena than co-living, particularly in Sweden. An independent evolution would raise other questions, particularly about more conscious intentions of less natural or economically and

functionally interdependent groups. For architectural examples of such housing, see McCamant & Durrett (1988).

9 For a more thorough discussion, again, of the structural characteristics of spatial expression, e.g. oppositions, axes, thresholds, etc., see Doxtater (1984).

10 The source mentioned in the preceding footnote used the terms "discursive" and "non-discursive" to distinguish "communicational" usages of architectural form from "ritually expressive" ones. This distinction seems now applicable in many respects to the notions of third order (discursive, rhetorical, presentational) and second order (non-sacred ritual practice). Both first and second-order uses of architecture are essentially non-discursive in their reliance upon ritual practice.

11 This observation is based on fieldwork during the period prior to the recession of the early nineties.

12 Wineman's survey of literature on work settings, defines three areas of research present at the time: (1) Physical comfort and task instrumentality, (2) Privacy and social interaction, and (3) Symbolic identification (1982). The introduction to the author's article on using ideas of ritual space in office design (1990), discusses the existing literature in reference to more culturally "deep" expressive possibilities in office environments--such as the present work hypothesizes.

13 The work of Deal and Kennedy (1982) recommends an analysis of the physical setting as the first step in reading corporate culture. They do not, however, develop this aspect of a much larger process to any degree of detail. Their intentions are naturally focused on third order meanings, perhaps including the possibility of expressing corporate metaphor. Their use of the terms "ritual" and "rite" in their title is inappropriate from our present viewpoint. By definition, events manipulated discursively or territorially by executives--however formal or "ceremonial"--are distinct from those practices based upon shared symbolic frameworks. Speer's designs for Hitler's rallies produced great effect, but perhaps should not be called "ritual" frameworks?

14 One might begin to look for answers here in Turner's and Schectner's work on performance (1986), where symbolism and ritual are being investigated in larger scale, syncretic, or even contemporary settings.

15 For a current discussion of the multiple guises under which human space falls in the field of anthropology, see Low & Lawrence (1990).

16 Certainly Gagliardi will see much in common between his ideas about the primacy of reason in Western thought and Bell's (more recently published) deconstruction of a similar or identical bias in anthropology, i.e. the causal preference of symbolic thought over action (see again footnote 1 in the Introduction).

Glossary

arbetare - worker
arbetsgäng - work "gang"
arbetsgiver - employer
arbetsgrupp - work group
arbetskamrat - work comrade
arbetsplats - work place
besökfica - visitor, break
by - Swedish village
bygata - village street
bygd - village, geographical area
bygdelag - social organization of the bygd
centrum - city center
chef - boss, supervisor
dugnad - rural group which exchanges labor (Norway)
fest - social event, party
fica - smoke break
flextid - flexible work hours
frukost - breakfast
gågata - walking or pedestrian street
gäng - traditional term for social group ("gang")
gård - enclosed exterior area, atrium, garden, farm
gårdstun - buildings of the Norwegian farm

gästgivargård - rural inn or farm
gästmatsal - guest dining room
gata - street
gille - traditional social event associated with cooperative work
gruppledar - work group leader
idrott kamrat - sports comrade
jämlike - equal
Jul - Christmas
kafferast - coffee break
kamratangivare - comrade informant
kamratkrets - circle of comrades
karriarist - achievement oriented office worker
kling-tun - village-like cluster of farms (Norway)
klubb - club
kombi-kontor - so-called combination of individual rooms and open landscape
kommun - city/county governmental entity
konferens - conference
kontor - office building

kontorist - ordinary office
worker
kontorshus - office building
kontorslandskap - office
landscape
lägenheter - apartment
ljusgård - skylight atrium
ljushall - skylight interior
space
Majstång - May pole
matsal - dining room
Medbestammanderätt - right
of co-determination
middag - dinner
Midsommer - summer
solstice, midsummer
mobbning - ostracism
möte - meeting
okamratligt - uncomrade-like
omgång - (taking) turns, shifts
pause - work break
pentry - wet bar
personalfester - employee
social event, party
personalmatsal - employee
dining room
platschef - plant superintendent
revir - territory
rokrum - smoke room
rum - (dwelling) room
samarbete - cooperative work
samarbetsovillig - unwilling-
ness to work cooperatively
sammanträda - conference
skrivcentralen - typing pool
(place in office)
smårumskontor - small room
office building of
individual rooms
social utfrysning - ostracism
sociala huvudrum - central
social space

sommer stuga - farm dwelling
used for summer vacation
stad - city
stuga - principal farm dwelling
tacktal - dinner speech which
thanks the host
tjänsteman - traditional office
worker, person in "service"
tomte - elf
torg - market
uteslutning - ostracism
vardagsrum - living room.
everyday room
ven - friend
verksledning - work
supervision
verkställande direktör - chief
executive officer (CEO)

Bibliography

ABV (1987), *Televerket Radio*, (brochure by the construction company ABV), Solna.

Affärsekonomi (1972), 'Bygg inte om små rum till storrum', Vol. 11, pp. 42-43.

Ahlin, Jan; Carlsson, Leif (1985), *Planlösning vid tre statliga verk*, Byggnadsstyrelsen tekniska byråns information No. 71 (11), Stockholm.

Arbetsmiljö (1982), Statens Planverk, Stockholm.

Arkitektur (1986), 'Ideon i Lund', Vol. 2, pp. 14 - 18.

Bedoire, Fredric (1979), 'Trällhav, Landskap, och Celler', *Arkitektur*, Vol. 1, pp. 16-26.

Bedoire, Fredric (1985), 'Large-Scale Work Places', *L'Ètude Et La Mise En Valeur Du Patrimoine Industriel*, Èditions Du Centre National De La Recherche Scientifique, Paris, pp. 436-461.

Bejne, Åke (1979), 'Canonhuset', *Arkitektur*, Vol. 4, pp. 18-22.

Bell, Catherine (1992), *Ritual Theory, Ritual Practice*, Oxford University Press, Oxford/New York.

Berg, Arne (1968), *Norske Gardstun*, Universitetsforlaget, Oslo.

Berg, Marjanna (1987), *Spatial Aspects of Social Organization: A Study of Buildings for Daycare*, Dissertation: Chalmers University of Technology, Göteborg.

Berg, Per Olof; Kreiner, Kristian (1990), 'Corporate Architecture: Turning Physical Settings into Symbolic Resources', in Gagliardi, Pasquale (ed.), *Symbols and Artifacts: Views of the Corporate Landscape*, Walter de Gruyter, Berlin.

Boëthius, Hans (n.d.), 'SAS Frösundavik--Philosophy and Building in One', (reprint from Manager of Government Relations, SAS), 10 pp.

Bohman, Stefan (1987), *Mitt liv och arbete*, Nordiska Museet, Stockholm.

Boholm, Åsa (1983), *Swedish Kinship*, Acta Universitatis Gothoburgensis, Gothenburg.

Bradley, Gunilla; Börjeson, Karin; Lundgren, Margareta (1976), *Arbetsmiljö och Tjänstemän*, TCO, Stockholm.

Brill, Michael; with Margulis, Stephen; and BOSTI (1984), *Using Office Design to Increase Productivity*, Volume Two, Workplace Design and Productivity, Buffalo.

Brück, Ulla (1971), 'Byorganisationen', in Daun, Åke (ed.), *En svensk by*, Leksands Hembygdgemenskap, Falun, pp. 20-53.

Callmer, Johan (1985), 'To Stay or to Move, Some Aspects of Settlement Dynamics in Southern Scandinavia in the Seventh to Twelfth Centuries A.D. with special Reference to the Province of Scania, Southern Sweden', *Papers of the Archaeological Institute University of Lund*, 1985-86, New Series Vol. 6, pp. 167-207.

Campbell, Joseph (1969), *The Masks of God: Primitive Mythology*, The Viking Press, N.Y..

Carlzon, Jan (1984), *Moments of Truth*, Ballinger Pub. Co., Cambridge, Mass..

Christiansen, Palle Ove (1978), 'Peasant Adaptation to Bourgeois Culture?', *Ethnologia Scandinavica*, pp. 98-153.

Christiansen, Reidar (1964), *Folktales of Norway*, University of Chicago Press, Chicago.

Christiansson, Carl (1970), 'Trivs ni i Kontorslandskap?', *Form*, 66, nr. 3, pp. 124.

Christiansson, Carl (1977), 'Människan på kontoret', *Form*, Nr. 1, pp. 7-11.

Cole, Robert E. (1989), *Strategies for Learning: Small-Group Activities in American, Japanese and Swedish Industry*, University of California Press, Berkeley.

Colquhoun, Alan (1974), 'Centraal Beheer', *Architecture Plus*, Sept./Oct., pp. 49-54.

Conradson, Birgitta (1980), 'Kontorsliv På 1930-talet', *Fataburen*, Nordiska museets och Skansens årsbok, Stockholm, pp. 47-59.

Conradson, Birgitta (1984), 'Det manliga försprånget', *Fataburen*, Nordiska museets och Skansens årsbok, Stockholm, pp. 77-88.

Conradson, Birgitta (1988), *Kontorsfolket*, Nordiska Museets Handlingar 108, Stockholm.

Contract (n.d.), *Enator*, Reprint of Contract 23, Contract International, Båstad.

Daun, Åke (1991), 'Individualism and Collectivity among Swedes', *Ethnos*, 3-4, pp. 165-172.

Daun, Åke (1989), *Svensk Mentalitet*, Rabèn & Sjögren, Stockholm.

Daun, Åke; Forsman, Ingrid (1984), 'Gustav Sundbärg och det svenska folklynnet', *Att vara Svensk*, Kungl. Vitterhets Historie och Antikvitets Akademien, Stockholm, pp. 33-45.

Deal, T.E.; A. A. Kennedy (1982), *Corporate Cultures: The Rites and Rituals of Corporate Life*, Addison-Wesley, Reading, MA.

Dovey, K (1992), 'Corporate towers and symbolic capital', *Environment and Planning B: Planning and Design*, Vol. 19, pp. 173-188

Doxtater, Dennis (1971), *The Organization of Primitive Socio-Cultural Groups Via Places: An Essay*, M.A. thesis in sociocultural anthropology, University of Washington, Seattle.

Doxtater, Dennis (1981), *Thursday at a Crossroads: The Symbolism, Structure and Politics of "Center" in the Old Scandinavian Farm Culture*, Dissertation: University of Michigan, University Microfilms, Ann Arbor, MI.

Doxtater, Dennis (1981b), 'Cosmos in the Corporation', *Environmental Design Research Association*, 12, pp. 36-45.

Doxtater, Dennis (1984), 'Spatial opposition in non-discursive expression: Architecture as ritual process', *Canadian Journal of Anthropology*, 4:1, pp. 1-17.

Doxtater, Dennis (1989), '"Cultural Space" as a Needed Research Concept in the Study of Housing Change: The White Pueblos of Andalusia', in Setha Low and Erve Chambers (eds.), *Housing, Culture, and Design*, University of Pennsylvania Press, Philadelphia, pp. 115-140.

Doxtater, Dennis (1990a), 'Socio-political change and symbolic space in Norwegian farm culture after the Reformation', in Mete Turan (ed.), *Vernacular Architecture*, Gower Publishing Company Limited, Aldershot (Eng.), pp. 183-218.

Doxtater, Dennis (1990b), 'The Medial Role of Architecture in the History of Human Space: The Cosmic, Architectonic and Semiotic', *Culture, Space and History*, Proceedings of IAPS 1990, Vol. 2, Faculty of Architecture Press, Ankara, pp. 91-101.

Doxtater, Dennis (1990c), 'Meaning of the Workplace: Using Ideas of Ritual Space in Design', in Gagliardi, Pasquale (ed.), *Symbols and Artifacts: Views of the Corporate Landscape*, Walter de Gruyter, Berlin, pp. 107-128.

Doxtater, Dennis (1991), 'Reflections of the Anasazi Cosmos', in Grøn, Engelstad and Lindblom (eds.), *Social Space*, Odense University Press, Odense.

Duffy, Frank (1989), 'SAS co-operation', *Architectural Review*, 3, pp. 42-51.

Edman, Bengt (1986), 'Forskning utan by', *Arkitektur*, Vol. 2, pp. 19.

Ehn, Billy (1981), *Arbetets Flytande Gränser*, Prisma, Stockholm.

Ek, Sven (1970), *Östra Torn*, Hykon, Lund.

Ek, Sven (1980), 'Cultural encounter in industrial Sweden', *Ethnologia Scandinavica*, pp. 31-45.

Ericsson (n.d.), *Ett bra kontor ska vara som ett musikinstrument: Det nya Svenska kontoret*, (marketing publication), pp. 55-61.

Erixon, Sigurd (1960), *Svenska Byar*, Nordiska Museet, Stockholm.

Foucault, Michel (1977), *Discipline and Punish*, Random House, New York.

Försäkringstidningen (1970), 'Ja och Nej till kontorslandscap', 4/70, pp. 14.

Frykman, Jonas (1988), 'Fördelen mid att vara informell', in Löfgren, Orvar (ed.), *Hej, det är från försäkringskassan!*, Natur och Kultur, Malmö, pp. 17-46.

Frykman, Jonas; Löfgren, Orvar (1979), *Den kultiverade människan*, Liber Förlag, Malmö.

Frykman, Jonas; Löfgren, Orvar(1985), 'På väg--bilder av kultur och klass', in Frykman & Löfgren (ed.), *Modärna tider*, Liber Förlag, Malmö, pp. 20-139.

Gagliardi, Pasquale (1990), 'Artifacts as Pathways and Remains of Organizational Life', in Gagliardi, Pasquale (ed.), *Symbols and Artifacts: Views of the Corporate Landscape*, Walter de Gruyter, Berlin, pp. 3-40.

Gaunt, David (1977), 'Om fräsebönders sociala problem in Borgeby och Löddeköpinge under 1700-talet', *Ale: Historisk tidskrift för Skåneland*, Nr. 2, pp. 15-20.

Giddens Anthony (1987), 'Structuralism, post-structuralism and the production of culture', *Social Theory and Modern Sociology*, Polity Press, Cambridge, pp. 73-108.

Giddens, Anthony (1987), 'Time and Social Organization', *Social Theory and Modern Sociology*. Polity Press, Cambridge, pp. 140-165.

Gilmore, D. (1977), The social organization of space: Class, cognition, and residence in a Spanish town', *American Ethnologist*, 4:3, pp. 437-451.

Goffman, Erving (1974), *Frame Analysis*, Harper & Row, New York.

Grandlund, John (1943), *De Obesuttna, Arbetaren I Helg och Söcken*, Tiden's Förlag, Stockholm, pp. 13- 77.

Gustavsson, Bengt (1966), *Några Arbetspsykologiska Synpunkter På Kontorslandskap*, Psykotekniska institut vid Stockholms universitet, Solna.

Hansen, Judith F. (1976), 'Proxemics of Danish Daily Life', *Studies in the Anthropology of Visual Communication*, Vol. 3, nr. 7, Spring, pp. 52-62.

Hastrup, Kirsten (1985), *Culture and History in Medieval Iceland*, Clarendon Press, Oxford.

Helmersson, Stina (1987), 'Mobbning: konsten att plåga en arbetskamrat', *Statstjänstemannen*, 2/87, pp. 20-23.

Henriksson, J.; Lindqvist, S. (1977), *Lägenheter på verkstadsgolvet*, Statens råd för byggnadsforskning, Stockholm.

Hjelm, Åke (1967), 'En ny arbetsmiljö', *Form*, nr. 10, pp. 633-644.

Holm-Löfgren, Barbro (1980), *Ansvar, avund, arbetsglädje*, Askild & Kärnekull, Stockholm.

Hultin, Olof (1979), 'Introduction to Kommentarkontor', *Arkitektur*, h. 4, pp 2.

Hultin, Olof (1980), 'Kontor i Alvik', *Arkitektur*, h. 3 , pp. 14-17.

Hultin, Olof (1985), 'Tävling om SAS Huvudkontor', *Arkitektur*, h. 3, pp. 16-24.

Hunt, Geoffrey; Satterlee, Saundra (1986), 'Cohesion and Division: Drinking in an English Village', *Man*, 21 (3).

Jaynes, Julian (1990), *The origin of consciousness in the breakdown of the bicameral mind*, Houghton Mifflin Company, Boston.

Korda, M. (1975), *Power: How to Get It, How to Use It*, Random House, New York.

Kungl. Byggnadsstyrelsen (1965), *Kontorslandskap Rapport från Resor I Tyskland Maj och Oktober 1965*, Utvecklingsavdelningen, Stockholm.

Landberg, Gunnar; Uppman, Ragnar; Westerman, Allan (1979), 'Oxen Större', *Arkitektur*, h. 1, pp. 2-8.

Lawrence, Denise L.; Setha M. Low (1990), *The built environment and spatial form*, Annual Review of Anthropology, 19, pp. 453-505.

Leymann, Heinz (1986), *Vuxenmobbning*, Studentlitteratur, Lund.

Lindgren, Gerd (1985), *Kamrater, Kollegor och Kvinnor*, Research Reports from the Department of Sociology, University of Umeå: RR No. 86.

Link, Ruth (1974), 'Better Days', *Sweden now*, 8: h.2 pp. 38-46, h.3 pp. 44-49, h.4 pp. 44-49, h.5 pp. 71, 78, 80, 82, 84.

Löfgren, Orvar (1972), 'Historisk bakgrund', in Hellsprong & Löfgren (eds.), *Land och Stad*, Lund.

Löfgren, Orvar (1973), 'Arbetsgillen bland skånska bönder', *Skånska Årsfester*, Skånes Hembygdsförbund Årsbok, Malmö, pp. 11-40.

Löfgren, Orvar (1988), 'Omskoladed svenskar', in Löfgren, Orvar (ed.), *Hej, det är från försäkringskassan!*, Natur och Kultur, Malmö, pp. 11-16.

Löfström, Tomas (1985), 'Den Stora Bysprängningen', in Ambjörnsson, R.; Gaunt D. (eds.), *Den Dolda Historien*, Författarförlaget, Malmö, pp. 160-177.

Lyttkens, Lorentz (1985), *Den disciplinerade människan*, Liber Förlag, Stockholm.

Mazumdar, Sanjoy (1988), *Organizational Culture and Physical Environments: A Study of Corporate Headoffices*, MIT: PhD Dissertation.

McCamant, Kathryn M.; Durrett, Charles (1988), *Cohousing*, Ten Speed Press, Berkeley, Calif..

McLuhan, Marshall (1964), *Understanding Media*, Routledge and Kegan Paul Limited, London.

Medföljer AT (1987), *Arkitekttävlingar: Kontorsstad vid Norrviksstrand i Sollentuna*, SAR, Stockholm.

Meyrowitz, Joshua (1985), *No Sense of Place*, Oxford University Press, New York.

Minnhagen, Monika (1973), *Bondens bostad*, Folklivsarkivet i Lund, Lund.

Miskar, G. (1980), 'Domänverket Falun', *Arkitektur*, h. 7, pp. 34-37.

Mortensen, Kristine (1983), 'The American Experience', *Sweden Now*, 1, pp. 31-33.

Nivesjö, Lennart (1988), 'Mobbad på jobbet', *Kooperatören*, Nr. 18, Nov. 24, pp. 3-5.

Nyrén, Carl (1981), 'Förvaltningsbyggnad för länsstyrelse', *Arkitektur*, h.5, pp. 28 - 31.

Olivegren, Johannes (1975), *Brukarplanering*, FFNS--Gruppens Förlag, Göteborg.

Olivegren, Johannes (1985), *FFNS nu*, FFNS-Gruppens Förlag, Stockholm.

Olofsson, Gunnar (1984) 'Den svenska socialdemokratin-en rörelse mellan klass och stat', in Ambjörnsson, R.; Gaunt D. (eds.), *Den Dolda Historien*, Författarförlaget, Malmö pp. 431-449.

Ordets Makt (1974), 'Sekreterarna--arbetsmarknadens hemmafruar', Nr. 2, 1974/75, pp. 26-31.

Ortmark, Annika (1989), 'På vår arbetsplats mobbar ve inte varandra!', *Kvinna Nu*, 6/89, pp. 37-39.

Ottoson, Erik; Stephansson, Jan (1967), *Det Nya Kontoret*, Bokförlaget Prisma, Stockholm.

Örum, Leif (1980), *Människan i arbetsmiljön*, Liber Förlag, Stockholm.

Phillips-Martinsson, Jean (1981), *Svenskarna som andra ser dem*, Utbildningshuset Studentlitteratur, Lund.

Pred, Allan (1986), *Place, Practice and Structure*, Polity Press, Cambridge.

Rapoport, Amos (1990), *The Meaning of the Built Environment*, The University of Arizona Press, Tucson.

Rapport nr 20 (1980), *Hur jämställda är vi?*, Levnadsförhållanden: Sveriges officiella statistik, Stockholm.

Richardsen, Miles (1984), *Place: Experience & Symbol*, Geoscience Publications, Dept. of Geography and Anthropology, Louisiana State University, Baton Rouge.

Rissler, Anita; Elgerot, Anita (1980), *Omställning till arbete i kontorslandskap*, Rapporter Nr. 33, Stockholms Universitet, Psykologiska Institutionen, Stockholm.

Roberts, Fredric (1989), 'The Finnish Coffee Ceremony and Notions of Self', *Artic Anthropology*, Vol. 26, No. 1, pp. 20-33.

Rosen, Michael; Orlikowski, Wanda; and Schmahmann, Kim (1990), 'Building Buildings and Living Lives: A Critique of Bureaucracy, Ideology and Concrete Artifacts', in Gagliardi, Pasquale (ed.), *Symbols and Artifacts: Views of the Corporate Landscape, Walter de Gruyter*, Berlin, pp. 69-82.

Sahlin, Bernt (1979), 'Kommentar kontor', *Arkitektur*, h. 4, pp. 2-6.

Sandberg, Thomas (1982), *Work Organization & Autonomous Groups*, Liber Förlag, Lund.

Sandberg, Åke (1980), *Varken Offer Eller Herre*, Liber Förlag, Stockholm.

SAS Corporate Communications (1988), *Togetherness* (brochure), Brindfors Produktion, Stockholm.

Schneider, David (1968), *American Kinship: A Cultural Account*, Prentice-Hall, Englewood Cliffs, N.J..

Sjöquist, Kerstin (1964), 'Kulturhistorisk Jul På Skansen', *Fataburen*, Nordiska Museets och Skansens Årsbok, Stockholm.

Sjöman, Svante (1977), '80-talents kontor--en idéskiss', *Form*, Nr. 1/77, pp. 22.

Sjöstrand, Sven-Erik (1978), *Organisation för medbestämmande. En ny företagsekonomi?*, Sandberg, Åke (ed.), Liber Förlag, Stockholm, pp. 107-109.

Skare, Leif H. (1967), *Handbok för kontoret*, Bokförlaget Prisma, Stockholm.

Slater, Phillip (1970), *The Pursuit of Lonliness*, Beacon Press, Boston.

Social-nytt (1970), 'Kontorslandskapets inverkan på trivsel och effektivitet', *Social-nytt*, Nr. 6, pp. 62-63.

Sonnenfeld, W. & Stådal, K. (1970), 'Konventionellt kontor eller kontorslandskap?', *Affärsekonomi*, nr. 16, pp. 13-15.

Steele, F. I. (1973), *Physical Settings and Organizational Development*, Addison-Wesley, Reading, MA.

Stigsdotter, Margareta (1985), 'Den långa vägens män', in Frykman, J.; Löfgren O. (eds.), *Modärna tider*, Liber Förlag, Malmö, pp. 256-293.

Stigum, Hilmar (1971), *Var Gamle Bondekultur Vol. II*, J. W. Cappelens Forlag, Oslo.

Stone, Philip J.; Luchetti, Robert (1985), 'Your office is where you are', *Harvard Business Review*, March-April.

Stromberg, Peter (1983), 'An Anthropological Approach to a Swedish Popular Movement', *Ethnos*, 1/2, pp. 69-84.

Stromberg, Peter (1991), 'Cooperative Individualism in Swedish Society', *Ethnos*, 3-4, pp. 153-164.

Svensson, Sigfrid (1973), 'Föra sommar i by', *Skånes hembygdsförb. Arsb.*, Lund, pp. 93-107.

Svensson, Sigfrid (1977), *Från gammalt till nytt*, LTs Forlag, Stockholm.

Turner, Victor (1968), *The Ritual Process*, Penguin Books, Middlesex.

Turner, Victor (1969), 'Forms of Symbolic Action: An Introduction', *Forms of Symbolic Action: Proceedings of the 1969 Annual Spring Meeting of AES*.

Uggelberg, Georg (1975), *Samarbete på arbetsplatsen*, Hermods, Stockholm.

Veckans affärer (1971), '"Typisk svensk VD": Ung, rörlig, blygsamt betald', No. 23, pp. 14-16.

Veckans affärer (1982), 'Det osynliga kontraktet ersätter morot och piska', Nr. 43, pp. 54-58.

Von Friesen, Otto (1976), 'Bara missnöje med kontorslandskapen', *Tema*, Nr. 1, March, pp. 18-19.

Werne, Finn (1980), *Allmogens Byggnadskultur--Förvandling och Upplösning*, Dissertation, Chalmers tekniska högskola.

Wineman, Jean (1982), 'Office Design and Evaluation: An Overview', *Environment and Behavior*, 14(3), pp. 271-298.

Wolgers, Bo (1968), *Kontorslandskap*, Personaladministrativa rådet, Stockholm.

Yngvesson, Barbara (1978), 'Leadership and Consensus: Decision-Making in an Egalitarian Community', *Ethnos*, 1-2, pp. 73-90.

Åberg, Alf (1953), *När byarna sprängdes*, LTs Förlag, Stockholm.